Library of
Davidson College

METROPOLITAN GROWTH
Public Policy for South and
Southeast Asia

SOUTH AND SOUTHEAST ASIA URBAN STUDIES SERIES

Series Editors
　　Leo Jakobson and Ved Prakash
　　　Department of Urban and Regional Planning
　　　University of Wisconsin (Madison)

International Editorial Advisory Board
Jean Canaux　　*Director, Centre de Recherche d'Urbanisme*
Ruth Glass　　*Director of Research, Centre for Urban Studies, University College, London*
Jean Gottmann　　*School of Geography, Oxford University*
Bert F. Hoselitz　　*Director, Research Center in Economic Development and Cultural Change*
Reikichi Kojami　　*Director, Tokyo Institute for Municipal Research*
Aprodicio A. Laquian　　*International Development Research Centre, Ottawa, Canada*
John P. Robin　　*The Ford Foundation*
Khalid Shibli　　*University of Pittsburgh*
M. S. Thacker　　*Bombay, India, formerly member of the Planning Commission, Government of India*
Ernest Weissmann　　*Senior Advisor on Regional Development, UN Office of Technical Cooperation*
Edwin Young　　*Chancellor, University of Wisconsin (Madison)*

Volumes in this series:
Urbanization and National Development (available from Sage Publications)
Metropolitan Growth: Public Policy for South and Southeast Asia

METROPOLITAN GROWTH
Public Policy for South and Southeast Asia

Edited by **LEO JAKOBSON** *and* **VED PRAKASH**

SAGE Publications

Halsted Press Division
JOHN WILEY & SONS
New York–London–Sydney–Toronto

Copyright © 1974 by Sage Publications, Inc.

All rights reserved. No part of this book may be reproduced or utilized in any form or by any means, electronic or mechanical, including photocopying, recording, or by any information storage and retrieval system, without permission in writing from the publisher.

Distributed by Halsted Press, a Division of
John Wiley & Sons, Inc., New York

Printed in the United States of America

Library of Congress Cataloging in Publication Data

Jakobson, Leo.
    Metropolitan growth.

    1. Metropolitan areas--Asia, Southeastern--Addresses, essays, lectures. 2. Metropolitan areas--South Asia--Addresses, essays, lectures. I. Prakash, Ved, 1932- joint author. II. Title.
HT334.A8J3   301.36'4   74-103482
ISBN 0-470-43732-4

FIRST PRINTING

CONTENTS

	Preface	7
1.	On the Consequences of Urbanization: Contributions to Administrative Capacity and Development ARCH DOTSON and HENRY TEUNE	13
2.	The Measurement of Metropolitan Performance: Singapore and Bangkok as Pacemakers RICHARD L. MEIER	45
3.	Problems of a City State: Ethnicity in Singapore PETER A. BUSCH	75
4.	Metropolitan Planning in Karachi: A Case Study KHALID SHIBLI	109
5.	Metropolitan Problems and Prospects: A Study of Calcutta ARTHUR T. ROW	137
6.	Water Supply and Economic Development: The Scale and Timing of Investment IAN BURTON and T. R. LEE	177
7.	Housing Policy and Housing Standards: A Dualistic Dependency LEO JAKOBSON	197
8.	Financing Housing and Urban Development VED PRAKASH and J. P. SAH	227

9. *Urban Planning in the Context of a 'New Urbanization'*
   LEO JAKOBSON and VED PRAKASH 259

   About the Contributors 289

   Index 295

PREFACE

This second volume[1] of the South and Southeast Asian Urban Studies Series brings into focus several of the critical policy issues confronting the large metropoli of the region and relates them to the broader perspectives of national planning and urbanization discussed in the first volume of the series.

The introductory chapters present an analysis of two of the basic questions often raised in the debate on the role of the Asian Metropolis ... is it successfully manageable? ... is it performing a positive function in the context of development and modernization? Arch Dotson and Henry Teune suggest in Chapter 1 that urbanization yields administrative capacity, which yields national development. Their hypothesis is based on an examination of a variety of data which demonstrate that urbanization produces complex, cooperative structures and patterns of behavior which enable the social, economic and political systems to become more productive. In Chapter 2 Richard Meier examines Singapore and Bangkok as pacemakers for development and comes to the conclusion that there seems to be no barriers in sight that would prevent a continuation of that role.

The following three chapters present case studies of Singapore, Karachi and Calcutta. Peter Busch, in Chapter 3, describes the problems of ethnicity in Singapore, pointing out that social science theory can be put into practical use in Southeast Asia and that such a corpus could have great utility in the formulation of public policy for development. Chapters 4 and 5 describe the current planning efforts in Karachi and Calcutta respectively. In the former study, Khalid Shibli points out the futility of the traditional "master-planning" approach and describes the reasons for the current planning effort, supported by the United Nations through its technical assistance program. Arthur Row, in his Calcutta analysis, provides an excellent summation of possibly the most elaborate and costly foreign aid planning program undertaken anywhere in the developing countries. In this case the financial support for planning was provided by the Ford Foundation.

The next chapters discuss in conceptual terms three functional issues of critical concern in every Asian metropolis: water supply, housing, and urban finance. Ian Burton and Terry Lee, in Chapter 6, propose that notwithstanding emotion, ideology and politics, the scale and timing of infrastructure investment (in this case water supply) has to relate realistically to the overall state of the economy. They conclude that in the attempt to devise a policy for community water supply it may be advisable to be a little old-fashioned. The senior editor, Leo Jakobson, in his chapter on housing policy and housing standards follows this same theme, suggesting that not single but multiple standards must be developed and applied to the provision of shelter to the various segments of the metropolitan population. To do this, the formulation of standards must follow a dualistic principle which reorganizes the existence of cultural tradition, as well as the need for modernization. Ved Prakash and J. P. Sah discuss the problems of urban and housing finance within the context of national development, income and pattern of its distribution, and costs associated with urban infrastructure. They suggest that financing urban development—in terms of both the capital facilities and long-run maintenance and provision of urban services—is basically an intergovernmental process and requires both horizontal and vertical coordination among central (national), state (regional), and local governmental agencies. They argue the need for a national urbanization budget and present a conceptual framework for its development. In the context of municipal finance they feel that taxation of land and buildings should be viewed not only as a source of revenue but also as an integral element of land policies for urban development, and urge the utilization of tax credits and revolving funds.

In the last chapter the editors provide an overview of the planning efforts to date in the various metropoli of South and Southeast Asia. They present a conceptual framework for metropolitan planning based on the general state of development and urbanization on the one hand; and on the specific conditions of the metropolitan region on the other hand.

It can be argued that a collection of essays as presented in this and the previous volume of the series produces—at best—a loosely assembled, shallow overview of the topics discussed which is of value only to the general reader or novice. It is sometimes suggested that serious scholars will be better served by concentrating on the larger contributions of the various authors made individually and presented in book form or as articles in disciplinary journals. This is true if one takes the position of the disciplinary specialist. We contend, however, that most decisions in the sphere of public policy are made by individuals or groups of individuals who seldom have more than a casual acquaintance with the subject matter of their decisions—let alone understand its broader context. This is the universal curse of planning in the public sector, and it becomes more aggravated the lower in the governmental hierarchy the decisions are made. The sophistication which usually can be found at the national level, both among decision makers and among their advisors, vanishes rapidly when one begins to move to more local levels of government, though one can encounter a different kind of sophistication—a "bazaar sophistication"—in the smaller towns and villages where the modern ways of decision making have yet to penetrate.

As stated in the introduction to this series, we want to provide a forum for juxtaposing different viewpoints and different disciplinary approaches to metropolitan problems in order to create a broader frame of reference for those who are making the policy decisions. In other words, the intent is to serve the general reader and the policy maker rather than the scholar or expert in a particular problem area. Our professional experience in working with urban problems—not only in developing countries but also in the "developed" United States—suggests that a forum of this kind is needed and that it can help to expand both the time and the space horizons of those who decide the future of urban communities.

—Leo Jakobson
—Ved Prakash

NOTE

1. See Jakobson and Prakash, eds. *URBANIZATION AND NATIONAL DEVELOPMENT* (Beverly Hills: Sage Publications, 1971).

METROPOLITAN GROWTH
Public Policy for South and
Southeast Asia

CHAPTER 1

Arch Dotson and Henry Teune

ON THE CONSEQUENCES OF URBANIZATION:
Contributions to Administrative Capacity and Development

THE HYPOTHESES AND DESIGN

Introduction

The consequences of urbanization pose a serious and primary public policy question for national development. For example, if the phenomenal rise of urbanization in developing countries is producing a "wasteland," if that urban growth is "pseudo," as the orthodoxy so widely expounded now contends, then we face a crisis of catastrophic proportions.[1] The only prudent course, for survival if not welfare, is to attempt by all means available to stop urbanizing. At the very least, developing nations should try to regulate or modify the trend so as to ameliorate its consequences. Remaining resources, presumably, would be directed to other, more constructive non-urban and non-urbanizing investments. Public policy for both urbanization and national development would, therefore, be aimed at the arrestment and restraint of urban growth.

But is the apocalyptic thesis valid? Its factual, analytic, and interpretive defects were examined earlier.[2] Such error and illogic should call into question its estimates. One can conclude that they are not proven; and, on the contrary, are improbable. But the entire question suffers from want of empirical evidence and comparative tests. More systematic investigations might not only prove the thesis mistaken, but might also establish a more valid one. No such systematic investigation now exists.

Obviously, there need be no single relationship. And in the interdependence of such complex phenomena, variations are to be expected. But is there a central tendency? Were we able to establish this reliably, the variations and their conditions could better be explored.

During 1970-72, a SEADAG research project attempted to answer the basic question: What is the relationship of urbanization and national development?[3]

Partial results are reported here. They deal with some general relationships at the sub-national level in one country. They do not deal with the direct and immediate consequences of urbanization or the impact of urbanization on the nature of society or on the individual. Nonetheless, this approach to assessing the relationship between urbanization and development should at least provide some basis for evaluating two general and highly conflicting hypotheses of relevance for policy: that urbanization (in some time frame) has negative consequences for national development; and that urbanization (again in some time frame) is one of the necessary ingredients of national development.

This research began with a bias toward the latter hypothesis. The theoretical context of this hypothesis is political and administrative—that urbanization reduces the costs of social and economic interaction and thereby stimulates in part the growth of a social and political infrastructure (administrative capacity) which provides for a basis for political intervention and mobilization of the population. Such an infrastructure is a precondition for development, although urbanization might not be a necessary condition for the growth of the infrastructure. This developmental process was assumed to be manifest, albeit weakly, within Southeast Asian countries.

Development was defined phenomenologically as a variety of institutions, economic activities, and services. Such an empirical approach is fraught with difficulties. Rather than theoretically focused definition, there is a measurement question: in what ways can generally understood developmental characteristics within a country be dimensionalized? Such an empirically grounded approach, while less than theoretically satisfying, does, however, allow for more obvious transitions from research to policy-like predictions for specific cases.

Hypotheses

The general hypothesis concerning the impact of urbanization is at two levels and at two or more points in time: increases in urbanization within a country should lead to increases in national development of a country. In a language of association, increases in urbanization should be positively associated with increases in development (lagged). One assumption is necessary for this study: national developmental processes are manifest at the sub-national level, and, thus, the more urbanized the local political unit the higher its level of national developmental phenomena and the greater the increases in urbanization at the sub-national level, the greater the increases in these national developmental phenomena. The general hypothesis, along with this assumption, is the basis of predicting to data from the Philippines: (1) the more urbanized the province and the more urbanized the city, the greater the manifestation of national development; and (2) the greater the increases in urbanization of province and city, the greater the increase in national developmental phenomena.

Context of Confirmation

The general hypothesis speaks to a large variety of data. The data to be examined are from two levels and in most cases two points in time for one country. Thus the conditions under which such a relationship should hold, such as a particular level of national development of a country, are not specified.

The data are largely drawn from official sources and from a sample of cities (n=37) and nearly all of the provinces (n=54). Further, these data are limited to contemporary experience rather than the long-term developmental processes that require historical data. Also, this study did not systematically examine the intervening processes by which the urbanization sets the conditions for national development.

Because of the approach used in this study, several mixed results were anticipated—a positive association with respect to one dimension of development but not another. Thus the findings must be judged as a whole. Although any positive finding does not confirm the hypotheses (rather it tends to indicate that the evidence does not confirm), the absense of any findings also does not confirm the negative view that urbanization has a negative effect on development. The results of such a study, however, can at least inform some specific predictions that must be contained in any urban policy for a specific country.

Approach to Measurement

Approaches to social measurement reflect not only particular views of what is important to measure, but also different philosophies and purposes of measurement. The approach taken here is that items of information can be conceived as indicators of some general underlying social processes, such as urbanization and development, and can be used to measure several dimensions of those processes.

(1) Data as Indicators Within a Context: Most data which are defined, gathered, and processed by political systems come in discrete form, such as the number of factories and hospitals. As specific items they can be used to read what they appear to be and are intended to be—a more or less accurate count of hospitals, for example. Hospitals, however, are defined in a variety of ways, such as the number of beds, staff, etc. These different definitions create difficulties when comparing hospitals in India and the United States. In addition, the distribution of hospitals may reflect different social processes, such as the general level of health of a population, or governmental concern for welfare. As these data occur within the "contexts" of particular countries or cultures these contexts can be used to interpret specific items as reflecting some general processes—thus data are considered indicators.

The first principle on which measurement in this study is based is that, because social items of information are contextually defined, they can be considered as indicators.

(2) *Specific and General Differences:* Although particular political units may differ in practically an infinite number of ways, most of these differences may be reduced to a few general ones. Just as individual differences may be summarized into one or a few general differences—general "intelligence," reasoning, or spatial relationships—so can the many differences among political units be summarized into a few general differences, such as the involvement of the population or the effectiveness of institutions. The purpose of the reduction is to order complexity in such a way that general dimensions become more useful for general analysis and for policy.

The second principle of measurement involves the assumption that many specific differences may be reduced to a few "more meaningful" differences.

(3) *Theoretical and Empirical Measurement:* Ideally, it is desirable to define those dimensions which are posited to be important for some purpose, particularly in constructing general theories, and then to develop measurement systems that would reliably and validly assess objects on those variables. In this study several very general dimensions, such as urbanization, were posited and then procedures were adopted to obtain the best measures with available data. Further, because of this approach it was necessary to redefine the general variables being sought, such as administrative capacity, to fit the salient differences or types of variance that could actually be isolated. General concepts were used as guidelines; but the empirical research considerably regulated what variables could be used. The definitions of dimensions, therefore, are largely determined by the major clusters of differences found. This approach, however, although practical in a specific research context, diverts investigation away from what is necessary for answering the questions of the research toward what can be assessed within a general theoretical framework with available data.

The third principle is an empirical, rather than a focused or theoretical orientation.

(4) *Multiple Indicators: Compensation for Error:* Many differences can be reduced to a few: this reduction is often necessary because each indicator "indicates" more than one phenomenon. The example of the number of hospitals indicating health, as well as governmental concern for welfare, applies to most "hard data." A specific indicator must be examined in terms of what it is most likely to indicate the "most" of in particular settings. Thus the indicators of any general phenomenon, in order to assure that they are properly evaluated as indicators, must be multiple. Further, any set of indicators is assumed to reflect not only "true" measurement, but also error. Any assessment (measurement statement based on a set of indicators) will contain different sources of error which are assumed to interact, to cancel out, or to reduce to insignificance, any systematic error.

The fourth principle is a reliance on multiple indicators to compensate for the error in any single indicator. (In certain cases this principle was not used because of the absence of multiple indicators.)

(5) *Criteria of Validity:* The common-sense formulation of the problem of

validity is evidence that what is claimed to be measured, is indeed being measured by the indicators used. Several criteria and kinds of evidence can be used, such as predictive validity, the ability to predict from one variable to another in a way known to be "true." The decisive validity test is the actual correlation of the indicator (item of data) with a "basic" measurement operation (e.g., social differences actually observed as correlated with differences in personal possessions which could be considered a valid indicator of social distance). Most criteria of validity are difficult to apply. One of the simpler tests was adopted in this research: convergence among a set of indicators hypothesized to reflect the same phenomena. This test is based on a general logic: if A is related to X (the underlying dimension) and if B, C, and D are also related to X, then because of their mutual dependence on X, they should be intercorrelated among themselves. Two operational criteria may be used for evaluating the resulting intercorrelations—the extent to which they are high and the extent to which they are higher than others. Thus A and B may be sufficiently correlated to be considered indicators of X by the first criterion; but if this correlation is not as high as between B, C, and D, therefore (assuming three items are a sufficient number of indicators), item A will be deleted. In addition to convergent validity among indicators, there is also divergent validity. Not only should the indicators be homogeneous among themselves, they should also be different from indicators that could be used to assess some other dimensions. Although demonstration of divergent validity is desirable, it has not been used systematically in this research for two reasons: because of the large number of indicators for a specific dimension (in some cases), and because the hypothesized relationships among specific sets of indicators. Health measures, for example, were considered to form a "natural" cluster among themselves, without regard to whether specific health indicators diverged sufficiently from educational measures.

The fifth principle of measurement is the convergent validity among indicators hypothesized to form certain substantive clusters.

(6) Contextual Differences and Comparability of the Measures: It is obvious that an indicator of health in one country may not be an indicator of health in another. Further, "valid" indicators of health for a city may not be equally valid for provinces, or for that matter for different points in time for the same cities. The assumption here is that the specific context—country, political unit, and a specific point in time—is the most appropriate context of validation.

The sixth principle of the approach is thus that the indicators must be validated in a specific context in time and space. (The corrolary is that the validity of the indicators of a general dimension supply the basis for determining the equivalence of measurement statements for different levels of social aggregation, for different systems, and for different periods of time.)

Measurement Operations

Measurement involved the following steps, although modified for specific sets of data:

(1) General definitions were formulated, for urbanization, development, etc.
  - (a) Urbanization: concentration of population in physical space. Although this is a "demographic" definition, it is at the core of any definition of urbanization. Thus the selection of more than one indicator of urbanization started from the assumption that concentration had to be, by definition, one indicator. The question is, concentration in what kind of space? Here, political units were used for assessing concentration: province and city.
  - (b) Development: in addition to the above a variety of other dimensions, albeit in many cases using conventional definitions, were employed, such as educational level, health, wealth. An attempt was made to assess as many of these dimensions as possible in order to portray the linkages between urbanization and development broadly.
  - (c) Administrative capacity: the presence of secondary economic, social, and political structures through which individuals do, and can, cooperate. The concept is intended to signify the condition that secondary organizational structures provide the basis for effective collective action.

(2) An attempt was made to collect as wide an array of social, economic, and political data as possible, on at least two levels, municipality and provinces, for at least two points in time.[4] One level was selected to examine the impact of urbanization beyond the city itself, but less than the country as a whole. Two points in time were needed to examine the impact of changes.

(3) A check was made to delete items on which data were missing (about 25 percent of the cases), or which displayed very little difference (no variance among the units).

(4) A correlation analysis was made of almost all of the indicators.

(5) The indicators were then clustered into a variety of dimensions, such as wealth, urbanization, and the like.

(6) After examining their intercorrelations, several more indicators were deleted. This was done because: the item generally had negative, no, or low correlations with the other items hypothesized to belong to the domain of that set of indicators; or the item correlated substantially below the average correlation of other items with each other. (As many indicators as possible were retained to increase the reliability of the measurement statements.)

(7) Those items known to meet at least one essential condition—that of belonging to a common domain, established in the general correlational analysis—were factor analyzed to find the dimensions underlying the general domain hypothesized.

After the first factor analysis the results were examined to delete additional items, particularly those that were not clearly homogeneous with the rest. Items would be deleted because they "loaded" on more than one factor. In most cases of clusters of more than four indicators, one, and in several cases, two or more, additional runs were made in order to "purify" the set of indicators to be used for scoring. (Where only two or three intercorrelated indicators remained, these were used for the score on the dimension.)

The indicators retained after these analyses were then used to score the cities or provinces on the dimensions defined in the analysis. Scoring was the average score of the unit for the indicators in the factor. Thus, standard scores (scores based on deviation from the mean score) were computed for each indicator, and a mean of those standard scores was used for the overall score on the dimension. In the case of missing data, the indicator was deleted from the computation of the mean standard score. This procedure was used rather than a factor score (which is based on the sum of the factor loadings multiplied by the standard score for each unit on each indicator, divided by the total number of indicators) because it requires no estimate of missing data.

Interpreting the Dimensions: The Factor Analysis

The factor analysis used to identify clusters of indicators was orthogonal, with varimax rotation. Although factor analysis can be used to make inferences about the interdependencies among certain kinds of variables, it was employed here to identify a set of indicators which could be used to score cities or provinces on identifiable dimensions.

Most of the factors have indicators with consistent loadings, that is, either all positive or all negative. In some cases there are "contradictory" loadings, that is, some items are loaded positively and some negatively. This was taken into account in the actual score: the indicator was reversed. For example, educational level contains positively loading items for percent of people completing schooling, but a negatively loaded item for the percentage of people with no schooling. As this is to be expected, the item is reversed in the actual score.

In a few factors all of the loadings are negative. The important consideration, however, is consistency rather than whether the loading is positive or negative. The negative loading is an artifact of the particular factor rotation. In such cases, all the items are reversed in the actual scoring, so that the variable can be interpreted as the higher the score, the higher the attribute.

The factor analysis had iterated rotation. This means that, in succession, rotations were performed in order to extract as many specific dimensions as possible. But because of the careful selection of the input items, one large, general factor with conceptual and substantive coherence could be expected. This is usually the factor presented. Many other factors are not as large in terms of variance explained, and are not presented.

The "variance explained" expresses the amount of interdependence among the variables. (Total variance would be 100 percent if all the variables were almost perfectly correlated, in which case a factor analysis would not be needed since there would be no specific dimensions.) As can be seen in the Philippine data the amount of variance explained is usually high. (In most social science data analysis anything over 50 percent would be considered very good.) Two reasons account for a high amount of variance explained: only those indicators that were highly correlated in the first place were put into the analysis, or many of the indicators were clearly redundant or tautological, such as the number of people literate and the number of people with no schooling.

In most analyses, tautologies or redundancies are to be avoided. However, the purpose of this factor analysis was to obtain as many indicators as possible, even though some might be redundant. Redundancy is permissible because what is intended is as close an approximation of what is being measured as possible. Where there is no redundancy in the indicators it is expected that competing and cancelling entries of error will tip only slightly the balance of "true" assessment in the set of indicators.

Occasionally an indicator may not "fit" on common-sense grounds. This is not serious to the extent that the indicator is highly correlated, or loads well with the other indicators, and to the extent that there are multiple indicators in the factor. Thus a substantively doubtful indicator, if it is highly correlated with a substantively sound factor, and if it is one of many rather than one of few, will not seriously affect the measurement statements based on the entire set of indicators.

Of course, all of the assumptions required by factor analysis were made, if not endorsed, including the one that is particularly bothersome: that the relationships being examined are linear.

URBANIZATION AND DEVELOPMENT DIMENSIONS: THE CITIES

Urbanization: 1939-1960

It was possible to use a variety of indicators for urbanization, built around the demographic factor of concentration. This factor reflects concentration in a variety of ways—people across land, the proportion of people in the urban area as compared to the total population in the province, and the total number of people. The results of the analysis clearly show a consistency of urbanization across time—from 1939 to 1960—meaning that those cities that would have scored high on this measure of urbanization in 1939 would have scored high compared to the other cities in the sample in 1948 and 1960. The amount of total variance explained means practically that it would have been possible to use any one, or two, or any combination of these indicators, and the urbanization score for the cities would remain almost identical to the one finally used.

FACTOR: URBANIZATION

		Loadings
1.	Percent of the province population in city	.959
2.	Population 1960	.974
3.	Population 1943	.993
4.	Population 1939	.980
5.	Estimated number of population 21 years and older 1960	.978
6.	Estimated number of population 21 years and older 1948	.995
7.	Persons per square kilometer total area 1960	.974

Missing data—3 percent.

14 original variables; 2 reruns; 7 final variables—96 percent of the variance explained.

Note: Only loadings .50 or above are presented.

City Salience: Industrial, Service, Commercial Concentration: 1960

One feature of urbanized areas is the concentration of industrial, commercial (wholesale and retail trade), and service establishments. Added to this is the size of such establishments. Two clear measures of a city's salience in the province of which it is a part were distinguished: the small establishment concentration and large establishment concentration. There appear to be two kinds of cities: cities that aggregate the small-scale establishments, and those that aggregate those of large scale—scale being determined by the number of employees in the establishment.

FACTOR I: SMALL-SCALE AGGREGATION*

		Loadings
1.	Percent manufacturing establishments, 5-9 employees	.908
2.	Percent manufacturing establihsments, 10-19 employees	.940
3.	Percent transportation establishments, 5-9 employees	.715

		Loadings
4.	Percent transportation establishments, 20-49 employees	.713
5.	Percent service establishments, 5-9 employees	.866
6.	Percent service establishments, 10-19 employees	.756
7.	Percent service establishments, 20-49 employees	.556
8.	Percent commercial establishments, 5-9 employees	.959
9.	Percent commercial establishments, 10-19 employees	.838
10.	Percent wholesale and retail establishments, 5-9 employees	.961
11.	Percent wholesale and retail establishments, 10-19 employees	.821
12.	Percent wholesale and retail establishments, 20-49 employees	.653

Limited missing data—3 percent.

*Data consists of the percentage of the type of establishment for the province in the city.

FACTOR II: LARGE-SCALE AGGREGATION

		Loadings
1.	Percent service establishments over 49 employees	.564
2.	Percent commercial establishments over 49 employees	.943
3.	Percent wholesale and retail establishments over 49 employees	.933

Missing data—3 percent.

26 original variables; 2 final dimensions: Factor I—12 variables, 67 percent of the variance explained; Factor II—3 variables, 69 percent of the variance explained.

Communications (Utilization of Libraries): 1960-1965

A clear dimension in the data was communications, actually a measurement of consumption of publications. Public libraries contributed the only part of this dimension. The measure might also express the availability of a public service, as well as its use.

FACTOR I: COMMUNICATIONS

		Loadings
1.	Circulation of publications/number of publications	−.705
2.	Reading room attendance/number of card holders	−.842
3.	Circulation of publications per 10,000 population	−.960
4.	Number of publications per 10,000 population	−.815
5.	Number of cardholders per 10,000 population	−.652*

On the Consequences of Urbanization

	Loadings
6. Circulation of publications 1965 per 1,000 population	−.924
7. Number of publications 1965 per 10,000 population	−.883

Missing data—from 25 percent to 60 percent.

17 original variables: 2 reruns; 7 final variables; 69 percent of the variance explained.

*Due to missing data, this variable is not included in final dimension.

Road Development: 1960

This analysis produced two dimensions. In each, however, there is a mixture of city and national efforts to develop and maintain roads. For the purposes of our research, the second factor is more interesting as it clusters municipal effort in roads. (Because of missing data, it could not be used in the analysis.)

FACTOR I: ROAD DEVELOPMENT

	Loadings
1. Percent of national roads earth 1960	.885
2. Percent of national roads bituminous 1960	−.760
3. Percent of roads city maintained 1960	−.742
4. Percent of city roads macadam 1960	−.882
5. Percent of city roads low type bituminous 1960	−.746
6. Percent of roads national maintained 1960	.749
7. Percent of national roads macadam 1960	.882
8. Percent of national roads low type bituminous 1960	.746
9. Length of macadam national roads per capita	.871
10. Number of cars per 10,000 population 1960	−.732
11. Number of cars per 10,000 population 1965	−.691

Missing data—3 percent for 9 indicators: 50 percent for 10 and 11.

38 original variables; 5 reruns; 2 final dimensions; Factor I—11 variables; 63 percent of the variance explained.

FACTOR II: ROAD DEVELOPMENT*

	Loadings
1. Percent of city roads bituminous 1960	.594
2. Percent of city roads high type 1960	−.861
3. Percent of city roads concrete 1960	.881
4. Percent of national roads high type 1960	.861

Missing data—3 percent to 50 percent.

*Due to missing data, this factor is not scored.

Education: 1960-1965

Because of the important role of private schools, measures of education development and utilization are perhaps more complicated for the Philippines than for any other country. The original analysis included over 120 indicators, most of which were deleted because of missing data. The problem appears to be that where there are large numbers of private (usually religious) schools, there may also be a substantial commitment to public education.

Two general factors with a large number of items emerge in the analysis. The first of these is the level of education in terms of percentages of the population with schooling (and literacy). Further, there are some positively loading items contradicting several of the consistently negatively loading items (indicating a contradiction of some of the other indicators having to do with the proportion of teachers teaching at the lower levels—teachers teaching kindergarten and teachers in elementary school as a percentage of the total teaching in both kindergarten and elementary schools). The second factor is largely a measure of public school enrollment and the presence of teachers, both public and private. Although in the first factor the measure is largely that of the educational attainment of the population, with contradictions introduced among the indicators because of the private-public school mix; the second factor indicates a convergence of private and public school facilities and enrollment, except for the total number of public schools. The latter contradiction in the direction of the loadings is perhaps due to the fact that public schools are larger than private schools and, although less numerous, they enroll a large number of students.

Because of the inconsistencies in the first factor, the second is used in the analysis. The first factor is presented to show the patterns attributed to private schools.

FACTOR I: EDUCATION

		Loadings
1.	Percent of population with no education 1960	.794
2.	Percent of population with high school education 1060	−.835
3.	Percent of population with college education 1960	−.914
4.	Percent of population over 10 and literate 1960	−.777
5.	Percent of population over 6 attending school 1960	−.896
6.	Enrollment/number of public schools 1961	−.805
7.	Teachers/number of public schools 1961	−.794
8.	Percent of teachers in elementary schools/teachrrs	.716
9.	Percent of teachers in secondary public schools/teachers	−.726
10.	Total number elementary public school/total number kindergarten and elementary school	.781
11.	Percent enrollment in kindergarten and elementary private school/total kindergarten and elementary school	−.862

Missing data—10 percent.

FACTOR II: EDUCATION

		Loadings
1.	Number of private schools/number public schools 1965	−.762
2.	Number of private schools/number total schools 1961	−.943
3.	Number of elementary private schools/total number of primary schools	−.941
4.	Total number of public schools/10,000 population 1960	.698
5.	Total number of elementary schools/10,000 population 1960	.698*
6.	Enrollment in private schools/10,000 population 1960	−.948
7.	Number enrolled in kindergarten and elementary private schools/10,000 population 1961	−.945
8.	Number enrolled in secondary private schools/10,000 population 1960	−.728
9.	Number enrolled in private colleges 1961/10,000 population 1960	−.884
10.	Number enrolled in private schools 1965/10,000 population 1960	−.931
11.	Number enrolled in primary private schools 1965/10,000 population 1960	−.892
12.	Number enrolled in intermediate private schools 1965/10,000 population 1960	−.884
13.	Number enrolled in private colleges 1965/10,000 population 1960	−.857
14.	Number enrolled in special private vocational schools 1965/10,000 population 1960	−.733
15.	Number of teachers in private schools 1965/10,000 population 1960	−.814
16.	Number of teachers in primary private schools 1965/10,000 population 1960	−.762
17.	Number of teachers in intermediate private schools 1965/10,000 population 1960	−.875
18.	Number of teachers in private colleges 1965/10,000 population 1960	−.881

Missing data—8 percent to 12 percent.

124 original variables—most of these eliminated because of missing data; 9 reruns; 2 final dimensions: Factor I—11 variables, 66 percent of the variance explained; Factor II—18 variables, 72 percent of the variance explained.

*This variable is eliminated from the final dimension due to its perfect correlation with variable 6.

Educational Change: 1960-1965

There are two very specific and clean (high level of clustering with consistent substantive content) factors of educational change. The first involves increases in total public school teachers and enrollment, and increases in public primary school enrollment. The change dimensions for the private schools are not meaningful. What change occurs is almost entirely public. The second factor parallels the first except for the emphasis on secondary schools rather than primary schools. (It was not used in the analysis.)

FACTOR I: PUBLIC SCHOOL INCREASES

		Loadings
1.	Percent of change in public school enrollment	.930
2.	Percent of change in public school teachers	.916
3.	Percent of change in primary public school enrollment	.921
4.	Percent of change in primary public school teachers	.920

Missing data—10 percent to 15 percent.

FACTOR II: PUBLIC SECONDARY SCHOOL INCREASES

		Loadings
1.	Percent of change in secondary public schools	.761
2.	Percent of change in enrollment in secondary public schools	.976
3.	Percent of change in secondary school teachres	.948

Missing data—10 percent to 15 percent.

31 original variables; 5 reruns; 2 final dimensions: Factor I—4 variables, 85 percent of the variance explained; Factor II—3 variables, 81 percent of the variance explained.

Administrative Capacity (Governmental): 1956

This measure shows a consistent pattern of the effectiveness of the municipal government in raising and spending revenues. All 13 indicators load consistently and positively in one dimension. Revenues and expenditures provide a highly interdependent cluster of indicators across the 36 cities.

FACTOR I: ADMINISTRATIVE CAPACITY

		Loadings
1.	Real property taxes/from 1956 taxation	.750
2.	Assessed value of taxable property/per capita 1960	.968
3.	Assessed value of exempt property/per capita 1960	.704
4.	Assessed value of total property/per capita 1960	.978
5.	Real property tax/percapita 1960	.965
6.	Revenues from taxation/per capita 1960	.871
7.	Total budget expenses/ per capita 1960	.793
8.	Assessed value of taxable properties/households 1960	.966
9.	Assessed value of exempt properties/households 1960	.715

On the Consequences of Urbanization

	Loadings
10. Assessed value of total properties/households 1960	.974
11. Real property tax/households 1960	.963
12. Revenue from taxation/households 1960	.868
13. Total budget expenses/households 1960	.821

Missing data on all variables in 11 cases.

13 final variables; 77 percent of the variance explained.

Administrative Capacity (Governmental) I: 1960

This measure is similar to that of 1956, including the high amount of total variance explained. It adds a dimension not available for 1956—payment of wages for workers in public works and projects.

FACTOR I: ADMINISTRATIVE CAPACITY I

	Loadings
1. Average monthly wages for skilled workers in public works projects	.590
2. Average monthly wages for unskilled workers in public works projects	.686
3. Average monthly wages for laborers in public works	.775
4. Assessed value of taxable properties/per capita 1960	.898
5. Assessed value of exempt properties/per capita 1960	.721
6. Real property tax/per capita 1960	.964
7. Gross revenue/per capita 1960	.957
8. Total budget expenses/per capita 1960	.890
9. Assessed value of taxable properties/households 1960	.889
10. Assessed value of exempt properties/households 1960	.726
11. Real property tax/households 1960	.959
12. Gross revenues/households 1960	.969
13. Total budget expenses/households 1960	.907

Missing data, 4 cases on all data.

13 final variables; 72 percent of the variance explained.

Administrative Capacity (Governmental) II: 1960

Again, this is a fiscal measure—revenue assessed, collected, spent, and available. Also again, the indicators are consistent and highly loaded, and the factor explains almost all of the common variance.

FACTOR I: ADMINISTRATIVE CAPACITY II

	Loadings
1. Total income RSBH fund/per capita 1960	.834
2. Total available funds RSBH/per capita 1960	.875

	Loadings
3. Total expenditure from RSBH/per capita 1960	.865
4. Total income from school fund/per capita 1960	.951
5. Total actual available income in school fund/per capita 1960	.956
6. Total expenditure from school fund/per capita 1960	.926
7. Gross fund balance in school fund/per capita 1960	.896
8. Income from revenue and other receipts/per capita 1960	.797
9. Total income for fiscal year/per capita 1960	.783
10. Total income in RSBH fund/households 1960	.853
11. Total actual funds/households 1960	.889
12. Total expenditure from RSBH fund/households 1960	.695
13. Gross balance at end of fiscal year RSBH fund/households 1960	.883
14. Total income in RSBH fund/households 1960	.954
15. Total actual available income RSBH fund/households 1960	.959
16. Total expenditures in school fund/households 1960	.934
17. Gross fund balance in school fund/households 1960	.915

Missing data—1 or 2 cases per variable.

17 final variables; 79 percent of the variance explained.

Administrative Capacity (Governmental): Change 1956-1960

Because of the small overlap in the indicators, only a few could be used in a measure of change. Three indicators remain: increase in assessed value, increase in the real property tax, and increase in the assessed value of taxable property. The positive loading of the first item is due to the particular way in which the ratio was computed—1956 base divided by the 1960 base. As in all such cases, a correction was made for the direction of the indicator in scoring.

FACTOR I: CHANGE IN ADMINISTRATIVE CAPACITY

	Loadings
1. Assessed value of taxable property 1956/assessed value 1960	.929
2. Percent of change in values of assessed taxable properties	−.966
3. Percent of change in real property tax	−.746

Missing data for 11 cases on all variables.

3 final variables; 79 percent of the variance explained.

Manufacturing, Service, and Commercial Activity: 1960

This factor is generally consistent except for manufacturing establishments with over 50 employees. The factor brings together all kinds of manufacturing, commercial, and service institutions for a particular population. It differs from the first measure of manufacturing discussed, in that it reflects the total number of such establishments of all sizes per capita: how much is available per person, rather than how many are present without regard to the size of the population. Further, it is interesting that in the first factor the size of the establishment as reflected in number of employees does not matter (with the exception noted above): it reflects a blanketing of these kinds of institutions across the population.

The second factor is more mixed; in some ways it is a residual of the first. Here, the size of the establishment does matter, and the differences in size are expressed in contradictory loadings—positive and negative. Although such a factor suggests some patterns for Philippine cities, its mixed character makes it of doubtful use as a homogeneous measure of some single, underlying dimension.

FACTOR I: DENSITY OF MANUFACTURING,
COMMERCIAL, AND SERVICE ACTIVITIES

	Loadings
1. Number of manufacturing establishments with 5-9 employees/per 100,000 persons	.849
2. Number of manufacturing establishments with 10-19 employees/per 100,000 persons	.751
3. Number of manufactuirng establishments with 50 or more employees/per 100,000 persons	−.552
4. Number of transportation establishments with 20-49 employees/per 100,000 persons	.598
5. Number of transportation establishments with 50 or more employees/per 100,000 persons	.588
6. Number of service establishments with 5-9 employees/per 100,000 persons	.754
7. Number of service establishments with 10-19 employees/per 100,000 persons	.754
8. Number of service establishments with 20-49 employees/per 100,000 persons	.606
9. Number of light industry establishments with 10-19 employees/per 100,000 persons	.592
10. Number of heavy industry establishments with 5-9 employees/per 100,000 persons	.801
11. Number of heavy industry establishments with 10-19 employees/per 100,000 persons	.587
12. Number of commercial establishments with 5-9 employees/per 100,000 persons	.854

	Loadings
13. Number of commercial establishments with 10-19 employees/per 100,000 persons	.933
14. Number of commercial establishments with 20-49 employees/per 100,000 persons	.818
15. Number of commercial establishments with 50 or more employees/per 100,000 persons	.749
16. Number of wholesale and retail establishments with 5-9 employees/per 100,000 persons	.845
17. Number of wholesale and retail establishments with 10-19 employees/per 100,000 persons	.920
18. Number of wholesale and retail establishments with 20-49 employees/per 100,000 persons	.778
19. Number of wholesale and retail establishments with 50 or more employees/per 100,000 persons	.676

No missing data.

19 variables; 56 percent of the variance explained.

FACTOR II: SIZE OF ESTABLISHMENT

	Loadings
1. Percent of manufacturing establishments with 10-19 employees	.723
2. Percent of manufacturing establishments with 50 or more employees	−.691
3. Percent of transportation establishments with 5-9 employees	.572
4. Percent of transportation establishments with 20-49 employees	−.617
5. Percent of transportation establishments with 50 or more employees	−.582
6. Percent of light manufacturing establishments with 5-9 employees	.803
7. Percent of light manufacturing establishments with 20-49 employees	−.727
8. Percent of light manufacturing establishments with 50 or more employees	−.778
9. Percent of commercial establishments with 5-9 employees	.867
10. Percent of commercial establishments with 10-19 employees	−.859
11. Percent of commercial establishments with 20-49 employees	−.646
12. Percent of wholesale and retail establishments with 5-9 employees	.888
13. Percent of wholesale and retail establishments with 10-19 employees	−.853

	Loadings
14. Percent of wholesale and retail establishments with 20-49 employees	−.644
15. Percent of light manufacturing establishments with 50 or more employees	−.541

Missing data—2 percent.

15 variables; 53 percent of the variance explained.

Wealth: 1960

This factor generally assesses the urban amenities available to households. The first factor—the quality of amenities—shows that cities that have electricity also provide the utilities that allow for household toilets. This incorporates a large amount of the total variance.

The second factor, in effect, measures the type of housing available in the city—in particular upper income type housing in the terms of single resident units and owner-occupied housing. The loadings further show a class difference among cities: those with a large population able to afford single residential units, and those with a population that have multiple dwelling units.

FACTOR I: WEALTH: HOUSEHOLD AMENITIES

	Loadings
1. Percent of homes with electric lighting 1960	.986
2. Percent of homes with kerosene lighting 1960	−.985
3. Percent of homes with radio 1960	.984
4. Percent of homes with flush toilets 1960	.938
5. Percent of homes withpublic toilets 1960	.596
6. Percent of homes with no toilets 1960	−.776

No missing data.

FACTOR II: WEALTH: UPPER INCOME HOUSING

	Loadings
1. Percent of single resident unit 1960	.867
2. Percent of duplex resident unit 1960	−.771
3. Percent of accessory unit 1960	−.954
4. Percent of apartment unit 1960	−.749
5. Percent of households, owner-occupied 1960	.815

No missing data.

19 original variables; 5 reruns; 2 final dimensions: Factor I—6 variables; 82 percent of the variance explained; Factor II—5 variables; 70 percent of the variance explained.

Administrative Capacity (Mobilization): 1959-1963

One of the most consistent factors is administrative capacity (mobilization). What these data show is a high consistency among voter registration and voter turnout for the years 1959-1963. Those cities with a population that registers has a population that also votes, and does so consistently across time. Again, because of high amount of total variance explained by this factor, cities would score about the same, if combinations of two or three indicators were used instead of the 16 that were actually used here.

ADMINISTRATIVE CAPACITY (MOBILIZATION)

		Loadings
1.	Number voting 1959/estimated 1960 eligible population	.969
2.	Number voting 1961/estimated 1960 eligible population	.959
3.	Number of registered voters 1959/estimated 1960 eligible population	.972
4.	Number of registered voters 1961/estimated 1960 eligible population	.982
5.	Number voting 1959/estimated 1959 eligible population	.965
6.	Number voting 1961/estimated 1961 eligible population	.959
7.	Number voting 1963/estimated 1963 eligible population	.956
8.	Number registered voters 1959/21 and over 1959 population	.962
9.	Number registered voters 1961/21 and over 1961 population	.984
10.	Number registered voters 1963/21 and over 1963 population	.965
11.	Number registered voters 1959/21 and over 1960 population	.981
12.	Number registered voters 1961/21 and over 1960 population	.983
13.	Number voting 1959/estimated 1960 population	.958
14.	Number voting 1961/estimated 1960 population	.953
15.	Number voting 1963/estimated 1960 population	.951
16.	Number registered voters 1959/estimated 1960 population	.947

Missing data—10-12 percent.

36 original variables: 2 reruns; 16 final variables; 93.3 percent of the variables explained.

Findings from the Philippine City Data

Despite the method of their generation, the city data are wide-ranging. The quality of the data is also high, having been checked several times. In all cases except those noted, missing data were not a problem. The data, however, are still

On the Consequences of Urbanization

less than ideal. There is a sound measure of urbanization which incorporates a variety of its aspects, although these differences are not basic to the definitional indicator used—population concentration.

The urbanization measure produced 8 out of a possible 16 correlations with the dimensions of cities that were assessed. In terms of the various specific dimensions, there were some interesting, unexpected findings. (For this discussion a .33 correlation will be taken as the cut-off point of significance for an n = 37.)

To test administrative capacity directly we had to rely on public and political indicators. For all three measures of the level of governmental capacity there are strong correlations with urbanization. Not only are these correlations strong and positive, but they increase over time with the 1960 level of urbanization: 1957—.56; 1960—.65; and 1962-63—.85. The increase in the strength of the correlation might be grounds to some extent for making a case for a plausible causal relationship. What the last two correlations mean is that the level of urbanization in 1960 not only predicts administrative capacity in 1960, but predicts it better in 1962-1963. This time difference, however, should not be considered decisive. With respect to change in administrative capacity from 1956 to 1960, a four-year period, nothing can be said. This last measure of capacity, however, is entirely based on the changes in property taxation. Although one image of urban areas is that of a more politicized and mobilized electorate, this does not hold for the Philippine cities. This finding is relevant to the issue of political participation.

The relationship between urbanization and industrial-commercial activities produces a mixed pattern. In terms of both the size of the (industrial-commercial) enterprises, the economic significance of the city in the province (city salience), there is no correlation. This means that the size of the industrial enterprises and the general economic importance of the city, relative to other areas in the province, have nothing to do with the urbanization level of the city. If we examine another infrastructure measure, road development, again we find no correlation. The correlation, however, between urbanization and the *concentration* of industrial, service, and commercial activities, of all sizes, is strongly positive: .53. (The second dimension is a weak, insignificant correlation: .30.) This relationship, perhaps more than others, suggests the linkage between urbanization and administrative capacity, for it implies the range of structures within which people interact and cooperate. The more urbanized the city, the greater the number (and presumably the wider the distribution) of such structures. It is the sheer number of such structures, per capita, not simply the size, that is positively associated with concentration. In other words, taking the definition of urbanization literally, the greater the concentration of the population, the greater the concentration of industrial, service, and commercial enterprises of *all* sizes.

The correlations support a generalization that the greater the urbanization, the greater the educational attainment of the population (first factor: .56).

There is no relationship, however, between the urbanization level and educational change; but all of the indicators of change refer to public rather than to private education. More urbanized cities are better able to provide educational facilities (or have provided them) than less urbanized cities.

The correlation between urbanization and the quality of the amenities, as they were measured, is negligible.

In sum, the highly urbanized cities in the Philippines, in contrast to the less urbanized ones: (a) have more manufacturing and service establishments for their population; (b) have a population that has a higher educational attainment and educational facilities; and (c) have governments that raise more revenues and spend more for public purposes. More urbanized cities, however, cannot be distinguished from less urbanized ones by the politicization of their population or by the size of their economic enterprises.

URBANIZATION AND DEVELOPMENT DIMENSIONS: THE PROVINCES

Although the data on Philippine provinces are not as comprehensive as those on cities, they reflect somewhat better some of the dimensions of development and extend in some cases over a longer period.

Urbanization: 1960

The urbanization factor for 1960 reflects not only concentration but also total population, the number of municipalities, and the ratio of urban to rural population. (One indicator that perhaps should not be included is the number of barrios in the province, perhaps a better indicator of political organization than of urbanization.)

FACTOR I

	Loadings
1. Total population	.836
2. Population per square kilometer	.656
3. Number of barrios per province	.575
4. Number of municipalities and municipal districts	.902
5. Percent of population urban	.792

Missing data—5 percent.

5 final variables; 58 percent of the variance explained.

Note: Because of fewer variables, information on processing will not be given.

Urbanization: 1970

Only two indicators were employed for the measure of urbanization: population in 1970 and estimated population density in 1969. These two indicators, which were summated, correlate at .57, From previous indicators of urbanization the mixing of the two years, 1969-1970, should make virtually no difference in terms of the standing of particular cities in this two-indicator scale.

Industrialization: 1960

This factor assesses the concentration of manufacturing establishments, along with the value of manufacturing, and the presence of large-scale establishments. Further, the measure incorporates the proportion of employment in the province of manufacturing and non-agricultural sectors.

FACTOR I: INDUSTRIALIZATION, 1960

		Loadings
1.	Manufacturing establishments per capita	.844
2.	Employed in manufacturing establishments per capita	.998
3.	Payrolls of manufacturing establishments per capita	1.004*
4.	Value of manufacturing receipts per capita	.984
5.	Employed in non-agricultural industries per capita	.883
6.	Females employed in non-agricultural industries per capita	.909
7.	Non-agricultural establishments with over 500 employees per capita	.832
8.	Employed in manufacturing per capita	.620

First four variables—50 percent missing data; last four variables—5 percent missing data; 8 final variables; 72 percent of the variance explained.

*Loading due to missing data.

Industrial Concentration: 1956 and 1962

These data measure the activity of large manufacturing establishments—assets, production, employment, and total payroll. This factor is extremely clear, accounting for over 90 percent of the variance. The 1956 factor closely parallels that for 1962.

FACTOR I: INDUSTRIAL CONCENTRATION, 1956

		Loadings
1.	Value of production of large manufactures per capita	.971
2.	Value of fixed assets of large manufactures per capita	.880
3.	Capital expenditures of large manufactures per capita	.910

	Loadings
4. Employment of large manufacturing per capita	.980
5. Total payroll of large manufacturing per capita	.971

Missing data—40 percent on all variables.

5 final variables; 88 percent of the variance explained.

FACTOR I: INDUSTRIAL CONCENTRATION, 1962

	Loadings
1. Value of production of large manufactures per capita	.916
2. Value of fixed assets of large manufactures per capita	.985
3. Capital expenditures of large manufactures per capita	.915
4. Employment of large manufactures per capita	.995
5. Total payroll of large manufactures per capita	.983

Missing data—40 percent of all variables.

5 final variables; 92 percent of the variance explained.

Public Service Institutions: 1960

One measure of a government's ability to reach its population is the number of points at which services can be dispersed. Two of the indicators reflect that—public hospitals and post offices. (Bed capacity is partially redundant with number of hospitals.) A negatively loading item here is the budget of agricultural extension offices, reversed in the final scoring. (This item although not decisive in the final score, should perhaps be deleted except insofar as it reflects something of the costs of such offices.)

FACTOR I: DISTRIBUTION OF PUBLIC SERVICE INSTITUTIONS

	Loadings
1. Population/points with post offices	.666
2. Agricultural extension office budget per capita	−.690
3. Population/public hospitals	.814
4. Bed capacity of public hospitals per capita	.771

Missing data—5 percent.

4 final variables; 54 percent of the variance explained.

Education: 1960

At the province level, there is a clear educational cluster—teachers and schools, including those that are private, sectarian, and Catholic. In addition, the number of colleges is reflected.

FACTOR I: EDUCATION

		Loadings
1.	Population/colleges	.479*
2.	Population/schools	.517
3.	Population/teachers	.782
4.	Population/private schools	.827
5.	Population/sectarian schools	.842
6.	Population/catholic schools	.824

Missing data—1 percent.

6 final variables; 53 percent of the variance explained.

*Loading below .5.

Educational Change: 1954-1960

A small set of indicators presents a very cohesive measure of educational change, incorporating schools, teachers, and pupils.

FACTOR I: EDUCATIONAL CHANGE

		Loadings
1.	Percentage change in the number of schools	.909
2.	Percentage change in the number of teachers	.940
3.	Percentage change in the number of pupils	.920

Missing data—2 percent.

3 final variables; 85 percent of the variance explained.

Communications (Libraries): 1960

This is generally a clear factor, although the amount of variance explained by it is not as high as for many others. What the factor does show is that where municipal library facilities and use are high, so are provincial facilities and use also high. (Missing data are, however, a problem.)

FACTOR I: LIBRARIES

		Loadings
1.	Municipal book circulation per capita	.827
2.	Municipal reading room attendance per capita	.887
3.	Provincial branch book circultaion per capita	.648
4.	Provincial branch reading room attendance per capita	.708

Missing data—40 percent.

4 final variables; 59 percent of the variance explained.

Road Development: 1960

This factor contains a number of obvious indicators. Roads reflect governmental capacity to deliver services and are also elements of the infrastructure necessary for development.

FACTOR I: ROAD DEVELOPMENT

	Loadings
1. Length of highways in kilometers per capita	.793
2. Length of bridges in kilometers—national highway system—per capita	.837
3. Length of bridges in kilometers—provincial highway system—per capita	.721

No missing data.

3 final variables; 61 percent of the variance explained.

Health: 1960

The general health dimension is based on three components: births, deaths, and deaths caused by tuberculosis. This factor to some extent reflects capacity for providing medical services to the population.

FACTOR I: HEALTH LEVEL*

	Loadings
1. Births per capita	.886
2. Rate of births per 1,000	.871
3. Deaths per capita	.925
4. Deaths per 1,000	.869
5. Deaths caused by TB per capita	.853
6. Rate of deaths caused by TB	.816
7. Births attended by non-medically trained personnel per capita	.799

Missing data—40 percent.

7 final variables; 74 percent of the variance explained.

*The first of the two indicators for births, deaths, and TB deaths were computed; the second taken from published sources.

Housing: 1960

This five-indicator factor measures quality of housing. That quality is based on type of construction material and presence of electricity and water. It is interesting to note that the quality of the housing is directly associated with the proportion of the housing that is rented, perhaps rented in multiple dwelling units.

FACTOR I: QUALITY OF HOUSING

	Loadings
1. Dwelling units built with strong construction material per capita	.817
2. Rented dwelling units per capita	.919
3. Dwelling units with electric lighting per capita	.866
4. Occupied dwelling units with piped water	.804
5. Occupied dwelling units with electric cooking fuel	.958

Missing data—1 percent.

5 final variables; 76 percent of the variance explained.

Road Development: 1968

Because of the lack of data, two indicators were summated into a general score: roads per hectares and roads per capita. This measure should reflect the distribution of roads both by area and by the potential number of users. The two intercorrelate .49.

Items of Infrastructure: 1968

Several conventional indicators of investment in infrastructure were available for 1968, especially the production and use of electrical energy. In addition, ports and developmental loans are included. Even with such diversity of indicators (particularly ports, obviously biased by geography), the six indicators account for nearly 70 percent of the common variance.

FACTOR I: ECONOMIC INFRASTRUCTURE

	Loadings
1. Number of customers of electric utilities per capita 1968	.852
2. Energy generated by power plants in 1,000s of KWH per capita 1968	.965
3. Total assets of utilities in 1,000s of pesos per capita 1968	.936
4. Number of existing ports per capita 1968	.714
5. Number of DPB loans approved pre capita 1967-1968	.735
6. Value of DPB loans approved in 1,000s of pesos per capita 1967-1968	.704

Missing data—5 percent.

6 final variables; 68 percent of the variance explained.

Investment of Infrastructure: 1969

A variety of indicators of investment in infrastructure in the provinces was available in 1969. These include, notably, cost of roads, bridges, ports, buildings, and water works.

FACTOR I: INVESTMENT IN INFRASTRUCTURE

		Loadings
1.	Population/number of roads completed 1966-1969	.957
2.	Cost of completed roads in 1,000s of pesos per capita 1966-1969	.919
3.	Cost of completed bridges in 1,000s of pesos per capita 1966-1969	.924
4.	Cost of completed buildings in 1,000s of pesos per capita 1966-1969	.816
5.	Cost per completed portworks in 1,000s of pesos per capita 1966-1969	.730
6.	Estimated population served by completed water works per capita 1966-1969	.867
7.	Cost of ongoing road projects in 1,000s of pesos per capita 1968-1969	.597
8.	Cost of ongoing bridge projects per capita 1968-1969	.711

Missing data—1 percent.

8 final variables; 68 percent of the variance explained.

Communications: 1969

A mix of data on modern communication facilities provides a cohesive set of indicators: radio, telegraph, telephone, and their use.

FACTOR I: COMMUNICATION FACILITIES AND USE

		Loadings
1.	Population/number of bus operators 1969	.926
2.	Population/number of radio-telegraph facilities 1969	.868
3.	Population/number of telegraph facilities 1969	.666
4.	Population/number of telephone-telegraph facilities 1969	.845
5.	Population/number of radio facilities 1969	.898
6.	Population/number of stations sending social telegrams 1969	.800
7.	Population/number of stations sending nightletters 1969	.830

Missing data—15 percent.

7 final variables; 70 percent of the variance explained.

Findings from the Philippine Province Data

The provincial data are of about the same quality as those for cities. But they tend to be more conventional, and are clearly more oriented to economic planning. Social and political data are generally lacking. In many cases, the information was too specific to be used as general indicators across several provinces. In certain instances, such data were summated into an overall indicator, such as total cost of facilities. Without specific information about the nature of these projects, some errors in grouping were undoubtedly made.

Urbanization correlates significantly with 8 of the 15 dimensions examined. (A .273 correlation is used as a cut-off point for n=54, and .34 for n=35.) It is striking that the measures of urbanization for 1960 and 1969, although expressing nearly a decade of urbanization, produce no differences in relationships. The relationship between the urbanization and developmental dimensions remains constant, regardless of the changes in the level of urbanization of the province.

The correlations between urbanization and industrial activity are, as might be expected, very high and consistent for the two time periods. The correlations remain high, even though there are several cases of missing data for the years 1956 and 1962.

	Urbanization 1960	Urbanization 1969
Industrial activity, 1956 n equals 35	.70	.62
Industrial activity, 1960 n equals 54	.72	.70
Industrial activity, 1962 n equals 35	.73	.70

Whatever other forms of economic activity occur there, industry concentrates in urbanized regions.

The availability of electrical energy, utilities, and developmental loans, is also associated with the more urbanized provinces. The correlation between these variables and urbanization in 1960 is .39; and in 1968, .44. On the other hand, there is no similar correlation between urbanization and governmental input into cost of roads, bridges, water works, etc. Indeed, outlays for roads are clearly rural rather than urban investments, with correlations from −.51 in 1960; −.60 in 1969; and −.31 for roads and urbanization in 1968. But in education and housing, the relationship reverts to positive. The correlation between urbanization and education in 1960 is .32; and between 1954 and 1960 the correlation between urbanization and education change is .29. But the view that the more rural the province, the more likely there will be both high birth and death rates, does not hold for the Philippines. Finally, there is one strong and clear relationship between the kinds of amenities available and urbanization:

housing. The correlation between urbanization levels, both for 1960 and 1969, and the quality of the housing, is .51 and .55, respectively.

Generally, then, even though differences within provinces might exceed differences among them, and even though urban populations may be quite concentrated in particular areas of provinces, the conventional measures of development at the provincial level are related to the level of urbanization. These correlations, especially if some error is taken into account, are very high—so high, in fact, that it is unlikely that a province would have modern economic growth without growth in urbanization. Despite the urbanization-industrialization nexus, more urbanized provinces do not appear to have achieved economic growth at the cost of critical items of the standard of living of the population.

While the changes in urbanization and development analyzed in detail above were taking place in the city and provincial levels, the nation was becoming more urbanized in both relative and absolute measures. Whereas in 1955 only 2,560,000 persons lived in cities of over 100,000, by 1965 the number had reached 3,651,000. In 1965, over 14 percent of the total population was contained in cities of over 20,000 population. Although the rate of increase slowed, gross domestic product advanced from $132 per capita in 1955 to $237 in 1965.[5] Our analyses would suggest that much of that growth is reflected in urban activity.

CONCLUSIONS

What do these findings indicate? What conclusions might they reliably support? While proofs in social science are never compelling or definitive, the present case seems persuasive. There is at no point any indication that urbanization in the Philippines is destructive, or even inhibitive, of development. On the contrary, it appears constructive and contributory. At the sub-national level, it is likely that:

(a) Increases in urbanization are positively associated with increases in development; and

(b) Higher levels of urbanization are positively associated with higher levels of development.

Of course offsetting decreases in development in non-urban sectors could diminish the positive association of urbanization with national development.

One of the most interesting findings from the case has to do with the dynamics of the relationship. The issue is functional: just how does urbanization yield national development? Many variables must intervene between such complex conditions; but one factor emerged persistently in the analysis, something designated "administrative capacity." In effect, what appears to occur is that urbanization produces complex, cooperative structures and patterns of individual and group behavior which, in turn, enable social, economic, and political systems to be more productive. As a nation increases this capacity, it is able to set higher developmental goals, and to approach them. The hypothesis suggested is that *urbanization yields administrative capacity, which yields national development.*

NOTES

1. See for example: James E. Bogle, "The Coming Urban Crisis in Asia," in Ministry of Public Works, Republic of Vietnam, United States Agnecy for International Development Contract No. AID-VN-86 (1971); Terry G. McGee, *The Southeast Asian City*, New York: Frederick A. Praeger, 1967; N. V. Sovani, "The Analysis of Overurbanization," *Economic Development and Cultural Change*, Vol. 12 (January 1964), pp. 113-122; and Ernest Weissman, "Introduction" to Aprodicio A. Laguian (ed.), *Rural-Urban Migrants and Metropolitan Development*. Toronto: Intermet, 1971.

2. Arch Dotson, "Public Policy and Urbanization," paper presented at SEADAG Urban Development Panel Seminar, Ithaca, N.Y.: July 1971.

3. This study focused on a central question addressed by seminars sponsored by the Southeast Asia Development Advisory Group of the Asia Society and was supported by a SEADAG research grant. A version of this paper was presented to a SEADAG Seminar in Manila, January, 1972. Though the research focuses on the Philippines, Malaysia and Thailand were also covered, but with a less extensive data base. We wish to thank Thomas Nowak of Michigan State University for providing most of the data on the cities and Richard Greenfield and Elizabeth Elder of the University of Pennsylvania for their work on processing the data which are presented here.

4. National data are taken from the estimates in A. S. Banks, *Cross-Time Polity Survey*. Cambridge: M.I.T. Press, 1971; the data on the Philippines were in addition taken from a variety of official governmental sources.

5. *Ibid.*

CHAPTER 2

Richard L. Meier

THE MEASUREMENT OF METROPOLITAN PERFORMANCE:
Singapore and Bangkok as Pacemakers

Two metropolises lead the way in the modernization and economic development of upwards of 250,000,000 people on the southeast fringes of Asia. They provide niches for the powerful technological concepts of our time, allowing them to activate a series of quiet revolutions in ways of life, philosophic outlook, and human relationships. Increasingly the bearers of the crucial capabilities are the multinational corporations that can swiftly build up regional headquarters, now that the telecommunications facilities allow continuous exchange of information with the other leading metropolises of the world.

Singapore and Bangkok have accumulated skilled multilingual personnel who can be recruited to management, intercontinental hotels for entertaining important visitors, comfortable homes, a good standard of security from violence, and suitable recreation. In them world markets are translated into bids and offers for smaller transactions within the region; world interests in health, education, and welfare are reworked into metropolitan-scale programs implemented by public agencies, and advanced by newly organized scientific research and scholarship. Metropolitan enterprises simultaneously subdivide the larger managerial concerns into local projects and field operations.

The primary function of the pacemaking metropolis in Asia is that of broker. One cannot understand the dynamism of Singapore and Bangkok without recognizing the variety of milieux for middlemen that they maintain. Dealing in commodities moving in international and regional trade is a traditional activity that remains important. More recently quasi-markets in human skills have come into being. Consulting groups have established themselves as knowledge distributors. Organizers of information acquisition systems have advanced far beyond simple journalistic endeavors. Tourism has become professionalized with hundreds of specialties evolving which buffer the visitor, so that he is usually kept from experiencing severe cultural shock. The wholesalers of popular culture, whether American, Japanese, Chinese (from Hong Kong and Taiwan), or European, are also proliferating. When exchanges are effected with the hinterland, modern styles and cultural responses are very often adopted sooner in the boondocks than are the related technological improvements. Steps in the diffusion path can be traced back to locales in these metropolises where a small community of entrepreneurs, brokers, and agents have been learning how to distribute non-material modern outputs.

Singapore's brokerage transactions are much more open to view than those of other metropolises, because almost all are cross international boundaries and are counted in one way or another as exports or imports. Recent trading data show a rise in the importance of Japan and the United States, displacing Great Britain and Western Malaysia (Table 1).

Urbanists and planners find that the models and analyses offered by social scientists for such rapidly modernizing metropolises are necessarily obsolete. The accepted methods for promoting studies, collecting data, analyzing that data, propounding generalizations, and publishing in accredited media takes five to seven years if the investigators are fortunate. Only then is the information and the conceptualization available for public decision making and higher education. However, in cities like Singapore and Bangkok the level of economic activity is likely to be double what it was at the time the study was designed, the social communications in the modern sector at least treble, while both capital formation and institution building proceed at an equally high multiple of former rates. Totally new, often ultramodern, organizations and activities will have appeared on the scene in the interim. Thus conditions already in existence often

Table 1. Principal Trading Partners of Singapore (Percentage Share of All Singapore Exports and Imports)

	1965	1966	1967	1968	1969
Import Sources					
Western Malaysia	23.2	23.2	19.3	15.9	17.5
Japan	11.1	11.4	12.4	13.6	16.3
United States	5.1	5.2	5.6	6.8	7.9
Great Britain	10.9	10.0	8.0	7.8	6.7
China	5.9	6.7	8.5	9.1	6.7
Others	43.8	43.5	46.2	46.8	44.9
Total	100.0	100.0	100.0	100.0	100.0
Export Destinations					
Western Malaysia	31.2	26.9	23.6	19.4	16.4
United States	4.2	4.8	7.0	8.5	10.7
Vietnam	3.7	7.6	8.7	9.0	9.4
Japan	3.7	3.6	4.5	7.1	7.1
Great Britain	6.4	5.5	6.1	6.3	5.8
Others	50.5	51.6	50.1	49.7	50.6
Total	100.0	100.0	100.0	100.0	100.0

contradict the preconceptions underlying the formulations of inquiries into the social system, the economic system, or the urban ecology now being published. Western social scientists take growth for granted, and are sometimes criticized for this underlying bias, but their methods and time scale do not fit the acceleration of growth now underway in Seoul, Singapore, Hong Kong, Bangkok, Taipei, and some of the lesser metropolises in that part of Asia.

A future-oriented, on-the-scene assessment of contemporary development applicable to such Asian metropolises was reported in 1971 by Meier.[1] This technique was applied to both Singapore and Bangkok in the period 1969-71, and then updated by review of current periodicals. The following report on the two metropolises is therefore designed to fit the needs of planners more than geographers, historians, and other urbanists; it is based upon future-oriented observation rather than documentation and analysis of what the metropolis has been.

Singapore's Takeoff

A review of the current literature on Singapore leads one through repetitious presentation of the same challenges, the same high points in achievements, and a virtually identical list of present difficulties. Whether one reads *Business Week, The Economist, Time,* the American Geographical Society's *Focus,* or the World Bank-IMF quarterly *Finance and Development,* the following points are encountered:

- Sir Stamford Raffles, founder (1819);
- Naval base and entrepôt;
- Japanese occupation in World War II;
- Battle against Communist guerrillas (Malaya);
- Housing Development Board (Queenstown);
- Malaysian independence;
- Separation from Malaysia (1965);
- Jurong Industrial Estate;
- Economic Development Board;
- Labor peace in Lee Kwan Yew's socialism;
- "Instant Asia" label for speedy building;
- Family planning progress, population levelling near 2,000,000;
- Overextension in hotel construction but more air flights;
- Per capita income, about U.S. $900 (1971 dollars);
- Fourth harbor of the world and still expanding;
- Petroleum processor for Southeast Asia.

All this consensus in the published reports seems to mean that the city-state has a consistent self-image which is credibly transmitted to journalists, economic development specialists, and geographers. Elaboration on such themes by men with very different backgrounds but high levels of intelligence suggests that the facts are true, but probably not complete, because no adequate explanation is given for the dramatic upsurge of development they report (Table 2).

Table 2. Composition of the Gross Domestic Product of Singapore (in 1969 Singapore $Million)

Year	GDP	Agriculture, Fishery (%)	Manufacturing (%)	Construction (%)	Trade	Tourism (%)	Military Needs, Services (%)	Others
1959	1,968.0	6.1	8.6	2.0	31.7	1.2	13.8	36.5
1963	2,683.8	5.5	11.0	3.5	32.0	2.0	12.0	33.9
1966	3,365.2	4.5	14.5	3.8	26.1	2.5	16.3	32.3
1968	4,257.0	3.5	15.9	4.2	31.7	3.4	10.7	30.6
1969	4,833.4	3.3	17.1	4.3	33.6	4.4	8.6	28.7

The Measurement of Metropolitan Performance

The most insightful theory explaining the accelerated growth is probably still unacceptable in Singapore. It is provided by W.L.C. Wheaton.[2] in a parable on regional planning where he presents some "outrageous hypotheses" about development in a hypothetical Asian metropolis:

Singkong divorced itself from its Mother Country in 1970. I will not go into the details, but the Mother Country was paralyzed by its fifth internal military revolution, and was powerless to resist the separation. Further there were marked ethnic and religious differences between Singkong and its hinterland. The people of Singkong were fundamentally of a vigorous and busy racial group, and they believed in a religion called economics. The dominant population of the Mother Country was not so hard-working. They believed in a religion called balanced regional growth. Clearly the separation was politically advantageous to both sides.

Singkong... announced itself as a free trade port on the gold standard. The leaders proclaimed that they would run their new state like a city-firm. They invited business investment, and proclaimed the conviction that nations did not need any resources other than people in the last quarter of the 20th century.

The leaders of the Mother Country scoffed at this outrageous notion. Cities, they said, were evil, corrupt, overcrowded, incapable of reproducing themselves, and dependent upon rural areas for food and raw materials. Singkong would soon starve. The rural constituencies of the Mother Country applauded these wise sentiments, and believed them, since they, too, were stalwart 19th century minds.

The first effects of independence were striking and unanticipated. Without thinking about it, the Government of Singkong had maintained the Mother Country's tax system and tax rates. These produced huge budgetary surpluses in the first year, since the city was no longer drained of tax funds to support farm subsidies, rural development, roads and schools for the backward and unproductive parts of the Mother Country.

Singkong historians later read the last National Regional Development plan of the Mother Country and discovered that, although the Singkong area had 30 percent of the population and produced 50 percent of the wealth of the Mother Country, it had only been receiving 5 percent of the development budget of the nation, 5 percent of transportation investments, 15 percent of power, 1 percent of community facilities and social welfare, 9 percent of public health and 6 percent of education expenditures. Accordingly Singkong was able to immediately increase its investments in these fields by three to 50 times the previous rates. This had startling effects upon both the contentment and the productivity of the people of Singkong.

Equally important, the city-state discovered that a large population of its employees were no longer needed. They had been engaged in protracted and futile negotiations with the central government of the Mother Country for grants-in-aid... Since government was momentarily embarrassed with a hugh revenue surplus... these services were quickly expanded to maintain the previous level of employment, but with substantially greater output.

Soon the government discovered that another form of efficiency was emerging. Decisions could be made promptly. Word began to spread that an industrialist who wanted to build a new plant could get roads, water and housing within a matter of months. More striking, he could get a final decision in a matter of days. Home builders learned that they could get government insurance of mortgages approved overnight, since cases were decided in the home office, rather referred to the former national capital. This reduced delay time 18 months, and costs by 12 percent.

The enthusiasm and optimism generated by these conditions, and the budgetary surplus, quickly convinced the leaders of Singkong that their economy would grow rapidly. They turned their energies to planning for economic development... the Singkong government agreed to provide all of the requisite services for industry promptly and efficiently, including transportation, sewer, water, housing and community facilities for employees, and all of the educational services required to make the employees efficient workers.

Orthodox 19th century economists, of which there are many, predicted the early bankruptcy of Singkong... Of course, Singkong prospered. It purchased raw materials on the world market, processed them and sold its products at great profit. It purchased food on the world market in exchange for a tiny fraction of its industrial output. Assured of sites at reasonable costs, and skilled and contented labor, industrialists flocked to Singkong, wages began to go up, migration from the Mother Country to Singkong began to soar. With prosperity, Singkong saw that it must soon inaugurate policies which would regulate industrial growth and migration.

Being convinced that a city must operate like a firm, the leaders of Singkong adopted some new rules. Preference was given only to those industries whose average return to the economy of Singkong exceeded marginal costs, and whose average return exceeded those of alternative industries. Similarly migration was permitted, but only by those prepared to invest an amount equal to the marginal investment per employee, or by those whose skills were such that their capitalized earnings would equal the average value of Singkongese by the same measure.

Time does not permit me to go into the subsequent history of Singkong. Suffice it to say the per capita income there doubled every seven years. Naturally, the people of the Mother Country resented its wealth and prosperity. Some even proposed a holy war to exterminate the heresy, and force Singkong to share its wealth. But Singkong cleverly offered to build Singkong II on the most barren desert island off the coast of the Mother Country, to demonstrate that anyone could do it all over again, if only they would be busy and energetic, and adopt Singkong's religion. Naturally the Mother Country refused this outrageous offer, for they still devoutly believed in agriculture and balanced regional development.

Further, they were not doing too badly, as Singkong's prosperity doubled their markets for food and raw materials every seven years, though per capita income continued at low levels . . .

Images of the Rugged Society in a Garden City

One exceedingly significant indicator of the place of a metropolis on the world scene is the image of itself that it presents to outsiders. This "face" appears in public statements by the Prime Minister, and is elaborated in detail by the output of the ministries wherever the leader strikes a chord of consensus and pride. Often the pictures speak louder than words; in the Singapore output they are very often glossy and in color, which indicates the priority level assigned to the maintenance of appearances. The imagery captured by the pictures raises questions of "Why?" and the explanations obtained from the residents are most often fragmentary accounts of recent history in the city-state. The items that follow are clearly important:

Singapore felt seriously threatened when the British announced that they were pulling out altogether. Was a city-state viable in a part of the world where guerrillas were attempting to take over two Asian countries to the north, and had just barely been beaten off in Malaya, when Singapore was the chief prize sought by the self-declared Communists? The government decided that it needed to become much more like the Israelis—rugged and quick to react. At an extraordinary high price they brought in Israeli military advisors. The period of military service for young men was raised to three years, which is even more than for South Korea.

Modern British military equipment is available at cut rate prices at the moment, but it must be replaced in a few years and the decisions have to be made shortly. Now that the American umbrella is being withdrawn in Vietnam, some soul-searching reappraisals are in order.

The rugged society has reached down into the schools. Physical fitness programs are emphasized, as well as parade ground exercises. This shows up in the self-image of Singapore as transmitted through the Ministry of Culture's booklet for tourists. There is a remarkable degree of unanimity among the people as evidenced by the rather trivial scale of the May Day bombs and demonstrations. The Chinese, who once resented the built-in Malay control of the Malaysian government and took pride in the achievements of Mao Tse-tung, now much prefer independence. Increasingly, Singapore is a nation worth fighting for. Business is very good, the schools are improving rapidly, and the government is sensitive to the needs of specialized groups.

The rest of the booklet for tourists transmits the theme of modernity—an excellent environment for conducting business. Another message that comes through is only understood if one compares photographs of Singapore with other cities dominated or strongly influenced by the Chinese—Hong Kong, Taipei, Bangkok, and Saigon. Singapore has a clean and tidy image.

The younger professionals say the clean-up from the conditions described in the novels about the Japanese occupation[3] began with indoctrination in the post-War Chinese elementary schools. Cleanliness came next to proper behavior in the presence of superiors. The other standard was set by the great houses and the clubs of the British colonial civil servants and the expatriate business class. They put great store in their gardens. Now perhaps three-quarters of those houses with sweeping lawns and manicured plots of flowers have Chinese names (printed in English) at the driveway entrance. Dust and smoke are also rare. Thus the tourist is very much reassured upon entering Singapore because he feels he is likely to leave with a functioning gastrointestinal tract. The local illness rate is, as expected, extraordinarily low, as is infant mortality.

The traffic circles and places are kept blooming the year round. Yellow, red, and green colors predominate. Similarly, the fringes around the tall white slabs of housing are planted in relatively formal gardens. This is a place for the tourist to rest for a few days from the emotional upsets of Saigon, the classical treasures of Thailand, or the inaccessible marvels of Angkor Wat. There is nothing special for the tourist to do except eat alfresco on Bugis Street watching the transvestites who hang out there. The government has clamped down strongly on beggars and all the addictive vices from drugs to gambling. Hippies are shorn at the quarantine stations, and homosexuals are jailed if they become too visible.

On the other hand city life is relaxed and casual, so that coats seem never to be worn by men, and even neckties are extremely rare. Skirts can be mini, but not micro, as they often are in the centers and sub-centers of Tokyo. A straitlaced Honolulu has been a source of inspiration for the planners of tourism in Singapore; not surprisingly, their advisers are drawn from among the most respectable professionals in Hawaii.

The street scene in Singapore is primarily automotive, with a heavy proportion of buses at peak periods. The pedicabs are the smallest seen anywhere, and are relatively undecorated; they move around on the fringes of traffic, primarily in the more traditional areas dominated by shop-flat combinations (mostly three stories). Bicycles come into view more often in the early morning, before the nine o'clock rush, and in the evening at dusk. Light vans are common, trucks of two to five tons are concentrated around the harbor, while the heavier trucks are seen mostly around construction sites and industrial estates. The weird shapes and cadmium yellow skins of American heavy duty construction equipment are sometimes seen on the roads. Singaporeans who have had a tradition of leveling hills ever since the 19th century, have been quick to import this equipment.

If the image of proper Singapore in the past had been a Southhampton and Torquay in the tropics, it is now surely a Tel Aviv-Honolulu restyling. No mention is made as yet of the future, when a strong influence will be the Osaka pragmatist. Singaporeans have gotten so used to looking East and West for visitors, they are not yet used to the idea that Japanese from the North will make up the principal flow of tourists and make up perhaps a majority of the sojourners in the future.

Already over a thousand Japanese are living in Singapore, as compared to perhaps 7,000 Americans. The Japanese families come in the second year of the residence of the employee. Since their salaries are double what they would make at home, they pick up the modern contractor-built houses in the suburbs. They concentrate their children in the same private nursery schools, and party each other in much the same way that the English did before the war. The women rarely learn English because they manage to get by with the Chinese characters used in the Japanese language, writing rather than speaking. Because most of the ultramodern technology installed in the Jurong Industrial Estate will come from Japan, this Japanese colony is likely to multiply by ten within a decade. Its institutions will be reinforced by the funds expended by tourists and sojourners.

It will be interesting to see what happens when a contingent of the Japanese "goes native" in Singapore and begins to interact with its culture. The urban Japanese are the most difficult culture in Asia to hybridize. (It was accomplished in America and Hawaii because the immigrants were extremely poor, rural, and comparatively uneducated.) However, the Japanese tend to respect very highly a society that tries to be both "rugged" and "clean and green," so that a much greater degree of compatibility is to be anticipated than, say, with Bangkok or Saigon.

Readying for the Future

To what extent can a city-state be a modern nation? There are insufficient precedents for Singapore to follow. Therefore it will have to innovate as it goes. The government has enough dash and vigor to be willing to innovate, but what should it do? What policies and projects would a planner advise, beyond what is already being done, to make it possible for an isolated, independent metropolis to reconstruct itself and still maintain a viable form?

There comes to hand a quite new volume called *Modern Singapore*,[4] very capably edited by professors Jin-bee Ooi and Hai Ding Chiang of the University of Singapore. It provides basic factual background before entering into some of the more sensitive social and political development analysis. The reader is introduced to an ethnically mixed society fused by an effective political party leadership but still containing disparate elements. Crucial decisions, such as the choice of English as the principal language of education, had been implemented. The task of the future is to apply scientific knowledge to modernize and build an Asian society. Most of that effort still lies ahead, with the warning that Westernization (of which English and science are two characteristic traits) involves a set of customs and taboos that may have little or nothing to do with modernization. Blatant examples of committing a Westernism are the presently accepted shaving and bathing customs, but the drinking of milk and the use of the private automobile comprise members of a large and expensive class of instances of Westernization that has yet to be critically analyzed locally. In the long run Singapore needs to select a resource-conserving set of customs because additional resource-based commodities must all be imported under conditions that keep foreign exchange scarce.

One contribution could not be included in that volume. Koh and Lim[5] very carefully reviewed the history of Singapore planning. They demonstrated that a plan derived from the philosophies of English intellectuals in the 1930s, greenbelt and all, and accepted as a statutory Master Plan in the 1950s, was becoming a straightjacket that would greatly reduce flexibility in the 1970s. The lack of variety in public housing, which constitutes 80-85 percent of all new housing, the difficulties put in the way of community formation in the relocated population, and the huge increase in traffic, were all unanticipated and are not yet provided for adequately. Somehow the government must move to a greater dependence upon market mechanisms in land use and land development, which means progressive de-control of rents. This would allow a more rapid response to opportunities in the business sphere, mostly existing in the world market.

The most fundamental policy problems, now that economic development is gaining momentum, are political. Thus far the principal actions have led to an homogenization of the vastly different ethnic and religious groups, first in unions, then in the vote and in party unification, followed by urban renewal and schools, and now the military. Recently even the Malays, who make up an element not too far different in outlook from that of the Spanish-speaking population in California, have been responding well to the incentives for integration in schools, housing, and labor force (but after two years they had yet to take up the first small business loan from the allocation set aside for them). In the future, Singapore will need to capitalize upon its diversity. Each of its ethnic and religious traditions should be encouraged to evolve a modern component. These include British, along with the Hokkien, Hakka, Cantonese and Chiu-Chow, Malabar Muslim and Tamil, Sikh and Malay. Almost certainly Sumatran, Japanese, and Vietnamese will have to be added over the next decade. Fortunately the restriction on immigration are relaxed for people who bring either a good education, a nest egg of capital, or a business opportunity. Therefore it seems likely that when the full force of the prospective labor shortage hits in mid-decade, the response will be more open than that exhibited by the Japanese, but more restrictive than that of the Western Europeans when they imported millions of peasants from Italy, Spain, Yugoslavia, Greece, and Turkey to man the machines in their factories. Singapore will probably accept immigrants as they are needed, but not before.

The city must evolve structural differentiation to become a home for all of these newcomers. The Japanese will probably want garden apartments, and the Vietnamese walk-up apartments, while the Sumatrans need aided self-help housing because they will be poorest of all. Many Malays might join them. Since the government cannot tell how many immigrants will be added, or how strong the brain drain to the West will be, land use allocations must be kept on a tentative year-to-year basis and be guided by a good data-gathering system. The government could remain agile by opening new land up for bids, with the

Housing and Development Board bidding against the open market, using its budget to best advantage.

This speed of adjustment will be made necessary by the fact that the way has already been cleared for the jobs to appear on the scene within a matter of months after a contract is signed. The Jurong Industrial Estate is fully serviced for all but the largest chemical plants and refineries, but even they can be installed at almost the same speed as in Japan.

Singapore's attention must remain fixed on the actions of the major actors on the world scene. During the year of 1971, for example, a multitude of adjustments had to be made to (1) postponement for a while of the pipeline from the Alaskan North Slope, (2) resumption of diplomacy between the United States and Communist China, (3) the inclusion of Great Britain in the European Common Market, and (4) the admission of Communist China into the United Nations. The first of these caused a quick transfer of oil well drilling capacity and all the ancillary service activities to the region served by Singapore. The second opened up a series of new entrepôt options for exploration by the respective communities of Chinese traders which would allow them to market the product from the cheapest labor in the world. The third represented a clear break in the trading arrangements left over from the days of the British Empire. The fourth resulted in a huge flow of funds from Hong Kong, and indirectly Taipei, to Singapore banks, which will be followed by a diligent search for opportunities to invest locally in land and short-to-middle term propositions. Since the respective trading groups often arrive at the same conclusions about the strategy for investment but operate under a cloak of secrecy, the supply of suitable land, or of specific skills and equipment, will sometimes become insufficient, and sharp price changes will be experienced. However these shifts present opportunities to other traders, who will bring in new sources of supply or substitutes from the outside, thus reducing the period of shortage to a matter of weeks or months.

On the whole then, a city-state appears to be as viable as Wheaton argues, but only if it bends its governmental efforts toward maximizing its freedom to jump, either to avoid the effects of disastrous tears in the fabric of world trade (e.g., the closing of the Suez Canal or the turn toward protectionism in America), or to take advantage of unusual new opportunities. Singapore should continue to have a strong developmental effect upon its suppliers because it could insist upon standards of accounting, quality, hygiene, and delivery that would raise the level of organization in its "hinterland" to a point approximating that of the rubber industry, and these improvements would feed back to support an organizing center in its own upgrading attempts. Telecommunications allow almost instantaneous adjustments to be initiated to keep the entrepôt in equilibrium with the other financial centers. Given a balanced and agile policy, the gross domestic product could grow more rapidly over the next decade than Japan has over the last, despite the greater proportionate costs of defense. It has already come close to matching the Japanese rate, so that the foregoing claim is not an extreme one.

MODERNIZING PEASANT CULTURE IN BANGKOK

The effects of growth in population, income, and organizational capability are everywhere evident in Bangkok. Most of the frustrations felt by the farang (the label applied to outsiders) with airport, telephone, transport, and governmental operations can be attributed to growth pains in the urban economy. Bangkok has reached a stage where the demand for such services is expected to grow much faster than the absolute dimensions of the residential population, which is about 3,000,000 and expanding by an estimated 5-7 percent per year, and more rapidly even than the gross regional product, which surely has been exceeding 10 percent per year prior to the levelling beginning in 1970. It is also one of the characteristics of Bangkok that the aggregate data are either not available or not trustworthy when reported.

Bangkok is different from Taipei, Singapore, and even Seoul, in that it has acted very much as a stopper that prevents further migration into the rest of the world. It contains many sojourners with the hope of finding a job. Formerly, most were carried in the boats that transported the rice, maize, jute, and minerals from the river ports upstream in the Chao Phraya basin. Now more common people arrive like the students and educated people on the buses and the trains. Most return home after a stay in the capital city, but quite a few do find reasonably steady employment and places to live in the soi (lanes) that invade the plantations surrounding the city. No real brain drain to the rest of the world has occurred because Thai students return, almost all of them, to Bangkok. There are no important foreign colonies which exchange personnel with the mother country. The Thai elite, made up of top military officers to a large extent, do get to the United States, but see little there to attract them for long periods of residence.

The physical installations and rolling stock needed to support a vastly increased circulation through the cities of Thailand have been largely completed. But this involves primarily the primate city, because Chiengmai, the second city, contains only about 100,000 population, and the other cities are proportionately smaller. The focus on Bangkok, at the head of navigation on the Chao Phraya, is due largely to physical geography, but centralism is reinforced by the politico-military system. What can be projected regarding the resulting flow and counter-flow? We are forced to depend heavily upon the performance of several key mobilizing institutions in the countryside.

Considerations of these questions strongly affecting the future of Bangkok were greately aided by a recent review of the experience with community development and decentralization.[6] In it the theory and practice are compared and a carefully annotated assessment of the academic literature is provided.

At present, the influence of the capital upon the peasant villagers (almost all of whom own their land and are not permitted by law to lose it to Chinese moneylenders) is felt most strongly through the Army. The Thai have a tradition of being military conquerors in Southeast Asia so the Army is a service in which most families take pride. The soldiers and police are most onerous in territories that had been conquered in the 18th and 19th centuries and have not yet been fully assimilated, such as the Muslim South and the Lao Northeast. Although these features are apparently the most important contacts, one finds only a few indirect references to their influence in scholarly studies. The most revealing statements are the matter-of-fact pronouncements of top Thai officials such as ". . . a pattern of local administration with a high degree of participation by the people becomes an effective tool of counter-insurgency. At the same time it provides a basic foundation at the grass roots for a truly democratic system." It is the general belief locally that the Thai survived as the only people in Southeast Asia not subject to colonization by the Western Great Powers because they paid attention to self-defense very promptly as compared to other matters. They also trained some astute diplomats, but that is a story that depends solely upon the outcome of Bangkok intrigues.

Bangkok rules through a chain that leads through 71 provincial governments (changwats), 539 districts (amphoes), 5,089 sub-districts (tambons), and 45,610 villages (mubans). The top two levels are filled by permanent government officials, but the latter two are selected from the community at the designation of the officials, but with the acquiescence of the local peasants. The tambon supports a wat, the Buddhist temple-monastery-school-hospital-meeting place complex (or a mosque in the South).

The equilibrium-maintaining feature of peasant society is the tie to the land. Social status among the peasants in the muban derives from the amount of land ownership. The bigger land owners among them are more likely to innovate in agriculture, make more trips to town, and send their sons to school longer. Their opinions dominate in the village councils for the simple reason that they are also more likely to be influential in obtaining Bangkok's help in restoring or improving the vicinity. Peasants normally wait upon government action and are reluctant to help themselves.

The central government has been engaged in experiments aimed at improving its effectiveness at the local level. One of these (Developing Democracy Program, 1966) allowed greater independence to a tambon leader by giving him some staff college training and providing grants-in-aid. The newly initiated projects include a volunteer defense corps (that works with the police and military in areas threatened by terrorists), health stations and midwifery centers, potable water projects and electrification. U. S. AID helps in the North and Northeastern provinces. Community development programs exist, but have little influence, despite the mobile development units that have been created to help remote areas.

These programs have a history of repeated failures; nevertheless the capabilities of the peasants have been noticeably increasing. Improvements in transport, use of fertilizer, health, the control of water, electrification, education, and handicrafts are accumulating. They can only be attributed to indirect, but reinforcing influences emanating from Bangkok.

Buddhist monks in Thailand are not politicized, as in Vietnam, but are becoming increasingly influential in secular matters in the countryside. The most respected of these are the "permanent monks" who have served for more than ten years in the predominant Mahanikai Order.

Teachers are influential for many of the same reasons, particularly if they live in the village and if they are headmasters. They validate a great deal of the technical knowledge that villagers would not be able to distinguish from braggadocio or rumor, and they help write official reports.

Traders are appearing in villages now who are not Chinese. They appear to have acquired capital by working on construction projects, or in cities, and combine it with their expanded experience and contacts. Thus many village-based middlemen with ties to regional centers and to Bangkok have been created since World War II. It would not be surprising to discover (though it is not reported) that experience with organization and equipment during military service was exceedingly important.

Many Bangkok-based "politicians" (a term which includes higher military officers) maintain contacts with client villages to which they have an obligation, usually through possession of family estates. They may find means for installing new services in "their" villages earlier than the others and therefore serve as an "outside" entrepreneur.

These combined forces bring about change among the peasants in a very patchy sort of way. They also insure that the standard approaches to planning by government continue to be ineffective. An AID administrator, after many frustrations, came to the conclusion that the proper model for implementation should not be based upon communications in an hierarchical pyramid but upon a pancake, a shape which forces the funds and information to diffuse laterally away from the center, but hinders them from moving very far.

I have yet to see an adequate explanation for the way that Thailand outgrew its feudalism and transferred title of the land to the peasantry. At any rate, the laws were carefully constructed so as to maintain a peasant society at equilibrium with its resources, even in the face of three decades of unprecedented population growth. It is evident that the system was refurbished after World War II when the grain collection channels were taken from the black market operators and centralized by the government. The government was aided by the food shortages in rice-eating countries during the 1950s and 1960s, because the sales were made on a government-to-government basis. But now, due to the "miracle rice" that has come out of Rockefeller Institute research in the Philippines, almost all Asian nations are becoming self-sufficient. The price of rice has dropped spectacularly and is likely to be driven even lower, so that it will sell again at only a slight premium over wheat or maize when measured as food value. The Chinese will continue to import wheat and sell rice until that equilibrium point is reached. This price drop forces the Thailand grain collection organization to put up huge subsidies, which probably cannot be sustained for more than a year or two. Already it is said that two-thirds of the farmers are in debt, almost all at usurious interest rates (say 3-7 percent per month) so the pressure on the peasant population will be extraordinarily severe, especially on the farmers living at a considerable distance from Bangkok.

This means that Bangkok and the regional centers are likely to receive an increasing flow of people who cannot make ends meet when living on their own land. A son or daughter will be sent to the city to get a job. They will find a way of squatting on governmental land and will search for work as servants or in construction. The government's control over Bangkok development is far too imperfect to stop them from staying, once they enter as visitors.

The Klong Toey Reception Center

Klong Toey is the name of the principal canal behind the large, modern port which serves Bangkok and all of Thailand. Ships from all over the world line up at quayside, drop off general cargo, and take on grain or logs for plywood. Their turnaround time is comparable with the best in Asia, and the port itself is well planned, clean, and commodious, but it is not big enough to cope with the future of a developing Thailand, so an expansion is planned to take care of the new containerized ships and the LASH ("lighter aboard ship") lighters.

Lying behind the harbor, in a patch of swampy land, is the Klong Toey community. It was founded just after World War II when the first stages of the harbor were constructed. To these inhabitants were added a number of squatters displaced by the road built to the harbor from the center of the city. Then, less than ten years ago, a series of disastrous droughts in the North and Northeast of Thailand added thousands of new families. By now it is believed that 25-30,000 people are in the path of the further modernization of the port of Bangkok. For years notices have been given to squatters to quit the location. However, when residents have been brought to court they have been able to obtain delays in putting eviction proceedings into effect, so that new notices no longer frighten the members of the community. This action indicates some kind of organization in the community, but none is admitted when first speaking to university investigators and higher government officials. The pattern suggests underworld control and organization.

Smuggling can be highly profitable in Thailand because the excise taxes are high, and the international authorities are doing their best to stop the flow of heroin. American cigarettes are highly prized also. Normally the contraband is dropped from the incoming ships at night to small boats so highly powered that they can escape from the police boats. The goods are taken to disguised godowns close to Klong Toey and distributed from there throughout the city by school age children who cannot get into schools because they live in unregistered residences. The children are not subject to severe penalties until the age of fourteen or more, so the risks are small. This mode of smuggling requires core organizations of thirty to a hundred men, and hundreds of contacts. Therefore, one would expect that several gangs will have formed, each of them somewhat specialized but having in common musclemen to coerce individuals, knife-men to keep contacts in line, and gunmen to protect the bosses of the rackets. Local police will have learned to live with the situation and have accepted tea money ($500 to release a smuggler if they catch him), but the special squads working with the international authorities remain a problem, and all other interferences to their operations must be blocked by higher up personages kept on retainer in the government.

Addicts to heroin and opium congregate in places like Klong Toey. The source of the drugs is advertised by a gray, weatherbeaten flag waving over a shack at the city dump. (Prostitutes are also available at a "hotel" in the log yard.) Users provide extensions of the underworld organizations. Therefore, if anything constructive goes ahead in the Klong Toey community, even a piece of research, the underworld needs to be assured that it will not "hurt business."

Nevertheless, changes can occur. For instance the solid waste of the city is being deposited as fill in low areas near the entrance to the community. Scores of residents go through the dumped loads for metal and unbroken bottles first. Later plastic trimmings are used to cover wet mud and allow people to walk over it the way that they might use a straw mat in the village, and waste paper may be collected and baled, although there was no direct evidence of that stage at the time of the visit (paper salvage depends upon access to a pulping plant). Similarly at the back of the community, in an area separating it from the fence of the Port Authority, a pipeline was delivering silt and sand dredged from the deep channel linking the port with the Gulf of Siam. The excess water would drain off to the river leaving a muck that resisted invasion by squatters, but would eventually make the community less and less livable due to a shift in the drainage system.

Already most of this community lives over water that is a few inches to several feet deep, varying according to the extent of the rain and, in the lowest places, the tides in the Chao Phraya and the klongs (canals). One gets to the doorway of a house by means of rickety boardwalks (usually one six-inch plank, supported by stakes). The houses have scrubbed wood floors, 2x4 framing on 4x4 posts, walls of lumber or woven nipa leaf strips, and roofs of rusting sheet iron, corrugated transite, or moldy canvas. Windows can be shuttered against the driving rain, but otherwise stand open. All sorts of lean-tos and extra rooms have been improvised so that no sense of order remains for the eye to grasp. Thin power lines extend in odd ways to connect up most houses and provide "street lighting" at crucial intersections of paths, thus supporting radios in most houses, television in about 10 percent and even hot plates for cooking instead of the more familiar buckets lined with fireclay and fed with charcoal. Provisions are obtained from a string of shops lining a recently constructed concrete road or by taking a bus up the road several miles. The bus terminal also appears to be a relatively recent addition. A few baht-buses (decorated light trucks that carry produce or up to twelve passengers at $0.05 per trip) and samlors (scooter cabs carrying up to three passengers) were standing nearby, but they could have been parked close to the residence of the entrepreneur-driver waiting for the noon traffic to build up. One loop of street was paved; it guaranteed access to the essential services.

Building a New Bangkok

Klong Toey lies within the oldest of the four corridors now building out and away from the original palace and the seat of government. Landings at the riverside are served by launches carrying workers from the dense inner city to factories downstream which are interspersed among the various port and naval installations. The more recently evolving corridors are based upon the original railway network, which moves out to the east, west, and south. Each of those lines was paralleled by one or two roads that bridged the klongs to dwindle away into the rice paddy, palm, and banana plantations interspersed with a few fruit trees.

Now tracts of middle class housing and squatter settlements are scattered along each corridor, separated by distribution centers, factories, private schools, and military specialization centers. All of these are remarkably automobile-oriented, as is the Don Muang Airport to the north. Round estimates suggest that as many as 50,000 households are living in the squatter settlements equivalent in most respects to Klong Toey. The number may well be an underestimate because it appears that neither the policy of registration of all members of the household nor the census can be assured of getting within 20 percent of the real figure.

How can the Thai Government promote housing and infrastructure that expands at least proportionately to population? It has had housing experience in the recent past at Ding Doeng with pukka apartments for the middle classes, but they cost about $4,000 per unit. With a rent of $10 per month such apartments require a considerable government subsidy, which it can afford less and less.

More promising by far is the "site and services" approach to housing, where the minimum requirements are made available through loans as needed and the householders produce their own housing. If all of squatter Bangkok is as poor as Klong Toey (Table 3) it appears that up to 75 percent can afford the rent levels implicit in the "site and services" schemes, allowing 10-20 percent of income to be applicable to shelter. The remainder may be able to achieve the minimum level after acquiring more experience and skill in the city or they may return defeated to the village, as many do, to be replaced by an even larger number of young and adventurous individuals.

One other feature inherent in such data is often ignored. Windfall sources of income, and ill-gotten gains of all sorts, are rarely reported to interviewers. The fact that quite sizable sums are obtained shows up in the number of television aerials and motor scooters, but more is undoubtedly hoarded and would be invested in property with a clear title, should it become available.

Table 3. Income Distribution in a Bangkok Squatter Community—1970

Monthly Income per Household	Percent of Households	
Under $ 20	5	(The median
20-40	23	figure in peasant
40-60	21	villages up country
60-80	16	is reported, by
80-100	13	newly returned
100-140	11	Peace Corpsmen,
140-220	7	to be in the $30-40
Over $220	5	monthly range.)

Source: Thammasat University, Survey of Klong Toey Slum, Bangkok, 1971.

Assessments of the cost of the "site and services" approach to housing reveal that a half to two-thirds must be allocated to land. The not inconsiderable development costs for filling and drainage are far overshadowed by the price of raw land. This finding causes one to investigate the land market in Bangkok.

Land price changes are an important indicator of confidence in the future of a metropolis if a land market is allowed to exist. Land price has not always been significant in Thailand because land was once almost totally in the hands of the Thai aristocracy, or the peasant farmer who was prevented from freely transferring his land. The government was the most common land developer, but it sold off plots to the private sector (after World War II reconstruction) at the same time that a demand for free standing houses began to appear due to a new and rapidly proliferating middle class. Thus a shadowy land market evolved. Everyone agreed that foreigners should be kept out of landholding, so the government enforces those laws even as it winks at other questionable transactions.

Over the past five years important amounts of official credit have flowed into real estate loans. Bank of Thailand figures show a 50 percent annual growth rate, resulting in an absolute total of $324 million in loans in 1970. The first quarter of 1971 was up 22 percent despite many blows to the economy as a whole. At least two-thirds of this lending is concentrated in the Bangkok region. The uncertain nature of the land market is fostered by murky titles—the recording office is at least three years behind, and many holdings already built upon are merely shares in a scheme which does not make specific assignments of plots. It is amazing how much concrete and steel has gone up on such a flimsy legal base!

According to *The Investor* (August, 1971, pp. 677-82), Bangkok land prices as a whole are down somewhat from 1970, having retreated to the 1969 level. Such generalizations are banker's estimates, not the movement of an indix figure such as is available in Japan and Korea. They are also based upon a turnover of a very restricted quantity of land released by the major land holding families, mostly aristocrats. The latter cannot very easily become "land poor," as has happened elsewhere in the world, because no tax has been laid upon land. What this means in Bangkok is that the values created by urban improvements in roads, drainage, and water supply accrue largely to the speculators. Because the government cannot recoup its funds directly, the supply of such services must remain scarce, land price high, and congestion close to tolerable limits.

Perhaps the most troubling indicator that is relevant to the immediate physical development of Bangkok is the rapidity of growth of the population of motor vehicles. Roads are now predominantly asphalted, even in the interior of the country, so that movement of people and produce has been vastly speeded up. The most recent data provided by the Ministry of National Development allow us to follow growth in the decade 1959-1968, which show that the number of motor vehicles has been expanding about 20 percent per year, with the countryside keeping up with the metropolis in the latter half of the decade. Compare this with Singapore, where growth was 3-7 percent per year and accompanied by strong complaints concerning congestion. Bangkok has reached a stage where there is one four-wheel vehicle for every 7-8 residents in the region while Singapore is still around one for each 10-11 persons. In Bangkok the congestion greatly reduces the quality of service provided by the buses, so that people will pay more and take the jitney-type baht-bus that can sometimes maneuver itself through the jams, or acquire a car themselves in the hope of beating the traffic tie-ups.

It has been obvious for some time that something has to be done about the population explosion in autos. This is a moment when foreign exchange is becoming exceedingly scarce, so rumors about a sizable addition to the excise tax have been persistent, but the denials (up to September 1971) were equally persistent. More than three-quarters of the new models on the streets are of Japanese origin, so that birth control for vehicles will have a selective impact. The idea of making automobile production a local industry has occurred to many; therefore first Ford and then General Motors were invited to look over the market. However, the fraction of components imported will remain high unless Thai consumers are willing to discipline themselves and accept an extremely standard vehicle, a situation no one expects at the moment. One must imagine some kind of political and administrative crisis in Bangkok before activities based on *structures,* and land use, such as residence, retail sales, light manufacturing, and cinema attendance, and on *networks,* such as transport, water supply, electric power, and telephone, actually grind to a halt. The city can be directed to a path of steady development only with the aid of some new institutions that accumulate highly competent local talent and yet remain open to imported ideas that are carried into Bangkok from all parts of the world.

Cultural Values in the Modern Institutions

The new metropolitan institutions must be operated by middle class Thai, products of the local educational system. They will be directed by Thai that have gone overseas, about 40 percent to the United States and almost an equal proportion to other English-speaking countries. The basic technology is transmitted either through the military, where the advisors are American, or through the multinational corporations where—out of 168 companies maintaining offices—68 were from the United States, 21 from the United Kingdom, and two apiece from Australia and India. However, the 28 Japanese firms operate much more often in the English language than in Chinese. Thus the remarkable openness of the Thai society is seen as being open only by those who use English; for the speakers of tongues other than Chinese it appears quite insulated. For the Chinese, if one gauges by the inscriptions on tombstones even in the villages peripheral to Bangkok where ancestor worship is still important, the absorption into Thai culture is largely completed, so the young people in particular think Thai, but learn English if they wish to rise in the world.

The Thai society is aware of the risks of alienation associated with the learning of English and therefore special care has been taken to counteract the evil to which the teenage youth are exposed. In Bangkok this is done by providing a "catechism" of Thai nationalism in the English language itself, so that fluency in English is reached by reviewing the dogma underlying one's own culture. This technique of teaching renders the subtle forms of English more understandable and therefore easier to learn. The textbook entitled *140 Essays and Letters for Advanced Students* was found in a state publishing house display window; it had just such an approach. A highly condensed treatment of Thai values to be transmitted to incompletely socialized adolescents is thus made available to the outsider in his own language. Imagine the following principles operating as part of the unspoken consensus in the modern sector of Thailand, much of it still in the early stages of institution-building, and compare it with the sophistication in content of parallel materials in South Korea (see footnote 1).

The first lesson asserts that Buddhism is the oldest of the great religions and based upon "Four Noble Truths" of "The Middle Way," one of which is the eightfold path. The message is laid out in twenty questions and answers with the following conclusion: "Under its good influence the Thais have become a peace-loving nation, with unrivalled tolerance and hospitality to people of different races and creeds. It is not too much to say that, in the past, this admirable characteristic of our nation helped a great deal in preserving our national independence while the neighboring countries all around us were losing theirs."

The second lesson continues this theme by describing the operation of the wat, the Buddhist monastery-school-temple establishment. It commits the citizen to assist the priests in obtaining food, clothes, medicine, and shelter so as to perpetuate Buddhism "in our beloved country." The third exhorts them to "Uphold the moral standard in this corrupted world" by observing the days of the waxing and waning of the moon called Wan Pra. The fourth takes up the ordination ritual for young men at age twenty-one, where they learn "how to curb their passions at an age when these passions are strongest." The fifth takes up a new holiday declared especially for the onset of the 26th century of

Buddhism. Asalaha Day commemorates the beginning of Buddha's teaching of the ascetics who became his disciples, a reminder of the "Triple Gems" principles.

Thereafter, the essays become more secular in character but no less serious. Essays cover nutrition, followed by traditional games, kite flying, and takraw—which uses a wicker ball. Then the famous Thai dramas, replete with dancing, are explained so that the popular version can be distinguished from the classical. The ritual of greeting, the wai, is justified on the bases that "it makes the Thai people look quite lovely and amiable ..." Note the attention paid throughout to the image the Thai national presents to the outsider.

Lessons in government start with a brief history of the Thai precedents of constitutional monarchy, showing that for almost a thousand years the king and the Buddhist religion have been traditional symbols of the nation. On the tricolor flag of the country, the white strip represents Buddhism, the blue the king, and the red the nation. The election mechanics are reviewed so that Thais need not be "tempted or bribed to vote for a bad candidate."

Once the truly important lessons have been learned, the professor can relax somewhat and translate familiar aspects of life style into English: transport means, modes of communication, influences of weather, recreational opportunities (which draw upon the 4-H principles so familiar to American farm youth), etc. Then the role of education (which "makes a full man") and its two streams, intellectual and manual, is elaborated according to structure and function characteristics. That sets the stage for a discussion of the progress of science, which glorifies technological developments from James Watt's steam engine to the communication between earth satellites which should soon be realized. A hope is expressed that science will be used for the welfare of the people, and it leads to a special essay that attempts to define the welfare of the people. The latter is particularly important because the extent to which a state provides for human welfare is seen as an index "of the efficiency and stability of the government." One sees in the argument a genuine recognition that the future elite can be secure only if it is based within an environment that it is able to improve through the use of modern technology.

Newspapers and books are also given due attention. The journalist is exhorted to avoid any taint of exaggeration and prejudice—he is responsible to the Minister of the Interior. Books are dissected—title page, preface, table of contents, glossary, index, etc., with a homily added that books may be dull or exciting, good or evil, and faithful instructors.

The chief lessons about an automobile are that they cost more than a good house or two, so that few people can afford them, and many accidents are caused due to crazy driving.

Athletics are important in the life of the nation, so the student will maintain interest in learning English in order to read a piece on interscholastic competition at the Gymkhana in Bangkok. However, the subsequent essays which are more in conflict with traditional values may encounter resistance on the part of the student. One is a piece on country life in which the authorities seem unable to defend that way of life except as it is necessary for the sustenance of the city. Another is a sermon on procrastination, "Life is a struggle against nature, against temptations, and against other human beings; only the fittest and the strongest will survive and prosper. Only a moment's delay will end in failure and defeat." The Thai educational administrators use these homilies as a common sense attempt to banish the traditional fatalism and apathy of the Orient. They anticipate creating a kind of society that might be called "urbane social Darwinism."

These arguments are followed by an essay on patriotism, another on SEATO, followed by a still longer one on the United Nations organization. The latter account clearly predicts that the Communists and the United States will engage in another great war which will set the whole world ablaze; yet I suspect that statement results more from clumsiness in the use of the English language because the authors are unable to use a kind of conditional phrasing not available in Thai grammar. Somewhat later the official history of the 20th October Revolution was taken up and then, without reference to chronology, the border incident with Cambodia where the United Nations "put things right," without a single mention that the contested Khmer hill fort was given to Cambodia.

Letter writing in English presents some real challenges. Naturally it begins with the letters of schooldays, but then introduces a father's letter to a schoolmaster with phrasings for the schoolmaster to employ for either a favorable or an unfavorable reply, excuses provided by a mother, or a clerk of an employer. How to borrow money, and how to decline politely, is included with a distinction being made as to whether it is inside the family or not. Letters of application for employment and recommendation naturally must be represented, as are orders for books or goods, paying under protest, getting service from the landlord, and complaining to the neighbors about a nuisance. The book finishes with a slightly sarcastic letter to the editor complaining about the inattention of the road repair administration to the sad state of the road in front of one's house. In such a manner are the proprieties of participation in urban and social affairs laid down. As yet there seems to be very little disenchantment with education in Bangkok, so the text would not normally be labeled as "preachy" or hypocritical by the students, but merely of use for conforming to modern ways of life in official circles, just as English is of use.

Thai views of popular culture in English-speaking countries can be obtained by going to the cinema. There the favorites seem to be war epics, Walt Disney, Westerns, and productions of literary classics. Melodramas are imported in Chinese from Taiwan, Hong Kong, and Singapore, which makes them more understandable. The media do not transmit much of the rock and country music that has won the attention of the youth elsewhere in the world, and sales of recordings of these themes began to increase rapidly only after 1970. Much of the popular Thai culture comes through the advertisements in cinema, television, and store fronts, so that consumerism is what is promoted in the loosely controlled, largely commercial institutions engaged in modernizing and internationalizing the Thais.

Building Ultramodern Organizations

Students steeped in these Thai traditions must become participants in the most modern institutions with the strongest technologies. When the Koreans faced the same problems they stressed the traditions and popular culture of the English-speaking peoples, and thus prepared their overseas students much better for the shock of cosmopolitan living in the West. Thus, the Koreans found it quite possible to adapt and transfer loyalties to the host country and suffered a considerable brain drain, while the Thai got homesick and accepted even the unrewarding posts back in Bangkok. Nevertheless, the social and economic development of Seoul is far more rapid than that of Singapore, and even further ahead of Bangkok, in large part because Koreans have learned to take advantage of opportunities in new technology that originate overseas.

An example of the means by which modern institutions are built in Bangkok is provided by the Telecommunication Training Centre and its spinoff, the Test and Development Centre, at Nonthaburi and Pathon Thani on the Chao Phraya River a few miles north of the city. It was founded upon a general recognition among the overseas-trained-members of the elite that telephones were an essential feature of the kind of modernization they thought appropriate for Thailand. Telecommunications increase the capacity to govern because they speed up the response of government to local emergenices and they permit a much higher degree of coordination between departments, agencies, offices, and enterprises in both government and the private sector. The government could no longer depend upon foreign concessionaires to develop such an essential utility once Thai engineers and technicians were available. The program was expedited by the International Telecommunications Union (ITU) and the United Nations Development Program.

Telephones have lagged in Bangkok. Only about 100,000 lines could be used in September, 1969, but expansion is due to be accelerated over this decade. According to plan the network size would be trebled by 1975 and almost doubled again by 1980.

The Training Centre had to start from the very beginning with translation of the training manuals used elsewhere in the world, establishment of dormitories, the acquisition of equipment, and formulation of a recruiting program for the various levels of trainee. Nevertheless, since 1965 it has produced 5,000 trainees and now operates at about 1,200 a year, almost double the planned rate. The Test and Development Centre provides a place for checking out new and existing telecommunications equipment, and a base from which improved operating procedures can be worked out as well as the plans for developing a system that fits the country's needs for communication. The extra push that was needed to overcome obstacles very often came from the Armed Forces of Thailand, but the military influence within the institution is difficult to isolate. The most effective technical assistance thus far has come from India, after a somewhat shaky beginning when the source of help originated in Australia.

From this base Bangkok is expected to link up the countries of Southeast Asia—Laos, Cambodia, Malaysia, Burma—tying them to the communications satellite already over the Indian Ocean. At present there is an impasse between the Telephone Organization of Thailand, which handles domestic telephones and the links across the boundaries, and the older Post and Telegraph Department which has the microwave relays transmitting television from Bangkok to the lesser cities of Thailand. Once the two systems are married to each other, the channels for modernization will be vastly amplified.

Ultramodern technology seems to be introduced into these societies much more rapidly and smoothly now than in the earlier era based upon the diesel engine, electric generator, and the printing press. The latter are now dependable, almost invisible mainstays in these metropolitan communities with mature, self-sustaining institutions to back them up.

The new contraceptives provide an opportunity for creating ultramodern organization aimed as achieving a greatly needed social adaptation.[7] The rate of population growth in Thailand is now estimated at 3.3 percent per year, which is among the highest in the world. Thai women average about 6.5 births over the reproductive period of life. All the concomitants of such growth are everywhere evident—a very youthful society, a housing shortage, schools that bring the population up to literacy but can take only about 2.5 percent of the age class to higher levels, and an expressed desire on the part of women for smaller families. In 1968 surveys showed that suburban women, who comprise a relatively educated population, were succeeding in reducing births by 15 percent over those in a rural district used as a control. Among the contraceptors, Thai women are distinctly under-represented, while Chinese most frequently use the available services. At the government level, recognition at the policy level has been given to the forthcoming population crisis, but it has yet to be followed through with the provision of adequate funds. A "Family Health Project" began in 1968 and became official in 1970; about 5,000 workers have been trained and 3,500 clinics organized. About 5 percent of the population in need is presently served.

The number of acceptors has roughly doubled each year, reaching 225,000 in 1970. The method of contraceptive now favored by more than half of the early adopters is the use of pills, while female sterilization is preferred by about a fifth. Now a five year plan has been formulated with the aim of doubling the number of acceptors in that period and establishing an integrated family planning program capable of much more comprehensive services in the decades to come. The aims are still modest, particularly those for reaching 7.5 percent of the target population by 1976. The project received only $500,000 from the Thai Government for 1972, a bit over a third of what was requested. However, four times that amount is expected from overseas sources, most of it in the form of pills and instruments with the major share of the aid coming from Germany.

Thus family planning is at an earlier stage of institution-building than telecommunications. The prospects of effecting a rapid demographic transition, the kind that has dramatically accelerated in South Korea and has gained great momentum in Taiwan, Hong Kong, and Singapore, does not seem likely in the Thai culture, even for Bangkok. The prospects are for the overall population to double in size over the next 20-25 years, and for Bangkok and environs to quadruple. This population pressure will spin new urban settlements into the adjoining countryside at an increasing rate.

URBAN FAMILY LIFE COMPARED

Recently a totally new approach to the comparison of metropolises has been started, and both Bangkok and Singapore were among the urban centers to which it was first applied. The basic hypothesis is that living in a large metropolis is subject to a number of extraordinary stresses, and the residents are forced to cope with them as best they can. The coping behaviors are adjustments, or indicators of strain. Thus it is possible to get reports by the residents themselves on the adaptive processes in their family life and their feelings. From a representative sample one can discover what psychic costs and gains are attendant upon the respective drives toward development led by Singapore and Bangkok. Robert E. Mitchell initiated such studies in Hong Kong in 1967 and extended them to Bangkok, Singapore, Taipei, and the six major cities of Western Malaysia in 1968.[8] Mitchell's study appears likely to become a major benchmark in sociology, although not yet published in full. It contains a multitude of comparisons, many of which show a mixed response of the residents to urban conditions. The findings are often not greatly different for the respective cities or the major ethnic groups living in them, nor are they strikingly new in the light of prior experience with urbanization. The surprises and major differences are worth noting, however, because they require explanation regarding the different histories of these metroplises, their expectations regarding the future, and the characteristics of the tools for data gathering and analysis employed. In the following discussion Hong Kong conditions are included for comparison because that city contains a population comparable in ethnic origin, and it serves as a major competitor for the two pacemaking metropolises reported upon here.

One significant indicator that allows direct comparison is the reported earnings per working individual in the families interviewed. They are calculated in U.S. dollars at a time when all currencies were freely convertible, so that the internal cost of living was not based by currency controls (Table 4).

The summary results suggest that Bangkok has 4 percent greater income per worker than Singapore and 10 percent greater income than Hong Kong. This observation is strongly in conflict with estimates of gross domestic product in Thailand versus those for Hong Kong and Singapore (which are approximately

Table 4. Mean Monthly Personal Income—1968 (U.S.$)

		Total	Men	Women
Bangkok:	Thai	97	103	84
	Chinese	75	87	44
Singapore:	Indian	92	97	60
	Chinese	85	98	56
	Malay	68	70	48
Hong Kong:	Chinese	79	96	43

equal to each other). The explanation seems to derive from the use of commercial surveys which, despite meeting tests for preventing bias, encounter the same difficulties as the census does in Bangkok. The latter seems to under-report by 30 percent or so, and many more low-income Thai seem to be missed than Chinese. Places such as the Klong Toey community described earlier would not have been represented in the sample. It appears to have been drawn from the accessible parts of Bangkok, the locales of the city the foreign visitor might be able to see under ordinary circumstances. On the other hand, virtually the whole of Singapore and 97 percent of Hong Kong is similarly accessible. Despite its limitations, the Bangkok sample shows much greater inequality of income than Singapore, while Hong Kong is in between them.

Employment among Bangkok Chinese is strongly within the family, usually in the family enterprise, or with that of a family connection. This is due to the fact that Thai are preferred in direct applications for jobs opening up in the various public and private organizations. In Singapore the family enterprise is more important by far for the Chinese than for Indian or Malay; nevertheless, friends rather than relatives are more likely to have provided the essential contact needed to obtain the current job regardless of ethnic origin. In Hong Kong friends are even more important for getting a job. The difference is between belonging to a minority population in the social system or the predominant one, even if the latter may not have political power, as in Hong Kong.

Singapore people are far more optimistic about life changes for the young than either the Bangkok or Hong Kong sample. However, within all the cities shared with significant numbers of other ethnic groups, the Chinese were significantly less optimistic than the other ethnic groups. (This question asked about the chances for a working class boy to become a medical doctor, and accepted "excellent" or "good" as indicators of optimism.) Hong Kong opinion may have been influenced by the uncertainty about whether the political turbulence of 1967—when the local Communist Party tried to deliver the Colony to Peking by means of a combination of strikes, street riots, and bombs—had not greatly weakened the long-term economic outlook for the metropolis. It was only a year or more later that the residents began to realize that the economy was seemingly unimpaired.

The reports regarding the high fraction of residents in these metropolises who

The Measurement of Metropolitan Performance

felt that they could not control the course of their life are similarly explainable. Bangkok Thai are least likely to feel that they are victims of fate, but Bangkok Chinese are nearly the same. Bangkok Chinese have also experienced relative stability in the social status of the family. So we encounter a peculiar difference in philosophy between the two cultures—Bangkok people do not feel that it is possible to achieve much in life, even with increased education, yet they are not fatalistic. Singapore people seem to think of education as a means of reaching the top in social status but their sample had acquired less schooling.

The Singapore sample contained the fewest migrants (32 percent versus Bangkok's 38 percent and Hong Kong's 70 percent), but those present had more rural backgrounds. Three dialects are almost equally represented among the Chinese of Singapore, these being Cantonese, Chiu Chow, and Hokkien, while in Bangkok more than four-fifths belonged to the Chiu Chow speakers, who come from very poor villages in the hinterland of Swatow. Although imported Confucianism seems to be declining, Bangkok families are actively religious, while Hong Kong seems not interested in religion, and Singapore people hold views that are very mixed.

Interchange of population between Singapore and Bangkok is very small; both are linked to Hong Kong much more closely than to each other. However, air traffic is building up 20-30 percent per year, and the staffs of multinational corporations and international government-oriented agencies are increasingly Asians, so it is anticipated that each will very soon establish a special enclave within the other where special services are more readily obtained. Then the Thai could get his peppery dishes, or even repair to a wat for meditation, while in Singapore; correspondingly, the Singaporeans and Hong Kong residents might find a new apartment in a high-rise building, handle legal work at a distance, and play mah jong in Bangkok. These districts are likely to combine tourism with business, and perhaps also a complete school system that meets the standards set at home, thus providing a compact set of services for those who stay for many months or some years. Such enclaves would constitute differentiated sectors in

Table 5. Backgrounds of Immigrants

		Spent most of ages 5-12 in a farming village (percent of migrants)	Spent most of ages 5-12 in small or large city (percent of migrants)
Singapore:	Malay	59	18
	Chinese	57	32
	Indian	23	64
	Total:	53	35
Bangkok:	Chinese	57	23
	Thai	37	42
	Total:	46	36
Hong Kong:	Chinese	40	42

the cosmopolitan ward of the metropolis. In this part of the world the demands of the Malay-Indonesian, Tamil, French, and English speakers already generate the markets that bring about cultural exchange at the individual, household, and small neighborhood level.

Inter-metropolitan exchange is also beginning in the area of popular culture—athletics, dance, music, Sunday newspapers. Each inter-metropolitan institution will develop a public of its own among the new cohorts completing secondary school who become minor experts in following the action. As income rises further, and the cost of group travel continues to decline, the new cosmopolitans may be expected to mix freely, rising above the barriers of language in ways that are familiar to the youth of Europe today. Enrichment of each other's lives should provide a partial substitute for looking to New York, London, Paris, Tokyo, and Los Angeles for models of modern behavior.

Potentials for the Future

There seems to be no barrier in sight that would prevent a continuation of the pacemaking function by both Singapore and Bangkok. Indeed, the overview of specific constraints experienced in these metropolises suggests that the pace may very well be stepped up over the next several years. Singapore in particular appears to be in a position to profit from the shifts in the world politico-economic system.

Many of the institutions that Bangkok needs have already evolved in Singapore and elsewhere. Thus the management techniques for the refining and petrochemicals complex, the telecommunications establishment, public housing management, family planning organization, and dozens of others can be learned and borrowed from Singapore, the next stages in transport organization can be adapted from Hong Kong, and industrial organization in export garments, appliances, and electronics from Taipei, Kaohsiung, and Seoul.

Interesting for the socio-cultural analyst is the observation that each of the transfers of a technology, mode of management, institutional structure, or legal instrument needed for installing a given institution seems to require translation into the English language between the Japanese, Chinese, or Korean version and the Thai before decisions can be made or action taken. Therefore the review of the policy for English-language instruction provided earlier becomes exceedingly significant; the institutions for extending the standard training in reading and speaking, and the comprehensiveness of the English language periodicals, become important for future development involving regional inter-society transfer.

The institutional solutions that Singapore needs are most likely to be found in Tokyo or the United States. Due to Singapore's former colonial status the teaching of English has made much more progress there, and no longer represents the eye of the needle through which modernization must pass. The university, for example, must now set itself standards equivalent to those of the leaders, rather than "developing country" type compromises, for research as well as teaching.

Exchange of these complex organizational concepts for both these cities is increasingly expedited by the regional offices of the United Nations agencies clustered around the ECAFE (Economic Commission for Asia and the Far East) headquarters in Bangkok. A number of special projects associated with them have begun to spill over into the nearby hotels in their search for office space. The ECAFE-related activities needing economic research are assembling on or near the campus of Singapore University. Another kind of international institution, the Asian Institute of Technology in Bangkok, is a graduate school drawing students from all of the Far East as a substitute for training in Western countries, but because textbooks and source materials are predominantly in English the language of instruction must also be English. The problems under investigation, however, are either contributions to theory or relevant to Asian development. The growth in these coordinating, promoting, and educating activities is far more rapid than the rates of economic growth experienced in these countries, but progress still seems to be proceeding at a snail's pace as compared to the modernization gap that becomes increasingly visible to the participants in the process. They are discouraged much of the time, and feel reinforced only occasionally. Yet any objective measurement of achievement seems certain to reveal that the groups with modern outlook indirectly affected by the coordinative work of the official and unofficial international institutions are rapidly expanding their influence. Moreover, careful questioning of some of the principals associated with a success reveals repeatedly a step or a stage in the ticklish process of promotion and reduction to practice that depended in a crucial manner upon the output of one of these international agencies or institutes. That kind of stimulus to development may be expected to increase as the colonial era recedes into history and more representative organizations struggle to be born.

NOTES

1. Richard L. Meier, "Exploring Development in Great Asian Cities: Seoul." Journal of the American Institute of Planners, Vol. 36 (November 1970), pp. 378-392. The findings from an application of this technique to Kanpur, Uttar Pradesh, India, was reported earlier: "Kanpur: A Metropolis Without a Face." Ekistics, Vol. 29 (May 1970), pp. 334-338.

2. W.L.C. Wheaton, "Singkong—A Parable on Regional Planning." Proceedings of the Third International Conference on Regional Development, Japan Center for Area Development Research, Tokyo, 1970, pp. 257-260. It was reported to me by the author of this paper that the Indonesian delegate to the Conference contributed in the course of the comment a competing parable that was unfortunately not recorded in the Proceedings. It portrayed the Asian intellectual view of the metropolis more or less as follows: "In my country there is a plant called singkong with somewhat unusual properties. It grows like a weed, extracting nutrients from the soil all around it. This enables it to grow large and overshadow the surrounding plants. They gradually wither and die while the singkong grows still larger. When the soil nutrients are exhausted the singkong dies, leaving a ghostly bare trunk in a patch of desert."

3. James Clavell, *King Rat.* Boston: Little, Brown, 1962; Nevil Shute, *The Legacy.* New York: Morrow, 1950.

4. Jin-bee Ooi and Hai Ding Chiang (eds.), *Modern Singapore.* Singapore: University of Singapore Press, 1969.

5. T.T.B. Koh and William S.W. Lim, "Planning Law and Processes in Singapore." Malaya Law Review, Vol. 11 (December 1969), pp. 315-344.

6. David A. Wilson, *The United States and the Future of Thailand.* New York: Praeger, 1970.

7. Allan G. Rosenfield, "Thailand: Family Planning Activities 1968 to 1970." Studies in Family Planning, Vol. 2 (September 1971), pp. 181-191.

8. Robert Edward Mitchell, "Levels of Emotional Strain in Southeast Asian Cities." The Urban Family Life Survey, Chinese University of Hong Kong, Hong Kong, July 1969, mimeo. A portion of the findings appeared as "Some Social Implications of High Density Housing." American Sociological Review, Vol. 36 (February 1971), pp. 18-29.

CHAPTER 3

Peter A. Busch

PROBLEMS OF A CITY STATE:
Ethnicity in Singapore

Because of Singapore's distinctive position as a city-state, this chapter is concerned not so much with uniquely urban phenomena as with problems that, while conditioned by their urban context, are essentially similar to those faced by many countries. In a study of politically subordinate municipalities such topics as transportation, housing, sanitation, or race relations would obviously merit attention. These issues are important in Singapore too, but in this setting they cannot be separated from foreign relations, national identity, and economic development policies. In short, analysis of Singapore must be guided by the coincidence of national and urban characteristics.

Like most Southeast Asian states, Singapore faces the necessity of building a politically coherent nation out of a multiethnic population—a task rendered difficult not only by the lack of common historical bonds among the island's peoples but also by the fact that the country's independent political institutions are younger than the children now in its secondary schools. The twin issues to which this paper is addressed are then, national allegiance and social harmony. Because of the brevity of a single chapter, these matters can be treated here only in their relation to the country's Chinese residents with a consideration of the Malays and Indians reserved for another work.[1]

This search for the causes of national political and social strength begins in the next section with a highly selective review of historical and contemporary Singapore. This will serve to introduce the reader to the island-state and to lay a substantive basis for the application of pertinent insights drawn from the social science literature. This latter task occupies the third part of this essay. The ideas that have emerged will next be operationalized and further explored with the aid

Author's note: Financial support for this project was provided by a Fulbright-Hays Fellowship, a National Science Foundation Dissertation Improvement Grant (Grant No. GS2452), and an Arms Control and Disarmament Agency grant.

of data from a survey of secondary school students which I conducted during 1969-1970 as part of a larger project.

The final goal of this analysis is a set of equations which explain the derivation of commitment to the state of Singapore and the causes of willingness to accept ethnically different citizens as fellow members of the same national society. In order to reach this point, however, we must wind our way through a variety of arguments and bodies of literature. This process may be facilitated by a brief summary of the major points made in the empirical analysis.

The fifth and sixth sections of this chapter deal with the causes of political support. One of the findings presented here is that the respondents apparently support their state more strongly to the degree that they feel their family and their ethnic group to have experienced economic improvement. This is in line with the observations of a number of scholars commenting on political development and it agrees with common sense expectations.

A more complex theme involves the effects of racial attitudes on commitment to the state. In the second and third sections of this paper I try to show that the present regime of Singapore has attempted to promote the legitimacy of the state by appealing to all citizens to accept each other as political partners regardless of ethnicity. This suggests that racial hostility would decrease political allegiance. On the other hand, the point is also made that pride in one's own group is compatible both with acceptance of other peoples and with allegiance to a multiracial state. The results of the quantitative analysis support this argument.

A number of other variables are also explored in the analysis of political attitudes although they cannot conveniently be summarized at this point. Included here are proficiency in the various languages spoken in Singapore, the effects of different types of school environment, and several aspects of the pupil's cultural heritage.

In sections seven and eight attention shifts to an explanation of the causes of ethnic hostility and amicability. This concern is due not only to the political role which such feelings play but also to the intrinsic importance of racial harmony in Singapore—a country which, like its neighbors, has a history of racial turmoil. In this part of the analysis, then, economic perceptions, school and neighborhoos, and linguistic ability are all found to have important impacts.

One of the motivations for this study is to show how this kind of research can be useful in guiding public policy. Some of the variables included in the analysis are directly subject to governmental manipulation while others can be controlled indirectly. Unfortunately a demonstration of these indirect effects, and hence, a picture of the overall policy implication of our findings, are beyond the scope of this chapter. Nevertheless, the issue is of sufficient importance to warrant a brief discussion of some analysis presented elsewhere.[2]

Before proceeding, I should stress that in talking about political support I mean allegiance to the state rather than the popularity of the present ruling elite (although the two are obviously related). For the really important issue for

Singapore is not so much whether Prime Minister Lee Kuan Yew and his party enjoy mass support—as they seem to. The more vital issues are the extent to which they are laying the foundations for an enduring polity and the reasons for their successes and failures.

INTRODUCING SINGAPORE

Since its expulsion from the Federation of Malaysia in 1965, Singapore's area of 224.5 square miles has made it the smallest independent state in Southeast Asia. Despite its size, the island manages to contain an amazingly diverse population. Of the two million residents, 76.2 percent are ethnic Chinese, 15.0 percent are Malays, and 7.0 percent are Indians.[3] The remaining 1.8 percent consists of Englishmen, Eurasians, Arabs, Iraqi Jews, and people who defy categorization.

The island is just off the southern tip of the Malay peninsula in the Straits of Johore. Its position between the South China Sea and the Indian Ocean and its excellent natural harbor were the main reasons why Sir Stamford Raffles acquired the then nearly uninhabited territory from the royal house of Johore for Britain in 1819.[4] Based on favorable geography, Singapore rapidly became a major entrepôt, not only for British trade but also for commerce conducted by the Chinese and Indian merchants who came to the area. Aside from its location and harbor, however, Singapore has no natural resources. The island has no valuable minerals and its high population density would leave it with little agricultural land even if its soil were not poor. Even water must be piped from the peninsula.[5]

Nevertheless, the country is relatively prosperous and compares very favorably with the rest of the region in such indicators as literacy, communications facilities, per capita GNP, and health. While the economic basis of this prosperity is predominantly commercial, substantial industrialization has occurred, fostered in large part by recent political stability, government incentives and support, and the continuing provision of trained manpower emanating from an educational system that is increasingly shifting from a white-collar, liberal arts tradition to a technical emphasis.[6] Indeed, much more industrialization is required to solve a continuing problem of unemployment aggravated by the British military withdrawal at the end of 1971.[7]

One of the most striking characteristics of Singapore's population is its ethnic, cultural, and linguistic diversity. The census figures cited earlier give only a slight feeling for this variety. Perhaps more revealing is the fact that the island supports newspapers in English, in Chinese, and in Malay and Tamil (the major Indian language in Singapore), and that radio and television are broadcast in these languages (Chinese programs being in Mandarin plus several dialects). Public education is also conducted in each of the four languages, with parents free to choose the one in which they want their children taught.

Table 1. Comparisons of Singapore with Other Asian States

	Singapore	Malaysia	Indonesia	Philippines	Japan
Per capita GNP for 1969 in U.S. dollars	$844	$349[1]	$96[2]	$340	$1,626
Estimated daily newspaper circulation per 1,000 inhabitants	154[5]	74[5]	7[3]	27[4]	503
Radio receivers per 1,000 inhabitants as of 1968	50	41	14	45	255
Population per physician	1,520[5]	4,220	27,560[5]	1,390[5]	910[2]

Notes: Unless otherwise noted, all figures are for 1969 and are from United Nations, Statistical Office, *Statistical Yearbook: 1970*. (New York: United Nations, Department of Economic and Social Affairs, 1971.)

   1. Bank Negara Malaysia, *Quarterly Economic Bulletin*, Vol. 3, No. 3 (September 1970), pp. 41, 60. The exchange ratio used here is M$3.055 to the U.S. dollar, as stated Ibid., p. 60.
   2. Estimate for 1968.
   3. Estimate for 1965.
   4. Estimate for 1966.
   5. Estimate for 1967

As shown in Table 2, communication among the various groups is facilitated by two common language media: English and Malay. Although the degree of multilingualism has probably increased greatly since the 1957 census from which these figures are drawn, there are, of course, many people who speak only their own ancestral tongue.

Turning from this snapshot of Singapore, we may ask why political allegiance and ethnic relations are major problems. The answer requires a brief historical review of the formation of political identities in Singapore. Apologies are rendered in advance to the historian for the necessarily cursory nature of so short an exposition.

Much of Singapore's history is encapsulated in J. S. Furnivall's classic depiction of colonial Burma and the Dutch East Indies:

> ... the first thing that strikes the visitor is the medley of peoples— European, Chinese, Indian, and native. It is in the strictest sense a medley, for they mix but do not combine. Each group holds by its own religion, its own culture and language, its own ideas and ways.[8]

Interaction among these groups, according to Furnivall, was limited to economic relationships, and did not embrace wider social intercourse. In effect, there was a single territory, inhabited by peoples who were linked only by trade and by their common subordination to the colonial suzerain.

Table 2. Persons 10 Years of Age and Over Able to Speak Malay and English by Percent of Each Ethnic Group, 1957

	Ethnic Group					
Language	Chinese %	Malays %	Indians, Pakistanis, and Ceylonese %	Eurasians %	Europeans %	Others %
Malay	29.4	98.9	87.5	93.7	49.2	87.9
English	21.0	25.8	38.6	99.2	99.4	56.8

Source: State of Singapore, Superintendent of Census, *Report on the Census of Population, 1957*. Singapore: Department of Statistics, 1964, pp. 162, 163.

Note: Ceylonese have been combined with Indians and Pakistanis in the table although they are presented separately in the census report. The category "Malays" has been used here rather than the census report's "Malaysian." "Malaysian" includes not only Malays born in Singapore and Malaya but also immigrants or descendants of immigrants from Indonesia. Of the latter group, some persons identify themselves as Javanese, Boyanese, Bugis, etc. The very small number of these persons who cannot speak Malay account for the fact that less than 100 percent of the "Malays" in the table are able to speak Malay.

In the case of the Chinese residents of Singapore, this separation from the rest of the populace was supported by a congeries of purely ethnic social structures that performed those functions which in other instances are usually thought of as governmental. Until their suppression in the late 19th century, the most prominent of these groupings were the "secret societies."[9] In China the secret societies had been devoted to the support of the Ming dynasty against the Manchu usurpers. But this aspect was carried over to Singapore only in a ceremonial version. Their real function on the island seems to have been to act as a quasi-government and family substitute with criminal ventures such as extortion and prostitution providing a profit motive.

The typical immigrant from China came in search of economic opportunity. He had left his family, planned to work as a laborer while sending money home, and he hoped to save enough to return to China with some capital. During his sojourn in the Nanyang (or "South Seas" as the Chinese called Southeast Asia), the secret society helped him find a job through employers who were society members, provided him with temporary housing until he settled down, tended to his religious beliefs, and if necessary buried him in a pauper's grave.

The secret societies also served a purpose for the British administrators during the 19th century. Unable to communicate in the various Chinese dialects and uncomprehending of this people's social patterns, the colonial rulers sought to use prominent Chinese as intermediaries in the few relationships that existed between the government and the administrators (such as tax collection and keeping the peace.)[10] Often these persons, the so-called "Kapitans China," were secret society members. Similarly, European employers seeking Chinese laborers would often use agents with such affiliations. The criminal activities of the societies eventually led to their suppression by the British in 1890. But their place was taken by a profusion of other groups such as clan associations, burial societies, school boards, etc.[11]

Typically the membership of such an organization was limited to a particular dialect group—a reasonable situation in view of the fact that the Chinese at this time did not have a common spoken language.[12] There was, of course, a single written language which was used by the imperial Chinese court in Peking. But this could hardly bind together the overseas Chinese since most of them were illiterate. This lack of linguistic unity seems to have been paralleled by the absence of common political feelings except, perhaps, the common desire to avoid governmental authorities. Indeed, the point has been made that in many ways the Chinese in the area did not constitute a meaningful social unit during the 19th century.[13]

During the first half of the 20th century, the emergence of a single spoken language, the rise of Chinese nationalism, and the formation of political organizations spanning the confines of dialect boundaries increasingly constituted the Chinese of Singapore and Malaya as a unified political community. As part of the nationalist upsurge in China, a modified form of the Peking dialect (Mandarin, or Kuo-yü, which means "National Language") was adopted as the medium of education and as the common spoken language of all Chinese.[14] The language of the imperial court was also displaced in favor of a transcribed version of Mandarin which could much more easily be learned by the common man. Singapore's Chinese language schools, which were privately run and often staffed by intellectuals from China, quickly adopted these changes.[15]

Corresponding organizational developments also appeared in the early decades of this century. Sun Yat-sen visited Singapore in 1900 to raise funds and to promote the new patriotism, a branch of the Kuomintang (KMT or Nationalist Party) was established in 1912, and a China oriented, Chinese composed Malayan Communist Party (MCP) was founded in 1927.[16] However, it was not until the Japanese invasion of Manchuria in 1931 that either the MCP or the KMT began to establish a mass following. From this point on, the structures and sentiments associated with Chinese nationalism became increasingly strong. One of the more prominent features of this development was armed opposition to the Japanese by the guerrillas of the Malayan Communist Party. This, as well as the MCP's insurrection against the British after World War II (the so-called Emergency which officially ended in 1960 but which really ceased in the mid-1950s) have been widely recounted elsewhere.[17] Suffice it to say that in Singapore, radical Chinese movements, including the Communists, operated a well-organized infrastructure that embraced not only armed groups but also Chinese-language primary and secondary schools, trade unions, sewing classes, etc.

This brief sketch of Singapore's complex past illustrates a theme that is essentially common to the island's Malays and Indians as well as to the Chinese: each of Singapore's respective peoples developed into a politically organized and politically conscious community independently of the others.[18] True, part of this politicization involved conflict among the races. During the Second World War, the Japanese used Malay security forces to fight the Chinese guerrillas—a situation resulting not only in attacks by each group on the combatants of the other but also in retaliatory raids on each other's villages.[19] Furthermore, as William Roff has pointed out, the Malay fear of submersion by Chinese economic power and culture was an important stimulus in the creation of Malay nationalist movements as early as the latter 19th century. But the general picture is one of a separate development of disparate political ideas and organizations.[20]

In view of such a past it is more comprehensible why there should be difficulty in evolving a common national identity and a strong sense of allegiance to a single nation-state. Indeed, the kind of political setting needed to foster such unity did not exist until the coming to power of the People's Action Party (PAP) in 1959. Prior to this, the official political institutions of the increasingly self-governing colony could not absorb the activism of the masses, and especially not that of the Chinese. The parties which governed were caucuses of notables without widespread extra-parliamentary organization—a situation made possible by the highly limited franchise prior to 1957.[21] The leaders of these parties tended to be English educated and were generally unable to speak any Chinese dialect. This not only inhibited communication but more importantly identified this elite as alien to the ordinary Chinese citizen.[22]

The People's Action Party was able to link government with society because it included leftist, Chinese educated militants who were leaders of the Chinese infrastructure described earlier. In alliance with this group were the English-educated, anti-colonialist, vaguely socialist party founders such as Lee Kuan Yew and Toh Chin Chye. These two wings of the PAP, however, never shared the same goals.[23] They eventually split in 1961 ostensibly over the issue of merger with the proposed Federation of Malaysia; but the real reason lay in the incompatible visions of the future held by the two segments of the party.

After 1961, Singapore entered Malaysia (only to be expelled in 1965).[24] The leftist opposition Barisan Socialis, formed by the departing PAP members, declined in strength nearly to the point of extinction. Lee Kuan Yew and his colleagues, confronted by the almost total loss of the party's mass base in 1961, utilized the governmental institutions to sink new roots into society. One example of this is the quasi-governmental Community Centers which co-opt neighborhood elites and provide such community services to the masses as sewing classes, Chinese operas, language lessons, and free kindergartens.[25] With a combination of such social services, economic progress, and political acuity, the PAP has managed to win all parliamentary seats since 1968.

Despite the present air of economic progress and political stability, the future is hardly certain. The racial and political riots of the past are too recent to be forgotten.[26] Predictions widely made in 1965 of economic collapse because of the island's loss of the peninsular hinterland have been temporarily refuted. But Singapore's prospects are too dependent on an uncertain world market to be taken for granted. Finally, Singapore is after all, a Chinese-run country with a Malay minority. While the Malays are economically depressed (as they are in Malaysia), and while they can have no hope of dominating the government, they need only look to Malaysia and Indonesia to see models of Malay political power.[27] Besides the demonstration effect of these two neighbors, regional demography presents another potential threat. Both Indonesia and Malaysia have had their share of racial problems, and tensions in these countries have spilled over to Singapore in the past. If more serious problems should develop in either of these two states it could mean intolerable turmoil for Singapore.

In Search of Theory: The Literature

With this background in mind, we may return to the central questions of this chapter: what are the causes of political commitment to the state of Singapore, what effect do ethnic attitudes have on such an allegiance, and what causes different levels of ethnic hostility? To answer these queries we must synthesize pertinent theoretical insights from the literature with lessons drawn from Singapore's history. The resulting set of propositions can then be applied to our survey evidence.

A primary theoretical issue here is the degree to which cultural pluralism is compatible with a shared national identity. Many of the classics on nationalism are somewhat ambiguous on this, but they generally seem to assume that a high degree of commonality in many aspects of life is required. Emerson, for instance, describes a nation as "... a community of people who feel that they belong together in the double sense that they share deeply significant elements of a common heritage and that they have a common destiny for the future."[28] Since this can also be characteristic of religious and other such groupings, Emerson adds:

> The nation is today the largest community which, when the chips are down, effectively commands men's loyalty, overriding the claims both of the lesser communities within it and those which cut across it ...s,29

The implication of this view and more typically of studies of nationalism is that loyalty to the national political community, and to the nation-state more particularly, differs in degree rather than in kind from attachments to such cross-cutting points of reference as race, religion, and culture.[30]

A problem with this perspective emerges when one considers the citizen who feels absolutely loyal to his church in religion and is equally devoted to his nation-state in political affairs. This distinction, it might be objected, is more congenial to certain Western states than to Asia, where life has traditionally been seen more holistically. But ethnic differences in Singapore—indeed in Southeast Asia—are simply not going to disappear. If it is not possible for strong, non-coinciding cultural and political attachments to coexist then there can be little hope for the countries in this region.

Problems of a City State

There are, however, grounds for believing that ethnic diversity and political coherence are compatible. If we hazard the assumption that a firm sense of nationality and widespread support for the political system have been prevalent in the United States for some time, then American ethnic experience is instructive. In their study of New York City, Glazer and Moynihan observe that:

> In the third generation, the descendants of the immigrants confronted each other, and knew they were both Americans, in the same dress, with the same language, using the same artifacts, troubled by the same things, but they voted differently, had different ideas about education and sex, and were still, in many essential ways, as different from one another as their grandfathers had been.[31]

This persistence of distinctive identities is a theme found in other studies as well. For instance, Parenti argues that ethnic groups in America tend to maintain their own value systems as well as their own sub-cultural structures, such as churches, fraternal orders, and neighborhoods.[32] Masuda's research on Japanese Americans contains similar findings.[33]

The moral of the American experience for Singapore, then, is that groups considering themselves to be importantly different *can* accept each other as fellow citizens and *can* support the same state. To identify the influences that promote such a situation we may turn to some of the studies dealing with the causes of "legitimacy." A typical view of this concept is that it consists of "... the quality of 'oughtness'. that is perceived by the public to inhere in a political regime."[34] That is, the citizenry feels that the country's political institutions are morally proper for the society and that there is an obligation to obey the incumbents of those institutions even when specific rewards or punishments are lacking.[35]

How then does a set of political structures become legitimate? Studies attempting to answer this question may be divided into two kinds: those dealing with the legitimation of new institutions and those treating the transmission of feeling of legitimacy from one generation to the next. The first variety is of more obvious pertinence in a country like Singapore where the state is so new and where effective contact between the individual and the national political scene was only recently established. The second approach is, as we shall see, also fruitful in this setting.

One of the better known observations on the establishment of enduring support for new nations comes from Lipset's *Political Man:*

> ... [P]rolonged effectiveness over a number of generations may give legitimacy to a political system. In the modern world, such effectiveness means primarily constant economic development.[36]

Along these same lines, a learning theorist, Richard Merelman, has suggested a paradigm in which the provision of material satisfaction by a regime conditions the citizenry to the point where the institutions are firmly associated with the benefits they provide.[37] Eventually the institutions are seen as intrinsically desirable. Finally, the political processes come to be represented by symbols which, when transmitted intergenerationally, propagate the legitimacy of the regime.[38]

An obvious hypothesis implied by this discussion is that Singaporeans will feel a greater attachment to their state to the degree that they think their lives have improved because of governmental policies. While this chapter's quantitative analysis will indeed support this assertion, our investigation must recognize that the connection between material gain and political support is not a simple one. As Lipset himself noted:

> In the late 1920s, neither the German nor the Austrian republic was held legitimate by large and powerful segments of the population. Nevertheless, both remained reasonably effective.[39]

In a society deeply cleaved along cultural lines, legitimacy is first of all determined by the ethnic label of the elite: one supports the ruler only if he belongs to the proper group. But as a general matter, even where politics have begun to separate from overarching cultural matters, legitimacy continues to be affected by expectations and political symbols not directly attached to tangible rewards. Murray Edelman illustrates this when he notes that the setting of political acts in the West is often as important as the acts themselves. For instance, "the judicial bench and chambers, formal, ornate, permanent and solid, lined with thick tomes, 'prove' the deliberateness, scholarliness, and judiciousness of the acts that take place in them..."[40] Similarly, Buddhist kings in historical Southeast Asia acquired legitimacy largely through the possession of the royal regalia, occupancy of the semi-sacred palace, and the performance of acts required to maintain harmony between the kingdom and the universe.[41]

In addition, then, to bureaucratic efficiency and economic satisfaction we must examine culturally rooted political expectations if we are to account for legitimacy in Singapore. In turn, this means that we must look to the processes by which politically relevant values are passed from one generation to the next, for it is this learning process which must be modified if support for a new state is to emerge.

The literature dealing with this subject, generally under the rubric of "political socialization," is unfortunately generally limited to American or Western European experience. Nevertheless, it provides some insights for an analysis of Southeast Asian political life. Typical of these studies is the finding by Hess and Torney that at a very early age American children develop "...a strong positive attachment to the country; the United States is seen as ideal and as superior to other countries."[42] As shown by Greenstein and by Easton and Dennis, this process begins before children have any real cognitive basis for political feelings. For this reason, the President is particularly important since he is salient, central to the political scene, and emotionally comparable to the young child's father. Indeed, Easton and Dennis suggest that the earliest attitudes towards the political arena are generalizations of family-oriented emotions.[43] As the child develops intellectually, he is able to extend his political

Problems of a City State

awareness and attachments to institutions less comparable to the family, such as Congress.

If the content of socialization depends on the structure and political values of the family then it also depends on the cultural-historical milieu of the family, including the latter's group affiliations. That such contextual influences are indeed crucial to what the child learns is shown by a study conducted by Dean Jaros and his colleagues[44] in the Appalachian area of Kentucky—a region very different from that examined by Hess, Torney, Easton, and Dennis. In this part of Appalachia there is a long history of hostility to the national government. In addition, the father occupies a much more tenuous position than he does in the middle class families appearing in most socialization studies. As might be expected, Jaros found that his respondents have much more negative feelings toward the President and toward politics generally than do the children studied by Easton.

The general import of the socialization literature for this investigation of political allegiance in Singapore is rather unsettling. For if legitimacy is largely determined by so complex a web of influences, then this analysis requires a corpus of psychological and cultural theory which simply does not exist. I have undertaken this project nevertheless for three reasons: first, because the questions are important; second, because some basis exists for answering them; and third, because research into such matters as non-Western socialization will be facilitated if the important gaps in our knowledge can be located more clearly. Nevertheless, it must be born in mind that a full specification of the derivation of legitimacy and the effect on it of ethnicity is not now at hand.

Some insightful comments on political socialization in new states have been made by Robert LeVine.[45] LeVine notes that in such societies there is likely to be a much greater discrepancy between the patters of the family and those of the national political scene than is true of older nations. Traditional modes may persist in the home at the same time that politics and economics are undergoing great change. Presumably this would be especially true where societal diversity is greatest, as in a multicultural society like Singapore.

One might assume, then, that "agents of socialization" other than the family are likely to be particularly important in new states. One such source of political ideas that has received some attention is the school. In their five nation study, Almond and Verba found that formal education does seem to modify basic political attitudes—in some cases, significantly.[46] Similarly, Langton found that the secondary school environment in Jamaica had some effect on feelings of political efficacy.[47] In line with these studies, the quantitative analysis to be presented shortly includes a number of variables related to features of the educational environment which have historically played vital political roles.

The second major set of issues requiring attention revolves around the topic of race relations. Earlier in this section we noted that diverse ethnic identities can be compatible with a common allegiance. More particularly, political coherence in Singapore requires neither that cultural differences disappear nor that the various peoples accept each other in all social situations including marriage. What is necessary, however, is that the peoples of Singapore accept each other as fellow citizens and support their common state. An important task of this chapter, then, is to support the assertion that intergroup attitudes conducive to political cooperation do indeed foster allegiance to Singapore. In addition, the causes of such racial amicability must be investigated.

An ethnic issue with direct political importance in Singapore is residential integration. Well over one-third of the island's population lives in government housing.[48] Believing that increased familiarity breeds better understanding, the government has allocated flats in such a way as to maximize integration here. As a result it is unlikely that persons who strongly oppose multiracial neighborhoods could support the regime.

To determine the consequences of integrated housing for racial attitudes it is instructive to turn to American research on this issue. The classic studies by Deutsch and Collins[49] and by Wilner, Walkey, and Cook[50] found that when Blacks and Whites became neighbors in public housing:

> The attitudes of the members of one racial group towards the members of another will tend to become more favorable if there is sufficient contact between the two groups, provided that (a) the contacts occur between individuals who do not differ markedly in their social status in the contact situation, and (b) the contacts do not occur under circumstances in which there is competition for limited goods or facilities.[51]

It is important to note that the White families who moved into these housing projects did so because they wanted good, inexpensive housing and despite the strong desire of many not to live near Blacks. In a more recent investigation by Works,[52] the same generalization was found to characterize reduction of anti-White prejudice among Blacks.

Although these findings are generally accepted in the social psychology literature, a number of qualifications have been pointed out.[53] For instance, even where the requisites of equal status and sufficient facilities are present, favorable attitudinal changes may not result where the housing in question is private. All too often those White residents who can move do so while the remaining ones become increasingly hostile to their new neighbors.[54] This does not always happen, of course, but the reasons for favorable outcomes are not fully understood. Evidence on status and competition for facilities in Singapore's integrated areas is quite sparse, hence a prediction as to the beneficial or detrimental nature of inter-ethnic contact in public housing must be tenuous at best. It is, however, clear that residential integration is likely to be an important influence on ethnic attitudes in Singapore.

Another site of interaction among different groups is the school. Indeed, this setting might seem to be a particularly appropriate instrument for effecting more harmonious ethnic attitudes since people learn as well as live in schools. Howeer, the evidence here is quite inconclusive. As Caruthers puts it, "We simply do not know what happens to whom under what conditions of school desegre-

Problems of a City State 87

gation."[55] While some studies have shown that contact in a desegregated school produces more positive intergroup feelings, others have shown negative changes or no changes at all.[56] Some influences are known to affect the situation, such as similar socio-economic status of pupils, and the existence of a situation requiring cooperation for the attainment of common goals.[57] But an adequate theory is not available.

Nevertheless, school settings are obviously important in Singapore.[58] The government maintains education in the English, Malay, Mandarin, and Tamil media. The Chinese schools are in some cases the direct heirs of the past association between Chinese radicalism and Chinese education. Some of the English medium schools have traditions of academic excellence extending back to colonial times, and they have provided much of the island's political and economic elite.

Besides having very different cultural and historical pasts, the schools differ in other ways. For instance, an increasing number are "integrated"; that is, they combine under one roof two or three distinct language streams which are equivalent to separate schools in that each set of pupils learns its subjects in its own medium of instruction. However, extra-curricular activities and other functions are held in common. Singapore's school system, then, presents a tripartite contrast: English medium schools where children of all three races learn together in the same classes; integrated schools where interaction is more limited; and the Chinese, Malay, and Tamil stream schools where ethnicity and language separate pupils. We shall see that these different educational modes have distinctive effects on ethnic attitudes.

Research Evidence

Thus far this chapter has summarized the historical and theoretical foundations upon which the hypotheses of this study are based. Before presenting these propositions along with the statistical analysis supporting them, a few words are in order concerning the nature of the survey evidence used and the techniques employed to evaluate the data. Since space is highly limited, only the barest outline of these matters will be presented.

Two central problems in conducting a survey are, what questions to ask, and what people to ask them of. The major decision in the construction of the sample was to interview secondary school students. The political socialization literature (some of which was reviewed earlier) indicates that education and the school milieu generally have a marked impact on many political and social attitudes. Furthermore, talks with educators and researchers in Singapore suggested that the kind of difference with which I was most concerned could best be observed among these pupils.

Singapore's secondary school population is, however, a distinctive group. Only about 50 percent of the island's primary school children go on to secondary education.[59] The hurdle is not in general an economic one since school fees are quite low and the government provides financial assistance to the needy. However, the examination system is rigorous and only those who do well in primary school can continue their studies.

For the purpose of this study, however, the academic superiority of this sample relative to the general population is not a hindrance. The future of Singapore depends very heavily on the middle and upper level personnel produced by these schools for industry, the civil service, and politics.[60] Furthermore, the political movements of the past have been intimately tied to the secondary schools, and this connection may well reappear in the future.

Consigning a more detailed description of the sample design to a later time, suffice it here to note that in consultation with Singaporean educators and researchers, a list was compiled of the various school environments that seemed most important to the political and social questions of this project. Since only the results for the Chinese respondents are presented in this paper, only the following categories are pertinent: (a) English medium schools, (b) Mandarin medium schools, (c) the English stream of English-Mandarin and English-Mandarin-Malay integrated schools, and (d) the Mandarin stream of the integrated types in class (c). In addition, the first category was divided into ordinary schools and those long-established schools generally considered to be academically elite. Schools were randomly chosen from each category and one class from each grade was chosen for each school (or each stream within an integrated school). Written questionnaires were then administered to entire classes by my wife and myself with the help of teachers who were briefed beforehand. The language of the questionnaires corresponded to the class's medium of instruction.[61]

A crucial problem in research such as this is the degree to which the questions asked and the numbers derived really reflect the feelings of the respondents. After determining the kinds of information needed to investigate this project's research questions, a preliminary list of queries was formulated by consulting questionnaires that had been used in Singapore, Malaysia, and other countries including the United States. The resulting lengthy schedule was checked by Singaporean scholars. Next came what is perhaps the most important step. Students from different backgrounds and language streams were each interviewed for eight hours over the course of several weeks. The tentative survey questionnaire guided the interviews with particular attention paid to why the students answered as they did, what the questions meant to them, and what alternative questions could better tap their political and social feelings. Naturally, a pretest of the refined instrument was also conducted with a larger sample. Finally, the statistical technique used to investigate these survey data was multiple linear regression.

POLITICAL ALLEGIANCE: HYPOTHESES

Economic Bases of Support. The section of this chapter on the literature cited studies of legitimacy which indicate that satisfaction with benefits deriving from government policies increases national commitment. A version of this proposition which is particularly appropriate to Singapore is that *economic* satisfaction, if it is attributed to the government, increases national commitment. This is an assertion of an "interactive" pattern of causality in that only the joint occurrence of the respondent's gratification and his belief in the political cause of his good fortune are assumed to promote loyalty. However, my intensive interviews and pretest survey results as well as the obvious salience of the PAP's economic activities convinced me that all except the most parochial Singaporeans link their economic happiness or discontant to PAP policies. Hence the original hypothesis was altered to state that the respondents will feel more committed to the country to the extent that they show high degrees of both economic satisfaction and political knowledge.

The demography and history of Singapore suggest the addition of a related hypothesis. In a society where ethnic cleavages are politically important, it is possible that each group might define its economic desires not only as a maximum improvement over the past but also as a maximum superiority over the other ethnic groups. If this were true, then the greatest political support should result from the respondent's belief that he has progressed more than the disliked peoples have.

A final hypothesis in this area concerns income levels. Because of the PAP's past association with the Communists and other radicals, and because it has more strenuously directed its appeal to the masses than to the wealthy few, one would expect an inverse relationship between family income and political support. However, since the country's industrial and commercial expansion has improved the lot of all classes, it is likely that income level and satisfaction will be unrelated to each other and that each variable will have its own separate political impact. In short, we anticipate finding that economic satisfaction increases allegiance to the state and that the poor are more committed to their country than the rich.

Ethnic Attitudinal Hypotheses: A theme stressed earlier in this paper is that hostility towards the island's other races is likely to preclude support for the avowedly multicultural state. One hypothesis, then, is that negative stereotypes of the Malay people should decrease the Chinese respondent's national commitment.

A somewhat different but also politically pertinent aspect of ethnic feelings in Singapore is the attitude toward integrated housing. The present government has devoted considerable resources to the building of public housing because of an extreme shortage of decent dwellings. Because of the authorities' systematic integration of these buildings it is likely that unwillingness to live among families of other groups would entail antipathy towards the state.

In contrast to the assumed effects of racial antipathy, our earlier discussion suggested that pride in one's own group need not conflict with national allegiance. Of course the applicability of this idea depends on the actual position of the state vis-a-vis the country's cultural groups. A regime premised on the suppression of a particular people is not likely to receive support from citizens who strongly identify with the national outcasts. In Singapore, however, the PAP has devoted considerable attention to identifying itself with the interests of Chinese and Malays alike (and with the other groups as well). In order to wean the Chinese-educated away from the radical opposition the present elite increased support for Chinese education, promoted cultural festivals, and undertook a variety of other practical and symbolic actions designed to demonstrate the PAP's role as champion of Chinese interests. Our hypothesis, then, is that ethnic pride should not decrease the Chinese Singaporean's attachment of his multicultural state.

The discussion of ethnicity thus far has focused on attitudes towards one's own group or towards other peoples. The final formulation concerning this issue concerns perceptions of the ethnic scene as a whole. In particular, if the multicultural basis of the state is taken seriously by the respondents, then they should support the country more strongly to the degree that they think that all groups are treated justly. What "justice" means in this context will be explained below.

Language and Loyalty: An important influence on political attitudes which was not discussed earlier is linguistic competence. While the literature provides almost no theoretical guidance on this matter, the history of this region makes it clear that language, both as a symbol of group identity and as a medium of communication, has played an extremely important historical role in the political and racial development of Singapore.

Authors such as Karl Deutsch[62] and Clifford Geertz[63] have suggested that linguistic affiliation often become major reference points in the formation of nationalistic identities during the course of "modernization." As the second section of this chapter noted, this has been particularly true of Singapore. Mandarin, for instance, has played a central political role on the island since the time of the revolution in China. Indeed, this language was introduced as the medium of instruction in Singapore's Chinese schools as part of the rise of nationalism in the ancestral country. That the significance of Mandarin as a major symbol of Chinese identity has persisted, moreover, is shown by the continued insistence of the Chinese speaking community that Mandarin not be slighted in favor of English in the educational system.

In its political import, it would seem that Mandarin is essentially the same as Chinese ethnic pride. However, this language is not the mother tongue for any Singaporean Chinese, and many who do not know this language at all are extremely proud of their cultural heritage. We might assume, then, that Mandarin ability represents a particular kind of immersion in Chinese culture. While it should have the same general effect as ethnic pride (either increasing loyalty or leaving it unaffected), the two should operate independently.

English language ability should also be important politically, although the direction of this effect cannot be predicted independently of our survey data. For example, fluency in English is necessary for promotion to the middle and upper ranks of enterprises in the newer parts of the economy. One might expect, therefore, that students who are proficient in English would more realistically identify their personal hopes with national progress and, hence, have a deeper attachment to Singapore than people with less ability in this medium. In addition, fluency in English is likely to bring the individual into more intense contact with the cosmopolitan aspects of life on the island via the cinema and other mass media. If familiarity breeds appreciation in this context, then the ability to speak English might intensify bonds to Singapore's variegated polity.

There is, however, a conflicting feature of competence in English. Prior to conducting the survey, I sought the opinions of educators and government officials in order to refine my hypotheses. During these conversations, I often heard the assertion that those Singaporean Chinese who speak only Chinese have no choice but to see their future in Singapore since they lack the ability in English which is essential for earning a living in the West. The assumed opulence of the West might well be alluring to my respondents and is certainly plausible in view of the popularity of Hollywood movies.

Expectations concerning the political import of Malay language fluency among Chinese respondents are even more ambiguous than those for English fluency. No predictions have been hazarded in this case.

Loyalty and the School System: Several characteristics of Singapore's school system seem likely to be important politically. For example, certain English stream schools which were founded during the colonial regime have long histories of academic excellence. The career prospects of pupils in these elite institutions are particularly good; not only do these students tend to do rather well in the national examinations but the prestige of their school is useful in securing employment. One might expect that these pupils would be among the most patriotic.

The role of Chinese medium education is ambiguous. The old focus on China rather than on Singapore and the radicalism of the past have been eliminated by such measures as the PAP's imposition of a common syllabus throughout the educational system and the government's stern security policies. Probably more important in its contemporary political consequences is a feeling on the part of many Mandarin medium pupils and graduates that their diplomas are not economically as useful as those of the English stream. There is indeed some basis for this fear. But whether this is the dominant political force in such a complex educational milieu cannot be stated a priori.

POLITICAL ALLEGIANCE: VARIABLES AND FINDINGS

Because of extreme limitations of space it is impossible to present in this chapter a full discussion of the independent variables used to operationalize our hypotheses (a complete treatment is available in another work).[64] The indicators will therefore be presented only in a summary fashion. A somewhat more ample delineation of the dependent variable—the measure of political allegiance—is necessary however, and we turn to this task now.

The variable labelled "Political Support" in Table 3 is derived from two questions, the first being:

> Imagine that you were married and had children. Imagine also that you had a good job that paid a lot of money. Now suppose the government asked that you give up your job and take a job that paid much less but would help Singapore. How willing would you be to take the government job?

The second is:

> Frankly speaking, how willing are you to fight and die for Singapore?[65]

For each of these questions, the respondents had to circle one of four answers forming an intensity scale.

Both of these queries are designed to tap the kind of feeling associated with the concept of "legitimacy" or an enduring support for the state (rather than for incumbent leaders) which is not based on specific rewards. My intensive interviews showed that the questions fulfilled their purpose. Furthermore, the interviewees were able to answer readily and seemed to find the topics familiar.

The "Political Support" measure is the sum of the scores for these two items. One reason for combining them, besides their substantive equivalence, is that their product-moment correlation is 0.45. More importantly, separate equations for each produce very similar regression coefficients indicating that both are affected in the same way by the same influences.

To facilitate comparisons among variables, the ranges of all indicators, including "Political Support," have been standardized to run from zero to one. The scale for "Political Support," then, has seven points in the zero-one interval, with higher scores showing stronger support for the state.

Economics: Two variables are used to test the economic satisfaction hypotheses: "Chinese and Family Economic Improvement" and "Non-Chinese Economic Improvement." The first of these is a composite measure of the degree to which the Chinese student believes his family and the island's Chinese as a whole have improved their economic position over the preceding five years and the degree to which they will, in the pupil's opinion, improve over the next five years. Perceptions of the family and of the Chinese are combined in this indicator because the intensive interviews showed that the student refers to both

Problems of a City State

groups in judging the extent to which the government has provided appropriate economic opportunities. "Non-Chinese Economic Improvement" represents the respondent's assessment of the past and future economic improvement of the Malays and Indians. Finally, "Family Income" indicates what its name implies. High scores (i.e., 1.0) show maximum improvement or income.

In the discussion of hypotheses, the idea was presented that economic satisfaction should increase the respondent's political loyalty—but only when the student was relatively aware of politics. Similarly, the effects of perceptions of other groups' progress and of income level were presumed to exist only for politically informed persons. To test these three propositions, the regression initially included not only the three linear economic variables described above but also the product of each of these variables and a measure of political knowledge. However, the coefficients of these three multiplicative (or "interaction") terms were not significant.

It seems that any effect of the economic variables is unaffected by political knowledge and that the hypotheses must be cast only in terms of the linear variables. Part of the explanation for this probably lies in fact that the PAP has devoted considerable attention to inculcating a sense of national commitment, a

Table 3. Chinese Political Support

Variable	Regression Coefficient	t Ratio
1. Chinese Family and Group Economic Improvement	7.91×10^{-2}	4.34
2. Non-Chinese Economic Improvement	1.23×10^{-1}	3.64
3. Family Income	-8.10×10^{-2}	4.15
4. Neighborhood Racial Preference	6.57×10^{-2}	3.72
5. Chinese Culture and Intelligence	5.98×10^{-2}	2.01
6. Malay Culture and Intelligence		
7. Elite English Stream School	-6.72×10^{-2}	4.57
8. Ability in English	4.37×10^{-2}	1.98
9. Ability in Mandarin	1.02×10^{-1}	5.17
10. Grade Level	-1.40×10^{-1}	8.47
11. Racial Justice in Singapore	5.31×10^{-2}	2.26

$F^{10}_{1899} = 25.85$
$R = 0.35$
Number of Observations = 1910
Degrees of Freedom for t ratio = 1899
Intercept = 4.24×10^{-1}

feeling of economic progress, and a belief that it is the government which is responsible for the island's material progress. It is entirely plausible that this effort has reached persons of virtually all degrees of political knowledge.[66]

There is, however, an additional possibility. Much of the political socialization literature generally agrees that the kind of political loyalties with which we are concerned are sentiments that are relatively independent of factual knowledge. If, indeed, the kind of support for the nation encompassed by the concept of legitimacy is more emotional than cognitive, and if our respondents do generally connect their political and economic feelings, then the irrelevance of factual political knowledge to national commitment is quite credible.

Having modified the hypotheses to omit their connection with political awareness we may turn to Table 3. The positive coefficient of "Chinese Family and Group Economic Improvement" shows that economic satisfaction does indeed increase national commitment, while the negative coefficient for "Family Income" supports the contention that the poorer citizens are relatively more allegiant than their wealthier co-nationals. Howver, "Non-Chinese Economic Improvement" has a positive effect, thus showing that these pupils do not use ethnically competitive criteria in judging whether the government has done a proper job with the economy.

Ethnic Attitudes: "Neighborhood Racial Preference" taps the pupil's desire to live in an integrated neighborhood after he or she is married. A value of one corresponds to a strong preference for integration while zero shows a determination to live only among members of one's own race (there are three scale values in between with the midpoint indicating neutrality).

More general, stereotypic views are represented by "Chinese Culture and Intelligence" and "Malay Culture and Intelligence." Each student was asked to rate each of the cultures in Singapore from "not at all advanced" to "very advanced" with two intermediate options. In addition, the pupils were asked if they believed that any of the world's peoples were born with superior or inferior intelligence and, if so, to list the superior and inferior ones. The respondent's cultural and genetic assessments of the Chinese and Malays respectively were used to form the two indicators of stereotypes. The score for the Chinese people corresponds here to "ethnic pride" as discussed previously. For both variables, values near one indicate positive attitudes while scores close to zero show negative opinions of the group.

The final indicator required by our ethnic hypotheses is one related to racial justice. "Justice" is, of course, a slippery idea in any context and it warrants some description here. The measure called "Racial Justice in Singapore" is based on two questions: "To what extent do you think all races *should be* treated the same in Singapore?" and "To what extent do you think all races *really are* treated the same in Singapore?" The reason for the combination of queries is that my interviews showed that equality of treatment is not considered to be just by all respondents (and this was true for respondents of all races). Some

Problems of a City State

pupils felt that the economically depressed condition of the Malays required somewhat more favorable treatment of this group in order to achieve equity. Others felt that equality is justice. By using the difference between the responses to the two questions to represent the pupil's view of the departure of reality from the ideal, comparability could be achieved. For this variable, high values correspond to maximum justice while low scores show injustice.[6][7]

Turning to the coefficients in Table 3 we find support for the hypotheses presented earlier. A desire to live in an integrated neighborhood increases allegiance to the state, as does a favorable view of the Malay people (as is shown by the "Malay Culture and Intelligence" variable). In addition, group pride, as represented by "Chinese Culture and Intelligence," is also conducive to national commitment (analysis showed that the coefficients for "Chinese Culture and Intelligence" and "Malay Culture and Intelligence" have the same value, hence only one number is entered for both coefficients in Table 3). Finally, the patriotism of the Chinese pupils is stimulated by the belief that all groups are treated justly. Here is evidence that the PAP has, to some extent at least, succeeded in the attempt to found a new legitimacy on the basis of multiracialism.

Language and Loyalty: "Ability in English," "Ability in Mandarin," and "Ability in Malay" are derived from the student's subjective assessments of his verbal and written proficiency in each of these languages. Objective tests of fluency were abandoned because they required too much time to answer. However, several teachers were consulted and they blieved that the distribution of answers for their schools seemed reasonable.

Earlier we noted that proficiency in Mandarin should play much the same political role as ethnic pride. The basic prediction was that neither the pride nor the language influence should decrease national loyalty, although whether they actually increase national commitment (as opposed to leaving it unaffected) depends on how successful the ruling elite has been in presenting itself as a promoter of Chinese culture.

We have already seen that "Chinese Culture and Intelligence" has a positive coefficient and Table 3 shows that the same is true of "Ability in Mandarin." The evidence, therefore, shows that the present leadership has at least partly succeeded in taking over the Chinese interests and symbolry that once formed the basis of radical strength.

The other two language variables, "Ability in English" and "Ability in Malay," have been investigated more in the spirit of a search than as a means of testing clear hypotheses. While impressionistic evidence indicates that both languages have important political ramifications, it is impossible to balance the positive and negative consequences without the aid of our survey data. The results show that Chinese students who are more proficient in English are also more loyal although this effect is smaller than that of the Mandarin variable. Apparently the fear of many educators and political leaders that a facility in this medium will encourage pupils to think of other countries as alternative homelands is unfounded. The coefficient for "Ability in Malay" was not significant and was, therefore, eliminated from the equation; no conclusion about this influence can be drawn.

Allegiance and the Schools: The earlier discussion of education was phrased in terms of the differences in levels of political allegiance which one would expect to find in the various kinds of schools. To pursue these ideas, "dummy variables" representing school types were included in the analysis. "Elite English Stream Education," for example, equals one if the respondents attends such a school but equals zero otherwise. Its coefficient shows the difference between the level of political support exhibited by pupils in this type of institution and students in other kinds of schools. Other school categories were also included initially, but since no significant differences among them were uncovered they were eliminated.

The findings for "Elite English Stream Education" contradicts our anticipations. Attending an elite English medium institution was expected to increase national commitment because of desirable career opportunities. However, the negative coefficient for this variable shows that these pupils are actually less committed to Singapore than are other students.

The reason for this last result is almost certainly related to a peculiarity of the sample. By chance the schools chosen for this category included disproportionately more children from wealthier English-educated, high status families than was true of other elite English stream schools. My intensive interviews showed that a distinguishing feature of many such youths is their concern for "democracy" in the Western sense of the word. To them the process of politics is an important as the mass benefits government can provide. Therefore, the lack of party competition in Singapore is very disturbing to these students, while to most others the meaningful issue is whether the party in power is doing a good job. While this elite group dislikes the PAP's ready use of police powers to crush public demonstrations of political protest, the more typical Singaporean interest lies in whether the repression is even-handed and whether it actually provides domestic peace.

This is not to say that the island's "average youth" is totally indifferent to popular control of the government. Rather, most Singaporeans do not think primarily in terms of democracy because there are so many problems—such as national and personal economic survival—which seem overwhelmingly important. Indeed, many upper class pupils share this perspective. But for a significant number of well-to-do English stream students, personal economic security allows them to see issues like democracy as well.

If other schools had been chosen for the elite English stream category it is very likely that no differences among school-types would have been uncovered. Nevertheless, our result is important since this particular subset of respondents is representative of a group which has been and will probably continue to be vital in the ranks of business and government.

Sex and Grade Level: Two variables which were not mentioned in the discussion of hypotheses are "Male" and "Grade Level." "Male" is a dummy variable which equals one if the respondent is male and equals zero if the respondent is female; its coefficient therefore shows the difference between the sexes in scores on the dependent variable. "Grade Level" shows what its name implies, hence higher values show that the pupil is further along in his school tenure (despite the fact that "Grade Level" has a "natural scale" running from one to six, this measure has been standardized to a zero-one range as is true of all other variables here).

Sex and grade were included only to take into account a possible artifact of the dependent variable. As many teachers suggested to me, boys who are closer to graduation are also closer to the time when they will be conscripted for military service. As both boys and girls approach the end of their schooling, the prospect of actually earning money also becomes more imminent. With increasing grade level, therefore, the pupils are less likely to be enthusiastic about giving up a good job or fighting in the army. "Grade Level" is included in order to control for this "reality factor." Similarly, sex has been included since boys are conscripted (although girls may volunteer) and because boys are more likely to have a job worth giving up for the nation than are girls.

The coefficient for "Male" was not significant and the variable was eliminated. The negative coefficient for "Grade Level" is significant but it shows the necessity for the "reality control" rather than that students become less patriotic as they grow older.

ETHNIC ATTITUDES: HYPOTHESES

Economic Bases of Prejudice: The racial attitudes of Singapore's Chinese pupils have thus far been treated only in the context of their effects on political allegiance. This is of course important and the link between national allegiance and ethnic hostility makes it desirable to investigate the causes of the latter phenomenon. But this issue also has an importance of its own. Singapore's racially troubled history has been mentioned; the various incidents need not be recounted here. The likely international consequences that Chinese-Malay disturbances in Singapore would have on the country's relations with Malaysia and Indonesia (both of which have their own Chinese problems) are clear. Finally, the advances being made in industrialization and housing will increasingly require that Singaporeans be able to live and work together in positive cooperation.

Since space is so limited in this chapter, only one aspect of prejudice will be pursued here: namely, the belief that Malays as a group are inferior to Chinese. The indicator used to tap this feeling is the difference formed by subtracting "Malay Culture and Intelligence" from "Chinese Culture and Intelligence" (the same variables which appear in Table 3). Thus, larger values of this new dependent variable lead, according to the last section's analysis, to a lessened attachment to the state. Stereotypic inferiority is also important since Chinese who subscribe to ethnic equality are more likely than their bigoted fellow-ethnics to be able to live amicably and cooperatively with Singapore's Malay citizens.

One of the impressions gained from the interview segment of the project is that respondents of all races partially based their stereotypic views of the Malays on perceptions of the Malay's economic condition. The Chinese pupils seemed to feel that every individual strives for economic advancement; whether he succeeds depends upon how hard he tries, his mental and physical abilities, and good luck. For most Malays to remain poor for generations, either because they fail as entrepreneurs or because they stay in menial jobs with no hope of advancement is possible, in this view, only if the entire race is genetically incapacitated.

The psychological framework that seems to fit this situation most closely is suggested by a number of studies on "attribution theory."[68] Unfortunately, scholars pursuing this relatively new approach have not yet investigated the attribution of group characteristics but have instead concentrated on how individuals account for their own and other individuals' behavior. Rather than attempting to recast all of attribution theory, we shall simply sketch those of its highlights which seem especially relevant in the hope that future research will provide a more complete formulation.

Attribution theory starts from the assumption that people seek to understand their own and others' acts and intentions in a manner roughly equivalent to an experimental procedure.[69] For instance, if an observer tries to explain why a person has accepted one of two job offers, he would first eliminate as possible causes the characteristics that are common to both jobs.[70] Similarly, in trying to understand whether a worker reacts to his job as he does because of some personality traits or because of the nature of his job, an observer would compare that worker with other employees and he would compare the subject's behavior at that particular time with the way he had acted previously. If, for instance, the worker is obsequious on the job, but his fellow workers are vituperative towards the employer, then an observer would probably conclude that the behavior is due to the individual rather than to the situation. This impression would be strengthened if the subject were known to have acted similarly in previous jobs. Finally, if the subject were not submissive in non-employment contexts, then the observer would conclude that some personal characteristic specific to employment was responsible.

A feature of attribution theory which makes it particularly useful for the Singapore situation is the hypothesis that people use basically the same criteria in assessing the causes of their own actions as in making attributions to other people.[71] Although the issue cannot be pursued here, I show in a larger study that Malays judge themselves in much the same way that they are judged by the Chinese.[72] This similarity in evaluative processes fits in well with the attribution theory formulation.

Clearly a highly simplified version of a psychological theory based on experiments involving American subjects must be applied to Asian survey evidence with great care. This is especially true since the theory has not been applied to perceptions of ethnic groups at all. Nevertheless, the venture seems useful here and may be fruitful for further research. In particular, an obvious generalization for a Singaporean to make is that Malays do not succeed economically while Chinese rise, even if it takes them several generations. Since the respondents see little individual variation, and since Chinese who were once as poor and uneducated as their Malay neighbors achieved some economic betterment, the tendency is to attribute this economic condition to some general racial trait rather than to individual luck, ability, or perseverance, or to the national economic situation.

The prediction implied by this discussion is that perceptions of Chinese economic progress and of a lack of Malay advancement should increase the belief in the Malays' inferiority relative to the Chinese. In addition, one would think that richer Chinese would have a particularly high opinion of themselves and of Chinese in general and therefore would be especially likely to have negative stereotypes of Malays.

Friendship and Prejudice: Earlier in this chapter we noted a variety of sources which suggest that increased contact among members of different ethnic groups causes changes in racial stereotypes. However, these changes are sometimes in the direction of greater hostility, while in other cases more positive attitudes result. In a study undertaken by Marian Yarrow and her colleagues,[73] a children's camp in the United States was examined where half the cabins were segregated and half contained both Black and White children. The authors found that in this specially controlled situation, integration increased cross-ethnic friendships and made for more positive racial feelings.[74] Other studies also seem to show that bringing about inter-ethnic friendships tends to induce more favorable views of the groups to which the new friends belong.[75]

My intensive interviews and informal conversations with Singaporean students not only seemed consonant with research such as Yarrow's, but also indicated that cross-group friendships among pupils were frequently formed between individuals who were initially prejudiced. In another study I have shown that a number of circumstances unrelated to the student's ethnic attitudes markedly affect the ethnic composition of his circle of friends. Indeed, many of these influences are connected with the school environment and are directly amenable to governmental manipulation. The important point here, however, is that the behavior of *individual* students can be modified and there is reason to believe that this can result in decreased hostility between *groups*. The hypothesis implied here is that the more Malay friends a Chinese pupil has, the more likely he is to think that Malays as a group are not inferior.

Education and Racial Feelings: The school environment is clearly important in influencing ethnic attitudes. But as was true in our discussion of education in the context of political loyalties, there is no obvious way of predicting what kinds of school should have positive effects and which negative effects. Among the features of the educational system which probably contribute to differing racial views are the very dissimilar political traditions of the Chinese and English medium schools, the stronger presence of Chinese culture in the Mandarin than in the English medium, and the brighter career prospects of English stream graduates than those of other students.

One aspect of the school situation which was not discussed in the previous section but which should be important as a determinant of ethnic stereotypes, is the opportunity for inter-ethnic contact afforded by the different kinds of schools. In the English stream, members of all ethnic groups attend the same classes and have a variety of opportunities to know each other fairly well. In the integrated schools which contain an English stream and one or more other streams in the same building, students study separately but participate in the same extra-curricular activities. Finally, the Chinese schools, of course, contain only Chinese pupils. While the effect of inter-ethnic contact cannot in general be predicted, it does seem reasonable to assume that the situations of maximum and minimum contact (in the English stream classes and in the Chinese schools respectively) should have opposite impacts on racial stereotypes. Students in the Chinese stream of integrated schools should fall between these two extremes.

Integrated Housing: Logically interracial contact in one's residential neighborhoos should have the same effect as contact in one's school. Here too, however, there are only tenuous grounds for predicting whether such effects will be positive or negative.

Language and Ethnic Attitudes: The effect of language on ethnic identification and racial conflict in many new states has been stressed by several authors. A common theme is that language is not only a vehicle of communication but also a symbol of group identity. Both aspects are important to race relations. Speaking a common language facilitates meaningful inter-ethnic contact and should, therefore, increase the salience of ethnic attitudes. Historically, Mandarin has served as a general symbol of Chinese nationalism and culture. However, while empirical research pinpointing the effects of linguistic proficiency on ethnic attitudes and identifications is lacking, some studies do indicate that language ability often has general psychological consequences.[76]

If knowing another group's language confers greater empathy for that group and its culture, then Chinese students who know the Malay language well should be relatively positive towards Malays. However, the role of the Malay and English languages as media of inter-ethnic communication, and the unpredictability of the consequences of greater contact between groups (which is likely to follow from the ability to communicate), renders a priori predictions impossible.

ETHNIC ATTITUDES: VARIABLES AND FINDINGS

The measure used to represent stereotypic comparisons of Malays and Chinese is labelled "Relative Malay Inferiority." As we noted earlier, this indicator is formed by subtracting "Malay Culture and Intelligence" from "Chinese Culture and Intelligence." As in the political analysis, the ranges of all variables, including "Relative Malay Inferiority," have been standardized to run from zero to one. This being the case, a value of 1.0 corresponds to an assessment of maximum Malay inferiority, 0.5 represents a belief in racial equality, and 0.0 shows that the respondent feels that Malays are superior to Chinese.

Economics and Race Relations: The first variable used to test the attribution theory hypothesis is "Chinese Family and Group Economic Improvement" which was defined in the previous section. Tapping Chinese estimates of Malay advances is "Malay Economic Improvement." For both of these variables a value of one corresponds to maximum improvement while zero shows retrogression. "Family Income" was also previously defined.

The results in Table 4 support the main hypotheses. The more progress the Chinese pupil believes his family and race have made and the less progress he thinks the Malays have made, the more inferior he thinks the Malays are (note the positive coefficient for "Chinese Family and Group Economic Improvement" and the negative coefficient for "Malay Economic Improvement"). However, the discussion concerning the effects of income is not supported by the data. "Family Income Level" was found not to have a significant impact, which indicates that poorer respondents are just as likely to see Malays as inferior as are wealthier students.

Friendship and Prejudice: "Proportion of Malay Friends" is designed to test the proposition that having a higher proportion of Malay friends inclines Chinese pupils to have a more favorable view of the Malay people as a whole. This indicator is a composite variable designed to show the ratio of Malay friends to total friends. A value of 1.0 means that the pupil has only Malay friends, 0.33 shows one-third Malay friends, and so on. The coefficient for this variable in Table 4 supports the hypothesis.

Education: The effects of different school environments are tapped by dummy variables corresponding to each of the following types: elite English, ordinary English, and Chinese medium schools, and the Chinese stream of integrated schools. Each of these is multiplied by the student's grade level. The resulting variables are labelled "Change With Grade in Elite English Stream Education," "Change With Grade in Non-Elite English Education," "Change With Grade in Exclusively Chinese Medium Schools," and "Change With Grade in Chinese Stream of Integrated Schools." The reason for casting the school indicators in this way rather than separately including school type dummy variables and a measure of grade level is the assumption that the effects of education on racial feelings should be cumulative and should differ according to school milieu.

Aside from the assertion that exclusively Chinese schools and English medium schools should have opposite effects, with Mandarin medium classes of integrated schools falling between these extremes, no hypotheses were ventured because of the complexity of the educational environment. Actually, however, a somewhat different set of distinctions emerged from the analysis. Exclusively Chinese medium schools were not found to differ significantly from Mandarin stream classes in integrated schools. Considering both types of Chinese education together it would appear that increasing tenure in this kind of education produces the greatest tendency to believe that Malays are inferior. This point must be seen, though, in the context of the fact that Chinese students in all kinds of schools show an increasingly strong disposition to think Malays are inferior.

The most favorable (or least unfavorable) trend is exhibited by the respondents in non-elite English schools. This is probably not only a result of greater inter-ethnic contact in this setting but also a consequence of joint participation in extra-curricular activities and of cooperation in such matters as homework (a phenomenon reported to me by many pupils in such schools).

Table 4. Relative Malay Inferiority (Chinese Respondents)

Variable	Regression Coefficient	t Ratio
1. Chinese Family and Group Economic Improvement	9.23×10^{-2}	5.01
2. Malay Economic Improvement	-9.21×10^{-2}	6.15
3. Proportion of Malay Friends	-1.07×10^{-1}	2.27
4. Change with Grade in Elite English Stream	1.23×10^{-1}	5.71
5. Change with Grade in Non-elite English Stream	6.26×10^{-2}	3.11
6. Change with Grade in Chinese Stream (Integrated or Exclusively Chinese)	1.72×10^{-1}	8.59
7. Ability in Mandarin	9.17×10^{-2}	4.06

$F^{7}_{2041} = 28.83$
$R = 0.30$
Number of observations = 2048
Degrees of freedom for t ratio = 2041
Intercept = 2.02×10^{-1}

Finally, elite English education lies between the two poles. One likely reason for this is that my sample indicates that almost no Malays attend elite institutions. Thus, the kind of contact that might induce positive change is lacking in the superior schools.

Residential Integration: To determine whether living in a racially mixed neighborhood had any effect on assessments of Malay inferiority a dummy variable was included in the analysis to indicate whether the respondent lived in an integrated neighborhood or in a predominantly or completely Chinese area. Analysis showed no effect.

Language Proficiency: As with cross-group interaction in neighborhoods and schools, the area of linguistic ability lacks specific hypotheses because of a lack of theory. Analysis showed fluency in English or in Malay produce no impact on "Relative Malay Inferiority." Fluency in Mandarin, however, seems to induce negative stereotypes.

Some light is shed on this finding if we consider that in Singapore the role of Mandarin is rather different from that of the other two languages. While fluency in English or in Malay is, for a Chinese, largely a matter of communication, Mandarin is probably less useful than the Fukien (or Hokkien) dialect for speaking to Chinese in this country. Mandarin, on the other hand, has great symbolic importance. Speaking this language well is a sign of being a cultured Chinese and having a proper Mandarin accent is a sign of prestige. In a sense, then, the variable labelled "Ability in Mandarin" taps not only a linguistic ability but also a particular kind of immersion in Chinese culture.

POSSIBILITIES FOR A POLICY MODEL

In the previous analysis of national allegiance and ethnic attitudes our focus has necessarily been on one limited type of relation at a time. Each influence on national loyalty and each circumstance affecting ethnic views had to be isolated and compared with our data in order to delineate the forces impinging on Singapore's political viability.

However, politics is not a set of independent phenomena but is rather a network of processes in which a change in one area is likely to have widespread and often unsuspected ramifications throughout the polity. The successful policy maker is necessarily aware of the wholeness of his state. The ability of religious, educational, or economic issues to inflame racial animosities which in turn threaten the nation, has been demonstrated often enough throughout the world.

How, then, does our investigation bear on politics as a unified phenomenon? Our major linkage between processes was suggested in the fifth section where the negative effect of racial hostilities on national allegiance was hypothesized, and our analysis has confirmed this connection. A deeper coherence among the forces we have studied is suggested by the importance of factors like education and economic perceptions in both the political and the ethnic attitude equations. Thus a change in the educational system would affect national allegiance not only directly but also indirectly through ethnic attitudes.

Clearly the net consequences of direct and indirect effects must be known if our analysis is to be pertinent to public policy. To derive a policy model meeting these requirements, several tasks must be undertaken. First, equations must b e formulated in which influences not obviously amenable to control (such as ethnic composition of friendship patterns) are cast as functions of readily manipulable factors. The various regressions can than be treated as a system of equations and the system can be solved in order to express crucial political and racial variables in terms of the policy indicators.

Although the suggested analysis cannot be presented here, an example of the findings is appropriate. We have already seen that the national allegiance of Chinese pupils is increased by the perception of Chinese economic progress and, to a lesser extent, by the observation of Malay improvement. On the other hand, favorable views of the Malays—which increase patriotism—are promoted by the belief that Malays are improving their economic position relative to that of the Chinese. Combining the various equations indicates that Chinese national commitment would be maximized if the Malays were to improve more rapidly than the Chinese—that is, if the economy were to accelerate with the Malays receiving a greater share of the new benefits than the Chinese.

The general point of this example lies not in this particular finding but rather in the idea that social science theory can be put to practical use in the context of Southeast Asia. Obviously there are hazards in doing this. Presently available theory is scanty and almost invariably based on Western experience. Nevertheless, the utility of attribution theory in explaining Singaporean race relations implies that Western-oriented formulations can be used to build a more solid and more extensive theoretical base directed to Asian politics and that such a corpus could have great utility in assisting in the arduous tasks of nation-building.

NOTES

1. Peter A. Busch, "Political Unity and Ethnic Diversity: A Case Study of Singapore." Ph.D. dissertation, Yale University, 1972.
2. *Ibid.*
3. Republic of Singapore, Superintendent of Statistics, *Census of Population, 1970: Singapore (Interim Release).* Singapore: Department of Statistics, 1970, p. 1.
4. Among the many sources on Singapore's history is K. G. Tregonning, *A History of Modern Malaya.* London: Eastern Universities Press, 1964.
5. Ooi Jin-bee, "Singapore: The Balance Sheet," in Ooi Jin-bee and Chiang Hai Ding (eds.) *Modern Singapore.* Singapore: University of Singapore Press, 1969, pp. 1-3. This article gives a brief account of the island's resources.
6. For a discussion of industrialization in Singapore, see Helen Hughes and You Poh

Seng, *Foreign Investment and Industrialization in Singapore.* Canberra: Australian National University Press, 1969, chs. 1 and 8; on the relationship between education and industrialization, see T. R. Doraisamy et al., *150 Years of Education in Singapore.* Singapore: Teachers' Training College, 1969, ch. 8; also see Tan Peng Boo, *Education in Singapore.* Singapore: Educational Publications Bureau, Ministry of Education, 1969.

7. A discussion of unemployment and efforts to solve the problem is found in Harry T. Oshima, "Growth and Unemployment in Singapore." *Malayan Economic Review* Vol. 12 (1967) pp. 32-58; Hughes, in Hughes and You, *Foreign Investment,* p. 43, notes that the British military in Singapore generated about 14 percent of the GNP in 1967.

8. John S. Furnivall, *Colonial Policy and Practices.* New York: New York University Press, 1956, pp. 303-312.

9. L. F. Comber, *Chinese Secret Societies in Malaya: A Survey of the Triad Society from 1800 to 1900.* Singapore: Donald Moore Press, 1959; Victor Purcell, *Chinese in Southeast Asia,* 2nd ed. New York: Oxford University Press, 1965, pp. 272-274; Norton Ginsburg and Chester F. Roberts, Jr., *Malaya.* Seattle: University of Washington Press, 1958, pp. 282-295.

10. Generally the immigrants were recruited in China by agents who, in effect, sold the laborers. The immigrant was then indentured. See Purcell, *The Chinese in Southeast Asia,* pp. 247-248.

11. Maurice Freedman, "Immigrants and Associations: Chinese in Nineteenth Century Singapore." *Comparative Studies in Society and History* Vol. 3 (1960), pp. 25-48 (see pp. 34-35); Rene Peritz, "The Evolving Politics of Singapore: A Study of Trends and Issues." Ph.D. dissertation, University of Pennsylvania, 1964, p. 26.

12. Freedman, "Immigrants and Association"; Taku Suyama, "Pang Societies and the Economy of Chinese Immigrants in Southeast Asia," in K. G. Tregonning (ed.), *Papers on Malayan History.* Singapore: Journal of Southeast Asian History (1962), pp. 183-213.

13. Ginsburg and Roberts, *Malaya,* pp. 131-138.

14. Purcell, *Chinese in Southeast Asia,* p. 253; Robert O. Tilman, "Education and Political Development in Malaysia." Symposium held in Brussels by the Centre du Sud-est Asiatique et de l'Estreme-Orient (April 1966), pp. 209-228; Ginsburg and Roberts, *Malaya,* pp. 131-138 (see pp. 234-235).

15. Doraisamy, *150 Years of Education in Singapore,* ch. 5. This is not to say that all Chinese learned Mandarin.

16. J. Norman Palmer, "Malaya" in George McTurnan Kahin (ed.), *Governments and Politics in Southeast Asia,* 2nd ed. Ithaca, N.Y.: Cornell University Press, 1964, pp. 281-371 (see p. 339 for date of MCP founding); for a good account of the KMT, see Png Poh-seng, "The Kuomintang in Malaya," in K. G. Tregonning, *Papers on Malayan History.* Singapore: Journal of Southeast Asian History (1962), pp. 214-225.

17. To cite just three: Gene Z. Hanrahan, *The Communist Struggle in Malaya.* New York: Institute of Pacific Relations, International Secretariat, 1954; Victor Purcell, *Malaya: Communist or Free?* London: Institute of Pacific Relations, 1954; Lucian W. Pye, *Guerrilla Communism in Malaya: Its Social and Political Meaning.* Princeton: Princeton University Press, 1956.

18. The best source on Malay nationalism is William R. Roff, *The Origins of Malay Nationalism.* New Haven, Conn.: Yale University Press, 1967; for the emergence of Indian nationalism in this area, see Sinnappah Arasaratnam, *Indians in Malaya and Singapore.* London: Oxford University Press (Oxford in Asia paperbacks) 1970; the various nationalisms of this area are covered in T. H. Selcock and Ungku Abdul Aziz, "Mationalism in Malaya," in William L. Holland (ed.), *Asian Nationalism and the West.* New York: Macmillan, 1953, pp. 269-345.

19. Purcell, *The Chinese in Southeast Asia,* p. 311.

20. This interpretation is based in part on a conversation with Prof. Harry Benda. On the defensive aspects of Malay nationalism, see Silcock and Aziz, *Asian Nationalism and the West,* p. 285; also see Roff, *Origins of Malay Nationalism,* ch. 3.

21. Thomas J. Bellows, *The People's Action Party of Singapore: Emergence of a Dominant Party System*. New Haven, Conn.: Yale University, Southeast Asia Studies Monograph Series, 1970, see pp. 67-68 for a discussion of the expansion of the electorate.

22. Yeo Kim Wah, "A Study of Three Early Political Parties in Singapore, 1945-1955," *Journal of Southeast Asian History* (Department of History, University of Singapore) Vol. X (1969), pp. 115-141.

23. Pang Cheng Lian, "The People's Action Party 1954-1963," *Journal of Southeast Asian History* (Department of History, University of Singapore), Vol. X (1969), pp. 142-154; Bellows, *The People's Action Party;* ch. 3.

24. Singapore's exclusion from Malaysia has been discussed in a great number of articles. One of these is R. S. Milne, "Singapore's Exit from Malaysia: The Consequences of Ambiguity." *Asian Survey* Vol. VI (1966), pp. 175-184.

25. Seah Chee Meow, "Community Centres and Political Development in Singapore: 1951-1969." M.D. thesis, University of Singapore, 1969.

26. A variety of such incidents are recounted in Peritz, "Evolving Politics of Singapore"; For the area's turbulent labor union history, see Charles Gamba, *The Origins of Trade Unionism in Malaya*. Singapore: Eastern University Press, 1962.

27. The effect on Singaporean Malays of perceptions of Indonesia and Malaysia would be a fascinating research topic.

28. Rupert Emerson, *From Empire to Nation*. Cambridge: Harvard University Press, 1967, p. 95.

29. *Ibid.*, pp. 95-96.

30. Much the same perspectives emerge from such studies as: Hans Kahn, *The Idea of Nationalism*. New York: Macmillan, 1944; Dankwart Rustow, *A World of Nations*. Washington, D.C.: The Brookings Institution, 1967; and Karl W. Deutsch, *Nationalism and Social Communication*. Cambridge: The M.I.T. Press, 1966. For a critical evaluation of the literature on "nations" and "nationalism" see Clifford Geertz, "The Integrative Revolution," in Clifford Geertz (ed.), *Old Societies and New States*. New York: The Free Press, 1963, pp. 105-157.

31. Nathan Glazer and Daniel Patrick Moynihan, *Beyond the Melting Pot*. Cambridge: The M.I.T. Press and Harvard University Press, 1963, p. 14.

32. Michael Parenti, "Ethnic Politics and the Persistence of Ethnic Identification," *American Political Science Review*, Vol. 61 (1967), pp. 717-726.

33. Minoru Masuda et al., "Ethnic Identity in Three Generations of Japanese Americans," *The Journal of Social Psychology*, Vol. 81 (1970), pp. 199-207.

34. Richard Merelman, "Learning and Legitimacy," *American Political Science Review*, Vol. 60 (1966), pp. 548-561 (see especially p. 548).

35. Herbert C. Kelman, "Patterns of Personal Involvement in the National System: A Social-Psychological Analysis of Political Legitimacy," in James N. Rosenau (ed.), *Internationla Politics and Foreign Policy*, Rev. Ed. New York: Free Press, 1969, pp. 276-288 (see especially pp. 278-279); David Easton and Jack Dennis, *Children in the Political System: Origins of Political Legitimacy*. New York: McGraw-Hill, 1969, pp. 61-64. Easton's "diffuse support" corresponds to "legitimacy"; Seymour Martin Lipset, *Political Man: The Social Bases of Politics*. New York: Anchor Books (paperback), 1963, p. 64.

36. Lipset, *Political Man*, p. 70.

37. Merelman, "Learning and Legitimacy"; see p. 551 for his stages of learning.

38. A rather similar view is found in Henry Teune, "The Learning of Integrative Habits," in Philip E. Jacob and James V. Toscano (eds.), *The Integration of Political Communities*. Philadelphia and New York: J. B. Lippincott Co. (paperback), 1964; see especially p. 272.

39. Lipset, *Political Man*, p. 69.

40. Murray Edelman, *The Symbolic Uses of Politics*. Urbana: University of Illinois Press, 1964, ch. 5.

41. Robert Heine-Geldern, "Conceptions of State and Kingship in Southeast Asia." Cornell University, Southeast Asia Program, Data Paper No. 18, 1956.

42. Robert D. Hess and Judith V. Torney, *The Development of Political Attitudes in Children.* New York: Anchor Books (paperback), 1968, p. 242.

43. Easton and Dennis, *Children in the Political System,* chs. 6-9.

44. Dean Jaros et al., "The Malevolent Leader: Political Socialization in an American Sub-Culture," *American Political Science Review,* Vol. 62 (1968), pp. 564-575.

45. Robert LeVine, "Political Socialization and Culture Change," in Clifford Geertz (ed.) *Old Societies and New States,* pp. 280-303.

46. Gabriel A. Almond and Sidney Verba, *The Civic Culture: Political Attitudes and Democracy in Five Nations.* Princeton, N.J.: Princeton University Press, 1963; see pp. 379-387 for a summary of their findings on education.

47. Kenneth P. Langton, *Political Socialization.* New York: Oxford University Press (paperback), 1969, ch. 6.

48. "Housing and Development Board, Annual Report, 1970." Singapore: Housing and Development Board, 1970.

49. Morton Deutsch and Mary E. Collins, *Interacial Housing: A Psychological Evaluation of a Social Experiment.* Minneapolis: University of Minnesota Press, 1951.

50. Daniel M. Wilner, Rosabelle Price Walkley, and Stuart W. Cook, *Human Relations in Interacial Housing: A Study of Contact Hypotheses.* Minneapolis: University of Minnesota Press, 1955.

51. *Ibid.* p. 147.

52. Ernest Works, "The Prejudice-Interaction Hypothesis from the Point of View of the Negro Minority Group," *American Journal of Sociology,* Vol. 67 (1961), pp. 47-52.

53. For a good summary of the literature on residential contact and ethnic prejudice, see Barry E. Collings in collaboration with Richard D. Ashmore, *Social Psychology: Social Influence, Attitude Change, Group Processes, and Prejudice.* Reading, Mass.: Addison-Wesley, 1970. The sections on ethnic prejudice are by Ashmore. See especially pp. 330-331 on the effects of contact.

54. Eleanore P. Wolf, "The Invasion-Succession Sequence as a Self-Fulfilling Prophecy," *Journal of Social Issues,* Vol. 13 (1957), pp. 7-20.

55. Martha W. Caruthers, "School Desegregation and Racial Cleavage, 1954-1970: A Review of the Literature," *Journal of Social Issues,* Vol. 26 (1970), pp. 25-47, see p. 43.

56. *Ibid.;* also see John Harding et al., "Prejudice and Ethnic Relation," in Gardner Lindzey and Elliot Aronson (eds.) *The Handbook of Social Psychology,* 2d Ed. Reading, Mass.: Addison-Wesley, 1969, Vol. V, pp. 1-76, see pp. 49-50 and passim.

57. Muzafer Sherif, "Superordinate Goals in the Reduction of Intergroup Conflict," *The American Journal of Sociology,* Vol. 63 (1958), pp. 349-356.

58. For a discussion of education in Singapore, see Doraisamy, *150 Years of Education in Singapore;* also see D. D. Chelliah, *A History of the Educational Policy of the Straits Settlements.* Kuala Lumpur, Malaya: Government Press, 1947. Note that the latter was reprinted in 1960 by G. H. Kiat and Co., Ltd., of Singapore.

59. For data on education in Singapore see Singapore, Ministry of Education, "Annual Report, 1951-1971." Singapore: Government Printing Office, issues for 1951-1971.

60. Naturally many of those destined for the higher elite go on to university education. However, this would be too restricted a sample.

61. Because of the complexities of Singapore's school system, a sample of over 3,200 students was required. The number of respondents plus rather limited resources was a major reason for making the final selection of students by class. Since the unit of analysis is the student, this design raises certain problems in terms of using the laws of probability to generalize the descriptive results of the entire student population. However, the aim of this design was to be representative of those influences assumed to be important in the causal processes under investigation; hence the sacrifice of randomness was accepted.

62. Deutsch, *Nationalism and Social Communication;* while Deutsch stresses language throughout this book, the centrality of this factor in Deutsch's formulation is particularly striking in chapter 6 where "assimilation" is operationalized.

63. Clifford Geertz, "The Integrative Revolution: Primordial Sentiments and Civil Politics in the New States," in Geertz, *Old Societies and New States,* pp. 105-157.

64. Busch, *Political Unity and Ethnic Diversity.*

65. This question was suggested to me by John MacDougall, then of the University of Singapore, Department of Sociology.

66. It should, of course, be remembered that a sample of secondary school students is used here and these people are likely to have more knowledge than less educated persons. Nevertheless, analysis showed that the variance of this variable is similar to the variance of other indicators used. Thus, secondary school students do differ in their levels of knowledge but the difference does not produce the kind of political differences required by our original hypothesis. Hence, I would conclude that the findings reported are probably due to the lack of importance of political knowledge in the context rather than to the nature of the sample.

67. A logically possible alternative is that a respondent might feel that Malays should be suppressed and that théy are suppressed. My interviews convinced me that this option was entertained by few, if any, of the respondents.

68. The following sources on attribution theory are particularly pertinent to this discussion: Edward E. Jones and Keith E. Davis, "From Acts to Dispositions: the Attribution Process in Person Perception," in Leonard Berkowitz (ed.), *Advances in Experimental Social Psychology,* Vol. 2. New York: Academic Press, 1965, pp. 220-266; Edward E. Jones and Richard E. Nisbett, *The Actor and the Observer: Divergent Perceptions of the Causes of Behavior."* New York: General Learning Press, 1971; Harold H. Kelley, *Attribution in Social Interaction* New York: General Learning Press, 1971; Harold H. Kelley, "Attribution Theory in Social Psychology," in David Levine (ed.), "Nebraska Symposium on Motivation, 1967," Lincoln: University of Nebraska Press, 1967, pp. 192-238; Charles A. Kiesler, Richard E. Nisbett, and Mark P. Zanna, "On Inferring One's Beliefs from One's Behavior," *Journal of Personality and Social Psychology,* Vol. 11 (1969), pp. 321-327; Richard E. Nisbett and Stuart Valins, "Perceiving the Causes of One's Own Behavior," New York: General Learning Press, 1971.

69. Kelley, "Attribution Theory in Social Psychology," p. 167.

70. Jones and Davis, "From Acts to Dispositions," pp. 225-226.

71. Kelley, "Attribution Theory in Social Psychology," p. 197.

72. Busch, "Political Unity and Ethnic Diversity," ch. V.

73. Marian Radke Yarrow et al., "Interpersonal Dynamics in a Desegregation Process," *Journal of Social Issues,* Vol. 14 (1958). This special issue, edited by Yarrow, contains five articles written by the editor and her colleagues on the same experiment.

74. Marian Radke Yarrow, John D. Campbell, and Leon J. Yarrow, "Acquisition of New Norms: A Study of Racial Desegregation," *Journal of Social Issues,* Vol. 14 (1958), pp. 8-28.

75. See, for example, John E. Hofman and Itai Zak, "Interpersonal Contact and Attitude Change in a Cross-Cultural Situation," *Journal of Social Psychology,* Vol. 78 (1969), pp. 165-171.

76. Elize Botha, "The Effect of Language on Values Expressed by Bilinguals," *Journal of Social Psychology,* Vol. 80 (1970), pp. 143-145; Margaret J. Earle, "A Cross-Cultural and Cross-Language Comparison of Dogmatism Scores," *Journal of Social Psychology,* Vol. 79 (1969), pp. 19-24.

CHAPTER 4

Khalid Shibli

METROPOLITAN PLANNING IN KARACHI:
A Case Study

The General Setting

Karachi enjoys a unique status within the national provincial and regional framework of Pakistan. It is the largest metropolitan area of Pakistan and the province of Sind, as well as the most important and vital industrial and commercial center of Pakistan. In 1966-67, Karachi contributed about 29 percent to the total industrial production of both East and West Pakistan. In the case of West Pakistan only, Karachi's contribution was about 40 percent. During this period Karachi consumed 50 percent of the total raw materials and spare parts, etc. used in the whole nation. Out of the country's 35 banks, 26 are located in Karachi, with branches in various parts of the country. Is is estimated that more than 53,000 commercial and service establishments are located in Karachi, and with the economic growth of the country the commercial and service sector is further expanding at a rapid rate. In 1968-69, the Government of Pakistan collected 60 percent of its total central revenues from Karachi. As of today, the Karachi metropolitan area has a total population of more than 3 million. Karachi is the only port serving Pakistan as well as catering to the needs of landlocked Afghanistan. In 1946-47, the port handled 2.71 million tons of cargo. In 1950-51, it handled 3.47 million tons and in 1963-64, it handled 5.85 million tons. The 1963-64 cargo consisted of 25.09 percent exports and 74.91 imports. Although reliable estimates for the current handling are not yet available, it is estimated that in 1970 Karachi port handled 9 million tons of cargo.

Karachi also serves as a major international airport as well as the headquarters of Pakistan International Airlines which serves all of Pakistan and many large

Author's Note: The views expressed in this paper are private professional views of the author and should not be considered as views of the Government of Pakistan or the University of Pittsburgh. The paper was written before East Pakistan became Bangladesh.

cities of Asia and Europe. Many international airlines stop over at Karachi and the airport is being expanded to meet the expanding national and international needs.

Table 1 gives some idea of the growth of Karachi since 1901. Pakistan had a total urban population of 17 million in 1970. Out of this more than 3 million were in the Karachi metropolitan region. According to the 1961 census, industrial workers constituted 2.1 percent of the total population, 6.56 percent of the total civilian workers and 16.7 percent of nonagricultural workers; 13 percent of these industrial workers were in Karachi and the balance were distributed in much smaller proportions over other metropolitan areas and large urban centers. Figure 1 shows the existing and developing metropolitan centers of West Pakistan.

Developmental History of Karachi

There is some evidence that Karachi served as an outlet for the Indus Valley and there are some historical descriptions of port Debul (used by Arabs in the 8th century) which resemble those of Karachi. However, the uncertainty about the location and history of this city for the pre-British period reflects the erratic development of the lower Sind region, of which Karachi has been, and is a vital part. The British period begins with Sir Charles Napier, who shortly after the occupation of Sind in 1843, transferred the administration from Hyderabad to Karachi. At that time it was a dilapidated small town of 10,000 people. Between 1851-59, a number of social and economic reforms were introduced which set the city on the road to economic and social development. He promoted the development of the harbor and Sind Railway, which later on linked the city to the whole hinterland of Pakistan. By 1890, the city had a population of about 87,000 persons. Major town planning efforts were directed toward the establishment of a planned new settlement for the armed forces, which in the Indo-Pakistani British parlance is called the "Cantonment." Such planned settlements were built all over the Indo-Pakistani sub-continent, on the outskirts of some major urban areas. Later on a municipal committee was developed which worked closely with the Cantonment Board to build a nice clean city.

Table 1. Growth of Karachi, 1901 to 1971 (Derived from 1961 Census Publications)

Year	Population	Percentage Increase Over Previous Census
1901	136,297	139.00
1911	186,771	37.00
1921	244,162	30.70
1931	300,779	23.20
1941	435,887	44.90
1951	1,137,667	161.00
1961	2,044,044	79.67
1975	3,883,677 (estimated)	89.00 (estimated)

Metropolitan Planning in Karachi 111

Figure 1. Developing Metropolitan Centers in West Pakistan (based on 1961 census)
SOURCE: Pakistan National Planning Commission

By 1926 the municipal government was handed over to local leaders. As the city had begun to grow rapidly, its status was changed to that of a Municipal Corporation, enjoying several autonomous powers and a high status within the governmental hierarchy. Local leaders who served as secretaries or mayors of the corporation provided a dedicated leadership, and men like Harchandrai Vishindas, Ghulamali Changla, Jamshed Nusserwanji, and Hatim Alavi devoted their lives to the expansion and development of the city and converted it from a small colonial seaport to a modern commercial town which could successfully compete with other large urban centers in the sub-continent. Although the old parts of the city were indeed crowded and unsanitary, the overall impression of the urban area was so favorable that it gained reputation as the cleanest city in

Asia. During this British period, which ended in August 1947, a very well-planned industrial estate covering more than 5,000 acres was developed for location of industries as well as industrial workers' housing. This estate, called Sind Industrial Trading Estate (SITE), as of today houses the largest number of factories in Karachi and is considered to be one of the best planned and maintained industrial estates in the Indo-Pakistan sub-continent.

The period from 1947 onwards is marked by a number of unexpected and rather trying demands and developments. Karachi was declared the interim capital of the new government of Pakistan. This created a sudden demand for office space for the government as well as housing for the central government employees. In addition more than three quarters of a million displaced persons migrated to Karachi, as a result of communal disturbances which followed the partition of the sub-continent into India and Pakistan. This created not only serious overloading of facilities and services, but the city was virtually thrown into a chaotic condition. The major priority issues facing the government were the housing of families and persons who had migrated from India, creation of a reasonably rational framework for metropolitan government, and provision of most essential facilities and services for the suddenly inflated population of the city. The government felt that Karachi should have a separate autonomous improvement trust to look after the planning and development of Karachi as far as new areas were concerned, while the existing built-up areas within the jurisdiction of the Karachi Municipal Corporation (KMC) should remain within its own jurisdiction.

In 1952, a new autonomous organization called the Karachi Improvement Trust (KIT) was created. One major factor responsible for the creation of KIT was the recommendation of a foreign consulting firm of town planners, which was brought to Pakistan to prepare a master plan for Karachi, at the request of the Government of Pakistan. The firm—Merz, Randel & Vatten, Ltd. (in short MRV)—was commissioned by the Central Engineering Authority of the Government of Pakistan for this task. They completed their surveys and analysis rather hastily and submitted their report to the Central Engineering Authority in April, 1952.[1] As the consultants recommended the creation of an improvement trust for planning and development of the Karachi metropolitan area, the government immediately created KIT. While creating the KIT, the government followed the prototype models which existed in other parts of Pakistan and India, and just duplicated one of these. This was quite tragic because these improvement trusts were created during the British period essentially to look after new development that had very little to do with urban planning.

The MRV Plan did make clear-cut recommendations for the planning functions of such a trust, but somehow these were overlooked, and KIT was erected exactly within the details of the Improvement Trust Act of Calcutta (which was formulated in 1911!). It can be readily comprehended that KIT, created on such an archaic foundation, did not have appropriate administrative, executive, or legal powers to enforce the MRV plan or to pursue any systematic urban

Metropolitan Planning in Karachi

development policy for the metropolitan area. The MRV plan therefore assumed a respectable place in the shelves of the KIT. Meanwhile the water, sewerage, and drainage problems of Karachi had become serious, and a large project for Karachi's water supply was taken in hand. A separate autonomous body called the Karachi Joint Water Board was established to look after this project. As regards electricity, this was already in the hands of a private company, the Karachi Electric Supply Corporation. Thus the whole picture became a curious mixture of KMC, KIT, Joint Water Board, Karachi Electric Supply Corporation, Karachi Port Trust, the Cantonments, the central government, the provincial government, and a host of other agencies.

This confusion was further aggravated by the rapid growth of the metropolitan area because most of the industrial and commercial enterprises were being located in and around Karachi. The government was indeed upset and frustrated. Following some earlier recommendations of UN advisers and other foreign consultants, etc., the Government of Pakistan decided to merge the Karachi Improvement Trust and the Karachi Joint Water Board into a new and more powerful organization called the Karachi Development Authority (KDA), which came into being in 1958. These recommendations were initially suggested by Harland Bartholomew & Associates (an American city planning consulting firm), who were assisting the government with water, sewerage, and drainage planning for the Karachi metropolitan area.[2] The KDA was created under a Presidential Order, by the then President Iskander Mirza.[3] With the later transfer of the central government to Islamabad, the role and control of KDA had to be changed. The President's order establishing the KDA made the organization responsible to a ministry of the central government (as the central government was still housed at Karachi). The major functions of the new Authority were to look after water, sewerage, and drainage needs, planning and development of new land for housing, as well as urban planning. The Authority could also execute and manage low cost housing schemes, if so asked by the government and given funds and powers for the same.

In October, 1958, due to serious political and social disturbances, President Mirza declared martial law and abolished the political parties. Later that year a group of senior army generals led by General M. Ayub Khan took over the government and declared their new program for economic, social, and political reconstruction. The major thrust in Karachi for the new regime was for slum clearance and low income housing, provision of amenities and services for lower income groups, general planning and development of the metropolis, and restoration of law and order as well as curbing of nepotism and corruption in the local government. Rapid industrial and commercial development of Karachi had created shocking slums, serious transport and housing problems, mounting shortages of water, and an overall chaotic development pattern of the whole metropolitan area.

The displaced families from India and the migrants from the rural areas in search of jobs had created squatter problems of a vast magnitude. KDA was designated to initiate a slum clearance program (popularly known as the Korangi Project) of a very large size, and adequate funds and powers were provided to backup this program. The program was executed at a total cost of more than Pakistani rupees 40 crores (approximately equal to 80 million U.S. dollars). Unfortunately, the program was a sad failure and had to be terminated after this massive expenditure, and the balance of the project was reconstructed as a normal scheme of KDA. The other large-scale project for water, sewerage, and drainage was a little more successful and with technical and financial assistance from the United States, the water and sewerage facilities were expanded.

At one time the government was quite upset at the heavy concentration of industrial and commercial activity at Karachi, and an order was promulgated that no more industrial and commercial activities should be allowed to locate within the metropolitan area. However, as the national plans and the government were pursuing a policy of encouraging the private sector to participate in national development, and since Karachi offered several advantages to private entrepreneurs, this order was later withdrawn and cancelled.

Since 1966 a number of new developments have taken place. The problem of rehabilitation of the displaced families was completed by the end of 1965. President Ayub's new regime was well entrenched and a degree of national political stability was achieved. The new regime decided to shift the national capital to Islamabad. KDA's status was then converted to an agency of the provincial government, and the central government began to concentrate on the planning and development of Islamabad and the transfer of central government departments and functions out of Karachi to the new capital. In terms of the growth of Karachi, this shift of the national capital had only a marginal effect.

Karachi's growth problems were becoming serious, and slowly they came to the attention of the National Planning Commission. The Commission was anxious to study the problem and recommend appropriate solutions. With the Commission's recommendation the services of a UN adviser were obtained and placed at the disposal of the KDA. Meanwhile a Presidential Order[4] and a Government of West Pakistan Notification[5] had changed the status of KDA from a central government agency to a local body of West Pakistan, reporting to the provincial Department of Local Bodies. This created complex bureaucratic hurdles for metropolitan planning. On the suggestion of the National Planning Commission, the UN adviser and the KDA prepared a preliminary evaluation of problems and needs of Karachi. The National Planning Commission, the provincial government, and the KDA felt that foreign technical assistance was needed for preparing a regional development plan for the Karachi metropolitan region. The National Planning Commission suggested that a request be made to the United Nations for such assistance. A formal request was made to the UN in December, 1967, which was approved in June, 1968, and in September, 1968, KDA created a separate planning unit called the Master Plan Department (MPD) to look after the needs of this new project. The National

Planning Commission made special financial allocation in Pakistani rupees to provide essential local support to the UN technical assistance. Besides financial support, the National Planning Commission assigned the project a very high priority and included it in the list of their National Pilot Projects for regional development, which were launched by the Commission on an experimental basis and enjoyed the Commission's support and technical and financial assistance, as well as sustained high priority for successful implementation. In March, 1970, a detailed Plan of Operations was signed by the Government of Pakistan with the United Nations.[6] A UN Project Manager and a number of UN experts have been appointed. A large part of the project work has been sub-contracted by the UN to an American-cum-Czechoslovakian consulting firm of regional and urban planners, who have recently opened their offices at Karachi.

To conclude this hasty synoptic developmental history of Karachi, we can state quite categorically that since 1947, the Karachi metropolitan area has not been planned systematically. The government did make an effort by commissioning the MRV consultants to prepare a plan, but did not provide the institutional, legal, and financial tools for the plan to be implemented. KDA was created, not so much for meeting or solving the planning problems, but essentially to perform the functions of a large-scale public corporation for isolated land development schemes, handling problems of water, sewerage, and drainage, and executing those projects for low income housing for which the government had provided necessary funds and relevant executive and other managerial powers.

Although in pre-1947 days Karachi gained the reputation as the cleanest city in Asia, since 1947 the unplanned sudden large-scale growth has strained the facilities and servics and physical environment, and working conditions have indeed deteriorated to an extent that Karachi is generally considered an unhealthy and undesirable area for living. In spite of this bad reputation the metropolis keeps growing, and most of the people continue pouring in and settling down. Appreciating this curious phenomenon an Australian architect in a recent study of Karachi has given an apt nickname to the metropolis: "City that nobody loves, but everybody is there."[7]

Major Current Problems and Issues

From 1947 until 1955 the nation was fully occupied with basic tasks of establishing a rudimentary framework of the new government and tackling a number of other urgent problems. The first five-year plan was launched in 1955 but national planning did not gain much political support until the revolutionary government of President Ayub came into power in 1958, and the Planning Commission was moved into the President's Secretariat, with the President himself assuming the chairmanship of the Commission. The second five-year plan (1960-65) therefore fared a little better than the first.

However, the Planning Commission and the plans were following a development model which assigned the highest priority to economic growth and assumed that economic growth was synonymous with community and national welfare. Such a comfortable assumption and a relentless pursuit of economic growth for the sake of growth created serious social, environmental, and political problems. The country was able to achieve a high rate of growth, but the growth concentrated itself around developed areas and developed regions. In terms of its distribution and social justice, it benefitted a very small percentage of the total population. Unemployment increased, real wages in the industrial sector declined by one-third, and per capita disparity between East and West Pakistan nearly doubled. The dramatic growth of existing urban centers and metropolitan areas was not only unplanned but in many cases even essential utilities and services were not provided in an integrated manner, long after the industrial and commercial establishments had moved in.

One of the basic problems was the lack of integration of social and physical planning with economic planning on national, regional, and local levels. The other stumbling block was that the national, provincial, regional, and local levels were not very well coordinated and integrated with each other. The national planners, therefore, were neither fully conscious of the spatial and social consequences of their decisions nor did they possess any effective tools or institutional mechanisms for manipulating these consequences in desired directions. The metropolitan areas were neither warned nor prepared for additional growth. Accordingly even the social and spatial pattern which emerged out of the pursuit of an old fashioned market oriented growth model did not perpetuate any social, cultural, or political harmony. On a purely economic performance level the country did achieve a noteworthy rate of growth. On qualitative and socio-political levels the whole exercise ended up in a fiasco, which eliminated Ayub and his regime in 1968-69; martial law had to be imposed to bring the social and political chaos within some controls. The National Planning Commission had become aware of these serious social, environmental, and political problems which were created by the end of the Second Plan period, and had initiated in the Third Plan some experimental efforts for integrating physical planning with economic planning, as well as focusing attention on regional and urban development issues. However the progress made was rather modest.

Metropolitan planning and development problems of developing countries have been the subject of several global seminars. For example, the United Nations held a seminar at Stockholm in 1961 and another one on New Towns at Moscow in 1964.[8] The United States Agency for International Development organized a conference at Honolulu in 1967.[9] These two important gatherings of experts and practitioners from all parts of the world discussed metropolitan problems and needs in detail and came to several vital conclusions. There was some feeling that in market-oriented economies, it may be difficult to implement a program of decentralization of industries without strong regulation

Metropolitan Planning in Karachi

and control which may be in contradiction to the overall economic and political philosophy of a particular country. Under such circumstances it may be advisable not to enact negative controls for expansion of existing metropolitan areas and larger urban centers. Instead it may be more practical to encourage growth, if feasible in other areas and secondary urban centers, and at the same time plan the metropolitan areas and large urban centers to receive additional growth.

The International Bank for Reconstruction and Development (World Bank), in a recent study of Urbanization of Pakistan, also recommends a similar approach for Pakistan.[10] The study concludes that with appropriate research and proper communication and promotion, economic activities can be attracted to other urban centers which may have either an under-utilized capacity of urban services or where these services may be created or expanded at a lesser cost than in large metropolitan areas. Such an approach may be able to promote a more balanced urban growth pattern, in which the metropolitan areas will continue to grow, as "growth poles," while the secondary centers may develop as "growth centers," each attracting functions most suited to its own particular potentialities and facilities. This notion of growth centers and growth poles originated with the ideas and discussions generated by the French scholar Perroux. The whole theme forms the basis of a research paper presented by Dr. Bernard to the United Nations Research Institute for Social Development.[11] He argues that growth poles (metropolitan areas) and growth centers (deliberately selected secondary urban centers) can carry out different functions quite efficiently according to their level of hierarchy within a regional framework—the basic notion is to consider the metropolitan area and its potentialities within a larger regional and even supra-regional (provincial or national) framework.

National and local efforts to solve the slum problem had concluded in most unfortunate failures and frustrations. It was found that in 1965 more than 72 percent of the urban households of Karachi were living almost a sub-human life, with a monthly income of less than Pakistani rupees 200 (approximately $40 U.S. dollars). Karachi had the largest number of slum dwellers and displaced families from India who were also living in slums. The Ayub regime had launched a vast program of slum clearance based on a purely architectural-cum-engineering and aesthetic approach. The scheme was designed to remove slum dwellers to a planned new township (Korangi) approximately ten miles away from the city, where single room nucleus houses were built for them by the government. It is estimated that approximately 50,000 slum dwellers were rehoused in these clean quarters during the Second Plan period (1960-65). The sponsors, the designers, and the executors of the scheme felt that the problem of slum dwellers was being effectively solved in this manner, and the new residents of Korangi should soon be absorbed in the economic activities which may be located near there in the near future.

However, a socioeconomic survey of Korangi in 1960 revealed some startling facts. These facts indicated that the slum dwellers who moved to Korangi could not be employed in the nearby industrial and commercial enterprises since they did not have the skills needed by those establishments; thus, they were forced to travel long distances back to their original jobs or back to the central areas looking for jobs. This imposed a heavy transportation cost on their meagre earnings, in addition to the subsidized rent which they had to pay for the new house. Originally most of these workers lived close to work or traveled by bicycle. Now 98 percent had to spend about 20 percent of their total earnings for transportation and 13 percent on rental and other utilities provided in the house. These additional expenses, which they were not incurring when living in the slum area, were a serious drain on their monthly earnings. As a result, the real level of living of these slum dwellers started to decline and many of them either sold their houses to others, or did not pay the rent, or just left for other slum areas in the city.

These findings were indeed alarming and the whole project, which had consumed local and foreign resources worth about 80 million U.S. dollars, had to be phased out. The new target was to try to rescue the built-up part of the area from becoming a new slum.

A more recent study of a slum area called Azam Basti, by a team of students of the Free University at Amsterdam (Netherlands) brings out similar, interesting facts.[12] Azam Basti is a slum area of about 52 acres housing about 11,000 people. Out of these 11,000 people a large majority of the male heads of the households were employed in various activities such as cook, servant, gardener, etc. Only 18 percent were skilled laborers and others were either retired pensioners, unskilled laborers, or unemployed.

The average monthly income of the household was Pakistani rupee 200 (approximately U.S. $40) and more than 50 percent of this was spend on food. Many households spent a considerable amount of money and effort to purchase a portable radio or a sewing machine or a bicycle. Poor hygienic conditions and bad diet resulted in the spread of several perpetual and seasonal diseases such as malaria, dysentery, typhus, and skin and eye diseases. There are only seven community water taps in the area, and a large number of houses have no lavatories or other arrangements for excreta disposal. There are no arrangements for drainage, and dirty water runs from houses into open cesspools. There are no paved roads, nor are there any arrangements for waste or garbage disposal. There is no gas or electricity. There is a high rate of illiteracy, and the percentage of boys and girls between the age of 5-20 years not receiving education varies between 40 to 60 percent. This is due either to lack of interest on the part of parents, or to financial constraints which oblige children to start working young. The pattern of leadership is diffused and those persons who have contacts with the government, or who have influence in securing jobs for the jobless, or who can assist community people with their problems and contacts with various private, semi-government, and government institutions, enjoy a position of leadership.

Religious leaders indeed also enjoy a position of privilege and high status, and in many cases the residents of the community, in case of illness, first consult

Metropolitan Planning in Karachi

their religious leader, popularly known as "pir." There are more than thirty resident pirs in the community and several practitioners of local medicine called "hakims." Modern medical care is very limited and the bulk of this limited care is provided by various missionary organizations working on religious or charitable grounds. The community does not trust the government or government-sponsored organizations but is still very anxious to solve the basic problems of water, drainage, roads, electricity, waste disposal, health, housing, education, and employment. This thumbnail sketch gives some impression of a typical slum of Karachi. Azam Basti is still better off than many other slums as the unemployment rate in this area is rather low. Lyari and many other slum areas are far worse.

The program of slum clearance adopted by the government, as described earlier, has been a massive failure as it was based on a purely engineering-cum-architectural approach of "bulldozing" the existing slums and transplanting the slum dwellers to government-built houses and communities, hoping that the slum dwellers would find employment in the industrial enterprises to be located near these housing colonies. This was found to be more of a utopian assumption than a feasible proposition. If the process of slum formation is analyzed critically and carefully, it will be found that the problem is rooted not only in physical but also in socio-economic causes, and as such it cannot be effectively solved purely by what might be called a "public works" approach based on emotional analysis and aesthetic distaste for such a chaos.

However disturbing these slums may be, they serve a purpose and have a vital function. The private housing market does not cater to groups and individuals who cannot pay an economic rent. The slums house these groups and individuals. Most of the slum families are so poor that even if each family were housed in an indpendent clean and healthy dwelling unit, it would not have the resources to pay even a nominal rent, maintain the unit, and then utilize the pitifully modest balance for the most essential items of food, clothing, transport, etc. As such, a program of slum clearance without an advance or integrated program of economic and social development is not only bound for failure, but will create additional problems and responsibilities for the government by increasing the dependence of the residents on the government and public resources.

In the case of Karachi, we can identify three broad categories of slums:

(1) Areas which begin to deteriorate due to changes in land use, especially in their near vicinity, e.g., slow creeping in of trade, commerce, and light industry, etc.;

(2) Areas which begin to break down due to overcrowding, lack or inadequacy of utilities and facilities, and general neglect;

(3) Growth of temporary shacks on open spaces and fringes of a community.

The first type of problem is rather simple and can be dealt with by appropriate controls. The last two types may be analyzed and discussed briefly.

Because of the prevalent socio-economic and cultural levels and norms, the concept of a nuclear urban family (of husband, wife, and children only) is as yet not viable in Pakistan. It is therefore essential to use the concept of an "urban household" which envisions a group of persons living together and sharing a common kitchen or cooking facilities. In addition, the present pattern and level of urban living may have to be taken as normative, but subject to a slow change. On a careful survey, it may be observed that the majority of middle income and almost all the lower income groups in Karachi are used to rather spartan space standards, and as yet have not adopted the complex and rigid practices of separating cooking, dining, and living functions. In most cases all these functions are performed in pleasant informal harmony without modern rigid divisions of space. As such it is incorrect to assess or evaluate the existing housing stock on modern standards of rigid and functional division of space. In this context, the physical structures have no independent existence of their own. People do not live in houses only, as such it is necessary to understand the intimate relationship between people's lives, their social and economic levels and potentialities, and the real capacity of the local, regional and national economies to cater effectively to radically different or luxurious standards. Even today in many regions of economically advanced countries like the Netherlands, France, etc., many urban families do not have a shower bath and use the community bathing facilities; and these modes of living are socially fully acceptable.

Using this type of realistic criterion, we can condemn only temporary and dangerous dwelling units and cannot afford to throw away permanent and semi-permanent habitable units. Thus in the case of Pakistan in general and Karachi in particular, a careful classification of slums with an eye to partial replacement or improvements, etc., and an intensive program of general amelioration of the overall neighborhood with special attention to drainage, excreta disposal, water supply, light and air, as well as provision of a few "lungs" (open spaces with a tree or a little greenery, or just a small square or a small plaza) to introduce freshness and variety into the neighborhood will be more useful and feasible. Except for major replacement of dangerous structures, the slum area in general may only require "partial surgery" and a general program of amelioration and conservation.

It is the third type of slum, the temporary shacks and all kinds of ad hoc improvised solutions, that pose some of the most serious problems for Karachi and its local government. The government has generally contemplated these temporary structures in a somewhat negative manner, in the sense that they must be eliminated at public cost and the residents somehow housed in a cleaner environment. Such an approach not only oversimplifies the problem but drastically curtails the opportunities for an effective exploitation of a number of vital potentialities, which though latent, could be tapped. A temporary shack is a living proof and symbol of the poor resident's will power and sustained efforts (against all odds) to survive in a hostile environment and build a shelter (on a self-help basis) for himself and his family, without any assistance except for

Metropolitan Planning in Karachi

forcible free acquisition of government land. This proves that the incoming urban residents and families have the potentiality and will power to use their own modest resources and labor for building a temporary shelter for themselves. If we are able to adequately tap and guide these resources of slum dwellers, a viable program of slum improvement, self-help, and cooperative housing can be launched.

Actually, the housing problem of Karachi has never been viewed as a whole. Its various parts and pieces are viewed separately as problems of slum clearance, needs for industrial workers, housing, problems of cooperative housing societies, problems and needs of middle and upper income housing, etc. For example in 1967 and again in 1969 the Government of Pakistan requested the United States Agency for International Development (AID) to provide advisory assistance for initiating a scheme for industrial workers' housing at the Sind Industrial Trading Estate.[13] The recommendations of the advisers and consultants could not be implemented due to non-cooperation of the industrial entrepreneurs in providing a small share of the total funds, as well as government's inability to create a separate institutional mechanism for housing of industrial workers only.

Cooperative housing is dealt with entirely separately by the Cooperative Housing Societies Union; public servant's housing is handled by the provincial and central governments' Public Works Departments; the Port Trust, the railways, and Pakistan International Airlines have their own arrangements, while lower income subsidized housing for slum dwellers is dealt with by KDA, if and when provincial government delegates this responsibility to KDA with adequate funds and necessary powers. As such, at the moment there is no central locus of responsibility for overall housing policy, planning, financing, programming, and execution. Responsibilities are scattered and diffused over several departments and agencies, with no coordination or overall guidance.

In case of utilities and services, KDA's major contribution has been the completion of water, sewerage, and drainage schemes and initiating expanded programs for future needs. The first phase of the scheme, which has been completed, is supplying 70 million gallons of water per day. In addition to the lower income schemes of Korangi and North Karachi, KDA has executed a large number of middle and upper income housing schemes. The Authority only develops the land and provides necessary facilities and services. The houses are built by the persons purchasing those plots of land.

On the administrative side, functional confusions had become so serious that the Governor of West Pakistan in 1967 appointed a high level committee to look into these problems and submit a detailed report with specific suggestions for solutions. The committee submitted its report in 1968 (popularly known as the KLARCO Report)[14] which brought some new facts into the limelight. It was found that over the years, Karachi had become a breeding ground for a number of new municipal and other autonomous local bodies, and as of 1968, within the metropolitan region, there were two Municipalities, four Cantonment Boards, twelve town committees, a large number of local union committees, several

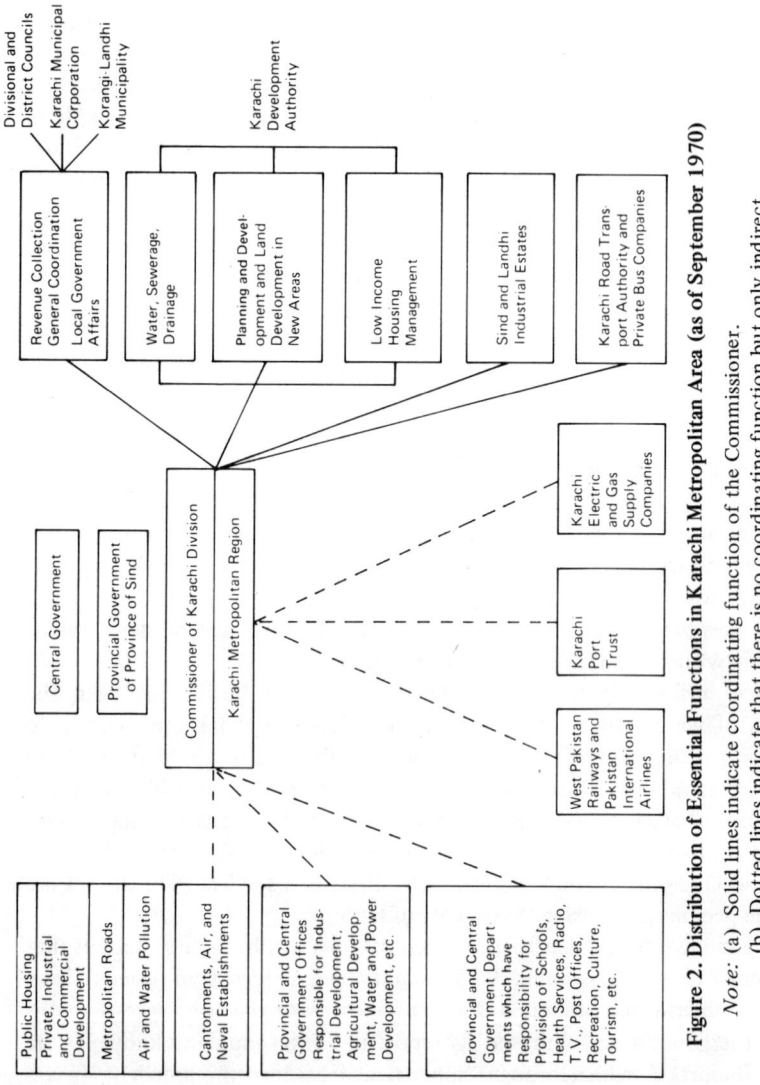

Figure 2. Distribution of Essential Functions in Karachi Metropolitan Area (as of September 1970)

Note: (a) Solid lines indicate coordinating function of the Commissioner.
(b) Dotted lines indicate that there is no coordinating function but only indirect persuasive and informal relationships.
(c) Boxes not connected by solid or dotted lines indicate that these problems and functions are not clearly placed in a related department and there is no formal or informal coordination with other metropolitan functions.

122

cooperative housing societies, two large autonomous industrial estates, and many other autonomous organizations such as the Karachi Port Trust, the Karachi Electric Supply Corporation, the Karachi Gas Company, and related units and offices of the central and provincial governments. The committee recommended creation of a Metropolitan Corporation by merging KDA and KMC and assigning overall planning and development functions to an appropriate unit of this Corporation. The Corporation was to develop appropriate working relationships with other units and bodies within the metropolitan area. The Committee's recommendations were reviewed but could not be considered seriously, as by this time due to social and political upheaval the martial law regime was forced to bifurcate West Pakistan into four separate provinces (based on ethnic and linguistic criteria as used by the British during their rule of the sub-continent). Karachi once again became the capital of Sind Province. Figure 2 shows the distribution of various functions within the Karachi Metropolitan Region. This helps to illustrate the atomization of the present planning system as well as some of its structural and functional weaknesses.

One fundamental problem, which is clear from Figure 2, is that even if Karachi had a very good planning system for the metropolitan area, it would not have been very effective, as the location of economic activities is in the hands of the central and provincial governments, their autonomous corporations, and the private sector. Unless and until this planning unit has some advisory or executive role in the locational decision making, its real effectiveness will be marginal.

The perspective for overall planning is far more fragmented and vague than in the area of housing. As clarified in the schematic chart, the planning responsibilities of KDA are of an extremely limited nature. The Karachi Municipal Corporation looks after the built up areas within its boundaries, and a host of other central and provincial government agencies, autonomous corporations, semi-public and private agencies look after their own affairs. The MRV plan was useful in guiding the development of the road network; beyond that it was neither used, nor had it any concrete practical recommendations for following a desirable and feasible pattern for the dynamic urban growth of the metropolitan area.

A far more serious problem, until very recently, was that there was no national or provincial urban development policy. Karachi's dramatic growth and serious shortages of utilities and services did not draw the attention of the National Planning Commission until the Third Plan period (1965-70), when steps were taken to initiate planning of the metropolitan region within a national and provincial framework. Figure 3 gives a general perspective of the accelerated growth of the metropolis since 1947. Due to an absence of national and provincial urban development policy, Karachi's expansion did not follow any preconceived notion of a general growth pattern. Neither KIT or KDA nor any other provincial or central government agency tried to analyze the pattern and structure of the growth that was taking place, or to crystallize any hypothesis out of such analysis. In some ways, one can take a daring step and generalize

LEGEND:
1948
1958
1968

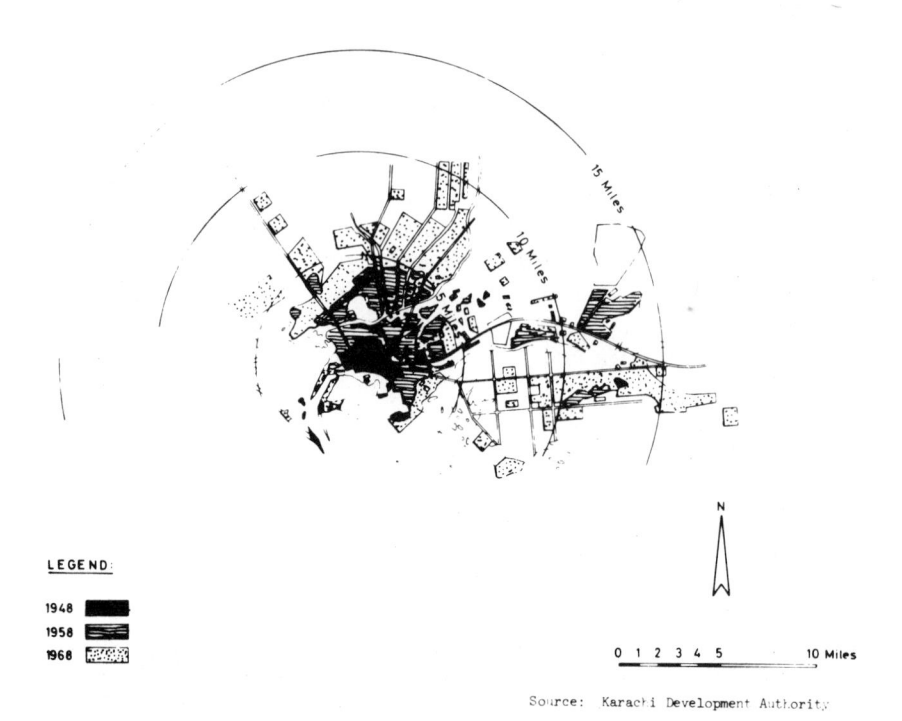

0 1 2 3 4 5   10 Miles

Source: Karachi Development Authority

Figure 3. The Growth of Karachi

that the pattern which has evolved is somewhat similar to the Multiple Nuclei Theory of Harris and Ullman.[15] The harbor, the airport, the Industrial Estates, the Business and Commercial Center, the Housing Societies, the University, and a host of other centers have agglomerated to form the growing metropolitan region.

Karachi has the largest number of automobiles, buses, and auto-rickshaws (rickshaws mounted on three-wheel scooters) as well as factories. All these combustion processes have indeed begun to create a pollution problem of their own. In addition there is the constant problem of dust, sand, and other contaminants. These free flowing gifts of industrialization and development naturally affect the health of all the residents and cause a considerable amount of respiratory and other diseases. Pakistani planners in general and planners of Karachi in particular are not concerned about these problems, and consider this area to be a major concern of the large metropolises of the developed economies of Western Europe and North America. Many of them are ignorant of the research findings and current thinking that is going on about the changes that are brought about in the atmospheric environment by urbanization and resulting damages.[16] Accordingly, so far pollution has received almost no attention.

The United Nations and the Dutch Projects

The major ongoing planning effort in Karachi was initiated in 1970 under United Nations auspices.[17] During the same year an agreement was signed between the Government of Pakistan and the Royal Netherlands Government to undertake joint research by the University of Karachi and the Free University at Amsterdam on slum improvement and urban development problems in Karachi.

The four-year UN project is aimed at assisting the Government of Pakistan in the preparation of a development plan for the Karachi metropolitan region. The general goal of the plan, as outlined in the Government "Request," is to create conditions under which the Karachi metropolitan region could develop in a coordinated and rational way, and the project has to recommend a desirable institutional framework for this. The plan will have the character of a comprehensive pre-investment study. It will formulate the broad directives on how to organize the region and how to establish guidelines for the planned development activities within the next 20-25 years. The project is expected to provide an answer to the questions, What, Why, Where, and When to invest, in order to ensure the harmonious socio-economic, functional, and spatial development of the region. The investment activities recommended by the project, commencing with the drawing up of detailed blueprints through to the actual construction and operation and maintenance, will be the responsibility of various Pakistani agencies. The multiplicity of executing agencies involved requires the creation of a high-powered body for the purpose of multisectoral planning for integrated physical and socio-economic development of the entire region, as well as for the actual coordination and planning supervision of the construction activities in conformity with the plan prepared for the region. Recommendations as to the set-up of the body (the planning organization) will also be formulated as an essential part of the project. The precise area to be covered by the plan will be defined by the planners on the basis of wider studies aimed at the delimitation of the metropolitan region. Those initial studies are expected to extend over an area of about 4,000 square miles (almost the whole Karachi District and part of Lasbella and Thatta Districts). The plan will be based on a thorough and detailed survey of the existing conditions in the city and its region, together with an analysis of prevailing economic and social trends.

The United Nations will provide fellowships abroad for the training of Pakistani counterparts working on the project; various types of specialized equipment and instruments necessary for the execution of the project; vehicles;

books and periodicals; printing of a final report, and other miscellaneous expenses connected with the operations. The total cost of the project is as follows:

Governing Council of the United Nations Development Program (including the Government cash contribution towards local operating costs of U.S. $135,500)   U.S. $1,208,100

Estimated value of the Pakistan Government's participation in Pakistani rupees, equivalent to   U.S. $ 625,268

The United Nations has been designated as the executing agency for this project. On the government side, the new Master Plan Department established for the purpose by the Karachi Development Authority is expected to be responsible for the preparation of the plan, and the UN personnel will assist this Department in the execution of that task. The wide scope, complexity, and coordinating character of the project requires that various agencies on the central and provincial government level collaborate with the project. The declaration of the project as National Pilot Project No. 3 of the National Planning Commission also necessitates special organizational arrangements facilitating the operation of the project. For that purpose special machinery has been established, and a high level steering and advisory committee, consisting of senior central, provincial and local officials as well as UN representatives, has been established by the National Planning Commission to assist with the implementation of the project and to insulate it from routine treatment and red tape.

The United Nations plan of operation based on the proposal worked out by the UN project manager, has been signed by the Government of Pakistan and the UN. The government has already appointed a Government Project Representative, a Project Commissioner, and a Project Director.

It is expected that as soon as the project is completed, and the plan approved, a number of actions will need to be taken for an appropriate follow up, such as:

(1) Based on the recommendations of the final plan and reports, and utilizing the physical base which would have been established in the shape of the operating Master Plan Department (MPD), the government is expected to convert MPD into a permanent planning organization. The main objective of that organization will be the carrying out of planning at the metropolitan regional level. In the process, it is expected to integrate physical planning with socio-economic plans and programs to be developed for the Karachi Metropolitan Region.

(2) The new planning organization will serve as a laboratory for learning and developing various techniques of regional development planning which may be applied in other regions of the country.

(3) In addition to formulating the general guidelines for development of the metropolitan region, the project will identify specific fields in

which training, technical assistance, and detailed pre-investment studies are necessary.

(4) As the result of the proposed program of development, essential investments and their order of priority will be identified, opening up the chances for undertaking new capital investments by the Pakistani authorities, private groups and individuals and also by foreign aid-giving agencies, as well as by investors and entrepreneurs.

The MPD has established a number of units for preliminary work, such as a unit for regional planning and development, an urban design unit, an economic and legal unit, a social analysis and social planning unit, a housing and utilities unit, a transportation unit, etc. These units have initiated and completed some preliminary research work. The consultants, to whom the UN has sub-contracted the major part of the project, have established their offices at Karachi and are now finalizing a detailed specification of work to be carried out within the broad framework of the plan of operations. The UN has also initiated the professional training program of the Pakistani counterpart staff.

The Dutch Project was to be a continuation of the previously mentioned detailed study of the Azam Basti slum area. The Azam Basti Report had come to the attention of the National Planning Commission. The Commission, which was still smarting from the painful experience of Korangi and similar slum clearance schemes taken up in various metropolitan areas of the country, was very much impressed by the work of the Dutch researchers and their suggestions for slum improvement instead of slum clearance. The Commission has tried to promote this notion of improvement instead of clearance since 1965 by propagating their policies on housing[18] as well as reprinting a detailed study by Patrick Geddes[19] which he completed for the old city of Lahore in 1917, with specific suggestions for "improvement" instead of clearance. The report was never implemented, and was buried in the records of the Lahore Municipal Corporation since 1917.

Conclusions and recommendations of the Azam Basti Report were very much in line with the policies promoted by the Commission for self-help and mutual aid housing, urban cooperatives, and general slum improvement. The report had come up with conclusions which the Commission had itself arrived at by the end of the Third Plan. The Azam Basti Report concluded that major problems of this slum settlement were: (1) employment and related economic issues; (2) basic utilities and services (water, roads, drainage, electricity, etc.); (3) medical care and health education; (4) education; (5) social planning and development; (6) community leadership; and (7) development of an integrated community out of diverse religious, cultural, ethnic, and linguistic groups.

The researchers interviewed the slum dwellers to find out what the residents considered their most urgent problems. The residents seemed to come up with the same list of problems and priorities as analyzed by the researchers. The report pointed out that the residents are willing to pool their own resources in cash, kind, and labor, to supplement a workable program to be initiated by the government, or to launch a program without government assistance but with technical guidance from an outside source. Both alternatives would of course require certain structural changes within the present system of the settlement as well as in the major outer systems and their relationship to the internal systems of the settlement. The report also proposed that most of the physical improvements be carried out in the local traditions and with local materials. The National Planning Commission adopted the report for implementation during the Fourth Plan period.

The commission felt that the Dutch students had done a pioneering job and requested the Royal Netherlands Government to assist with the promotion of a joint research project between the University of Karachi and the Free University of Amsterdam, which should expand the application of Azam Basti type of action-oriented research techniques to the overall problem of slum improvement and urban development of the Karachi metropolitan region (see Figure 4). The Royal Netherlands Government very graciously placed a grant of one million Dutch guilders (approximately 350,000 U.S. dollars) at the disposal of the Free University of Amsterdam for collaboration with the National Planning Commission and the University of Karachi for launching such a joint research project for the whole metropolitan region of Karachi. The National Planning Commission of Pakistan matched the Dutch grant by an equivalent grant in Pakistani rupees (approximately equivalent of U.S. $300,000), and requested the University of Karachi and the Free University of Amsterdam to prepare a detailed plan of operations for this joint research project to be executed over a period of five years (1970-75).

The project aims at carrying out in-depth action-oriented research in slums of Karachi and to evolve practical policies and programs for slum improvement as well as prevention within an overall framework of systematic urban development. The project is called Joint Research Project No. IV (JRP IV), and is titled: "Slum Improvement and Urban Development at Karachi." The detailed plan of operations was signed in 1970 with the cooperation of the Netherlands Universities Foundation for International Cooperation. Project directors were appointed within the Free University of Amsterdam and the University of Karachi. The Department of Non-Western Sociology of the Free University of Amsterdam and the Graduate School of Business Administration of the University of Karachi, have been designated as the respective coordinating units in the Netherlands and Pakistan. Young Pakistani and Dutch researchers have been recruited, and an intensive program of action-oriented research has been initiated in selected slums of Karachi.

The results of the research will be converted into policies and programs for slum improvement which will be executed by the provincial government of Sind, with necessary technical and financial assistance from the National Planning Commission, the Royal Netherlands Government, and the Free University of Amsterdam. The program is still in its infancy, as the actual work started in early 1971. A serious effort is being made to ensure that a new integrated approach is evolved for solving various problems of slums which have almost become

Metropolitan Planning in Karachi 129

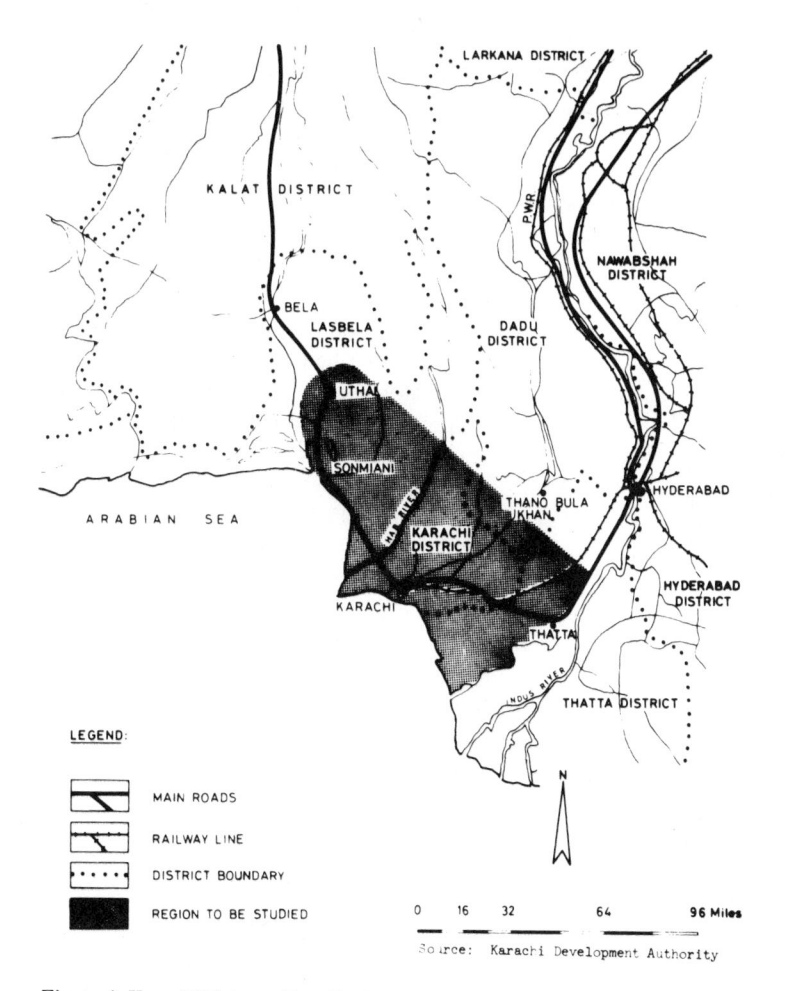

Figure 4. Karachi Metropolitan Region

chronic. Pakistani and Dutch sociologists, economists, physical planners, geographers, and development administrators are working hand in hand with sincerity and professional devotion to chart a new course of action. The project maintains very close liaison and working relationships with the UN project for metropolitan planning and all other relevant projects, agencies, and organizations of the central, provincial, and local governments as well as with semi-public, private, and voluntary organizations within the Karachi metropolitan region.

Future Directions

Recent social and political tensions and disturbances in Pakistan have forced the government and the National Planning Commission to do some serious soul searching. During the three plan periods (1955-1970) Pakistan pursued a goal of economic growth rather successfully. But this noteworthy growth was achieved at a serious social, environmental, and political cost. And worst of all, the growth solved neither the problems of poverty nor of unemployment. Most of the benefits seem to have gone to an extremely small number of entrepreneurs and others and the gap between the rich and the poor seems to have widened.

The Fourth Five Year Plan[20] admits these serious shortcomings and frankly states that it is groping for a new "planning model." Unfortunately the plan does not follow any new model. It simply states in a flurried mood that as the masses demand social justice and better living conditions, it aims for a lower rate of economic growth in order to accelerate social development by allocating more resources and a higher priority to the so-called social sectors. Such an ad hoc surgery of the old planning model is not possible. The whole model needs to be replaced by a new one, and more precise definitions of growth and development need to be stated within the framework of broad social objectives which the government and the plan profess to achieve. We may need to devise new indicators of measuring development instead of growth of per capita income of the GNP.[21] Adequate steps will have to be taken to ensure that social and physical planning are integrated with economic planning in such a manner that the national plans have adequate cognizance of the regional and spatial dimensions of the investments proposed by the plans.

Jagdish Bhagwati brings out this serious shortcoming of the national plans and finds that due to this neglect of the spatial dimension two serious problems have been created.[22] There is a scramble by regions, metropolitan areas, and their political leaders to grab industrial projects, and this free-for-all scramble then generates all kinds of inefficiencies, not only in terms of economic planning and performance but also in terms of spatial planning and organization, as areas which get these projects are not necessarily planned in advance for such growth, rational or irrational.

Besides the need for introducing a spatial component to the national planning efforts, there is also the need to establish a communications network between national, regional, and local level of planning. A very vital and important component of such an approach will be the role and place of popular participation. The United Nations has recently made some useful recommendations in a special study of the subject[23] as well as in a study group report[24] dealing with promotion of urban cooperatives. The search for new planning models formed the basis of a recent detailed discussion in the last meeting of the Institute for World Affairs.[25] There seemed to be a general consensus that the traditional growth models for economic development need to be replaced by a more integrated approach towards economic, social, and physical development. In such an approach a clearer and more potent policy for metropolitan, urban, and rural development will need to be spelled out. Rodwin considers this as a prerequisite, if any reasonable degree of success is to be achieved for promoting a more livable, healthy, and balanced urban growth.[26]

Pakistan does deserve some credit in that, as a result of her own experience of fifteen years of planned development following an archaic version of the capitalist model, the Planning Commission has now at least admitted the need for a new planning model (many other developing countries have not yet even admitted this and continue to prepare plan after plan within an archaic framework), and has floated some national pilot projects and joint research programs for regional and urban development, as well as slum improvements. What are the chances of success of these new pilot projects, and if successful what real impact will this success have on the larger and mounting problems of poverty, unemployment, the sub-human living conditions of the masses, and the overall process of social and economic change? This process of change at the moment is causing serious tensions, frustrations, and sometimes even deceleration of national and international integration of a pre-industrial society like Pakistan. These sweeping questions cannot all be answered in this brief paper, but we can at least frankly examine the role and impact of the UN and the Dutch project on the problems and needs of Pakistan in general and Karachi in particular.

There is no doubt that both these projects are trail blazers within the new and very young discipline of development planning. National planners and policy makers of Pakistan will indeed benefit from these experiences to chart new courses of action for national, regional, and local planning and development. However, there are some basic problems which cannot be solved by simple research and regional and urban plans, however well intentioned or well prepared. These are fundamental problems brought out by Myrdal in his *Asian Drama*[27] and by Lewis in his review of the Indian scene.[28] So far India and Pakistan have been carried away with preparation of plans and with presenting these to various aid-giving agencies, especially the World Bank and other multilateral and bilateral organizations such as the UN, U.S. AID, the Canadian International Development Agency, etc., for securing loans and grants for schemes and projects which could not be planned and executed without international financial, commodity, and technical assistance.

If one reads the plan, all seems to be ultra-progressive, and a sense of euphoria and confidence begins to envelop the reader, carrying him away to the dreamland of new societies projected with dramatic labels of Indian or Islamic socialism. The extremely clever editing and imagery of these plans are not revealed until one visits and lives in an Indian or Pakistani village or in an urban area or large metropolis. The rigid social and administrative institutions, the absence of social and civic discipline, the fossilized and creaking bureaucracy, the sub-human living conditions, the mounting urban unemployment, the widening gap between the rural and the urban areas, provide a severe jolt with two types of reaction. One type may be "Why plan?"—why not attack the most vital problems on a priority basis without cumbersome national planning? The other type of reaction may be, "How can we plan better" for a society which closely resembles the pre-revolutionary days of the Soviet Union or the Peoples

Republic of China? Can such a society be planned on a Western model. The answer naturally is in the negative. The central issue then is that no amount of metropolitan planning, however good it may be, can be a replacement for an enlightened and serious effort by the political leaders and the society itself to "will" the change that is needed and create a milieu which will accelerate social mobilization and the "will to work."

Metropolitan plans cannot be implemented without appropriate urban land policies as well as urban land reforms. New institutional, financial, and legal arrangements are necessary to implement these plans. Planners cannot provide these basic prerequisites for an effective implementation of their plans, and that is where the rhetoric of the national plans needs to be converted into political action leading to basic institutional reforms and changes.

Having clarified the issue of some of these basic changes, we may now briefly review a few substantive problems within the field of metropolitan planning which will pose some dilemmas in case of developmental needs of Karachi. The new discipline which is called by such diverse names as "Town and Country Planning" or "City and Regional Planning" or "Urban Affairs" or "Environmental Planning" or "Urban Development Planning," etc., is currently going through some self-criticism, review, and metamorphosis. For approximately fifty years, the profession has gone through what may be called the classical period of "master-planning," where in millions of land use type of master or urban plans were prepared and efforts made for their implementation. This experience provided some new insight into the process and problems of urban growth and development, and it was felt that urban areas were neither static nor isolated entities. This gave rise to the expansion of the concept to city and regional planning. However, further experience indicated that many of the locational and growth decisions and factors were beyond even regional boundaries and were direct functions of national development policies. This has set into motion a new stream of thought related to national strategies and policies for urban development. The experience of the classical period also brought out the need to prepare these plans within a broader socio-economic framework instead of within a purely physical or land use approach. Another vital area of concern was the whole problem of implementation of these plans. As soon as we start relating implementation to the planning proposals, we need to further broaden the general base and overall planning framework, to converge the exercise more towards local development planning instead of using a purely physical or economic or social or administrative and budgetary approach.

Recently geographers and urban economists have provided new insights and techniques for guiding urban growth. Richardson[29] and Hoover[30] have not only summarized the whole state of the art regarding urban spatial structure, urban growth, and urban public economy, but have also added new perspectives to urban and regional economic development. These new findings and experiences have radically altered the concepts and theories of metropolitan and urban development beyond the simple "master planning" approach to a more intricate and analytical exercise geared to agreed upon goals and targets. New techniques for preparing such plans with a built-in implementation component are being developed within the framework of a systems approach.[31] These new developments will need to be recognized and included in the current planning efforts for Karachi.

In the case of slums and slum improvement the United Nations has gained substantial new and useful experience. Some of these experiences were discussed in a recent seminar held in Latin America.[32] The seminar dwelt on a number of basic issues highlighted earlier in this paper, and agreed upon a number of new strategies and policies for handling this urgent problem. One vital conclusion was that the whole problem of slums and slum formation should be handled within the development policies of a nation and its urban development strategy in particular. Besides the UN, the U.S.A. has also gained a lot of experience in problems of slum, slum clearance, welfare of lower income groups, and programs for eradication of poverty. So far the U.S. experience has not resulted in any systematic new strategies or policies, but parts of this experience have some value for developing countries in terms of "what not to do." A recent experiment of the U.S. government and business organizations, launching joint programs for slum improvement and creation of job opportunities for slum dwellers, may also be interesting for developing countries[33] in general and Karachi in particular.

These two different scenarios of the state of the arts of metropolitan planning and slum improvement were created purposely in order to measure the potentialities and future directions of the Dutch and the UN projects.

As regards the Dutch project, the future survival of the project depends directly on a successful implementation of policies and programs emanating from the research. If the project boils down to simple report production and statement of wise and desirable policies for slum improvements, there is bound to be serious disappointment. The Azam Basti Report has still to be implemented. The Dutch researchers' approach is nothing very new in terms of the accumulated global knowledge of slum improvement. As mentioned earlier, Patrick Geddes recommended such an approach for the old city of Lahore as early as 1917, but no action has been taken on this even today. Lahore has gone through the disappointing experience of slum clearance types of projects (similar to the Korangi project at Karachi), and has recently completed a new scheme called the Lahore Township, with Canadian financial, technical, and commodity assistance. The scheme, which was supposed to assist the slum dwellers in relocation and possibly employment in the adjoining industrial estates, has not done much for them. It has of course helped in providing some relief to the serious housing shortage for the lower income groups. These experiences and problems raise serious questions as to whether any new research efforts and recommendations will be considered sympathetically and how these new suggestions and schemes for slum improvement will be launched. The basic support will need to come from the political and top levels of government, local, provincial, and central. Appropriate institutional, legal, and financial reforms, as well as new structures, will need to be created to cater to an efficient implementation of the new policies, plans, and projects. Pakistanis will need to be trained for handling these new tasks on professional, sub-professional, and skilled levels. Unless these preconditions are satisfied, there is a great danger that the findings of the Dutch project will as usual be read with great interest, and then like the Geddes report on Lahore and the MRV plan for Karachi, be forgotten and shelved.

Reviewing the planning side, it may be noticed that although Karachi had a master plan (the MRV plan described earlier), it could not be implemented, due to lack of institutional, legal, and financial support. Myrdal, recently, in one of his articles, has urged that there be no diplomacy in research, that we not try to cover up or avoid stating awkward facts which are necessary to carry out reforms.[34] Following his advice, it can be stated rather clearly that unless and until a number of prerequisites are created, the new UN plan may also meet the fate of the MRV plan. The National Planning Commission has taken certain steps to get the project initiated and to assign it a high priority. However, still on the provincial and local levels, there is neither conceptual awareness of the need for integrated planning nor appropriate institutional mechanisms for planning and implementing a plan. KDA and KMC both still consider "planning" as planning of projects, or at best, as "zoning" of new land. Neither has any controls or powers for guiding the location of economic activities. There is no arrangement to view the total investment program, public and private, within the metropolitan region as a whole and its spatial consequences. There is a danger that the present project may still utilize the classical "master planning" approach instead of trying the new innovations and changes which have come about in the whole field of urban and regional planning, converging it more towards local and regional development planning. These new ideas demand a much wider socio-economic framework as well as in-depth socio-economic analysis.

Then there is the whole question and problem as to what is to be done until the plan is ready. Every year several million Pakistani rupees are being invested in Karachi, in the public, semi-public, and private sectors. These investments can neither be delayed nor stopped for a period of four years, when the plan would be ready. Once the investments have been made, certain types of physical development would have taken place and the plan will not be able to change it later. The whole planning exercise therefore needs to be divided into phases—the long-range plan, the interim plan, the outline plan, and the general development policy. It will be essential to have some kind of general development policy to use as a yardstick for guiding these large-scale investments. This may be translated as soon as possible into a rough outline development plan which may later be refined to an interim plan. This can then be finalized, after discussion, etc., into the long-range development plan. The present approach does not follow this sequence, and as such it is completely divorced from the actual investment process, which is going along its own merry way. After four years the plan will be brought out of the bag, only to find out that a considerable amount of landscape has already been changed by large-scale investments during these four years.[35]

The provincial government of Sind has created a Provincial Planning Board for planning and development of the whole province. It is essential that the UN project work very closely with the Provincial Planning Board, if not become a part and parcel of it. KDA is neither an appropriate home for it, nor has it the mechanism to provide necessary socio-economic tools for analysis as well as planning within a wider regional and provincial framework. As explained earlier, KDA is essentially a construction agency for new land development, water and sewerage projects, etc. It neither has, nor will have in the near future, any analytical framework or powers for socio-economic development. Either such a framework will need to be created, or a new institution will have to be created, or the project will have to be attached to the Provincial Planning Board of Sind, which does have a framework for the whole province and can provide an appropriate regional setting.

It is urgent that besides concentrating on the long-range plan, the project should provide guidance for the large-scale investment decisions being made now in order to avoid some disastrous mistakes, which may be beyond correction once the investments have been made. Pakistan's national plan proposes to bring more structural changes in the economy and it is expected that manufacturing and non-agricultural employment will increase considerably in the coming years. Karachi will get a substantial share of it, and the project will need to provide guidance for this, and for when these new investments are to be made.

NOTES

1. MRV (Pakistan) Ltd., "Report on Greater Karachi Plan," submitted by Mr. Lindstrom of Vattenbyggnadsbyran, Stockholm, Sweden, in 1952. Full report was reprinted by Karachi Development Authority, Karachi, in 1967, and is available in their records.

2. Harland, Bartholomew and Associates, "Water and Sewerage Problems of Greater Karachi." Karachi: 1952.

3. Government of Pakistan, "President's Order No. 5: Karachi Development Authority." Karachi: Gazette of Pakistan, December 13, 1957.

4. Government of Pakistan, "President's Order No. 6: Amending KDA Ordinance." Karachi: Gazette of Pakistan, March 31, 1962.

5. Government of West Pakistan, "KDA Amendment Ordinance 1962." Lahore: Gazette of West Pakistan, September 26, 1962.

6. Economic Affairs Division, Government of Pakistan, "Plan of Operations for Master Plan for Karachi Metropolitan Region." Islamabad, Pakistan: March 1970.

7. G. Rudduck, *Urban Biographies.* Karachi: Pakistan National Planning Commission's Publication No., P.P. and H. 19, April 1965.

8. United Nations, *Planning of Metropolitan Areas and New Towns.* New York: 1967.

9. U.S. AID, *Pacific Conference on Urban Growth–The New Urban Debate.* Washington, D.C.: U.S. AID, 1969.

10. International Bank for Reconstruction and Development, *Current Cost of Urban-*

ization in Pakistan—A Cost Model for Urban Planning. Washington, D.C.: Economics of Urbanization Division, World Bank, 1970.

11. P. Bernard, *Growth Poles and Growth Centres in Regional Development.* Geneva: UNRISD Report No., 70/14, United Nations, 1970.

12. T. J. Segaar and J. H. de Goede, *Azam Basti—A Sociological Inquiry.* Amsterdam: Free University at Amsterdam, Department of Non-Western Sociology, 1969.

13. George Duggar, "Industrial Workers Housing in Pakistan: Problems and Prospects." Washington, D.C.: U.S. AID, 1969; also, "Report of the First Mission to Karachi." Washington, D.C.: U.S. AID, 1967.

14. Karachi Local Authorities Reorganization Committee, Final Report. Karachi: International Press, 1968 (restricted distribution). Copies available from Planning Director, Master Plan Project, KDA, Karachi.

15. J. H. Johnson, *Urban Geography: Theories of Urban Structure.* London: Pergamon, 1969, ch. 9.

16. H. E. Landsberg, "City Climate," in Landsberg, *Weather and Health.* New York: Doubleday and Co., 1969, ch. 8.

17. Karachi Development Authority, "Master Plan for Karachi: Metropolitan Region," Bulletin No. 1 (MP=B/1). Karachi: KDA, 1970.

18. Khalid Shibli, *Housing: Short Range Tactics and Long Range Strategy.* Karachi: National Planning Commission's Study No. PP and H., January 15, 1965.

19. Khalid Shibli and P.W.G. Powell, *Urban Improvements: A Strategy for Urban Works.* Karachi: National Planning Commission's Study No. P.P. and H., June 12, 1965.

20. Government of Pakistan, *The Fourth Five Year Plan (1970-75).* Islamabad: Pakistan National Planning Commission, July 1970.

21. "The Concept of Development and its Measurement," International Social Development, Review No. 2, United Nations (New York, 1970).

22. Jagdish Bhagwati, *Economics of Underdeveloped Countries.* New York: McGraw-Hill, 1970.

23. United Nations, *Local Participation in Development Planning.* New York: United Nations, 1970.

24. United Nations, *Report of the Study Group on Social Aspects of Urban Co-operatives.* Geneva: United Nations, 1968.

25. W. A. Beling and G. O. Totten, *Developing Nations: Quest for a Model.* New York: Van Nostrand Rheinhold Co., 1970.

26. L. Rodwin, *Nations and Cities.* Boston: Houghton Mifflin and Co., 1970.

27. G. Myrdal, *An Approach to the Asian Drama.* New York: Random House, 1970.

28. J. P. Lewis, *Quiet Crisis in India.* New York: Doubleday and Co., 1964.

29. H. W. Richardson, *Regional Economics: Location Theory, Urban Structure, Regional Change.* New York: Praeger, 1969.

30. E. M. Hoover, *Introduction to Regional Economics.* New York: Alfred Knopf, 1971.

31. J. B. McLoughlin, *Urban and Regional Planning—A Systems Approach.* New York: Praeger, 1971.

32. United Nations, "Proceedings of Inter-regional Seminar on Improvement of Slums and Uncontrolled Settlements," held at Medellin, Columbia, February/March 1970. New York: United Nations, 1971.

33. S. A. Levitan, G. L. Magnum, and R. Traggart, *Economic Opportunity in the Ghetto: The Partnership of Government and Business.* Baltimore: The Johns Hopkins Press, 1970.

34. "I have no respect for diplomacy in research." G. Myrdal, in Ceres, review of the F.A.O. (March/April 1971).

35. See Chapter 9 for some laudatory as well as critical comments on the plan as it is emerging "out of the bag."

CHAPTER 5

Arthur T. Row

METROPOLITAN PROBLEMS AND PROSPECTS:
A Study of Calcutta

Calcutta is important as the home of eight million people; it is important as the capital and only significant city of West Bengal with its population of 45 million people; it is important as the primate city of Eastern India with its population of some 150 million people; and it is important as one of the three national cities of the world's largest democracy. In itself it is larger than 85 independent nations, and its hinterland, if it were a separate nation, would rank fifth in the world in population.

In the context of this paper, however, Calcutta is important for a different reason. In terms of its complex mixture of the primitive and sophisticated, in terms of the population pressures with which it has had to grapple over the past quarter century, and in terms of the continuing deterioration in the quality of its urban life, Calcutta probably represents the leading edge of the urban situation in the developing world.

Calcutta has been described in numerous books, newspapers, journals, and television programs.[1] Its problems have been cataloged more completely and frequently than those of any other city in the developing world. There is no point in attempting to reproduce that catalog here—Calcutta is in difficult straits by whatever measure one chooses to use: deficiencies in housing and public services; a deteriorating quality of life for an increasing number of its inhabitants; precarious to disastrous states of local fisc; increasing unemployment with an increasingly restless and vocal educated segment. These aspects of contemporary Calcutta are probably more advanced than in most, if not all, of the developing cities of the world. But they are by no means unique to Calcutta.

But there are three aspects of Calcutta which are given too little notice in the spate of words written about it. The first is the astonishing vitality of the city and its environs. The second is the complex and intricate mixture of the primitive and the sophisticated. The third is the difficulty of providing an adequate urban environment with its necessary supporting facilities for a population in which two-thirds of the families have incomes of less than Rs.200 a month or about $26.00 (one U.S. dollar equals Rs.7.50).

Calcutta is an exceedingly vibrant and vital city. Politically, it is the liveliest and noisiest of the cities of India. Culturally and intellectually it is India's premier city. Although it is a Bengali city with all of the social accoutrements one would expect the Bengali society to produce, it is still a highly cosmopolitan city in which the public rituals of numerous Indian communities are regularly in evidence. Despite its squalor it is by no means moribund. All of this should not be surprising in view of Calcutta's primacy in a hinterland region of some 150 million people. And that hinterland will be in one sense increased now that East Bengal has become independent Bangladesh. There is no question of Calcutta's vitality and capacity for life.

The second point is more important to the professional planner. Calcutta represents on the same piece of landscape a spectrum of urban activities, forms, apparatus and machinery, and life styles that range from the oldest and most primitive to the most contemporary and sophisticated.

A principal task of the city planner is to resolve or alleviate conflicts between competing activities for urban space. It is also his task to improve the linkages spatially between related activities. In the modern Western city carrying out these tasks is difficult enough. It is immensely more difficult in Calcutta where the components in the urban mix are so much more numerous and where modern devices like the motor car are forced to operate in an environment of ancient forms.

The third point, the level of income, raises very serious questions of priorities and of standards. For example, the Basic Development Plan states "It appears then that the conventional housing objectives not only cannot be attained but probably should not be given priority until the economy has developed much beyond its present status." And again, "An interim public strategy for their fulfillment must concentrate on increasing local families' abilities to pay for housing—not on the direct provision of housing. Thus, programs for economic development must be given a higher priority and direct efforts in housing must be designed to keep to the lowest possible levels, the use of resources which might otherwise go to agriculture or industry."[2]

Although housing represents the largest single urban investment it is by no means the only one. What about schools, hospitals, recreation and other community facilities, and the priorities to be assigned to them and the standards of service to be provided? These are very difficult questions indeed in a society with the income distribution that characterizes Calcutta presently.

The Context

In this situation, there has now been for ten years an extensive and heavily manned effort to devise plans and programs to alleviate current problems and to turn Calcutta on a road toward gradual, if not dramatic, improvement. This paper sets forth a description and evaluation of that effort with emphasis on those aspects of it that may have more or less general application to other major cities in the developing world.

Perhaps it is necessary at the outset to identify those aspects of the situation which are more or less unique in order that the reader can identify those aspects which are more or less universal. The aspects peculiar to Calcutta would tend to fall under the following headings: the character of the population pressures; the character of the metropolitan economy; the relationship between Calcutta and its hinterland; the Bengal political situation. These aspects are all related one to another.

The population pressures on Calcutta have over the past quarter century been no greater than those for most major cities of the developing world. But the time pattern and the character of the in-migrants is probably unique. Indian independence was simultaneous with the Partition of the sub-continent. The effects of that Partition were most extensively felt in Bengal. At the time of Independence, 1947, Calcutta's population was nearly five million people. Between 1947 and 1961, Calcutta absorbed some one million refugees from East Bengal. Whereas in Western India the exchange between Hindus moving from Pakistan to India and Muslims moving from India to Pakistan was more or less even, in Eastern India, the Hindus moving into India outnumbered the Muslims moving into Pakistan. At the same time that Bengal in general, and metropolitan Calcutta in particular, was faced with the problem of absorbing three million new citizens, Calcutta's economy was severely damaged by the removal of its eastern hinterland. East Bengal became East Pakistan. Thus the city was confronted with the problem of somehow absobing an enormous number of refugees at the same time that its economic capacity to provide employment was severely curtailed. The refugees themselves represented a very mixed group ranging from intellectuals and professionals to large landowners to landless laborers. They did not come to Calcutta in the voluntary sense of the rural migrant seeking urban employment but in the involuntary sense of people fleeing their homeland. Some of them moved easily into the Calcutta society; others have not been integrated into society to this day. The refugees of course were not the only migrants to Calcutta. They represented an additional burden to the normal flow. In 1961, for the City of Calcutta itself, 53 percent of the population were born outside Calcutta and 42 percent were born outside West Bengal. These are the normal pressures one might expect. The refugees were an added burden.

Partition dealt a serious blow to Calcutta's economy. East Bengal supplied 90 percent of the raw jute which fueled Calcutta's largest industry; and East Bengal provided rice and other foodstuffs to West Bengal, which traditionally has a food deficit. East Bengal's 42 million people provided a huge market for Calcutta's manufactures, particularly textiles, steel, and engineering goods. Ironically, the most recent document of the Calcutta Metropolitan Planning Organization (CMPO), "A Memorandum on a Perspective Plan for Calcutta Metropolitan

District and West Bengal 1971-1989," argues that the only way in which Calcutta's stagnant industrial base can be resuscitated is through the medium of increasing the strength of Calcutta's rural hinterland . . . a belated recognition of the importance of the rural hinterland to the viability of the economy of the metropolis. As this is being written, East Bengal has just become the independent nation of Bangladesh and the complementarity that existed prior to Partition may once again come into being and help to recharge Calcutta's economy. The old colonial relationship, however, between Calcutta and its hinterland cannot (nor should not) be re-established. A more balanced relationship will have to be developed.

Partition dealt another kind of blow to Calcutta's economy. The rail system of Eastern India including East Bengal obviously was focused on Calcutta. And transport between East and West Bengal was also heavily dependent on river transport. Partition cut these direct lines of communication and heavily increased transport costs for Calcutta's imports and exports.

Bengal represented the focal point of British exploitation of India. British industrial investment was heaviest in Calcutta. Prior to Independence the dominant industries of engineering and jute were largely British-owned and managed. Indian investment and management began earlier in Bombay and proceeded apace after Independence. Ranajit Roy quotes Nehru as having said "Bombay became the center and headquarters of Indian-owned industry, commerce, banking, insurance, etc. The Parsis, Gujarathis, and the Marwaris were the leaders in these industries." Continuing the reference Roy quotes Nehru as saying that Calcutta "had been and continues to be the chief center of British capital and industry."[3]

The British attitude toward Calcutta was anomalous. In 1910 they moved the capital to New Delhi. When the Reserve Bank of India was established in 1928, the head office was in Bombay. Yet industrial investment continued most heavily in Calcutta. Following independence, the Government of India established most of its financial headquarters in Bombay, the most important being the Reserve Bank of India, the State Bank of India, and the Life Insurance Corporation of India. Calcutta's economy depended heavily on India's most important but rapidly deteriorating port and on the declining jute industry. In 1951, the 278,000 workers in jute represented 43 percent of registered factory employment in West Bengal. At Independence there was a heavily obsolescent component in the Calcutta economy. A further aspect of the Calcutta situation is the degree of its primacy in its region. In 1971, Calcutta had 8.3 million people. The next largest city in West Bengal was Durgapur with 207,000, and in the four states of Eastern India the next largest was the Patna urban area with just under 500,000. In Maharashtra on the other hand, although still heavily dominated by Bombay, Nagpur had 866,000 and Poona 853,000. Calcutta's hinterland is the least urbanized of all of the major regions of India and its agriculture is the poorest and least modernized. Thus Calcutta represents the most obvious target for rural/urban migration, although it must be pointed out

Metropolitan Problems and Prospects

that Calcutta's growth in the last decade has slowed down the growth of smaller cities has increased. But the absolute numbers are obviously still heavily weighted toward Calcutta. Worse, not only does the poverty of Calcutta's hinterland induce migration, but the hinterland itself represents a weak market for the products of Calcutta.

The final aspect of Calcutta that must be understood in context is the political situation in West Bengal. It is just as difficult to deal with this intricate topic in a synoptic sketch as with the preceding summary observations. Yet, it would be inexcusable to omit some reference to Calcutta's and West Bengal's politics. Historically, three themes have recurringly exhibitied themselves in the politics of Bengal: Bengal nationalism; radicalism; violence. Although the Congress party dominated Bengal until 1967, its domination did not go unchallenged, particularly by the parties of the left. And in some ways, it was a different Congress than elsewhere in India. For example, Bengal's hero is Subhas Chandra Bose, who left the Congress in 1939 and whose route to Independence was to have led through armed resistance to British power. With the departure of Bose from the Congress, Bengal's importance in the party went into eclipse. During the two decades of Congress rule from Independence to 1967, the only significant contribution made by the Center to West Bengal was the Rs.700 million investment in the new steel city of Durgapur, 150 miles northwest of Calcutta.

Within the state of West Bengal itself, Calcutta was no better appreciated by the state government. Congress strength lay in the countryside and there was little apparent willingness in the Congress high command to raise resources to cope with the deteriorating situation in the metropolis... with one exception. That exception was the establishment by the dominating Chief Minister, Dr. B. C. Roy, of the Calcutta Metropolitan Planning Organization (CMPO) in 1961.

In the Calcutta Corporation itself, the three million person central city, petty politics on the one hand and grand national and international resolutions on the other hand, excluded serious concerted political commitment to the state and fortunes of the city.

In 1967, Congress lost control of the state government and of the Calcutta Corporation. The United Front government that was formed lasted only 11 months. President's Rule was imposed at the time of its dissolution. In 1969, a new election was held and the leftists once again captured power. But again a coalition had to be formed to produce a government. This government lasted only nine months and failed when the Chief Minister resigned saying "his Government could not give to the people the minimum security of a civilized society." The law and order situation in general and the labor/management situation in particular had reached new lows. Once again President's Rule was imposed in March of 1970. At this point, for the first time since Independence, and including periods of President's Rule, the central government responded to the heavily deteriorated Calcutta situation.

A development program of Rs.1,500 million for a four-year period was adopted. A new tax to provide partial support for it was imposed and an extremely powerful Metropolitan Development Authority was established. Under the driving leadership of the Principal Advisor to the Governor, Mr. B. B. Ghosh, and an exceptional Secretary, Mr. K. C. Sivaramakrishnan, an extensive and impressive beginning on Calcutta's development was initiated.

In March of 1971, Bengal went to the polls again, this time in a national election. Despite the overwhelming victory gained nationally by the Congress-R led by Mrs. Gandhi, the largest number of seats in the West Bengal Assembly was won by the Communist Party of India (which was Marxist and at that time the larger and further left of the two major Communist parties). But the number was insufficient to provide the basis for a government as the other Communist Party of India (CPI) refused to join them. Once again a coalition government was established, this time dominated by the Congress-R with the support of the CPI. But this coalition could not function either and fell in July, 1971. President's Rule was imposed once more.

The importance of the political context does not lie in the series of failures of representative government to function in West Bengal. Indeed the effective performance of representative government in India as a whole is almost unique in the developing world. The importance in the Bengal situation lies in the increasing tempo of the politics of violence. Bureaucratic energies have been diverted to the problems of law and order, not development. And in an already serious economic situation the politics of violence have drawn down the functioning of the West Bengal economy to a dangerously low level.

As this article is being written, the Congress party has achieved an astonishing recovery in West Bengal, capturing 216 seats in the 280-seat State Assembly in the recent March elections. Hopes for a stable government and for a resurgence of the West Bengal economy are running high. But that is of the future and this article deals with the recent past and the context of the planning and development effort for Calcutta as sketched above.

THE MAJOR CHARACTERISTICS OF THE EFFORT

Given this context then for Calcutta's planning and development, what have been the primary characteristics of the effort? And to what degree are some of the lessons learned transferrable to other urban situations in the developing world?

The major characteristics of the planning effort are:

(1) It has been a very large effort in terms of budget and manpower;
(2) From the outset the effort was conceived within the larger regional context of Eastern India which Calcutta dominates;
(3) The planning effort was conceived in remarkably broad and inclusive terms;
(4) The principal product, the Basic Development Plan published in

December 1966, was considered to be a policy-oriented, dynamic, options-open plan, as distinct from conventional metropolitan or urban master plans;

(5) The plan and succeeding work have set standards and devised programs that are consistent with the resources of the metropolitan district and of the nation;

(6) The plan recognizes those areas of intervention that may move the area toward its chosen goals and explicitly rejects intervention in areas that may inhibit economic growth;

(7) The plan concludes with an immediate action Development Program designed to make the city livable ... "not the city beautiful but the city livable."

Size and Continuity of Effort

At its peak the CMPO had 600 employees, of whom about 100 were gazetted officers, either professional or administrative officers of the West Bengal Government. Its annual budget is Rs.3,500,000. Over the ten years of the Ford Foundation's involvement the Foundation has spent about $5 million. Obviously large staff size and significant budget amount are no guarantees of effective planning. But it is important to recognize that effective planning for cities of Calcutta's size and complexity requires large inputs of money and manpower sustained over a considerable period of time. Most of this manpower, and in some cases all of it, can be national. In the Calcutta case the international input was, by any standards, very large, probably uniquely so. At its peak the Ford Foundation had some 25 foreign experts working with the CMPO. This scale will probably never be repeated elsewhere. Nor is it the intent here to argue that it should. The intent here is to argue that very large amounts of professional manpower are required. (And in the Calcutta case, even with the heavy foreign involvement, the involvement of national professionals was, by any measure, much much greater.)

The above may appear to be a truism. So be it. The fact remains that most governments have not recognized the enormous complexity of their urban problems ... and the scale and breadth of effort required to cope with them. Where foreign assistance has been available the agents of assistance have not recognized the period and degree of tenacity that is required if the problems are to be understood and effectively grappled with.

As noted earlier, the Calcutta Metropolitan Development Authority (CMDA) was established as a separate coordinating and executing agency in 1970. It currently has 800 employees—of whom 400 are technical and professional personnel—and it is still seeking professional employees in certain critical areas.

Although the Basic Development Plan was completed five years ago, and the development effort itself begun in 1970 has reached the level of Rs.450 million a year, the prospects are for greater demands for professional manpower in both the planning and development fields. The CMPO staff has declined in size from its peak so that today there are some sixty-odd gazetted officers in an organization of about 500. This attrition took place in a period of non-activity. Today demands for systems plans and project designs are heavy on the CMPO. And the CMPO is engaged upon a new and extensive state economic planning effort. These demands are bound to increase its personnel.

An intriguing question has arisen in the argument for merger of the two organizations. Although this question is yet to be resolved, the probable outcome is that project designs and programming will increasingly fall within the purview of the CMDA, whereas systems planning, long-range planning, and planning for the state as a whole will remain with the CMPO. In any case it is fairly certain that there will continue to be two separate organizations. It is tempting to spin out the arguments as a case in the evolution of planning and development machinery in one of the major cities of the developing world but that is best left as the subject of a further paper.

The Regional Character of the Effort

Most urban plans devote space to consideration of the city's hinterland. This is obviously necessary as a basis for any kind of demographic and economic projection. But few plans come to grips with the problems of the region and make estimates about the development of the region with clear and explicit policy recommendations. Let me give an example.

The population of the metropolitan district in 1961 was 6.7 million. The 1986 population was projected to be between 12 and 13 million "if there is no change in Calcutta's position relative to the other existing urban centers in the region." This is a conservative position ... and many critics have argued that it is much too conservative a position. Yet the projection estimated a 1971 population of 8.7 million as against a 1971 census count of 8.3 million. It is much easier of course to project the population of the Eastern India region which is a reasonably self-contained demographic unit than to project the population of a metropolitan district. The region contained 111 million people in 1961 and is expected to contain 191 million by 1986, a staggering increment of 80 million people. The eastern region is the least urbanized of the major regions of India with, in 1961, 14.4 million people living in urban areas, or 13.1 percent of the total population. A critical question was (and is) what the rate of urbanization will be over this 25-year period. Four sets of assumptions were made in which the urban population would increase to a figure between 22.2 million and 39.6 million by 1986. For working purposes the two intermediate projections were taken in which the urban population would range from 25 million to 35 million by 1986. If one took the higher figure this would give an increase of 20 million in the urban population of Eastern India over this period. This would require urban areas in the region other than Calcutta to absorb 14 million people in this quarter century. For working purposes a somewhat lower figure of 30 million urbanites was used. Even this figure would require urban areas other than Calcutta to absorb 10 million people.

Planning for Calcutta did not stop with making these estimates of the future. It went on to attempt to assure them as a complement to the development of the metropolitan district. Thus plans were prepared for the Asansol/Durgapur urban region in the coal and iron-ore heart of West Bengal, for Siliguri, a major railhead and transfer point in North Bengal, and for Haldia, a new port city being built 60 miles downstream from Calcutta. These plans were prepared by planning agencies established by the Government of West Bengal administratively under the Commissioner of Town and Country Planning and the Director of CMPO in his capacity as Deputy Secretary for Town and Country Planning. They were provided additional technical support both by the CMPO and by the Ford Foundation Advisory Planning Group.

Although planning with clear relationship to the CMPO and its plans for the metropolitan district could only be carried out within the limits of the Government of West Bengal, planning efforts were also undertaken in the adjoining states of Assam, Bihar, and Orissa in order to help these states devise policies of urbanization that would be consistent with the general aims and plans for the Calcutta metropolitan region.

The Breadth of the Effort

The planning effort was conceived and largely carried through in remarkably broad and inclusive terms. Its major components were:

(1) Systems plans projected to the year 2001 for water, sanitation, and drainage;

(2) A system plan for transportation divided into a ten-year plan and a further plan to 1986;

(3) A plan for the improvement of 3,000 bustees;

(4) The outlines of a plan for economic development;

(5) A plan for governmental reorganization in the metropolitan district;

(6) Targets for housing, education, and health;

(7) An Immediate Action Program to constitute the Fourth Plan investment for the metropolitan district;

(8) A generalized schema for the future form of the metropolitan district and a generalized land use plan.

By any standards this is a very broad and inclusive list. This is not to say that the work across these fields was all of similar quality. But it is to emphasize that it is across this array that work is necessary if the problems of a huge metropolis in a developing economy are to be effectively tackled. It is also to say that problems range from the most elementary (e.g., sanitation) to the most sophisticated (e.g., economic development). Finally, it is to say that with a couple of exceptions, this array sets points of beginning and a framework of logic from which and within which sustained successive efforts are necessary.

It would be absurd to suggest that all of the effort across this spectrum of activities have been successful. Obviously the manner in which the components identified above have been described suggests that production has been uneven. There have been three areas in which work has been less than successful so far: economic development planning; planning for education and health; housing. Work is now underway in all three of these areas.

Let me dilate a bit and make some critical observations on these topics. The Basic Development Plan set forth employment targets by industry-type based largely on the projections of industrial activity, using as a base the trend in the years since Independence up to 1965. It was clearly the intent of the CMPO to expand this effort into a separate economic development plan. A tremendous amount of work has been done in the field of economic analysis, much of it of a very high order of craftsmanship. The Industrial Planning Team of the CMPO has undertaken studies of both the jute industry and the engineering industry, the major employers in manufacturing in the metropolis, and have made recommendations for the enhancement of these industries. But no coherent overall economic development plan has emerged.

There are a number of reasons for this. Let me cite two. First, the economic recession that struck India in 1967 hit Calcutta hardest. And although the rest of India began to recover in 1969, the recovery never gained momentum in West Bengal. The second half of the decade 1965-1970 has seen a decline in real incomes and an absolute decline in employment. Table 1 summarizes the employment picture.

This situation has meant a recasting of points of view and ideas for Calcutta's economic expansion. The crisis has been such that emphasis has been on short-range planning. In 1970 however, a new view toward the composition of long-range economic planning emerged. Before discussing this it will be useful to make a second point in regard to the ineffectiveness of the economic development planning.

The second point is that economic development for the metropolitan district

Table 1. Registered Factory Employment in Different Industry Groups, West Bengal, 1951/1970 (Hundreds of Thousands)

Industry Group	1951	1961	1965	1969	1970
Engineering	1.58	2.50	3.24	2.95	2.94
Jute	2.78	2.02	2.59	2.04	2.25
Others	2.16	2.66	2.97	2.92	2.90
Total	6.52	7.18	8.80	7.91	8.09

Source: A. N. Bose, *A Note on the Economic Development Programme for the Calcutta Metropolitan District* (draft), March 1972.

is probably impossible outside the framework of an economic development plan for the State of West Bengal as a whole and desirably for Eastern India. It was on this point that economic development planning re-emerged. In August of 1971 CMPO published "A Memorandum on a Perspective Plan for Calcutta Metropolitan District and West Bengal, 1971-1989." This memorandum is the bais for a new planning effort which in effect involves the preparation of an Economic Development Plan for the State of West Bengal. The main thrust of the current argument is that the economic base of the metropolitan district can only be resuscitated through a significant increase in the productivity of the state's agricultural sector. And that such an increase in the agricultural sector will not only generate increased incomes and demands for Calcutta products but will also generate increased employment in the agricultural sector, thus taking some of the pressures off urban areas already overburdened with unemployed manpower. Work on the Economic Development Plan outlined in the Memorandum is underway.

Probably the weakest part of the planning effort between 1961 and the publication of the Basic Development Plan in 1966 were the efforts to deal with deficiencies in the fields of education (primary and secondary) and health. In regard to the former, current deficiencies were noted and quantitative targets were set. But no spatial plans were prepared, no building programs were devised, and no consideration whatever was given to the form and content of primary education and its relevance to the situation in Calcutta and the needs of the future. In terms of the latter, only hospital bed targets were quantified. The need for neighborhood clinics and health centers was noted. But no attempt was made to conceive a total program of integrated health services, let alone to devise a plan and program for their establishment and operation in the metropolitan district.

It should be noted that there is one extenuating circumstance for this significant lapse. In an internal Foundation document I have written "the planning of social services requires a much higher degree of involvement in the planning process by the (operating) departments than does the policy and system planning of physical facilities. And during these years the CMPO was, in the eyes of many operating departments an upstart. Cooperation was not easy to come by." But extenuating circumstances do not change the fact that little or no planning was done. The CMPO was keenly aware of this gap but with no resources in sight during the period 1967-1970; there was little motivation to enter into the kind of aggressive interdepartmental negotiations and planning necessary to produce useful plans and programs.

In 1970, the situation underwent radical and dramatic change. The Development Program of Rs.1,500 million for the metropolitan district included approximately Rs.50 million for the building of primary schools. Depending upon the design and the cost of land, this would be enough money to build 600 to 700 new schools. Although building designs have been prepared, no systems plan exists. There is now a feverish hunt for sites.

Two efforts are now underway to remedy this serious deficiency in planning and programing. The first of these steps is the establishment by the CMDA of an Interdepartmental Programing Committee. Obviously the CMPO Is represented on this committee. It will grapple with short-range decisions in terms of sites and in terms of providing money to existing schools for modernization and expansion. Particular emphasis will be laid on the needs of low income families. The importance of this committee can be inferred from its membership; the Chairman is the state's Development Commissioner and an ex-officio member of the Development Authority.

The second is the belated beginning on a long-range spatial plan for education facilities for the metropolitan district.

The situation in the field of health is somewhat better . . . but by no means satisfactory. The Development Program provides Rs.95 million for investment in health facilities. The Health Department has plans for hospital expansions which will use some Rs.75 million of the Rs.95 million. But the requirements for the improvement of health services in the metropolis go well beyond the simple provision of additional hospital beds. It can be argued that the primary problem is the delivery of health services to relatively small communities throughout the entire metropolitan district, with emphasis on the low income communities, and that in such an array of facilities and services, the provision of additional hospital beds would not have high priority.

A cell has been set up by the CMDA to devise short-range immediate programs. These programs will emphasize delivery of services to local areas through the establishment of both mobile and static dispensaries, the establishment of polyclinics, and, on a sector basis, the relationship of these field stations to major hospitals. The theoretical program exists and work is underway on making the first operational decisions. Because the primary investment in these localized facilities will be in manpower rather than in facilities, the CMDA is prepared through the Fourth Plan period to meet the recurring expenses of these activities. This is an important departure from CMDA's accepted role of providing money only for capital investment. It has important implications in the field of improving the delivery of social services in a metropolis. Certainly it can provide immediate support for an expansion of an array of activities. But the CMDA cannot be expected to carry such recurring expenses indefinitely. Parenthetically it should be noted that a significant power deriving from the CMDA's autonomous status is that it can make expenditures without reference to the Finance Departemtn for approval. In the labyrinthine bureaucracy of the government this power is very real indeed in moving projects rapidly. But it is a power that is tempting to use whenever procedures appear to block or retard the expenditure of money for an activity deemed important in the development process. And the use of this money to meet recurring expenses in health may well generate demands from other departments for this kind of finance.

Meanwhile the CMPO in conjunction with the Health Department is undertaking the preparation of a long-range plan for health facilities and health services for the metropolitan district. This plan and program will include, besides curative medicine, preventive medicine, nutrition, maternal and child health care, family planning, and health education as an integrated package.

The question of the delivery of social services has important implications for strategy in the development process for cities of the developing world. To quote again from an internal Foundation document, "in a resource-poor situation ... the capital required for investment in facilities to meet even modest standards must be spread over a long period before anything representing complete coverage can be achieved. Significant investment in services as substitutes for facilities is the only alternative."

The third area that has been less than successful is housing. On the face of it this will appear to be inexcusable. Yet the fact is that this has proved to be a most intractable problem for almost all of the large urban areas of the world. In Asia there have been spectacular successes in Hong Kong and Singapore but even in those cities there are cogent critics of the programs. And the relevance of Hong Kong and Singapore to the Calcutta situation is remote at best.

As one would expect, housing has been a preoccupation of the CMPO since its inception. In the "Bibliography of Papers and Reports produced by CMPO 1962-1969" there are 64 entries in the section on Housing and Slum Clearance (see appendix to this chapter). Yet, with the exception of a long and effective section on the proposed Slum Improvement Plan, the Basic Development Plan includes only descriptions of the housing situation, estimates of deficiency, numerical targets, and a very brief and general policy statement. In the field of housing the foreign consultants attached to the CMPO have been particularly active. Of the 61 papers published, 24 were authored by foreigners. Nor did work on housing analysis, planning, and programing stop with the publication of the Basic Plan. Numerous papers have been prepared since. In March of 1971 a major program was prepared by Foundation consultants to the CMPO, utilizing and integrating data and ideas that were largely generated over the years in the CMPO. CMPO is revising that document. Meanwhile CMDA has made a programed building start.

The one successful area of planning, programing, and now work on the ground, in this field has been the Bustee Improvement Program. This type of program is now familiar throughout the developing world. It was not so when it was first published by the CMPO in October of 1965. The argument is now a familiar one.

A bustee is the hut slum of Calcutta, in some ways similar to the favela of Rio de Janeiro. For the most part they are not recent squatter colonies but settlements of long standing ... indeed the word "bustee" means settlement. In the metropolitan district at least two million people live in such settlements. They vary in size from a few thousand people to as many as 50,000 people in the area's largest bustee. It was determined by the CMPO in 1964 that any program of clearance and reconstruction that would improve the lot of a significant proportion of the bustee dwellers was beyond the financial capacity of the government to undertake. Therefore it was decided that the program should be one of environmental improvement: introducing water lines and water taps, sanitary latrines and sewers, paving of lanes, street lighting, improvement of small open space, and eventually inserting facilities such as schools and health centers. The standards selected were low, in keeping with the objective of a program that would have saturation coverage within estimated resource capacity. For example, 33 persons per water tap; 25 persons per sanitary latrine.

It was not an easy program to sell. To most bureaucrats and politicians it meant admitting that India could not rehouse these people, and it implied that the bustee would become a permanent fixture on the Calcutta landscape. By 1970 however, enough viewpoints had been changed so that the Development Program included Rs.100 million for slum improvement. The target set was the improvement of 3,000 bustees, housing some one and one-half million people over a two-year period ... a program staggering in scope. At this writing some Rs.42.5 million have been spent and improvements are underway in bustees affecting a population of 800,000.

In 1969, a modification to the program was introduced entitled "Slum Modernization." On an average, about 20 percent of the land in a bustee is open space. The idea is that very low-cost housing would be built on such space. Inhabitants of huts on land with market potential such as a major street frontage would be moved to the new housing, thus freeing the more valuable land for an economically higher use. Thus gradual improvement could take place in selected areas without any expenditure for land acquisition, and even some return to be plowed back. Pilot projects will shortly be underway. But on the broader housing front little progress has been made. The Basic Development Plan stated a recommended housing policy which had three components: preservation of the existing housing stock; elimination of barriers to efficient market functioning including "the evolution of a larger, more stable and effectively liberalized system of housing finance"; and direct public investment in shelter. But the last point would be limited in view of the fact that "housing's capital-output ratio is extremely high; each rupee invested adds a neglibile amount to the growth of the economy directly while it takes some away from other forms of investment which do add directly to economic development and rising incomes."[4] The plan quantified need at 65,000 new units per year over a 20-year period. With a policy limitation on the amount of direct public investment, a completely inadequate housing finance system for private housing, an income distribution that showed that (in 1966 prices) nearly half the population could afford no more than Rs.30 in monthly rent and 85 percent no more than Rs.78, it is clear that there is a dilemma between need and policy. The Basic Development Plan stated but did not resolve this dilemma.

The CMPO continued to hammer at the problem and produced an "Interim Report: Housing, Calcutta Metropolitan District" in 1967. This document set forth 14 points reiterating earlier positions such as emphasis on preserving existing stock, making environmental improvements, primarily in the bustees, and pressing hard the reduction of space standards, urging the use of new designs and undertaking a "massive 'new urban settlements program.'" The CMPO's major efforts on housing during the period between the publication of that document and 1970 were in the field of design, seeking to produce livable but minimum cost designs. Several were designed, built, and tested. But with no resources for major housing construction during this period, and little money available in the private market, these efforts remained simply experiments.

But the question of a broad and inclusive program continued to nag. In early 1971, a program was designed for consideration by CMPO and CMDA by two Ford Foundation consultants. This document, completed in March of 1971, synthesized most of the work that had been done and produced a proposed construction program for the Fourth Plan period. It laid a major stress on using government money to write down interest rates and to write down the cost of land so that hire-purchase housing could be made available to a large section of the market. It included within a comprehensive program the use of the government's Industrial Workers' Scheme and Slum Clearance Scheme, the Bustee Improvement Program, the Slum Modernization Program, land development schemes and open plot housing, an infill program of public housing, and an estimate of non-publicly assisted housing that might be expected in the decade of the seventies. The CMPO is now engaged in preparing a housing program using the above document as a point of departure but modifying the relative importance of the various components, the chief effort being to get as much housing for the very low income groups as possible. The CMDA is going ahead with a first construction program. In this most intractable of the metropolitan district's problems there now appears to be light on the horizon.

In this section I have chosen to use the greater part of the space to discuss the less successful aspects of the planning effort. This may give the misleading impression that I am judging the effort negatively. Nothing could be farther from the truth. I have chosen this mode because I think more can be learned from such a discussion than from simply repeating the successful efforts. But the successful efforts should be noted. The two systems plans, one for water, sanitation, and drainage, and the other for transportation, are well along in the current Development Program. The only deficiency in these two fields is that the pace of development is now beginning to outstrip the availability of project designs for execution.

Two observations on transportation are relevant. The first is that transportation is the most obvious and the most influential of the several technologies that serve and change the city. It is in this field that the combination of the primitive and the sophisticated, and the conflicts between them, are most apparent. It has been said of Calcutta that of all the forms of transportation ever devised by man, only one is now missing from the streets ... the palanquin ... and sometimes even that can be seen in wedding processions. The weakness of the otherwise excellent transportation paln is that it concentrates its efforts at the more sophisticated end of the scale: motorways and rapid transit.

Despite much discussion, no sensitive efforts have yet been made to deal with slow-moving vehicles, including the man-drawn, which not only represent an important component of the intricate transport system but which are important to the functioning of the Calcutta economy. With most employment figures stated in terms of "registered factories" it is frequently forgotten that 350,000 people are employed in industries employing less than ten persons. The handcart is the mode of transport for the goods of this important segment of the local economy.

The second point relates to the proposed rapid transit system. It is frequently pointed out by foreign observers that an economy in which 46 percent of the households have incomes less than Rs.200 a month and 73 percent have incomes of less than Rs.400 a month, a modern rapid transit system is simply beyond the capability of the society to support. If the city were entirely a handicraft city in which people were clustered in residences about small shops using primitive handicraft methods, that might be a valid argument, but to repeat what has been said many times, the city is also a contemporary industrial and commercial city composed of large firms using sophisticated techniques and technologies, its workers dispersed throughout the fabric of the metropolitan district and even beyond. If that economy is going to function effectively, it is important to the city, to the state, and to the nation that intra-metropolitan transport be radically improved. Further it should be recognized that the amount of space devoted to streets in Calcutta is only 6 percent, as compared to the Western norm of 25 percent and Bombay's 16 percent. If additional capacity is to be added to the transport system then it has to be overhead or underground. It is probable that the rapid transit system will have to be heavily subsidized. And one can argue that because of the importance of the local economy to the national economy that subsidy should be national.

Little need be said about the effectiveness of the plans for water, sanitation, and drainage. These were prepared by a special division of the CMPO with the assistance of two consulting firms provided by the World Health Organization. They were large in scope and provided not only for the major system designs but for a series of project designs. Because project designs were carried through in greatest number in these fields the current Development Program is spending more for water, sanitation, and drainage than for any other category. Perhaps this is just as well. For the low state of the health of the citizens of the metropolitan district cannot be significantly improved without an adequate supply of potable water and a system of disposal for storm water and for human and animal waste.

Two of the more striking features reflecting the breadth and inclusiveness of the planning effort are the recommendations for governmental reorganization, and analysis and recommendations in regard to fiscal resources. The CMPO has recommended the establishment of a Metropolitan Water and Sanitation Authority; a Metropolitan Traffic and Transportation Authority; the Hooghly River Bridge Commissioners; a Metropolitan Parks and Recreation Authority;

three geographically defined Development Authorities; consideration of a Metropolitan Commission on Education; and a statutory State Housing Body. Of these recommendations the Water and Sanitation Authority and the Hooghly River Bridge Commissioners are now in existence. One overall development authority, the very powerful CMDA, is functioning. The legislation has been drawn for a Metropolitan Traffic and Transportation Authority and the Rapid Transit Study Team of the National Railways has recommended it. The Secretary of the Education Department has recommended the establishment of a Metropolitan Education Authority. And the current session of the State Assembly will probably establish a State Housing Board. In the field of recommendations for governmental reorganization this is a remarkable record.

There remains the problem of the low estate of local government. Tens of millions of rupees are being spent by the CMDA to reconstruct old facilities and to build new facilities throughout the metropolitan district. Yet the only agencies responsible for ownership and management, and henceforth sustaining the value of the effort, are local governments with a very low record of performance. Restructure and reform of the system of local government is of the highest priority.

THE POLICY ORIENTATION OF THE BASIC DEVELOPMENT PLAN

Early in the planning effort, the Foundation's advisory team and the CMPO staff rejected the convention of the more or less rigid physical master plan being prepared for cities in the developing world by expatriate teams. The objective chosen was to enter upon a course of selective planning, of planning that would be dynamic and responsive, of planning that would set certain forms and norms but would leave certain major development options open. This is a tall order, more easily verbalized than accomplished.

In an internal paper of the consultancy written in 1962, it was stated that "to see these things (problems) may be to understand some of the key considerations concerning Calcutta's development problems, and of a development plan for dealing with them. For example, from a methodological point of view it becomes clear that the focus of the development plan must be *problems* . . . it makes a great difference whether problems, or goals, or standards and other regulating concepts are used . . . the planning process becomes essentially a problem-solving approach to redevelopment and development.[5]

And again in another paper, "since developmental planning implies a dynamic directed change in the economy and physical environment in which people move, the task of the social analyst is to indicate the change in population and their changing needs and the adjustments in the social pattern that may be anticipated as a result of choice of one alternative planning decision over another."[6]

In 1969, Colin Rosser, an early member of the team, wrote "What Calcutta clearly needed it seemed to us, was not a negative, restricted, regulative land use plan with the heavy commitment of scarce administrative resources that such a system of control requires, but rather a positive *development plan* in the full sense with the emphasis on a development action directed at priorities of social and economic change, of selected capital investment in the physical infrastructure, of administrative and fiscal reorganization, and of the systematic generation and mobilization of resources (fiscal, administrative, technical capacity, and the largely unutilized efforts and commitment of the population at large)."[7]

In January of 1967, a group of distinguished planners from abroad were invited to evaluate the recently completed Basic Development Plan. Following that evaluation William Wheaton wrote, "the CMPO Plan for Metropolitan Calcutta has pioneered in a new definition of a metropolitan plan. This is a significant professional advance in planning, as well as a significant attempt to grapple with the most desperate metropolitan situation in the world today. Only in England with the Southeast England Plan and with the plan for Greater Paris, do we find the concept of a land use plan, a rather primitive notion, abandoned in favor of a development policies plan such as that devised in Calcutta."[8]

This was high praise and well deserved, but in a sense of policies plan is only a beginning. It establishes a verbalized and generally quantified framework, sets relative priorities and targets, and sets design specifications. But sewers have to be laid, roads built, schools established, houses constructed. The plans for these constructions are presumably more sensitive to need when cast in terms of well-thought-through policies. And systems plans may be devised in such a way that they reflect not only the policies, but are responsive to changes in an evolving metropolitan situation. But systems plans and project designs there must be. A policies plan is not a substitute for systems plans; it is a precursor.

Unfortunately, with the exception of the systems plan for water, sanitation, and drainage, and for transport, further systems plans between 1967 and 1970 were not prepared. There are several reasons for this. Of them the two most cogent are, first, that the CMPO and Foundation leadership was heavily preoccupied with trying to move the then Rs.1,000 million Development Program through the Center, and second, that with no resources in sight, there was little motivation for the professional staff of the CMPO to get on with the planning and design job. The Development Program is suffering from that lapse now. There is a heavy bias in current public investment toward the fields of water, sanitation, and transport as against housing, education, and health simply because project designs are available for the former group and not for the latter.

Most of the policies of the Basic Development Plan have stood up well over time. The objectives for example, are even more relevant to the 1972 situation than to the 1966 situation. It may be useful to quote them:

(1) To promote a more dynamic growth of the metropolitan economy with increased production and income, with sufficient employment opportunities, and with close integration with the economic development of the region for which Calcutta provides vital economic functions.

(2) To develop an urban environment which is socially satisfactory and capable of sustaining with appropriate facilities and services a population of about 12.3 million in the CMD by 1986.

(3) To create the machinery for sustained development planning and for effective plan implementation within a coherent growth framework for the CMD and the State.

(4) To strengthen local self-government and citizen participation in the development of the metropolitan district through a more effective mobilization of local fiscal resources, civic leadership and voluntary citizen effort.[9]

The assumptions underlying the plan however, have not stood up. Population growth has been slower than projected. This would be a blessing if it were not for the probable reason ... the decline in the metropolitan economy. Assumptions regarding future employment have been far off the mark. Both employment and real income have declined absolutely.

The basic policies and targets set have stood up reasonably well. There is an inconsistency between the geography of the project composition of the current Development Program and the metropolitan form objectives of the Basic Development Plan. The former concentrates heavily in investments for the metropolitan center with its enormous backlog of deficiencies, whereas the latter recommended the development of a major new growth center to the north. Given the dismaying level of deterioration of public services in the heavily populated area this distribution of effort is probably inescapable. But if the bipolar notion of the metropolitan district's geography is to be advanced, then significant expenditures have to be made in other areas during the Fifth Plan period beginning in 1974. Whether or not the form objectives of the plan will be pursued is therefore still an open question.

In the current resurgence of planning effort, motivated largely by the establishment of the CMDA, but also by changes in the political situation, four threads are evident ... all of them consistent with the argument of the Basic Development Plan but modified to be responsive to a changed situation and to new ideas derived from a deeper understanding of the problems of the metropolis. The first of these threads is the new effort in economic development planning. It has become apparent that this planning must be done on a statewide basis and that attempts to deal with a resuscitation of Calcutta's economy on a purely metropolitan basis is myopic. The new planning effort is based heavily on the need for modernization of agriculture and the demands that that will place upon the metropolitan economy.

The second thread is a major thrust in the programing and delivery of social services, primarily education and health. Planning for health will not be restricted to programs for bringing hospital beds up to an acceptable standard but will include the planning of an integrated set of health services to be delivered to the local communities of the metropolitan district. And planning for education will not be limited to the identification of school sites and the provision of standard building designs but will include experiments in a variety of ways to improve current education and to expand the provision of education with emphasis on the primary grades but including secondary and adult education.

The third thread is the devising of project plans. A major new entrant on the scene is a proposed Fifth Plan Urban Renewal Program amounting to some Rs.1,250 million. This will be the first major attempt to go beyond planning for survival to planning for rejuvenation.

The fourth thread is the initiation of work on a structure plan for the metropolitan district. The general argument of the Basic Development Plan will be subjected to review and a selective plan will be devised to provide the frame for new investment in the Fifth and Sixth Plan periods.

These new efforts will require considerable new professional manpower. The Foundation will continue to assist but the Foundation's role will be quite different than in the earlier period. There will never again be a heavy input of expatriate experts. Foundation assistance will be largely in the area of training and applied research and that largely through the use of Indian institutions. Furthermore, the Foundation will be more selective in its areas of emphasis; in the current grant those areas are employment and economic development, health, and education, although continued assistance will be given in the field of urban and regional planning.

On Planning Standards and Costs

Cities are expensive. A well-equipped and well-administered city is more expensive in both worlds than most national governments realize, but relatively much more expensive to the economies of the developing world. Costs obviously vary by item. The cost of a sewer line per mile in Calcutta is about one-half the cost of a similar facility in the United States. A bridge costs about the same in both places. The proposed rapid transit line will cost the same per mile as the recently completed Bay Area Rapid Transit System in San Francisco. Simple structures cost much less in Calcutta: minimal housing can be built for as little as Rs.15 a square foot, about two dollars. This subject has not been researched as thoroughly and systematically as one would like. But it is clear from the work that has been done that even for facilities that cost less in the developing world, the relative cost to the society in terms of its income, say on a per capita basis, is many times higher than the cost in the developed world.

Initial planning efforts with assistance from developed countries did not adequately recognize this fact. It became evident first in the field of housing. It is rapidly coming to the fore as one of the important aspects of planning for urbanization in the developing world.

There are several ways in which costs can be marginally reduced. It is doubtful if any significant cost reductions can be made either across the board or by major category. But the combination of several approaches may produce some effective cost reduction. Among these are:

(1) The reduction of standards from Western norms, or the setting of standards consistent with the economy resources;

(2) Intensive and multiple uses of existing and new facilities;

(3) The conservation of existing investments;

(4) The substitution of intensive manned services for capital facilities;

(5) Research into the technology of cities aimed at cost reductions.

Let me remark on each of these points.

The minimum standard set by the Government of India for public or publicly assisted housing was, until very recently, 250 square feet per dwelling unit or 50 square feet per person. This may seem in itself a low standard established in recognition of India's limited resources for housing. But Hong Kong in its first resettlement housing provided less than 100 square feet per household. And some of the current designs of the CMPO go as low as 130 square feet per dwelling unit. For primary schools the Government of West Bengal has set a standard of 10 square feet per pupil. The standards for per capita water supply for the Calcutta metropolitan district are 60 gallons per capita per day for the Calcutta city area and 50 gallons per capita per day for suburban areas. In the bustees the standards are one bathing tap for 50 persons and one drinking water tap for 100 persons.

Initially Indian planning standards were largely adopted from the West. It should be self-evident that such standards are not only beyond the economic capacity of the nation to achieve at the present time but in many cases are culturally inappropriate. Yet there has been no concerted and systematic attempt to produce a set of standards either for urban India in general or for Calcutta in particular. Nevertheless, ad hoc standards are evolving in most fields. It would be exceedingly valuable if these were cataloged and analyzed as a beginning in establishing a set of standards for urban India. Standards of course are always in a process of change and any attempt to organize planning standards for India should be particularly alert to the need for rapid change.

It is self-evident that facilities requiring scarce capital investment should be very intensively utilized. Probably the most obvious is the school. It is ironic that multiple shifts and multiple use of school buildings is probably more practiced in the West than in Calcutta.

The conservation of existing investment has been a thread that has run through almost all of the CMPO's planning policies. Preservation of the existing housing stock is one of the principal elements of housing policy. One of the keystones of industrial development policy has been the use of idle industrial capacity. This now figures strongly in the government's efforts to resuscitate the economy of Calcutta and of West Bengal. Unfortunately, the high standards of maintenance required to preserve building stock are not practiced. This is particularly ironic in a heavily labor surplus economy. Like New York, Calcutta City has a rent control law. Perhaps this has inhibited investment in maintenance and repair. Whether it has or not, there has been surprisingly little agitation to lift it ... probably because of the unpopular political position this would imply.

The present public transport system consists of buses and trams. The standards of maintenance are abysmally low. Of a fleet of 904 buses, the Calcutta State Transport Corporation can only put on the street each day 494 . . . and these suffer 225 breakdowns on the average.

The idea that the intensive use of professional and semi-professional manpower can partially substitute for facilities is gradually being accepted. The 60 static dispensaries to be established in the current health program will be in rented space. The primary expense will be for doctors, nurses, and supporting personnel. The crash program of the CMDA will employ 10,000 medical and para-medical personnel.

A small urbanization study group established by the Ford Foundation in 1969 has completed its assignment. One of the studies commissioned by them was an exploration (by the Tropical School in London) of technological research now underway that might reduce the costs of urban facilities. The results of that study are largely negative. Only some work in the continuing quest to lower housing cost show some promise.

In Calcutta the CMPO and the Ford Foundation group have pursued the aim of reducing costs through prefabrication. This prefabrication has been based on three factors: the reduction in the use of materials; speed of construction; the use of units small enough and light enough to be manhandled. This last point obviates the need for heavy and expensive equipment and partially compensates for the offset of labor. All in all, however, the outlook for significant cost reduction through technological changes in the manner of construction and operation of the apparatus of a city does not appear to be very promising.

Choice of Areas of Intervention

One of the most hotly debated aspects of the Basic Development Plan was its explicit rejection of a system of overall land use controls. This significant departure from universal urban planning practice aroused considerable controversy in Indian planning circles. Nor has it been completely accepted to this day by the public and by government agencies. This is not to say that a land use plan was not proposed for the metropolitan district. An important aspect of the planning effort was the preparation of the land use plan . . . although admittedly generalized at the metropolitan level. But the plan argues that the land use objectives are to be achieved through positive developmental actions rather than through land use controls . . . and implicitly acknowledge that there will be land use mixtures and even conflicts. With the exception of the old European and Zamindari sector of Calcutta, the land use scene is one of highly mixed activity . . . and of apparent disorder. To many observers, particularly to foreigners, but even to such local organizations as the Citizens' Club, the picture is unacceptable. For the most part these observers are intelligent and concerned people. How then can one justify a massive and for the most part sophisticated planning effort that rejects the establishment of machinery to reorder this apparently inchoate situation?

First, Indian local government is strewn with the failures of development controls. Administrative resources are thin at best and they are thinnest at the level of local government. Where administrative resources are thin all decisions tend to float to the top ... with two consequences. The first is inexcusable delays described locally as "red tape-ism" and the second is a flouting of the regulations. In either case regulations have not only not achieved their objectives, but have slowed down development.

Second, and more important, the basic issues are increased incomes and employment, and anything that stands in the way of this must have powerful arguments to be acceptable. Actually, the situation is not as uncontrolled as it may appear. The Calcutta Municipal Act and the West Bengal Municipal Act include lists of uses that are permissible only in certain areas and with explicit government approval. Furthermore, the plan recognizes that in selected locations, land use controls may well be paramount in the public interest. But, generally speaking, it is argued that comprehensive land use control machinery will probably do more harm than good to the local development process.

Third, the intricate and interdependent nature of cities in general has only been perceptively recognized in fairly recent years. The fact that Indian cities are even more intricate means that much of the apparent disorder is not disorder at all but represents a very complicated interplay between a large variety of activities in quite limited space. It has been frequently noted that Calcutta represents a mixture of the primitive and the sophisticated. It should not be inferred from this that there are two separate unrelated cities ... the pucca and the kutcha. In fact, the two are very closely related. For example, some of the small parts used in the assembly of motor vehicles in one of India's most modern industrial establishments are made in small three- or four-man shops in the bustees. Likewise, domestic servants, still a source of major employment in Calcutta, are housed in bustees adjacent to middle and upper income housing.

If controls are to be rejected, then the other side of the coin, the emphasis on positive development actions, must be aggressively and systematically pursued. It must be recorded that the proposals of the plan in this wise were not aggressively pursued until the initiation of the large-scale Metropolitan Development Program in the latter part of 1970. And as of this writing only the first of a recommended series of actions is being prosecuted.

It is difficult to summarize the array of proposed development actions because they relate so directly to the local geography and the geographic or spatial objectives of the plan. But it is necessary if one is to understand the current state of events.

Grossly simplified, the proposed actions fall into the following categories:

(1) The arrest of deterioration and the removal of deficits in selected areas throughout the Calcutta metropolitan district with particular emphasis on the large concentration of Calcutta and its sister city, Howrah;

(2) Further development in partially developed areas of the metropolitan center including emphases for different types of development for each area;

(3) Specific new growth areas;

(4) Aggressive and accelerated development of a new metro sub-center, some 40 miles north of the existing center, by building on and expanding a premature investment in a satellite town and improving its connections;

(5) Major investment in transportation.

The use of spatial and functional targets for development is possible within the Indian context. But it is not easy. It requires the coordination of a variety of public actions with private actions susceptible to influence and control. The Indian economy is a complicated mixture of the private and public sectors. Two factors in Calcutta tend to provide government with considerable power in influencing spatial patterns of development. The first is that, with the exception of the northwest corner of the metropolitan district where the new center is proposed, there is very little buildable land in its present form. Most land not yet urbanized is intensively cultivated, much of it in paddy. To be developed for urban purposes, the land first has to be acquired from a large number of small owners and then filled, since it has been trained for years to hold water for paddy cultivation. Any significant new development perforce requires government acquisition and preparation of the land. The land obviously can then be planned and developed in accordance with the government's objective.

The second factor is that any new industrial enterprise using electric power and employing over 50 persons must be licensed. The plan argues that in the course of issuing a license the location of the proposed investment can be influenced, if not determined (there are a variety of criteria ... this is an oversimplified statement).

In the current Development Program only the first of these steps is being pressed in any significant manner. This is understandable since the present Development Program is aimed at rescuing the city from potential disaster. But it means that the verbalized and diagrammatic arguments of the Basic Development Plan must rapidly be transformed into site plans and project designs for the Fifth Plan period, if the argument for positive developmental actions as distinct from regulative controls is to have validity.

An Immediate Action Program

The Basic Development Plan concludes, not with a ringing call for a new, greater, more beautiful Calcutta, but with a highly specific set of recommendations for immediate action. The proposed actions are aimed, in the words of the Secretary of the Calcutta Metropolitan Development Authority, to produce "not the city beautiful but the city livable." From the inception of a first program note prepared in 1965, through the expanded and more highly rationalized program set forth in the Basic Development Plan and continuing with successive revisions up to the completion of the Rs.1,500 million program

Metropolitan Problems and Prospects

adopted in 1970, the acceptance of the Immediate Action Program by the Government of India was the consuming interest of the planning and development leadership of the Government of West Bengal. This intense interest and its continuing and aggressive presentation to the national government went well beyond the professional leaders to include the senior bureaucrats, the Chief Minister, and in the periods of President's Rule, the Governor. It is important to record that this work of the CMPO engaged the intense interest and concern of both the bureaucratic and the political leadership of the State of West Bengal.

The Immediate Action Program has three components:

(1) Identification of the subject matter of immediate concern (new township development, urban renewal, shelter, utilities, community services and facilities, traffic and transportation, industrial and commercial development) ... and it divides these for purposes of clarity between those proposed in the earlier 1965 program and those proposed in the Basic Development Plan;

(2) A specific investment program identifying projects, the agency responsible for the development of each project, and proposed method of financing;

(3) Proposals for new government agencies necessary to initiate and expedite the Development Program.

One of the criticisms frequently directed at the Immediate Action Program is that it is not a coherent set of projects aimed at achieving the objectives of the Basic Development Plan; it is in large part a collection of projects identified during the planning process but prior to the completion of the plan itself. This is an accurate criticism but not a cogent one, for three reasons.

First, one of the critical requirements of development planning is that it be built into the government decision making process as early and as effectively as possible. Judgments have to be made before all of the facts are in. Certain prior commitments have to be accepted. And a certain amount of project bargaining is inevitable. If the finally agreed upon project array is less coherent than some of the planners may wish, the loss of coherence in this particular case is more than offset by the governmentwide acceptance of the program. Obviously there are dangers in such a position ... the most apparent being that the planning agency is simply a kind of collector and cataloger of projects. This is by no means the case in the CMPO effort. A full 90 percent of the projects in the program are projects conceived within the CMPO itself.

Second, there is a serious intellectual and emotional conflict between emphasis on projects aimed at meeting current deficiencies and arresting further deterioration on the one hand, and emphasis on projects leading toward achievement of future land use goals on the other. Understandably, the Immediate Action Program tilts heavily toward the former.

Finally, it should be pointed out that the program was not a static one during the period 1967-1970. Three significant alterations were made and reflected in

Table 2. Calcutta Metropolitan District Development Schemes, Fourth Plan Period (in Millions of Rupees)

Water Supply	288.1
Sewerage and Drainage	289.4
Traffic and Transportation	418.1
Bustee Improvement, Housing, and New Area Development	309.1
Health Facilities	95.5
Primary Education	49.2
Other	47.5
Total	1,496.9

the adopted program of 1970: a significant increase in the amount of money allocated to the Bustee Improvement Program; an increase in the amount of money devoted to housing; and the insertion of important amounts of money for programs in primary education and in health.

In sum, the Development Program for the period through fiscal 1973-74 breaks down as shown in Table 2.

In addition to the above commitments there are two major investments in the metropolitan district which will be initiated during the Fourth Plan period and extended into the Fifth Plan period. Both are transport investments proposed in the CMPO Traffic and Transportation Plan. One is the new Hooghly Bridge across the river which will cost Rs.300 million. Second, is the first major component of the proposed rapid transit system which will cost in the order of Rs.1,400 million.

It is clear, looking at the above figures, that the heaviest investments are in basic infrastructure. And it is further apparent that, with the addition of the two major transport expenditures outside the program the total investment package is heavily biased in terms of transport. Perhaps this is necessary if the first objective of the plan is to be achieved, namely, promoting a more dynamic growth of the metropolitan economy. For the city as an economic machine cannot function well without radically improved transport. Nevertheless, it must be admitted that there has been inadequate debate on the distribution of funds across the several fields of investment. One of the continuing mysteries of urban planning is how to devise an optimum distribution of investment across the array of capital needs that face every metropolitan area. Perhaps the best test is the political one. Work is now underway on a program for the Fifth Plan period. With a new government just installed with its heavy majority, it is probable that the Fifth Plan program devised by the CMPO will be subjected to considerable political debate.

CONCLUSION

The future of Calcutta as a reasonably coherent society is by no means assured. From time to time in the recent past it has appeared to be on the verge of breakdown as an organized society. At the moment that danger has been averted, but there is no guarantee that such crises will not recur.

Nevertheless, on the record of the last year and with the new government in power, the future appears reasonably bright. The planning products of ten years are being put to work in an astonishingly rapid fashion. The rusty development machinery of the government has responded, with one major exception, to the challenge of manifold increases in the demand for project execution. (The one exception is the Calcutta Corporation, which at this writing has just been superseded by state government in one of the first acts of the new government.) From an expenditure on public works of Rs.40 million in the fiscal year 1969-70, expenditure rose to Rs.150 million in 1970-71 and an estimated Rs.500 million in 1971-72.

This is an extraordinary performance by any measure, but in view of the obstacles in the Calcutta situation it is even more so. Let me note four of those obstacles. First, the implementing agencies are manned by professional personnel who have had an opportunity to build very little over the past twenty years. Experience, and the confidence that come from it, is thin indeed. Second, with minimum public investments over this period Calcutta has not developed a strong contracting industry. Third, during this same period, there has been minimal demand for the materials of construction: cement, stone chips, steel, bricks. Acquiring these materials at short notice has been a very difficult task. Fourth, in a situation of chronic shortage in railway wagons there has been little excess capacity in the transport system that could be used to move the materials of construction to the metropolitan district. Yet these obstacles have been overcome and the program continues to gain momentum.

In conclusion, rather than attempting to summarize what has gone before I shall simply make some brief observations which may have applicability in other urban situations.

First, it is clear that the effort to raise Calcutta to an acceptable standard of livability could not be done without a commitment of national money. Both local and state fiscal resources are inadequate to the task. National cities require national investments. Second, the program could not be initiated without national political commitment. Third, the planning effort must be a very broad one. Although selective, it must cover a wide array of needs. Certainly the breadth of the CMPO's planning efforts have been remarkable. Fourth, the planning effort and the recently initiated development effort must be sustained efforts. Improving cities like Calcutta is a long hard task. Tenacity is an essential ingredient. Fifth, a large amount of trained manpower is needed. And training must be built into the planning process as a continuing effort.

Finally, strong metropolitan organizations are needed. At the apex there should be a triumvirate composed of a planning organization, a development organization, and a training and research organization. In Calcutta the first two are in place. Hopefully the third will soon emerge.

EPILOGUE

—December, 1973

This article was written in March 1972, nearly two years ago. Rather than try to modify the article to bring it up to date, I choose to add this epilogue.

Significant organizational changes have taken place in the meantime. In May of 1972 the West Bengal State Planning Board was established by Cabinet resolution. The Board has seen its responsibility as the development of the state as a whole. Its basic policy position is that the renaissance of Calcutta can only come about if there is a significant increase in income, employment and output from the agricultural sector. In internal debate the position has been put forward that public investment in the Calcutta metropolitan district should be reduced in order to provide a higher level of resource for investment in the rural areas. The outcome of the debate, however, was to support the CMDA's Fifth Plan proposals. But much the greater effort on the part of the Board has gone into devising programs for rural development, the central component of which is the proposed Comprehensive Area Development Program.

The CADP is a program which brings together technological improvements in agriculture (better seeds, irrigation, fertilizers, pesticides) with agro-service centers, along with an integrated program of crop planning, marketing and bank loans, and new programs in health and education. Because the program is so intricate and so ambitious, it is to be carried out in units of 10,000 acres each. In the first year, one such CADP area would be developed in each of the state's seventeen districts. By the end of the Fifth Plan the target is 310 such projects. It is intended that about 75 percent of rural West Bengal would be covered by this program at the end of the Sixth Plan. Much of the input required for the CADP would be produced in the state's urban areas. And increased income in the rural areas would raise consumer demand for products made in the urban areas. Finally, increased agricultural employment would reduce pressure on metropolitan Calcutta and other cities. This central policy of the State Planning Board represents for the first time a recognition of the complementarity of urban and rural areas expressed in programmatic terms.

The CMDA continues to move the Development Program forward. There have been major obstacles which have been noted in the article earlier. Of the programed Rs.150 crores for the Fourth Plan period, it is currently estimated that Rs.130 crores will have actually been spent when the Plan period ends in March 1974.

One of the problems of CMDA has been that, as the funding agency, it has been held responsible by both the Central Government and the general public for the progress and effectiveness of the Development Program. But it has no immediate authority over the performance of the implementing agencies. Hence, it is heavily criticized for failures in situations in which it does not have the requisite authority. An ordinance has been enacted which will bring a significant number of the implementing agencies into the CMDA. Three important ones are the Calcutta Improvement Trust, the Howrah Improvement Trust, and the Calcutta Metropolitan Water and Sanitation Authority. CMDA will expand from an agency of some 800 persons to an agency of 6,000 to 7,000 persons.

As CMDA expands its role in the implementation field, it continues to press for responsibility in the planning field. Yet the question of the distribution of planning responsibility between the CMDA and the CMPO continues unresolved.

As the Development Program has proceeded, a serious question has arisen in terms of maintenance of investments made. It has been calculated that maintenance costs of the new investments exceeds by Rs.3 crores annually the fiscal capacity of the local governments. The poor performance of local government in the Calcutta metropolitan district is a chronic problem. The Development Program has brought this long-standing problem to the forefront. The World Bank will provide technical assistance to improve the performance of local governments in raising their resource capabilities, but to many informed observers it is clear that some major restructuring of the pattern of local government is necessary. Proposals of the Basic Development Plan in this regard have been noted in the article. More recently, there have been proposals to establish a two-tier system: a metropolitan government and a series of borough governments. But these proposals lie dormant.

The resource front for the CMDA Program for the Fifth Plan period is much less bright than it was a few months ago. This, of course, is a reflection of the straitened circumstances of the Indian economy in general and the West Bengal economy in particular. The State Planning Board approved a Rs.340 crores program for the Calcutta metropolitan district for the Fifth Plan. Preliminary discussions in New Delhi made clear that this was too ambitious and the planners trimmed their sails to an anticipated program of Rs.250 crores. The Fifth Plan has just been approved by the Central Cabinet and submitted to Parliament. State shares and their composition remain subject to some negotiation, but it now appears that Rs.200 crores will be the outside figure.

The World Bank has loaned the Government of India $30 million (about Rs.23 crores) for the Calcutta Development Program. Included in that loan is $500,000 for technical assistance. Welcome and important as this money is, it is not an incremental addition to the Government of India's Fifth Plan Program for Calcutta, but forms a part of it.

An important aspect of Calcutta's Bustee Development Program is the emergence of a social and economic development program to parallel the physical development program. The program is built upon the premise that bustee dwellers can, with sensitive assistance, help themselves. Thus programs have been initiated in education—both primary and adult—and education that is work-related; in health, nutrition, and family planning with voluntary contributions by medical practitioners of their own time; and in employment training with emphasis on the potentials of self-employment. A European Consortium stands ready to provide substantial funds for a social and economic development program that is coordinated with CMDA's effort. A plan has been devised to that end.

A central and chronic problem of Indian development has been the gap between the elegance of plans and the relatively poor performance in the implementation of those plans. In early 1973, a report was completed proposing a training program in development planning and management for the state of West Bengal. Disenchanted with the inadequate performance of many new institutes, both the academic community and the government were reluctant to establish a new one. Further, the thin supply of persons available in the field raised the concern that any new institute could only operate by taking people from existing institutions. Thus, the program for training in project execution and management, which is so badly needed, still remains a matter of discussion. But existing institutions like the Indian Institute of Management are beginning to develop programs focused on training and research in urban development.

Thus, the metropolitan mill grinds slowly. Calcutta improves but not as rapidly as was foreseen in 1970. Politicians, bureaucrats and citizens rarely understand the intricate nature of cities. Hopes are easily raised and as easily belied. Improvement of cities like Calcutta is a long, slow, hard job. Tenacity and conviction tempered by sensitivity are requisites if progress is to be made. Perhaps that is the primary lesson of the Calcutta project.

NOTES

1. For good portraits of Calcutta see Nirmal K. Bose, "Calcutta: Premature Metropolis," Scientific American, Vol. 213, No. 3 (September 1965); and Geoffrey Moorhouse, *Calcutta*. London: Weidenfeld and Nicolson, 1971.
2. "The Basic Development Plan for the Calcutta Metropolitan District, 1966-86," Government of West Bengal, Calcutta Metropolitan Planning Organization, Calcutta, 1966, p. 88. For a list of the papers and other internal reports prepared by the Calcutta Metropolitan Planning Organization and the Ford Foundation Advisory Planning Group, see Appendix A.
3. Ranajit Roy, *The Agony of West Bengal*, Calcutta: Ananda Bazar Patrika, 1971, p. 100.
4. "Basic Development Plan for the Calcutta Metropolitan District," *op. cit.*, p. 87.
5. "Some General Characteristics of Development Plans and of the Planning Process," Ford Foundation Advisory Planning Group, Calcutta Metropolitan Plan. Calcutta: mimeo, April 1962.
6. *Ibid.*
7. Colin Rosser, *Urbanisation in Eastern India: The Planning Response*. Calcutta: Ford Foundation, mimeo, 1969.
8. William L.C. Wheaton, letter of February 7, 1967, to Douglas Ensminger.
9. "Basic Development Plan for the Calcutta Metropolitan District," *op. cit.*, p. 6.

APPENDIX
A Selected List of Working Papers—
Calcutta Metropolitan Planning Organization

This list of selected titles from "Bibliography of Papers and Reports, Produced by Calcutta Metropolitan Planning Organization, 1962-1969" is presented for several reasons. First and foremost, we feel that many of these papers are of high professional quality and warrant being known outside the limited circle of co-workers and persons with a special interest in the Calcutta planning effort. In general, our experience suggests that planning agency working papers and other similar "fugitive materials" often make significant contributions to the art of planning, notwithstanding possible flaws when examined from a strictly scholarly point of view.

Our second reason for presenting this selected list is to demonstrate the breadth of the Calcutta program. The total bibliography, which covers the formative years of the program, contains 585 entries divided among 17 subject headings. Although there are a number of multiple entries, and no cross references are given, the number of papers classified under more than one subject heading probably does not exceed 100. It is also of interest to point out that despite the massive support given to the project by the Ford Foundation —with well over 60 foreign advisers and consultants participating in program development and plan preparation—the majority of the papers in the bibliography are written by Indian staff members of the CMPO or affiliated organizations. The author index, for example, contains 88 Indian names of a total of 135 names listed.

By subject heading, the bibliography represents the following breakdown:

	Number of Entries	Percent of Total
CALCUTTA METROPOLITAN DISTRICT PLANS AND METHODOLOGY	31	5.3
GEOGRAPHIC DATA	25	4.3
DEMOGRAPHY AND MANPOWER	33	5.6
ADMINISTRATIVE ORGANIZATION AND LEGISLATION	42	7.2
ECONOMICS AND INDUSTRY	52	8.9
FISCAL PLANNING AND MUNICIPAL FINANCE	32	5.5
WATER SUPPLY, SEWERAGE, SANITATION AND REFUSE DISPOSAL	43	7.4
TRAFFIC AND TRANSPORTATION	66	11.3
HOUSING AND SLUM CLEARANCE	68	11.6
SOCIAL PLANNING AND COMMUNITY FACILITIES	37	6.2
LAND USE SURVEY AND PLANNING	13	2.2
NEW AREA DEVELOPMENTS	15	2.6
URBAN REDEVELOPMENT	18	3.1
CALCUTTA PORT AND HOOGHLY RIVER	6	1.0

	Number	Percent
	of Entries	of Total
HOWRAH	8	1.4
REGIONAL PLANS AND STUDIES	77	13.1
DATA PROCESSING	19	3.2
TOTALS	585	100.0

As pointed out in this volume in Chapter 9 on metropolitan planning, the Calcutta planning effort represents a drastic departure from previous work of similar nature in Asia. The above bibliography breakdown bears out this contention. For example, only 14 percent of the papers deal with such issues as land use and transportation, which are of central concern in traditional planning programs. In contrast, 21 percent of all entries represent papers dealing with population and social and economic issues, and as many as 74 titles (or 13 percent) are classified under the headings of administrative organization, legislation, fiscal planning and municipal finance. Finally, the national, regional and state perspectives are represented by 103 entries, or 18 percent of the total.

Only 29 of the papers in the bibliography have been published in various professional journals. Thirteen of the planning reports listed are available in printed version.

—The Editors

ASANSOL PLANNING ORGANISATION. Interim development plan: Asansol-Durgapur. 1966. Printed. 73p. Maps, tabs., diagrs. Rs.20/-.

ASHRAF, A. The city government of Calcutta: a study of inertia. Bombay, Asia Publishing House. 1966. Printed. 126p. Map.

BANERJEE, H. Projection of industrial employment in West Bengal: sectoral and spatial distribution. Undated. Mimeo. 40p. Tabs., diagrs. Unbd.

BANERJEE, H. Socio-economic plan frame. July 1964. Mimeo. 30p. Unbd.

BANERJEE, T. K. and M. K. BHATTACHARYYA. Municipal finance in the Calcutta Metropolitan District: an historical survey: 1951-2 to 1960-1. March 1964. Typed. 53p. Illus. Unbd.

BASU, C. Statement on recreation and the role of the urban community development units. April 1965. Typed. 15p. Unbd.

BASU, D. N. A note on the projected employment pattern by broad sectors for the Asansol sub-division. (1961-86). 1965. Mimeo. 5p. Unbd.

BASU, D. N. A general review of housing conditions in Asansol-Durgapur region. Jan. 1969. Mimeo. 28p. Tabs. Unbd.

BELCHER, D. J. Proposals for the restoration of the Port of Calcutta and the unification of the Calcutta Conurbation. Jan. 1962. Mimeo. 6p. Unbd.

BERRY, B. Note on the research programme for regional resource development. 1961. Mimeo. 28p. Unbd.

BHATTACHARYYA, A. Under-utilisation of industrial capacity in Asansol-Durgapur region. 1964-65. 1968. Mimeo. 24p. Unbd.

BHATTACHARYYA, A. Problems and possibilities of growth of ancillary industries in the Asansol-Durgapur area. 1968. Mimeo. 4p. Unbd.

BHATTACHARYYA, A. A comparative analysis of the industrial structure industrial mix of Asansol-Durgapur belt. 1968. Mimeo. 6p. Tabs. Unbd.

BHATTACHARYYA, M. Rural self-government in metropolitan Calcutta. Bombay, Asia Publishing House. 1965. Printed. 106p. Tabs.

BHATTACHARYYA, M. K. Financial feasibility of water supply projects in the Calcutta Metropolitan District: a case study—emergency water supply scheme, 1962. Feb. 1965. Mimeo. 46p. Unbd.

BHATTACHARYYA, M. K. Local government and Calcutta metropolitan plan: a treatise on the need for institutional reformation. *Local-Self Government Quarterly,* January-March, 1968.

BHUTA, B. M. Metropolitan regional planning: technique and survey. Sept. 1960. Mimeo. 9p. (Paper read at the 9th Annual Town and Country Planning Seminar, 1960.) Unbd.

BHUTA, B. M. Methods and techniques for the preparation of interim general plan I. June 1963. Mimeo. 23p. Unbd.

BOSE, A. N. A note on the plan for industries in the Maniktala prototype work-living project—a preliminary draft. Sept. 1962. Mimeo. 24p. Unbd.

BOSE, A. N. A report on the industrial estates in the Calcutta Metropolitan District. June 1963. Mimeo. 51p. Unbd.

BOSE, A. N. Economic development and regional development. A preliminary draft for discussion. 1967. Mimeo. 33p. Tabs.

BOSE, A. N. Draft of statement of industrial policy and a system of incentives, and a framework of study elements. 1967. Mimeo. 27p. Unbd.

BOSE, A. N. Survey of manufacturing industry—1962 Calcutta Metropolitan District. Volume I. Calcutta City. Jan. 1967. Mimeo. 181p. Bd.

BOSE, A. N. Survey of manufacturing industry—1962 Calcutta Metropolitan District. Volume II. Howrah City. March 1967. Mimeo. 110p. Bd.

BOSE, A. N. Survey of manufacturing industry—1962 Calcutta Metropolitan District. Volume III. Other C.M.D. Dec. 1967. Mimeo. 160p. Bd.

BURTON, I. Towards a more rational decision-making in India's water resource development. 1965. Mimeo. 16p. Unbd.

BURTON, I., S. C. CHATTERJEE and S. K. GHOSAL. Policy and recommendations for water supply, sewerage and drainage. Sept. 1965. Mimeo. 35p. Tabs. Unbd.

CALCUTTA METROPOLITAN PLANNING ORGANISATION. The setting up of Calcutta Metropolitan Planning Organisation and some general characteristics of development plans and the planning process. 1961. Mimeo. Various p. Unbd.

CALCUTTA METROPOLITAN PLANNING ORGANISATION. Work-cum-living centre project at Maniktala: conception of a neighborhood pattern. June 1963. 35p. Appendices. Unbd.

CALCUTTA METROPOLITAN PLANNING ORGANIZATION—21 POINTS PROGRAM.

Vol. 1: Comprehensive planning for the Calcutta Metropolitan District and its relation to the improvement programme. 1964. Mimeo. 58p. Bd.

Vol. 2, 2a: Master plan for water supply, sewerage and drainage in the Calcutta Metropolitan District. 1964-65. Mimeo. Tabs., appendices. Bd. Volume 2—138p. Volume 2a—102p.

Vol. 3a, 3b: Interim water supply project. 1964. Mimeo. Maps, tabs., appendices. Bd. Volume 3a—35p. Volume 3b—128p.

Vol. 4: A multiple and concerted attack to eliminate endemic cholera. 1965. Mimeo. 16p. Appendices. Bd.

Vol. 5: A massive bustee improvement programme for Calcutta and Howrah. 1964. Mimeo. 69p. Maps, appendices. Bd.

Vol. 6a: A note on the subsidised housing needs generated by the improvement programme. 1965. Mimeo. 23p. Tabs. Bd.

Vol. 6b: Demonstration of new techniques in housing construction and management. 1964. Mimeo. 59p. Diagrs. Bd.

Vol. 7: Concentrated improvement programme for Howrah and Tollygunge. 1964. Mimeo. 89p. Maps, tabs. Bd.

Vol. 8: Design for an urban re-development programme for the Calcutta Metropolitan District. 1964. Mimeo. 18p. Bd.

Vol. 9: Suburban development in Sonarpur, Kona and Salt Lake and its relation to the planned growth of the Calcutta Metropolitan District. 1964. Mimeo. 201p. Maps, tabs. Bd.

Vol. 10: Modernisation of traffic operations in Calcutta. 1964. Mimeo. 25p. Maps. Bd.

Vol. 11: Interim major street and highway plan for the Calcutta Metropolitan District. 1964. Mimeo. 103p. Maps. Bd.

Vol. 12a, 12b: Rapid transit proposals for the principal passenger traffic corridors in Calcutta. 1964. Mimeo. Maps, appendices. Bd. Volume 12a—95p. Volume 12b—65p.

Vol. 13: Proposed Calcutta-Howrah high-level bridge across the Hooghly. 1964. Mimeo. 54p. Maps, appendices. Bd.

Vol. 14: Modernisation of refuse collection and disposal in Calcutta and Howrah. 1964. Mimeo. 102p. Bd.

Vol. 15: Application of national goals and standards for education to the Calcutta Metropolitan District. 1965. Mimeo. 65p. Bd.

Vol. 16: A proposed network of community service centres for the Calcutta Metropolitan District. 1964. Mimeo. 15p. Bd.

Vol. 17: Urban community development as a method of government-citizen partnership for improving living conditions in metropolitan Calcutta. 1964. Mimeo. 37p. Diagrs. Bd.

Vol. 18: Parks and recreation needs of the Calcutta Metropolitan District and how they can be met. 1964. Mimeo. 28p. Tabs., appendices. Bd.

Vol. 19: Development of Haldia with respect to the Port of Calcutta and the metropolitan region. 1964. Mimeo. 40p. Maps, appendices. Bd.

Vol. 20: The relationship of Farakka Barrage to the planning of the Calcutta Metropolitan District. 1965. Mimeo. 18p. Bd.

Vol. 21a, 21b: Regional planning in Eastern India and its relation to urbanisation in West Bengal and metropolitan Calcutta. 1965. Mimeo. Tabs., diagrs. Bd. Volume 21a—65p. Volume 21b—171p.

CALCUTTA METROPOLITAN PLANNING ORGANISATION. Memorandum on development plan for Calcutta Metropolitan District, 1966-1971. 1965. Illus. 28p.

CALCUTTA METROPOLITAN PLANNING ORGANISATION. Basic development plan for the Calcutta Metropolitan District, 1966-1986. 1966. Printed. 179p. Photos., maps, tabs., diagrs. Rs.30/-.

CALCUTTA METROPOLITAN PLANNING ORGANISATION. Howrah area development plan, 1966-1986. 1967. Printed. 66p. Maps, tabs., diagrs. Rs.20/-.

CALCUTTA METROPOLITAN PLANNING ORGANISATION. Traffic and transportation plan for the Calcutta Metropolitan District, 1966-1986. 1967. Printed. Photos., maps, tabs. Rs.30/-.

CALCUTTA METROPOLITAN PLANNING ORGANISATION. Interim report: housing Calcutta Metropolitan District. 1967. 67p. Tabs.

CALCUTTA METROPOLITAN PLANNING ORGANISATION. Bustee improvement programme: Calcutta and Howrah. 1967. 100p. Tabs.

CASTREN, R. Papers on the mass transit problem of the Calcutta zone of influence. 1968. Mimeo. 66p. Tabs. Bd.

CHAKRAVARTY, K. R. Labour force by age-group and an estimate of volume of unemployment in Calcutta Metropolitan District. (1961 census). 1965. Mimeo. 10p. Tabs. Unbd.

CHOUDHURY, G. K. A short term project for environmental improvement for the benefit of refugees in Tollygunge area. 1968. Mimeo. 10p. Maps. Unbd.

CULLEN, G. A design study of the Maidan. Nov. 1962. Mimeo. 24p. Illus. Unbd.

CULLEN, G. Dalhousie Square. Dec. 1962. Mimeo. 29p. Illus. Unbd.

DAS, JHARNA (Nee Roy) and C. ROSSER. Provision of basic educational facilities for metropolitan Calcutta—the role of the planning agency. Sept. 1965. Mimeo. 15p. Maps, tabs. Unbd.

DAS GUPTA, P. and R. GHOSH. Migration in West Bengal. Part I: Population of West Bengal and its 16 districts and 12 cities classified according to place of birth (1961 census). Oct. 1966. Mimeo. 33p. Unbd.

DAS GUPTA, P., R. GHOSH, and A. ROY. Migration in West Bengal. Part II. Migrant and non-migrant population of West Bengal and its 16 districts and 12 cities classified according to industrial categories of workers and non-workers (1961 census). Jan. 1967. Mimeo. 29p. Unbd.

DAS GUPTA, SUNITA. Report on incidence of infectious diseases in Calcutta slums. May 1964. Typed. 15p. Tabs., diagrs. Unbd.

DAS GUPTA, SUNITA. Family planning services programme of the urban community development units. Preliminary report. Dec. 1964. Typed. 12p. Tabs., appendices. Unbd.

DATTA, A. Inter-governmental grants in metropolitan Calcutta. Bombay, Asia Publishing House. 1965. Printed. 50p. Tabs.

DATTA, A. and D. C. RANNEY. Municipal finances in the Calcutta Metropolitan District. I.P.A., New York. 1964. Printed. 123p. Map, tabs.

DATA GUPTA, JOYA. Social areas of Serampore town. 1962. Typed. 39p. Map. Unbd.

DATTA GUPTA, JOYA. Housing cooperatives in West Bengal. 1963. Mimeo. 16p. Unbd.

DEV GHOUDHURY, B. C. Economic justification of Haldia project with an outline of the plan project. April 1967. Mimeo. 17p. Unbd.

DUTT, A. K. Determination of daily influence area of Calcutta. Undated. Mimeo. 19p. Unbd.

DUTT, A. K. An analysis of commutation to Calcutta and Howrah with suggested improvements. July 1963. Mimeo. 25p. Maps. Unbd.

DUTT, A. K. Delineation of hinterland for Calcutta Port. Jan. 1964. Mimeo. 13p. Maps, diagrs. Unbd.

DUTT, A. K. Railway goods flow Calcutta. March 1966. Mimeo. 139p. Unbd.

DUTT, A. K. and A. K. MAIKAP. Determinants of composite index of developments micro-regionally. Undated. Mimeo. 11p. Maps, tabs. Unbd.

DUTT, A. K. and A. K. MAIKAP. Social development index for West Bengal. Aug. 1968. Mimeo. 14p. Maps, tabs. Unbd.

ECHEVERRIA, E. Land utilisation studies for the Calcutta Conurbation. Oct. 1962. Mimeo. 17p. Unbd.

ECHEVERRIA, PAULA. A note on community organisation in the implementation of slum improvement programmes. Dec. 1962. Mimeo. 22p. Unbd.

GRENELL, P. Cost of urban services in West Bengal. 1967. Mimeo. 33p. Tabs., appendices. Unbd.

KAPLAN, M. A proposal for slum improvement legislation. 1963. Mimeo. 11p. Unbd.

KAPLAN, M. Ingredients of legislation for acquiring land. May 1964. Mimeo. 23p. Unbd.

KAPLAN, M. State legislation for supporting instrumentalities. 1966. Mimeo. 54p. Unbd.

KAPLAN, M. and ELIZABETH WOOD. Preliminary notes on legislation for urban development. April 1963. Mimeo. 13p. Unbd.

KHANNA, T. S. A preliminary report on pedestrian traffic in greater Calcutta. Aug. 1962. Typed. 58p. Appendices. Unbd.

KINGSLEY, G. T. Housing for Durgapur: framework for a new strategy. 1967. Mimeo. 43p. Tabs. Unbd.

KUTTY, M. G. Government and administration in Calcutta district. (Background paper for C.M.D. plan). Feb. 1966. 75p. Unbd.

KUTTY, M. G. The administrative vacuum in Indian planning law. Oct. 1966. Printed. 28p. Unbd. (Paper submitted to the 15th Annual Town and Country Planning Seminar.)

KUTTY, M. G. Metropolitan and regional planning problems of organisation. *IULA Journal.* Spring 1968. No. 2.

LAHIRI, T. B. Urbanisation in Southern Plains–West Bengal. May 1963. Mimeo. 12p. Maps, tabs., diagrs. Unbd.

LAHIRI, T. B. A study of urban geography. *The Indian Geographer,* Dec. 1963, Volume 8. Nos. 1 and 2.

LAHIRI, T. B. Regional study. Southern Plains–West Bengal. Feb. 1964. Mimeo. 29p. Unbd.

LAHIRI, T. B. Haldia region: preliminary report showing major characteristics of region. Nov. 1966. Mimeo. 28p. Tabs. Unbd.

LAHIRI, T. B. Service costs and size of towns–with special reference to Calcutta Metropolitan District. Jan. 1967. Typed. 6p. Tabs., diagrs. (Paper read at the 54th Session of Indian Science Congress at Hyderabad.)

LAHIRI, T. B. Planning regions: an approach towards delineation with reference to West Bengal. 1967. Mimeo. 6p. Maps, tabs. Unbd.

LAHIRI, T. B. Impact of port construction–a study in spatial context with reference to Haldia region of West Bengal. Jan. 1968. Typed. 10p. Unbd.

LEE, T. R. Some aspects of the perception and use of water in bustees. April 1966. Mimeo. 7p. Tabs. Unbd.

LUDWIG, H. F. Report on interim water supply and sanitation scheme for Metropolitan Calcutta. July 1963. Mimeo. 33p. Unbd.

MacDOUGALL, J. Ancillary industries in Asansol-Durgapur. Bombay, Asia Publishing House. 1965. Printed. 59p. Tabs.

MADHAB, J. Notes on plan allocation, financing principles, unit and operating cost of some community facilities. 1965. Mimeo. 37p. Tabs. Unbd.

MADHAB, J. Resources for urban development. *Indian Journal of Public Administration.* July-Sept. 1968. Vol. XIV No. 3.

MADHAB, J., NIRMALA BANERJEE, T. K. BANERJEE and P. MUKHERJEE. Development resources for the fourth plan for West Bengal. June 1967. Mimeo. 71p. Tabs., appendices. Bd.

MADHAB, J., NIRMALA BANERJEE and T. K. BANERJEE. Crisis in Calcutta Corporation: a programme for action. Aug. 1967. Mimeo. 96p. Tabs. Bd.

MADHAB, J., M. K. BHATTACHARYYA and T. K. BANERJEE. A five-year capital improvement programme for the Calcutta Metropolitan area: 1961-66. (Financial analysis.) Dec. 1964. Mimeo. 43p. Unbd.

MADHAB, J. and J. J. CARROLL. A note on the local resource potentials for financing Calcutta plan 1966-71. 1965. Mimeo. 10p. Unbd.

MADHAB, J. and J. J. CARROLL. Financial powers of the States and the local bodies in India. Jan. 1965. Mimeo. 27p. Tabs. Unbd.

MADHAB, J. and J. J. CARROLL. Notes on some significant aspects of Government finances: centre, state and Calcutta Metropolitan District. April 1965. Mimeo. 25p. Unbd.

MADHAB, J., S. DUTTA and J. J. CARROLL. Development agency study: 1. Calcutta Improvement Trust (financial and administrative analysis.) July 1965. Mimeo. 39p. Unbd.

MADHAB, J., M. G. KUTTY and J. J. CARROLL. Revised proposals for financing the 100-crore plan for Calcutta Metropolitan District. Oct. 1965. Mimeo. 10p. Unbd.

MADHAB, J. and A. P. VAN HUYCK. Work programming in the planning process. *Journal of Indian Institute of Public Administration.* Jan.-March 1965. Volume 11, No. 1.

METCALF & EDDY LTD., and ENGINEERING SCIENCE INC. Master plan for water supply, sewerage and drainage–Calcutta Metropolitan District (1966-2001). (Report prepared for the World Health Organisation, acting as executing agency for the United Nations Development Programme.) Mimeo. Bd. Volume I: detailed report, photos, tabs.–397p. Volume II: appendices and drawings.

MUKHERJEE, B. N. and D. WILLCOX. A constitutional balance: the need for government planning vs. the "when" of procedural reasonableness–a draughtsman's task. *Journal of the Indian Law Institute.* July-Sept. 1967. Volume 9, No. 3.

MUKHERJEE, S. Studies on slums in the Calcutta Metropolitan District. Dec. 1963. Typed. 71p. Maps. Unbd.

MUKHERJEE, S. B. Pattern of fertility in West Bengal and its economic consequences. Sept. 1962. Mimeo. 12p. Unbd.

MUKHERJEE, S. B. Demographic-economic aspects of small and medium towns in Calcutta Metropolitan District. *Journal of the Institute of Town Planners, India.* Jan.-April 1963. Volume 33-34.

MUKHERJEE, S. B. A note on housing situation and projected housing needs of the Calcutta Metropolitan District. (1961-81). 1964. Typed. 18p. Unbd.

MUNICIPAL ENGINEERING SECTION, CMPO. Interim report of the removal and collection of garbage in Calcutta. Feb. 1964. Mimeo. 45p. Unbd.

OLGYAY, A. Climate and building: climatalogical evaluation and architectural recommendations for the Calcutta region. 1963. Mimeo. 164p. Graphs. Bd. (Edited by F. C. Terzo and S. Ghosh, 1968.)

PRAKASH, V. Some financial aspects of improvement scheme at Chetla. (Bustees nos. 2, 4 & 5.) June 1963. Mimeo. 11p. Tabs. Unbd.

REGIONAL PLANNING WING, CMPO. As assessment of urbanisation potential of villages in Southern Plains, West Bengal. Oct. 1964. Mimeo. 11p. Unbd.

REGIONAL PLANNING WING, CMPO. Roads: West Bengal transport survey. Report 1965. Mimeo. 215p. Maps, tabs. Bd.

REGIONAL PLANNING WING, CMPO. The industrial perspective for the census sector: national targets and West Bengal's share. 1966. Mimeo. 10p. Tabs., diagrs. Unbd.

ROSEN, G. Projected growth of the economics of West Bengal and the Calcutta Metropolitan District. (1960/61-1975). 1962. Mimeo. 39p. Unbd.

ROY, JHARNA. A report on the existing educational facilities in Calcutta Metropolitan District (1961) and preliminary assessment of the needs for primary and secondary education during the fourth plan period within the municipal areas of Calcutta Metropolitan District. (Revised version.) March 1964. Mimeo. 72p. Unbd.

SAHA, P. K. The crisis of water supply and sewerage in urban West Bengal. (A study of the problems and remedies with special reference to the Asansol region.) Thesis submitted to the Johns Hopkins University, Baltimore, Maryland, U.S. in conformity with the requirements for the degree of M.S. in engineering. 1968. 91p. Tabs. Bd.

SAHA, P. K. and A. BHATTACHARYYA. Rainfall study in Asansol-Durgapur region. 1967. Typed. 85p. Graphs, tabs. Unbd.

SAMANTA, M. A note on the problem of optimum transaction of a bivariate population in stratified random sampling. *Annals of the Institute of Statistical Mathematics, 1965.* Vol. 17, No. 3.

SAMANTA, M. A stochastic approach to determine the probable structure of Indian towns in 1971 census. 1965. Mimeo. 21p. Tabs. Unbd.

SARKAR, R. L. Income of the Calcutta Metropolitan District. 1961-62. 1964. Mimeo. 29p. Tabs. Unbd.

SARKAR, R. L. Agriculture and the growing needs of urbanisation. (An appraisal of comprehensive concept of town and country planning.) 1965. Mimeo. 66p. Unbd.

SARKAR, R. L. and A. R. CHOUDHURY. The rural economy of the Calcutta Metropolitan District. Part I and II. 1964-65. Mimeo. Unbd. Part I: 29p. Tabs. Part II: 34p. Tabs.

SARKAR, R. L. and D. P. JANA. Agricultural and urban growth—Part I. (Trends of agricultural income and employment in West Bengal—Preliminary.) June 1966. Mimeo. 61p. Tabs. Unbd.

SHARMA, M. N. Techniques of land use survey for the development plan of a city from aerial photographs: a case study of Calcutta and environs. *Journal of the Institute of Town Planners, India.* Jan.-April 1963. Vol. 33-34.

SILIGURI PLANNING ORGANISATION. Interim development plan for Siliguri. 1965. Printed. 54p. Maps, diagrs. Bd. Rs.20/-.

SINGH, M. M. Municipal government in the Calcutta Metropolitan District: a preliminary survey. I.P.A., New York. 1963. Printed. 44p. Diagrs. Bd.

SINGH, M. M. and A. DATTA. Metropolitan Calcutta: special agencies for housing, planning and development. I.P.A., New York. 1963. Mimeo. 171p. Bd.

SINGH, M. M. and A. DATTA. Passenger transport agencies in metropolitan Calcutta. I.P.A., New York. 1964. Mimeo. 125p. Tabs. Bd.

SIVARAMAKRISHNAN, K. C. Planning for a resource region—A case study— 1968. Mimeo. 25p. Maps, tabs. Unbd.

SIVARAMAKRISHNAN, K. C. Durgapur as a new town. Nov. 1966. Mimeo. 14p. Unbd. (Paper submitted to the 15th Town and Country Planning Seminar.)

TAYLOR, J. L. Analysis and projection of urban population, Bihar. Aug. 1967. Mimeo. 23p. Tabs. Unbd.
TRAFFIC SECTION, CMPO. Recommendations for short term actions relating to traffic and transportation activities in the Calcutta Metropolitan District. March 1964. Mimeo. 36p. Unbd.
TRAFFIC SECTION, CMPO. Travel analyses and projection procedures. Draft. Sept. 1965. Mimeo. 17p. Illus. Unbd.
TYSEN, F. J. District administration in metropolitan Calcutta. I.P.A., New York. 1964. Printed. 53p. Diagrs. Bd.
VAN HUYCK, A. P. Economics of urban renewal. May 1964. Mimeo. 19p. Unbd.
VAN HUYCK, A. P. The role of urban renewal in India: with special reference to Calcutta. Mimeo. 36p. Unbd. (Prepared for IULA Conference, Belgrade, June 1965.)
VAN HUYCK, A. P. and G. T. KINGSLEY. Interim report: housing—Calcutta Metropolitan District. 1967. Mimeo. 67p. Bd.
VAN HUYCK, A. P. and K. C. ROSSER. An environmental approach to low-income housing. *Ekistics,* Jan. 1967. Vol. 23, No. 134.
VINCENZ, J. L. Report on the modernisation of refuse handling in Calcutta. Nov. 1962. Mimeo. 78p. Unbd.
VICKREY, W. Economising in the use of electric power by suburban trains. Jan. 1963. Mimeo. 5p. Unbd.
WELLISZ, S. Report on the economic effects of the ban on slow-moving traffic in the bara bazar area. July 1962. Mimeo. 8p. Unbd.
WELLISZ, S. The economics of housing developments. Oct. 1962. Mimeo. 21p. Unbd.
WELLISZ, S. A housing program for the Calcutta Metropolitan District: interim general plan 1. 1963. Mimeo. 11p. Unbd.
WELLISZ, S. India's slum clearance policy. An economic evaluation. 1963. Mimeo. 14p. Unbd.
WELLISZ, S. The control of urban rents in West Bengal. April 1963. Mimeo. 11p. Unbd.
WILBUR SMITH and ASSOCIATES. Hooghly River Crossing study: a report to the Calcutta Metropolitan Planning Organisation. Sept. 1964. Mimeo. 42p. Illus., appendices. Bd.
WOOD, ELIZABETH. A preliminary note of a proposed social management program for the multi-purpose center in Manicktala. 1962. Mimeo. 4p. Unbd.
WOOD, ELIZABETH. Preliminary notes on housing legislation applicable to the Calcutta Plan. March 1962. Mimeo. 38p. Unbd.
WOOD, ELIZABETH and M. KAPLAN. Preliminary notes on legislation for urban development. 1963. Mimeo. 13p. Unbd.

CHAPTER 6

Ian Burton and T. R. Lee

WATER SUPPLY AND ECONOMIC DEVELOPMENT:
The Scale and Timing of Investment

Defining the Problem

Water is a peculiar commodity but nonetheless a commodity, and like all commodities, subject to rules of supply and demand. The position of water as a vital fluid essential for the existence of man and society obscures its larger role as an economic commodity. Unfortunately, the discussion of the development of the water resource too often assumes emotional overtones stemming from its elemental role in human life. Such an attitude can be perceived lurking within the policy adopted towards the provision of water supplies in underdeveloped countries. There is no doubt that these countries have a universal need for new and improved water supply systems. Urban water supply is undeniably a necessary part of the infrastructure required to attain the goal of social and economic development, the raising of the level of living. But, there is also a need for an evaluation of the nature of the role of urban water supplies in the development process and of the priority which should be given them amongst the multitude of necessary services and activities the underdeveloped countries so critically lack.

Ostensibly, the present policy adopted towards urban water supply is predicated upon the recognition of the role of a safe water supply in controlling the occurrence of certain diseases. The waste and human misery caused by such diseases as cholera, typhoid, and dysentery does not, however, excuse the water supply planner from the responsibility of establishing the extent of the need for water supply. It is not enough to accept that a safe water supply is a good thing.

Authors' Note: An earlier version of this paper was presented at a World Health Organization Inter-Regional Seminar on Integration of Community Water Supplies Into Planning of Economic Development, held in Geneva, September 19-28, 1967 (CWS/WP/67.8). The views expressed in this revised version are the responsibility of the authors alone.

If urban water supplies are to play their optimum role in the development process, changes in the demand for water as economic growth proceeds and per capita incomes rise must be understood. Patterns of water use and demand will alter as a society moves from being predominantely rural to more urban, and from smaller to larger cities, as well as with improvements in housing and increases in income.

There are a number of investment programs in public water supply. These include the Community Water Supply Program of the World Health Organization, bilateral aid programs in which a developed country aids a developing country directly, and the independent efforts of the developing countries themselves. While it is not possible to estimate accurately the total world expenditure on community water supplies for developing countries, limited evidence suggests that on a global basis, expenditures are low in relation to most definitions and estimates of need, and are probably not keeping pace with the growth of the population to be served. This state of affairs persists, even though international agencies report that funds are available if sound and "bankable" projects can be found. Estimates of investment in community water supply from all sources would serve as a guide to policy formulation. These should be compared with up-to-date estimates of need, and of population now served.

It is perhaps fair to say, in the absence of very precise information, that the view that we are failing to grapple with the problem on a sufficiently large scale is mainly expressed by community water supply engineers and public health officials. An outsider might be excused, therefore, for attempting a more skeptical scrutiny on the problem and for asking to what extent more piped water supplies are really needed. There is no doubt that modern piped water supply systems will eventually have to be built for all cities in the developing countries. What is in question is the scale on which systems should be built in the next decade or so, and the strategy of timing investment in community water supply in relation to the expanding economies of the countries themselves.

In theory, benefit-cost analysis might be used to show the extent of social benefits in relation to costs of public water supply systems. Where social benefits are found to outweigh costs by a substantial margin, governments and international agencies should have greater confidence in deciding to invest. The benefits of community water supply in economic terms may be either in promoting economic development and a rapid rate of growth, or in improving the welfare of the citizens. Both economic development and improved social welfare are high on the lists of priorities of the developing countries.

Experience with the benefit-cost analysis in the developed nations is not encouraging. Even in such fields as hydroelectric power development, flood control, and navigation, great difficulties have been encountered in attempting to reach agreement on estimated benefits. These difficulties are likely to be compounded in the developing countries and in relation to public health where the benefits are of a less tangible kind. Some studies have been made in developing countries which have shown very favorable benefit-cost ratios. In

Venezuela, for example, the total annual benefits to be expected from the provision of public water supplies in rural areas were estimated at 170 million bolivars, while the total annual cost was estimated at only 22 million bolivars, a ratio of over 7 to 1. The high benefits were based mainly on an estimate of 75 percent of the value earnings lost due to premature deaths. In another study in Puerto Rico, the benefit-cost ratio was found to be much smaller, although the major component again turned out to be the mortality benefit.

Continuing and intensified efforts are needed to improve techniques of measuring the benefits from community water supply in developing countries, but the problem is likely to remain with us for some time without very satisfactory solutions being reached.

A partial list of benefits for community water supply projects has been given by John Logan,[1] as follows:

(1) Health:
    (a) Basic physiologic need for water;
    (b) Reduction in costs of medical care;
    (c) Increased efficiency in human-energy utilization due to reduction in illness and debility;
    (d) Reduction in time losses due to illness;
    (e) Increased manpower availability.

(2) Economic development:
    (a) Attraction and growth of commerce and industry;
    (b) Contributions to production efficiency;
    (c) Tourism;
    (d) Improved food production.

(3) Public cleansing;

(4) Fire protection;

(5) Savings in cost and time over use of primitive water supply facilities;

(6) Encouragement of stable urban development;

(7) Increase in property values.

To these benefits, most of which could be approximately measured, can be added a range of other intangible benefits such as improvement in receptivity to new ideas and a faster learning rate by healthier students, a higher standard of public morale, perhaps contributing to greater political stability, and the incentive effect of the promise or realization of an improved standard of living.

It may be assumed that all these benefits do contribute in a direct or indirect way to economic development. The dialectic of community water supply engineers and public health officials tends to emphasize this view by ascribing to water supply a necessary role in economic development. Thus John Logan states: "It can be argued that, if health is fundamental to development, water supply is fundamental to health, and therefore water is a key to development."[2] Similarly, Abraham Horowitz is quoted as saying,

> If a single program were chosen which would have the maximum health benefit, which would rapidly stimulate social and economic development, and which would materially improve the standard of living of the people, that program would be water supply with provision for water running into or adjacent to the house.[3]

Such statements are even translated into an either/or choice, particularly in political speeches. The problem becomes transformed into the issue as to whether health is something which must first be earned by economic development, or if rather it is not a prerequisite without which economic development is impossible. The framers of such dichotomous choices intend to leave us no choice—we are clearly meant to choose health first. "Health first and economic development later" is quite misleading, however. The real issue is rather one of quantity—how much health can we afford at each stage of economic development? Or, how much health is really a necessary prerequisite for economic development? Such questions raise fundamental issues of choice. We all recognize that India could spend more money on the health of its population and less on steel production or running a national airline or building dams. But we do not really know what the returns would be from an additional rupee spent in any one of these areas. In the absence of a comparative and operational economic technique for measuring the marginal return to investment in all these and other areas, our decision makers must make value judgments in the light of what they think the people want and what they think will be best for the country in the long run (sometimes irrespective of what people want now). We all acknowledge the right of societies to make choices for themselves in these matters. The Americans have a high rate of per capita ownership of automobiles because evidently that is what people want, or, as Kenneth Galbraith would say, are persuaded by advertising that they want. On the other hand, automobile ownership is much lower in the Soviet Union, but they do have more doctors and more hospital beds per capita than the Americans.

The decision making problem faced by the developing countries, therefore, is primarily one of priorities, and this is related strongly to a value judgment about the type of society they wish to build. The choices can be clarified and exercised more effectively, however, if there is a clear understanding of their consequences. While it is often not possible to ascribe a precise quantitative or monetary value to particular choices, the consequences can often be described qualitatively in general terms. An improved benefit-cost analysis would help in formulating decisions by reducing still further the areas in which choice has to be exercised with a very hazy knowledge of the likely outcomes.

In the absence of a reliable and operational economic technique ready for immediate use in evaluating investment in community water supply, there are three things that might be done. The first is to search the economic development literature for theoretical guidelines about the level and timing of investments in community water supplies. The second is to ask what happened to community water supply investment in the developed countries at a comparable stage in their evolution, and what possible relevance this might have; and, thirdly, to examine the actual situation among the developing countries in terms of level of supply and level of development.

Economic Development and Social Overhead Capital

A water supply system is part of that category of economic activities subsumed under the heading of the social infrastructure, or social overhead capital. These are activities which in themselves are not directly productive but are the necessary basis for the successful growth of productive activities. The term "social overhead capital" is normally applied to such disparate categories as education, electricity, the transportation system, health services, systems of administration, as well as to various aspects of water development, among which urban water supplies are only a part. Attitudes towards the place of social overhead capital in the economic growth process vary considerably. The need for social overhead facilities is one which cannot be disputed, but debates on their importance leave room for considerable doubt and uncertainty.

A number of questions have been raised about the level of investment that should be made in social overhead or infrastructure facilities. The breakdown of gross fixed investment in an advanced economy as estimated by Lewis is shown in Table 1.

Social overhead investment, including housing, commonly accounts for over half the total of all investment. This is so in an advanced economy with a large existing stock of social overhead capital. In an underdeveloped economy, this stock does not exist and one might expect a policy of heavy initial investment in the social infrastructure.

There is reason to believe that the proportion (of social overhead investment) is particularly high in the first decades of development and declines thereafter. This is because initial development calls for the establishment of a framework of utilities, and though it is necessary to spend money on maintaining and improving and extending the framework, it is possible that these later expenditures are relatively not so heavy as those which have initially to be made.[4]

Such investment is characterized by a lengthy gestation lag between the

Table 1. Gross Fixed Investment in an Advanced Economy

Sector	Percentage of Total
Housing	25
Public Works and Utilities	30
Manufacturing and Agriculture	30
Other Commercial	10

Source: W. Arthur Lewis, *Theory of Economic Growth.* London: Unwin, 1955, p. 210.

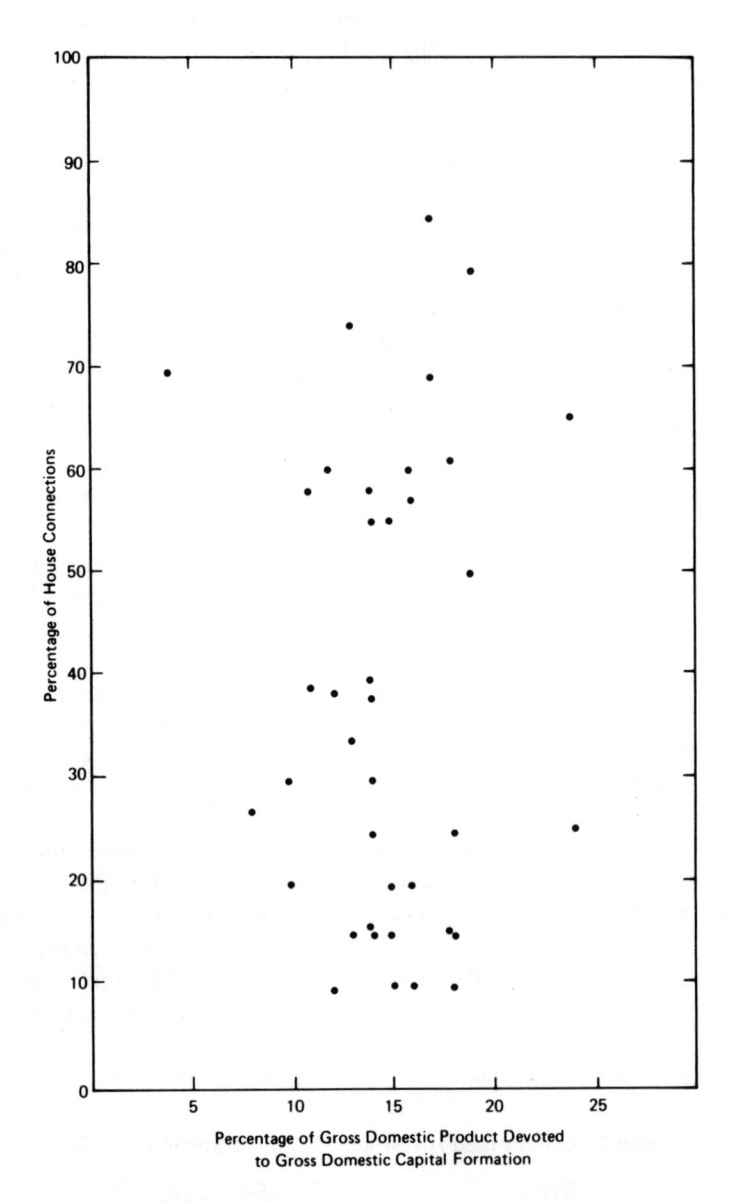

Figure 1. Percentage of Gross Domestic Product Devoted to Gross Domestic Capital Formation and Percentage of Urban Population with House Connections (n = 39; r = 0.259)

Source: United Nations, Yearbook of National Account Statistics, 1963 (New York: United Nations, 1964); United Nations, Statistical Yearbook 1963 (New York: United Nations, 1964).

original investment and the beginning of a return. The very nature of the activities undertaken accounts for this lag. It is most marked in education but holds for all types of social overhead investment. The contribution of these activities is, in addition, very dependent upon the development of the related productive activities. Investment in social overhead facilities is largely made in the public sector due to these long gestation periods and the size of the individual projects. In India, public investment in this sector accounted for 88 percent of the total in the period 1951 to 1960.[5] Investment in water supply is normally entirely within the public sector in all countries.

In the West the development of urban water supplies showed what can be described as a permissive sequence—permissive in the sense that the expansions to the systems were made with little attempt to evaluate the benefits to be gained from an increased consumption of water. Water for domestic supply was, and still is to a very large extent, not treated as an economic commodity. Such an approach is in every case of doubtful validity or wisdom but is particularly so in the underdeveloped countries with their shortages of capital and high rates of return on investments.

There is a strong priority basis, therefore, for the argument that the expansion of water supply facilities will be closer to an optimum rate if the amount of water supplied is kept at a level sufficient for the prevention of waterborne diseases. This argument is found in the economic development literature; Hirschman stresses that social overhead capital investment is largely facilitative, and directly productive, and has agreed that it might be better to allow a shortage of overhead capacity. Where a shortage is experienced,

> it is bound to lead to attempts to remedy it on the part of those who suffer from it or who stand to gain from its elimination. In situations where motivations are deficient it therefore seems safer to rely on development via shortage than on development via excess capacity. In other words, if we endow an underdeveloped country with a first-class highway network, with extensive hydro-electric and perhaps irrigation facilities, can we be certain that industrial and agricultural activity will expand in the wake of these improvements? Would it not be less risky and more economical first to make sure of such activity, even though it may have to be subsidized in view of the absence of adequate transportation and power, and then let the ensuing pressures determine the appropriate outlays for SOC and its location? As examples of this type of sequence, one may cite the development of Japan, Turkey and, to a considerable extent, of the U.S.S.R.[6]

It is not surprising, given the differences of opinion amongst economists about the role of social overhead capital investment, that no significant relationship appears between the percentage of the gross domestic product devoted to gross domestic capital formation and percentage of urban population with house connections (Figure 1). The data used are very crude but they do suggest that the high priority accorded water supply has not resulted in a high provision of supply systems.

Experience Among the Developed Nations

The analogy between past events in developed countries and the developing world today is weak because the situations differ markedly in several respects. Foremost among these are the facts that population growth in those nations which transformed their economies early was not generally so rapid as it is in many developing countries today, and that the improvements in public health and hygiene were introduced incrementally as they became known, whereas today, the developing countries have the benefit of all modern medical knowledge and only lack the funds and trained personnel to apply it fully. One consequence of this situation is the urge in many developing countries to attain present standards of the developed countries immediately, including present design standards. The first nations to develop, having no such models to follow, were able to make progress deliberately, but without widespread pressures for the attainment of (present) high standards at once.

Also, in a sense Hirschman's "development by shortage" is a closer approximation to what took place in the developed countries than "development by excess capacity." In proposing Western standards and levels for the developing countries, it is often asserted that provision of safe and adequate amounts of potable water in Western cities resulted in dramatic improvements of public health, and that it is necessary to do the same in the cities of the developing world today. While there is no question that waterborne diseases are a significant factor in public health, it is also clear that they are not the only factor. There are many other disease factors, including flies, human artifacts, and people themselves. The elimination of water as a source of disease may be a necessary condition for improvement of public health, but it is not a sufficient condition. As long as sewage collection systems are inadequate, and as long as food remains exposed and habits of personal hygiene remain unchanged, then disease will continue to be spread, no matter how good the water supply.

While it is true that these conditions were also obtained in many cities of the developed world, two factors are different. First, other environmental conditions were improved at the same time as water supply, whereas in the developing countries there is a strong impetus to improve water supply conditions quickly and to let other improvements follow. Second, the tropical climate of many of the cities in the developing countries is more conducive to the spread of disease by non-water vectors than is the climate in more temperate latitudes. It is by no means safe, therefore, to assume that equivalent improvements in water supply will produce equivalent improvements in public health. The climatic and environmental differences strengthen the case for caution in the avoidance of over-investment in community water supplies on the basis of assumed public health benefits. These may not be realized unless the water supply program is accompanied by improvements in other aspects of the environment, and by changing patterns of behavior.

Non-economic Criteria

Would it then follow that the developing countries should make no effort to provide public water supplies? There may be those who would support such a view. There are perhaps two reasons for opposing it. One is that unless water is publicly supplied in some cases at least, and on some occasions, people may not be able to obtain the minimal quantity of water for survival. When people are starving to death, we do not usually ask what the benefits are of giving them enough food to stay alive—rather we do what we can to provide the minimal food requirements. Insofar as a community water supply system constitutes a safeguard against drought, or the destruction of a community by fire, it may be justified on non-economic grounds or without resort to economic arguments. Clearly, however, the amount of water that needs to be supplied to permit survival is very small and will not normally require a piped system. Distribution by truck could be relied upon to meet this need.

A second argument is based on welfare considerations. It merely states that no country is so poor that it cannot provide its citizens with some welfare or some social services. Every country recognizes the need to provide roads, electric power, hospitals, schools, and water. The question is rather how much of each and of what kind? Where economic criteria are not available to give answers to this question, there are four other alternative ways of arriving at an answer. These may be categorized as (1) experienced judgment and rules of thumb; (2) strict financial criteria; (3) popular demands; and (4) minimal standards. At the present time the first three of these criteria are all used to some extent in some places. The fourth is as yet little used.

(1) Experienced Judgment: This type of criterion is most widely used in the engineering aspects of community water supply. When pushed to explain the reasons behind engineering design choices, the professional sanitary engineers responsible often talk about "sound engineering judgment and experience." Undoubtedly this is an important criterion. The major drawback of this approach is that it tends to become quickly codified into strict and arbitrary rules which are followed faithfully and often unquestioningly by other engineers who come after and who may be less gifted or more overworked. The rules then tend to become embodied so deeply in institutional practice that they become obstacles to change and continue to be applied in inappropriate situations.

(2) Financial Criteria: Under the conditions of great capital shortage which prevail in the developing countries, there is a case to be made for the argument that community water supplies should only be provided up to the ability of the community to pay. This "banker's approach" to the problem, superficially at least, offers promise of a sound and workable criterion. The challenge is to demonstrate that the system can be operated effectively and that revenues can

be collected in sufficient quantity to cover operating and maintainance costs and pay off the capital debt, including service charges. Its weakness is that it demands too much too soon at a low level of economic development. Such a policy is all right for the middle income countries of Southern Europe, or parts of Latin America, but for the majority of underdeveloped countries it imposes an insuperable obstacle. It is not surprising, therefore, that developing countries do not strictly enforce financial criteria for investment in water supply systems. It is recognized that the financial return on the investment may be long delayed even though considerable social benefits may accrue in the meantime. The external financial agencies, however, both international and unilateral, are wont to insist on sound financial status of a project before making an investment loan. This is, of course, perfectly reasonable from a banking standpoint. It goes a long way towards explaining why investment in community water supply projects with the help of external support has remained very small in most of the developing countries, and has been concentrated in the "middle income" countries.[7]

(3) Popular Demands: Another way to allocate limited financial resources in social overhead capital is to follow Hirschman's advice and seek "development via shortage." According to this philosophy, money would be expended in those areas where need was proven, rather than in advance of need. A danger of this method for community water supply is that the ill effects of inadequate water supply (ill health and higher death rates) may not be ascribed by the population to the water problem. On the other hand, there is evidence to show that where popular demands are respected, a high priority is given to community water supply among other environmental improvements. In interviews with bustee dwellers in Calcutta, for example, one of the authors found that water supply improvement was the first-choice improvement for a majority of the population over alternative improvements in drainage, street paving, lighting, and even housing space.[8] There are indications that Calcuttans are not alone in their assignment of a high priority to water supply.

The indications of popular choice are therefore on the side of a high priority for community water supply. Since water supply is evidently highly desired by the population, and since it can be supplied relatively cheaply compared with other social services, there appears to be a strong political argument for according some level of community water supply a high priority in social overhead capital investment.

(4) Minimal Standards: The criterion of popular demand points to some provision of community water supply. The criterion of experienced judgments leads to a warning to avoid over-investment and the results of applying strict financial criteria suggest that this method will have to be modified if much investment is to take place. In view of these cautions and in view of the absence of other economic guides to the level of investment, an answer seems to lie in

the direction of making investments subject to the requirement that they be at a minimum level commensurate with the attainment of the task they are intended to perform. In other words, community water supply systems should be designed so that they operate effectively at the lowest possible cost that makes possible an acceptable level of improvement in public health. All other investment should be regarded as luxurious frills to be delayed until a later time. The crucial question that emerges from this conclusion is, What level and type of community water supply can be designed to meet the minimal standard criteria proposed? Before considering this issue, an examination of current practice as indicated by some aggregate statistics seems necessary.

THE CURRENT SITUATION

To what extent are community water supply systems regarded as a prerequisite for economic growth and to what extent are they regarded as a consequence of economic growth? Accepting the conclusion previously reached that a minimal amount of water should be provided as a social service, and that beyond such a level it should be regarded as a public utility, we may examine existing policy on the basis of the relationship between the level of per capita gross national product and the per capita level of water consumption. The former is taken to be an indicator of the level of economic development. The authors recognize the comments that are being raised about such a simplistic measure of a very complex phenomenon.

It is possible to postulate a relationship between GNP per capita and investment in water supplies as shown by the theoretical curve in Figure 2. The curve shows three phases of the relationship.

Phase I represents the period in which water supplies are needed for public health requirements and as a minimal social service. In this phase there is urgent need for urban water supplies, and it may be expected that investment levels would be high. This corresponds to the period of high initial investment in social overhead capital that development economists generally agree is a prerequisite for growth.

Then follows Phase II in which minimal public health and social service needs have been met, and there is a transfer over to treating water supply as a public utility subject to strict financial criteria. In this phase per capita income would be expected to rise while investment in water supply would be stable in absolute terms, and would fall as a percentage of GNP. During Phase II, additional and extended systems would be made highly dependent on ability to pay and collect, and to administer and manage the system. This phase would correspond to the Hirschman strategy of "development by shortage." Water would not be supplied as a free or subsidized commodity.

Phase II is likely to be prolonged, but it is eventually terminated when the society has accumulated a greater basis of wealth. Per capita income is now much higher, and without any change in policy more water will be demanded by

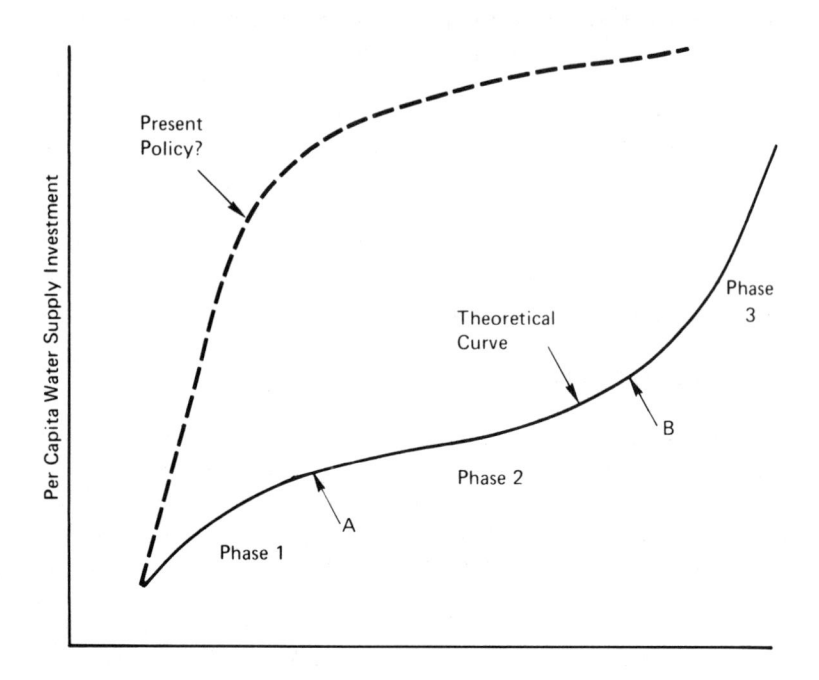

Figure 2. Per Capita Water Supply Investment and Per Capita Gross National Product

the population at a higher price for non-productive purposes. Phase III thus presents a level of investment now found among the highly industrialized nations.[9]

There is some evidence to suggest that the pattern of investment has not been following the theoretical curve in Figure 2, but in some countries has approximated the curve marked "Present Policy." A higher level of investment has been attained than might appear necessary from the previous discussion. This probably arises from an eagerness in the developing countries to attain advanced standards as quickly as possible; from the use of experience, rules of thumb, and sound engineering judgment as developed and used in the more developed countries; and from a public health concern to ensure that absolutely all hazards to public health are removed from community water supplies. Such policies are advocated by public health officials and sanitary engineers, and where applied can lead to over-investment in community water supply and a misallocation of resources. On the other hand, those countries that are in the Phase I period might find themselves subjected to strict financial requirements that they cannot meet, and even minimal supplies might be neglected.

These differences between countries might also be found between cities within one country where some regions have lagged behind others in pace of development. The statistical evidence to support this point of view is not very

Water Supply and Economic Development

strong, due mainly to data deficiencies. There are no readily available data on investment in community water supplies in developing countries. It is, therefore, necessary to find surrogate measures. One of these might be per capita water consumption.

Figure 3 shows an almost random scatter of per capita consumption levels in relation to GNP per capita. It demonstrates that a wide variety of levels of per capita consumption are found at essentially similar levels of income. There are, however, a lot of deficiencies in the data. To name a few of them, the observation of consumption are for urban supply systems, whereas the GNP data are for whole countries; some observations distinguish between domestic and total use, while others do not; some figures include industrial water use, others do not; many observations are estimates of total amount supplied, divided by population served, and are not based on metering; the percentage of water loss is not uniform, and is not accounted for; there is a bias towards countries with a dry climate; and the data do not show how the water is consumed and how much is supplied through house connections.

There appear however to be two quite distinct groups of consumers of water, those with house connections and those with access only to street supplies of differing sorts. Detailed studies of patterns of water demand in developing countries show that the demand for residential water supply is a function of accessibility to water, housing conditions, the level of income, and water using habits.[10] Accessibility to water appears to be the most significant factor

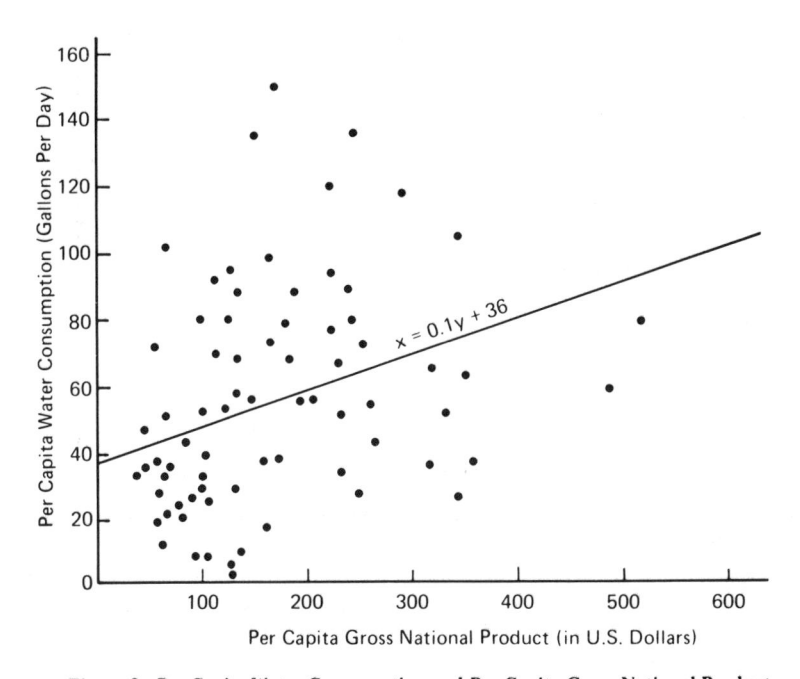

Figure 3. Per Capita Water Consumption and Per Capita Gross National Product

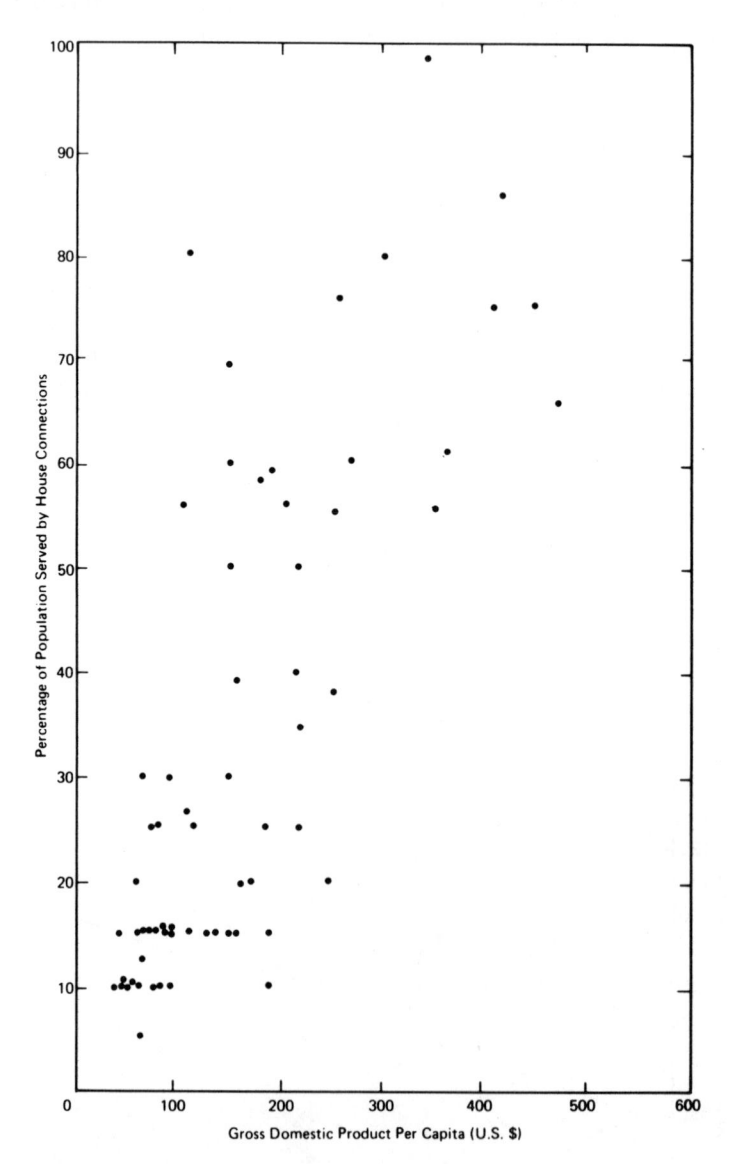

Figure 4. Percentage of Urban Population with House Connections and Gross Domestic Product Per Capita (U.S.$)

Source: United Nations, Yearbook of National Account Statistics, 1963 (New York: 1964). B. H. Dieterich & J. M. Henderson, Urban Water Supply Conditions and Needs in 75 Developing Countries, Public Health Paper No. 23 (Geneva: W.H.O., 1963).

influencing the level of water consumption. There remains, however, a large range in the per capita level of consumption within the two basic groups of households. The demand for water is far from constant even within households with a kitchen, bathroom, and flush toilet.

If it can be established that access to piped supplies meets the minimum public health standard, then it can be argued that this should be done on a free basis. This would correspond to Phase I of the curve of Figure 2. Further expansion by the provision of house connections would be made strictly dependent on financial criteria or the ability to pay and collect.

Such a strategy of the timing and scale of investment in community water supply raises several further problems. How many street taps or standpipes are needed in relation to population, to ensure that contamination of water supplies does not occur, or rarely occurs, between the source and its point of use? What is the relationship between distance to standpipe and per capita use? Can the rate at which house connections will be demanded be forecast accurately, and allowed for in design?

It is claimed that only by bringing the water supply directly into the house or courtyard can all contamination be avoided. What level of risk remains to public health when all urban populations have access to street supplies and can this risk be kept to an acceptable level? The future rate at which house connections will be demanded is important for system design. Small diameter pipe along a street intended to supply street taps, might quickly have its capacity exceeded, if house connections become common. Figure 4 provides an approximate guide, and for particular cities estimates might be improved on the basis of local forecasts of rise in income level. Even if more applications for house connections were received than could be provided, however, the deficiency would be less severe than where urban populations have no access to piped supplies. Development via shortage would operate and those desirous of having house connections would be asked to pay at a rate sufficient to cover the long-term marginal cost of water supply, and not simply the cost of installing a new house connection. This might also be an appropriate point at which to install meters and charge for the amount used.

Such a system would subsidize water use by those having access to street supplies only, and it would place a heavier cost on those with house connections. In so doing, the policy would recognize two distinct kinds of water supply. First, water supply as a public service for social welfare reasons and to obtain most of the public health benefits that contribute to economic development, and second, water supply as a public utility to be supplied through house connections as and when it can be afforded on the basis of long-term marginal cost pricing.

If water supply is accorded a high priority in the developing countries, and if systems are built, as appears to be the case, irrespective of the rate of saving, then the danger of over-investment is further substantiated. Such a conclusion is borne out by Figure 5. The highest correlation that we have been able to find with percentage of population served by house connections is the percentage of

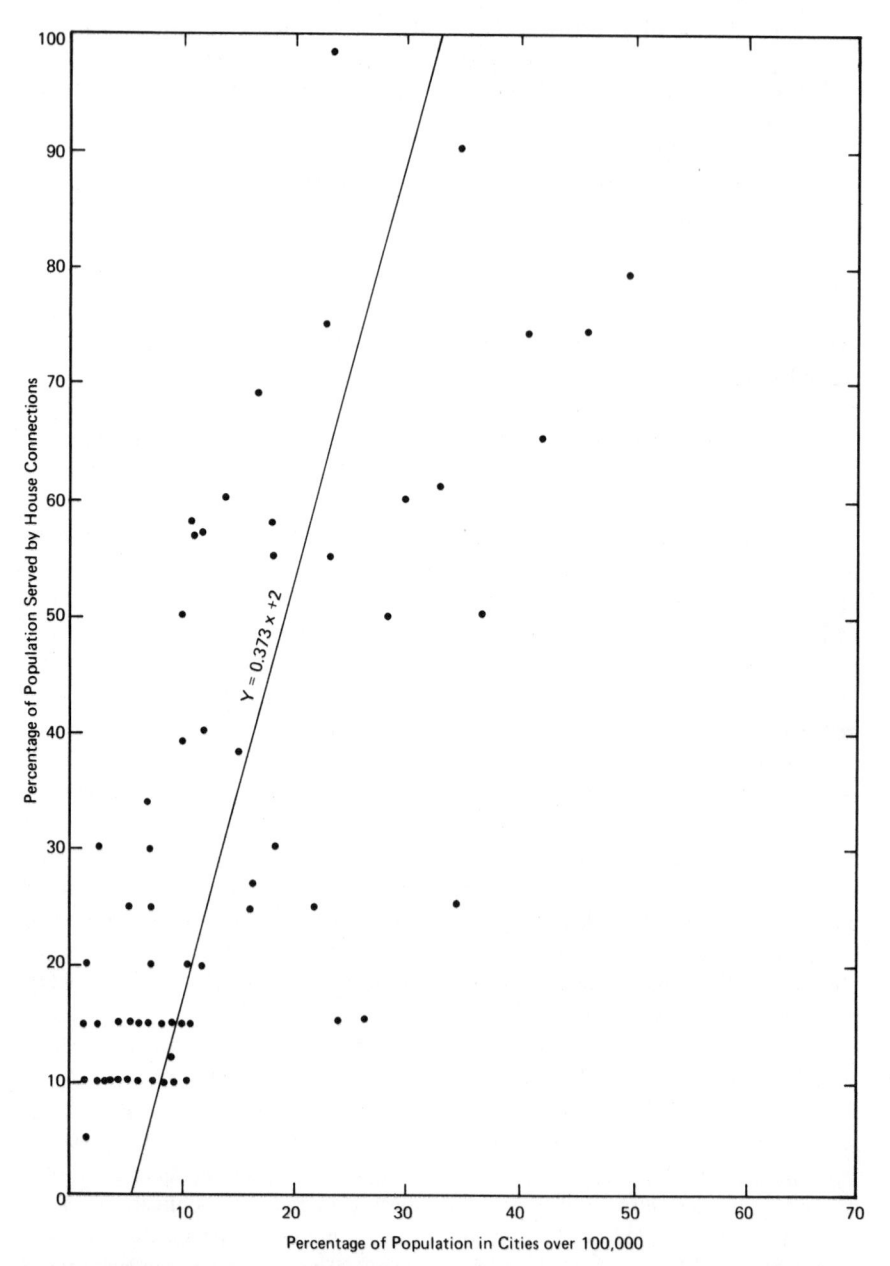

Figure 5. Percentage of Urban Population with House Connections and Percentage of Population Living in Towns of 100,000 and Over (n = 72; r = 0.752)

Source: United Nations, Demographic Yearbook, 1964 (New York: United Nations, 1965).
B. H. Dieterich and J. M. Henderson, Urban Water Supply Conditions and Needs in 75 Developing Countries, Public Health Paper No. 23 (Geneva: W.H.O., 1963).

population in cities of over 100,000. In other words, if you want to know what the water supply conditions are like in any given country, the best predictive variable is neither the level of national income, nor the rate of saving, but simply the degree of urbanization.

Are these findings equally applicable to all social overhead investments? Some evidence to the contrary is provided in Figure 6. Electricity generation shows a more direct relationship to gross domestic product per capita than provision of water supplies. It thus appears that new electricity generating capacity grows step by step in keeping with increasing GDP per capita. That water supply does not follow such a pattern is indicative of the recognition of water as a priority public service. However, electricity is paid for by amount used, whereas this is rarely the case with water. A danger to be avoided in public water supply systems, therefore, is letting the public service argument proceed beyond the criterion of minimal supply.

A NEW STRATEGY FOR COMMUNITY WATER SUPPLY IN DEVELOPING COUNTRIES

This paper has attempted to present a case for viewing community water supply in a distinctive way. It has been suggested that the relationship between the level of water consumption and living conditions is such as to suggest that large increases in water consumption can be expected only with a general improvement in the living environment. This close connection between the level of consumption and living conditions suggest that if water supply is planned in isolation from the wider effort to raise the level of urban housing conditions then serious benefit allocation problems will arise.

The raising of urban living conditions is tied very closely to progress in overall economic development. The existing low level of the living environment is a reflection of the economic poverty of the society. The dramatic repercussion of poor living conditions on the widespread occurrence of certain diseases may have to be accepted until the productive level of the economy is raised. Specifically, in the planning of water supply systems the emphasis should be placed on providing a skeletal but widespread system rather than attempting to raise levels of supply. The tendency of existing policy is the reverse in that standards are too often set rather arbitrarily based upon Western experience and the system designed around these standards.

If this new approach to system design is to be instituted, we need more precise estimates of the level of consumption from public standpipes. We also need estimates of the effect on standpipe consumption of such variables as frequency of standpipes, or number of people served per tap, standard of housing or density of occupancy and level of income, education and family size. It is also necessary to know the relationship between disease incidence and type of water supply. In particular, studies are needed to find ways of achieving substantial improvements in public health by reliance on public street taps only.

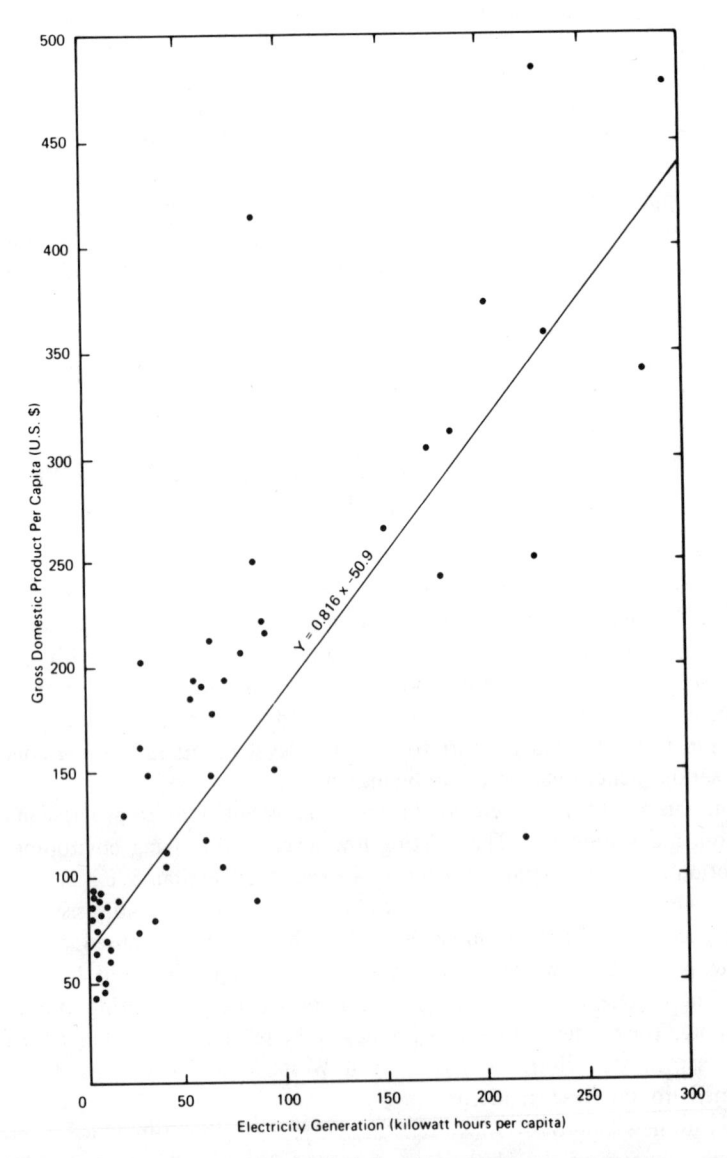

Figure 6. Gross Domestic Product Per Capita (U.S. $) and Electricity Generation Per Capita (Kilowatt Hours) (n = 56; r = 0.823)

Source: United Nations, Yearbook of National Account Statistics (New York: United Nations, 1964). United Nations, Statistical Yearbook, 1957 (New York: United Nations, 1958).

Water Supply and Economic Development

Can an acceptable standard of public health for developing countries be attained without or with very few house connections? This is a crucial question. If an affirmative answer can be found, then the public health benefit from community water supply and their contribution to economic development can be obtained at minimal cost and without resort to the construction of a large-scale expensive Western type system.

The importance of income and living conditions in influencing the level of water consumption accords with the hypothesis that the need for residential water supply varies with the level of economic development. It suggests that the planning of water supply systems should stress the widest coverage of the population rather than the raising of levels of consumption. There is the possibility of over-investment in water supply if the emphasis is placed on raising levels of consumption. The demand for water must be given an important place in the planning of water supply systems. A lower level of supply could lead to a higher level of total welfare. If this line of thinking is correct, then there are severe deficiencies in the present arrangements for financing community water supplies on international or bilateral bases. Frequently these arrangements require financial soundness as a basis for investment. This criterion should be removed when water supply as a social service is under consideration and replaced by a social and economic soundness criterion.

Since present institutional arrangements do not permit this, present institutional arrangements need to be changed, or at least supplemented with other arrangements. In practice, this probably means that new loan funds are required from individual countries, or from international agencies or groups of countries on a long-term, low interest rate basis. In offering such loans, the strict financial criteria of ability to pay and ability to collect would not be applied. Rather, the key questions would relate to the effectiveness of the systems designed in relation to their costs and to the proviso that they are minimal systems. Considerably more thought needs to be given to the design of minimal systems. This would be a useful exercise for the developing countries to attempt in relation to their own expenditures, and it might help set a pattern that external financing agencies might be persuaded to follow.

For community water supply of the public utility sort, beyond the level of social service, the present arrangements and criterion of strict financial viability still suffice. Under such arrangements, not a lot of construction seems likely in the next decade, but this is of lesser importance, provided strong efforts are underway to ensure that all urban populations in developing countries have access to piped supplies from street taps. One possibility is that the two kinds of financing could be tied together. For example, an external aid agency might come to a long-term agreement with a developing country whereby an initial loan would be made on very "soft" terms for a minimal community water supply system. The agreement might also provide that a fuller "hard" loan would be made for improvements of a public utility kind and that these would be priced at such a level as to pay off both loans. At the present time, some urban populations are being denied access to public supplies of water because there is insufficient demand for house connections. In the future, the growth in numbers of house connections could be more heavily used to help pay for the system which supplies people through standpipes. But in many cases, this cannot be done immediately. The provision of water supply as a social service should have priority over the provision of a public utility.

Recent studies of the water supply industry in developed countries have demonstrated that it has often been run on unsound financial and economic grounds, which may have resulted in a misallocation of resources.[11] Policies are now under critical review, and are likely to be reshaped in the near future. Let us not make the mistake, however, of assuming that the latest ideas in the developed countries are automatically appropriate in the developing countries. There is a great temptation among experts to advocate the latest ideas in the latest terminology. In attempting to devise a policy for community water supply in the developing countries, it may be a good time to be a little old fashioned.

NOTES

1. John Logan, "The International Municipal Water Supply Program: A Health and Economic Appraisal," *American Journal of Tropical Medicine and Hygiene*, IX, No. 5 (September 1960), pp. 469-476.
2. *Ibid.*
3. Abraham Horowitz, as quoted by A. Wolman and H. M. Bosch in "U.S. Water Supply Lessons Applicable to Developing Countries," *Journal of the American Water Works Association*, Vol. 55, No. 8 (August 1963), p. 954.
4. W. Arthur Lewis, *Theory of Economic Growth*. London: Unwin, 1955, p. 22.
5. J. M. Healey, *The Development of Social Overhead Capital in India, 1950-60*. Bombay: Oxford University Press, 1965, p. 11. Healey only includes power, transportation, and communications in his definition of social overhead capital: with the wider definition taken here the proportion of public investment would be higher.
6. Albert O. Hirschman, *The Strategy of Economic Development*. New Haven, Connecticut, and London: Yale University Press, 1966, pp. 93-94.
7. In a recent World Bank progress report on water supply and sewage investment only 16 percent of the funds allocated in 1962-71 were to "poor" countries. "World Bank Water Supply and Sewage," Sector Working Paper. Washington, D.C.: October 1971, p. 14.
8. T. R. Lee, Residential Water Demand and Economic Development, University of Toronto, Department of Geography, Research Publication No. 2. Toronto: University of Toronto Press, 1969, pp. 92-118.
9. This argument is elaborated in Lee, *ibid.*, pp. 19-37.
10. See T. R. Lee, "Residential Water Demand and Economic Development," paper presented at Association of American Geographers Conference, September 1968; and Gilbert F. White, David J. Bradley, and Anne U. White, *Drawers of Water: Domestic Water Use in East Africa*. Chicago: University of Chicago Press, 1972.
11. See for example, J. Hirschleifer, J. G. Dehaven, and J. W. Milliman, *Water Supply, Economics, Technology and Policy*. Chicago: University of Chicago Press, 1960; P. A. Bird and C. I. Jackson, "The Scope for Pricing in Maximising the Efficiency of Resources," in *Readings in Price Theory*. London: Institute of Economic Affairs, 1967; A. P. Grima, *Residential Water Demands: Alternative Choices for Management*, University of Toronto, Department of Geography, Research Publication No. 7. Toronto: University of Toronto Press, 1971.

CHAPTER 7

Leo Jakobson

HOUSING POLICY AND HOUSING STANDARDS:
A Dualistic Dependency

Introduction

Even a cursory examination of the literature on housing reveals that the term "housing policy" mostly refers to five issues: (1) the generation and allocation of financial resources for new housing construction; (2) the development of a more efficient housing industry; (3) the requirements for occupancy eligibility; (4) the management of public housing; and (5) the concern with slums, deterioration, squatters and shantytowns, however defined. In all instances, references are made to "standards" or the yardsticks whereby the particular concern is being measured. However, little attention is given to the manner whereby standards are being established, and virtually absent is the recognition that standards might be an integral element of housing policy. The fact is hardly acknowledged that notions like "a two-room house" or "200 square feet per person" or "an occupancy ratio not to exceed 1.5 persons per room" not only determine the quantity of housing that can be provided within a given allocation of funds and other resources but also determine the quality of the housing environment.

This lack of recognition of the role and importance of standards in the formulation and implementation of housing policy is not limited to the developing countries. In the "developed" nations of the West, including the United States, a similar void is apparent. For instance, Allan Twichell pointed out in his study on housing quality that the test applied by the U.S. Housing Act of 1949 for measuring overcrowding "is a brutal one." He gives the following illustration:

> More than 1.5 persons per room means, for a four room dwelling, that seven persons must occupy it before it shows up in the block statistics for crowding. By this standard, (if, in fact, the word is appropriate here),

occupancy by six persons—four sleeping in two bedrooms and two in the living room—is not overcrowding regardless of the size of the rooms and of the age and sex of the members of the family.[1]

Some ten years later Glenn Beyer observed that "standards" should define the housing goals toward which a nation strives, but that despite the many social and technological advances which have been made no concise definitions of "a decent home" or "a suitable living environment" have yet been established. He recognizes that it is not difficult to arrive at a desirable level of housing based on construction standards, but that it is more difficult to take proper cognizance of technological advances, environmental concerns, and in particular of human requirements, because of differences in housing goals and lifestyles between the various socio-economic and ethnic groups. Most importantly Beyer points out that:

> Unfortunately, most so-called housing standards today reflect minimum situations; that is, they reflect the level below which housing is considered to be unsafe or unsanitary. However, *a house that is safe and sanitary does not necessarily represent an adequate or a desirable home.*[2]

He goes on to suggest that much more attention must be given to standards and concludes that "we really don't know what the standards should be for the more than one million new homes which are being built each year."[3] More recently, the National Commission on Urban Problems (the Douglas Commssion), and the President's Committee on Urban Housing (the Kaiser Committee), submitted their respective reports and recommendations which discuss in depth the economic, social, political, and technological ramifications of the urban housing situation and the apparent deficiencies in the supply of housing and in the urban living environment. However, standards are not mentioned except at the most generalized level of "a decent home in a suitable environment."[4]

In the Scandinavian countries, noted as exemplary for their progressive housing policies, the problems associated with standards have been less critical because of their relatively homogeneous populations. However in recent years questions have been raised there too with respect to the role of standards in housing policy. For example, at the end of 1970 a Government Commission was appointed in Sweden to prepare recommendations for a national housing program for 1975-1985, including proposals for a new housing policy to replace current policies which were conceived in the 1930s and put into effect through legislation enacted in 1946-1948.[5] In addition to the usual references in regard to financial, technical, and demographic requirements, several of the directives to the Commission make reference to standards and their formulation. Among these were:

> The aim of the housing policy has long been to ensure that a healthy, spacious, well-planned and properly equipped dwelling is available to everyone at a reasonable cost, and this is still the fundamental objective; but it must be constantly redefined in the light of changes in the demands

and needs of the individual, the living habits and technological development. The definition of the goal is also affected by changes in the economic resources of the community. An assessment of future housing requirements must therefore include an examination of the definition of the housing policy aims, the means for realizing these aims and their effect on the housing needs.

* * *

Attention should also be given to the distribution of the housing production among dwelling units of different sizes, a question to which special importance attaches in view of the expected relative and absolute increase in the number of one- and two-person households.

* * *

As regards the ability of the consumer to pay for the dwelling, consideration must be given to questions relating to the general level of rents. A special problem is presented by the groups that *cannot afford a dwelling complying with the standards recommended by the authorities.*

* * *

Increasing emphasis is being placed today on the need for a good standard of indoor and outdoor amenities, and this is also a subject that should be considered by the Commission. The dwelling and this "immediate environment" together form a functional unit.

* * *

To achieve a more representative population of the residential areas it is essential to eliminate the differences in standard between areas. The many small apartments from the thirties and forties are one of the factors creating problems in this connection. Much importance therefore attaches to the question of the distribution of the total housing investments between new construction and modernization, between different kinds of houses, between dwellings and amenities, and between amenities in new and older residential areas, etc. The Commission should examine ways in which the distribution should be effected so as best to promote a fairly representative residential structure.[6]

Among the few attempts that have been made to develop housing standards which not only take into account economic resources and the state of the building industry but also incorporate such variables as "general family needs"—like the need for individual privacy in contrast to collective family life, or the need for relations with persons outside the family context—the "special needs" of the various member groupings within a family—total family, parents, children—and "environmental needs"—in the form of walking, shopping, recreation, cultural activities, etc.—are the "Cologne Recommendations" of the Standing Committee on Rent and Family Income of the International Federation for Housing and Planning.[7] Originally published in 1957, they were revised in 1971 to account for changes in family structure and lifestyle resulting from rapid social, economic, and technological development. Among the factors

General Needs	Collective Life in the Family Context	Life of the Parts of the Family	Private Individual Life	Relations with Others
Relations				

	1. The Family Life	2. The Life of the Couple	3. The Children's Life	4. The Life of the Individual	5. Common Cares	6. The Environment

Special Needs	family life
	
	movement relaxation
	
	meals reception
		common life
		
		intimity rest
		
		cares
			play — collective
			    — individual
			work recreation rest
			
			reception cares
				formation — profession
				         — cultural
				work, movement recreation rest
				(eventually:)
				life cares meals reception
					storage
					
					kitchen
					
					hygiene
						walking and shopping (work)
						recreation, play cultural & cultural life
						direct contacts indir. contacts addit. leisure time at home

PARTS OF THE DWELLING

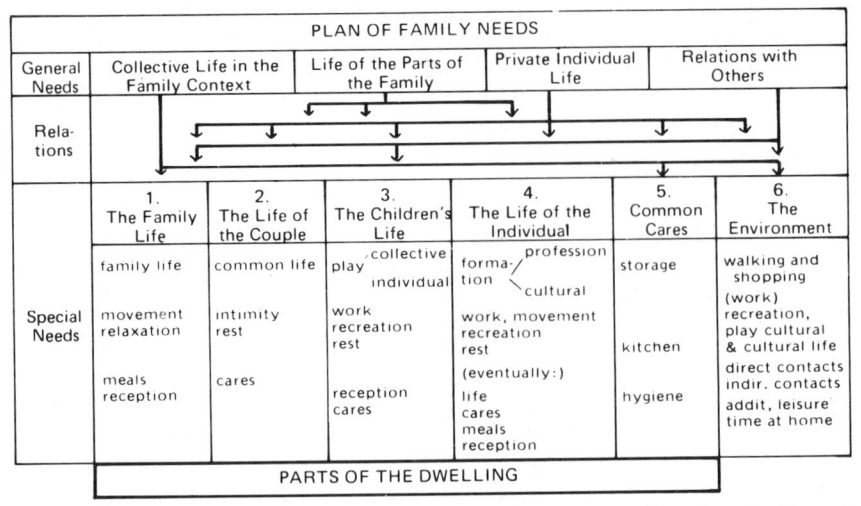

(For other structures, there are specific and additional needs (3rd age, persons living alone, handicapped persons, etc.)

SOURCE: Revised Cologne Recommendations, p. 10.

Figure 1. Plan for Family Needs

justifying the revisions, the report mentions the increasing number of working wives and of older people, the rise in the standard of living, the increase of leisure time, improvements in the housing- and living-related technology, e.g., mechanization of household chores, and the desire to control further degradation of the environment.

The interrelationships of the various "family needs" are shown diagrammatically in Figure 1.

In addition to conceptualizing this "Plan for Family Needs" the committee in the 1954 recommendations introduced a "capacity index for family occupancy" which expresses the ratio between the number of bedrooms in a dwelling and the number of beds that the bedrooms can accommodate. The rationale for this index is simple:

> Among the more or less necessary desiderata that have to be fulfilled for a dwelling to be considered rational, there is one essential need that takes precedence over all the others, and that is sleeping-space. If the worst comes to the worst, a human being can, if need be put up with a bit of a table in a corner to take his meal or with a bowl standing on a chair, to perform his ablutions. What, however is strictly incompressible, is the surface, indispensable for putting up his bed and lying down in it. Thus the essential element in the capacity of a dwelling is the space given to the bedrooms: consequently the index of occupation must contain two fundamental criteria: the number of bedrooms and the total number of persons that the whole of these bedrooms can normally accommodate.[8]

The committee feels that the index is a better housing standards measure than the traditional number of rooms or floor area measures because it allows for the recognition of the type of household for which a dwelling is intended. On the basis of the index the "Cologne Recommendations" outline in detail a diagrammatic representation of the characteristics of dwellings for different family sizes.

Glenn Beyer's remarks, the Swedish Commission directives, and the Cologne Recommendations all point to the need for the development of a better understanding of the role of standards in housing policy. At the same time they also suggest that this understanding must be based on a broad concept of housing that exceeds a mere dwelling unit definition by including the environment and the performance of the units as integral parts of a standard's definition.

In the developing countries too a growing concern is noticeable for improved understanding of the complexities involved in the formulation of housing policy in general, and of housing standards, in particular. For example, Gerald Desmond and Ved Prakash have recently submitted their housing policy recommendations for the United Nations Economic Commission for Asia and the Far East.[9] Though the paper is primarily concerned with finance, the role of standards as a critical variable in housing policy and housing programs is acknowledged:

> But there are additional costs which are not compelled by physical determinants. These are the costs of increased standards. If standards of construction, space and amenity are also increased together with location preference and in proportionally greater degree than the increase in realized income, it is obvious that there will be shortages with respect to those standards. Many substandard units will be constructed and occupied by families whose personal income plus supplements are not sufficient to compete for the higher standard/cost units. They automatically reduce standards and costs but may still be considered as part of the housing shortage by those who establish the standards.
>
> This is not to argue against higher standards but simply to point out that the concept of housing shortage is a very relative one and should not be viewed as a fixed and inflexible statistic. What we are all after is an improvement in the quality of housing conditions and related services and in the quantity of units available.[10]

The authors recommend that an ECAFE task force on housing and urban finance be organized. Among other things the task force should:

> Persuade economic and financial planners to broaden their understanding and treatment of housing and the related financial structure within national development plans and decisions regarding the mobilization and allocation of financial resources; and to develop a theoretical framework within which alternative choices can be evaluated" and "help define the principal economic, financial and administrative issues for further ana-

SOURCE: Revised Cologne Recommendations, p. 47.

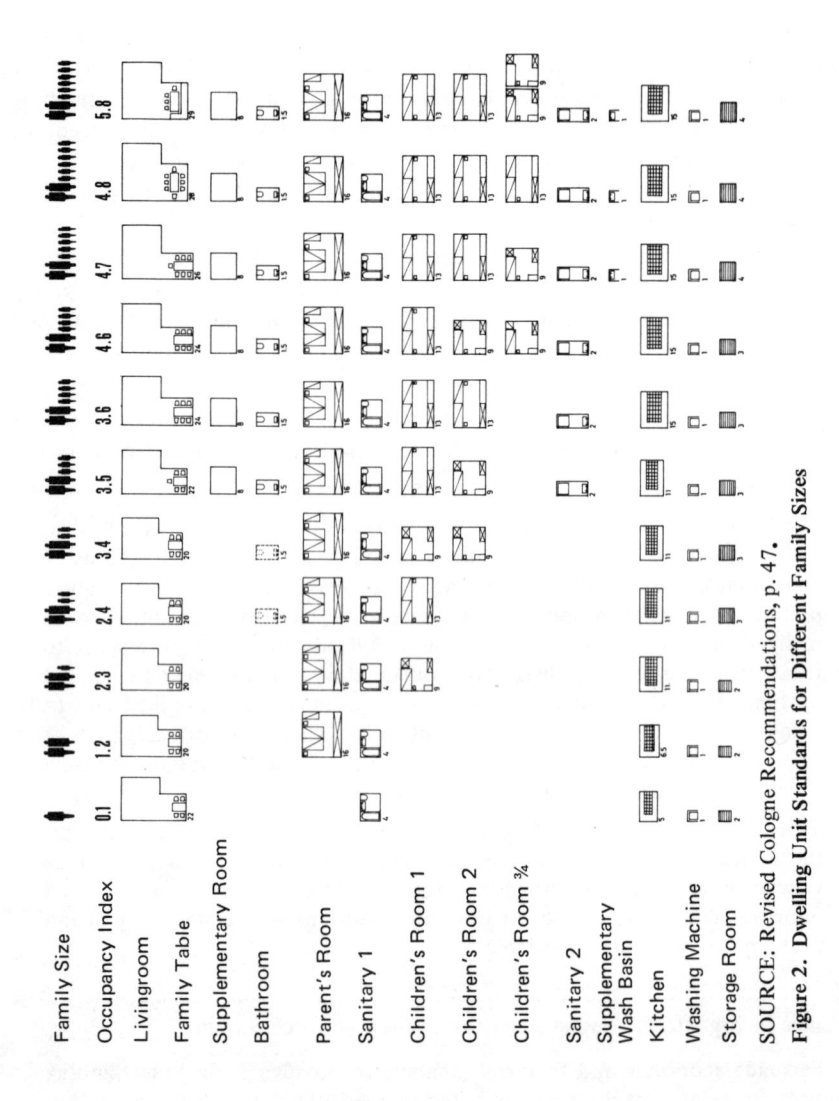

Figure 2. Dwelling Unit Standards for Different Family Sizes

lytical and feasibility work by both national Governments and regional organizations. Among the issues which the Task Force might consider, the mission suggests including the following:

"(1) *The setting of standards based on national and sub-national goals* which are commensurate with a realistic assessment of the level and kinds of resources likely to be available under alternative planning possibilities."[11]

The reference to theory and the recognition that goals may differ not only between nations but also among various groups within a nation are of importance because they represent a significant departure from past efforts in the formulation of housing policy which have been dominated by dogmatic, global concepts of what constitutes "adequate" housing.

In the following, then, an attempt is made to present a description of the role of standards in policy formulation and a conceptual definition of housing and of the manner in which standards evolve from within this definition. The last part will discuss the implications of these models for policy formulation with particular reference to some pluralistic concepts of society which have been presented in recent planning literature.

The Policy Formulation Process

In most discussions of housing policy attention has seldom been given to the process between policy formulation and policy implementation. In other words, the problem of moving from the general goal of "decent housing" to the specific standard of "a two-room house of 200 square feet" is assumed to resolve itself somehow if sufficient attention is given to fiscal programs which stimulate and subsidize housing construction. Though this may not be an important issue in countries at the threshold of affluence, in the developing countries the policy process lacuna can lead to many negative consequences. For example, the grand abstractions which often characterize national goals, e.g., "a two-room house with a garden" are taken as specifications for implementation, and become, hence, the standard for housing construction. Furthermore, long-range strategic objectives like "the elimination of slums" are often being confused with the tactical requirements of an immediate operational situation, e.g., the need to provide substitute shelter for those affected by slum clearance in advance of such clearance.

If, however, policy formulation is considered analogous to the processes which are applied in developmental planning in general, then a policy statement can be defined as a plan which identifies the means, the principles, and the actions required for achieving certain agreed-upon developmental goals. This definition sets forth three major conditions to which the policy planning process must conform. First, developmental goals must be established as a prerequisite to policy formulation. This, in turn, requires that some means of interaction between the public and the political-administrative structure are established in order to assure that conflicts are reconciled and that goals are the object of general agreement and are therefore capable of practical implementation. Second, the policy formulation process must involve exploration of the means available for achieving these goals, including the entire range of actions, from the long-range and general to the immediate and specific, which will be necessary for the attainment of each stated objective. Finally, policy planning must address itself to the political process which is to serve as the organ for implementation; since adoption by a governmental agency is in most societies a prerequisite to the effectuation of any public program, the process of policy formulation should result in a clear statement of the alternative courses which are open to the political and administrative decision maker.

Within this framework one must develop a systematic method for identifying policy content, policy level, and the types of action required for policy implementation.[1,2] Three aspects of policy content were suggested by the definition set forth in the previous paragraph: Objectives or developmental goals; Means for the achievement of these objectives; and Locations in the sense of the physical locale or administrative unit where implementation will be accomplished. In addition, comprehensive statements should include reference to the Priorities which affect both the means and the locations for implementing various objectives, and to the Standards which will be used as measures of control, accomplishment, and evaluation. These five aspects of policy content fall into two broad categories according to the nature of the issues addressed: objectives and priorities are Strategic in nature, while means and standards are Operational in that they are concerned with the actual execution of the strategies set by objectives and priorities. Locations have both strategic and operational qualities and thus serve as a bridge between the two categories.

With respect to policy level, five similar levels emerge as expression of the degree of generality or specificity of the actions required to implement each policy. According to the nature of such actions, policy statements will range along a spectrum from general policies to control policies, with program policies, plan policies, and implementation policies occupying intermediate points. General policies and program policies, which have to do with the setting of broad objectives and directives for development, are largely determined by legislative action, while the more specific forms of response with which implementation and control policies are concerned fall primarily within the administrative domain. Plan policies provide the vehicle for translating programs into action and serve as a link between the broader legislative and administrative categories. Diagrammatically this policy scheme can be presented as a 5x5 matrix.

Within the framework of this model, a policy may fall into one of four quadrants according to content and the level of action required for implementation. A strategic policy, whose content deals with objectives and priorities, will require legislative action to set up general directives and long-range programs for implementation; policies falling into this legislative-strategic quadrant are

Housing Policy and Housing Standards

		Legislative			Administrative	
Policy Level						
Policy Content		General Policy	Program Policy	Plan Policy	Implementing Policy	Control Policy
Strategic	Objectives	Basic Policy			Administrative Policy	
	Priorities					
	Locations					
Operational	Means	Programmatic Policy			Technical Policy	
	Standards					

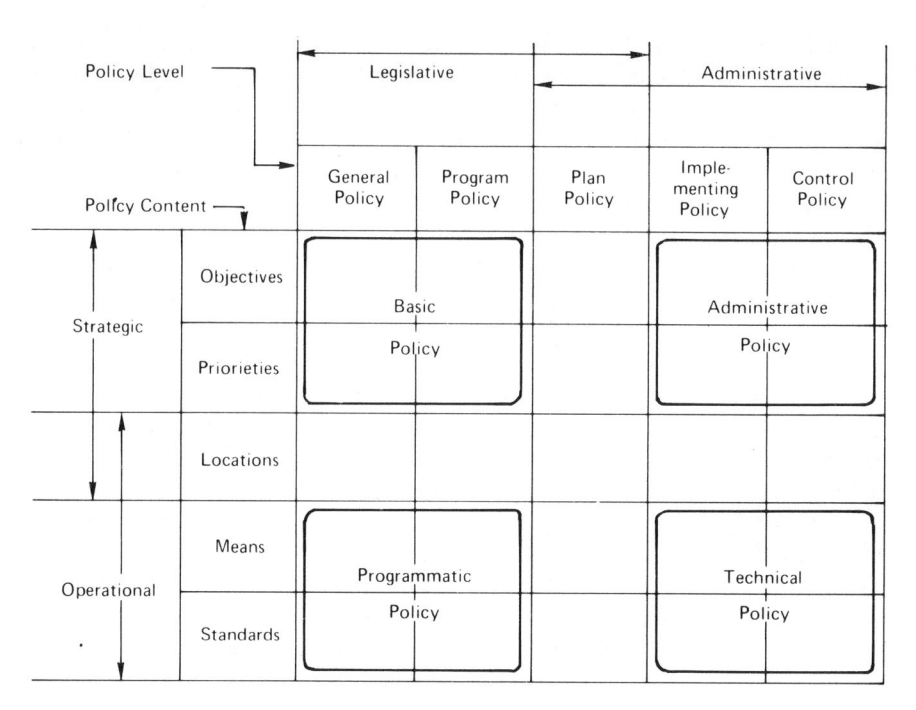

Figure 3. The Policy Formulation Matrix

identified as basic policies. Operational policies, containing identified means and specific standards for the achievement of more immediate objectives, also require legislative action when they are involved in the establishment of general and program policy; statements falling into this quadrant formed by the juncture of operational content and legislative action levels are termed programmatic policies. Strategic policies dealing with the general objectives and priorities of implementation and control are, on the other hand, set in motion by administrative action; policy statements in this strategic-administrative quadrant are denoted as administrative policies. Finally, policies with operational content at the administrative action level, setting forth the immediate means and specific standards of implementation and control, form a quadrant labeled technical policies, due to the technical nature of such concerns. The four quadrants are separated by the cross shaped area formed by legislative and administrative trade-offs required at the plan policy level and by the strategic and operational linkages inherent in the policy content element concerned with the choice of locations. It is in this intermediate area, where actual plans are established and the locations are chosen where implementation will be accomplished, that conflicts between policies will emerge. These conflicts can be accommodated through the formulation of policy sets representing alternative courses of action.

The model presented above was stimulated, in part, by Bertram Gross, who in his discussion of social systems accounts suggests that "another set of conceptual difficulties is found in the problems faced at the various points in the long ladder from vague but grand abstractions down through intermediate abstractions to very specific kinds of information."[13] He goes on to say that "for centuries the grand abstractions have been the ideas that have stirred men's souls."[14] However, "when we come down to earth and spell out what we mean by a grand abstraction like 'abundance,' we can now attain much greater precision.... At the same time, greater precision may eliminate the possibilities for consensus and coalition that stem from vagueness and ambiguity."[15]

Gross' abstraction-specificity ladder suggests that the possibilities for conflict increase if we, for example, descend from the national level to that of a locality or an individual. In terms of housing, the abstraction-specificity ladder and the policy model propose that through the simultaneous application of multiple sets of standards, conflict can be reduced in horizontal as well as in vertical conflict situations. The grand abstraction of "a decent home" can be deduced from the legislative-strategic corner to the operational-administrative box of specificity through two channels: one, from goals and objectives to priorities, to locations, and via the identification of means to standards; second, from general policy to its programmatic description, and from plan through implementation to control and evaluation. In the latter deduction standards must be considered at each of these levels. Thus, general policy describes standards in goal terms, e.g., a decent home; program policy states the legislative targets for housing production to accomplish agreed upon goals, e.g., the number of units in a given program. Plan policy identifies the spatial structure—locations, densities, housing types, service facilities—for program implementation within the framework of a comprehensive plan which is a statement of standards per se. The standards for implementation discuss in quantitative and qualitative terms the kind of housing that should be provided under the more general terms of the entire policy structure, e.g., the precentage of distribution between various dwelling unit types by the number of rooms per unit. Also, requirements defining the arrangement of buildings and facilities on the site, coverage, yards, courts, playgrounds, etc., should be considered standards for implementation. Finally, the standards for control would describe in detail the structural and spatial characteristics of the various units including their distinct appointments.[16]

A framework for policy formulation is but one of many tools needed in the design of policy. Its meaningful application will depend, in part, on understanding in analogous format the issues to which the model is applied. In the following section housing is, therefore, discussed in conceptual terms. First, in terms of a general definition, and, second, in terms of the processes required for the determination of standards.

A CONCEPTUALIZATION OF "HOUSING"

A mere description of a part of a complex phenomenon seldom leads to the discovery of the manner in which the part observed coalesces into the whole. Arnold Kaufman suggests that phenomenology is like frame-by-frame analysis of film: the scene on each frame will be subject to concise description but the tale behind the scenes may escape the attention of the observer.[17] Therefore, one could propose that the many policy questions in housing must be evaluated within a comprehensive framework which not only distinguishes the tangible physical dimensions of housing from those which are the product of mental imagery, but also provides the means whereby grand mental abstractions can be reduced to operational levels of specificity.[18] Diagrammatically this framework can be shown as a Cartesian plane (Figure 4) in which the abstract and the imaginary coalesce at the point of origin of the abscissa and the ordinate describing the degrees of specificity and reality, respectively. Using a modified terminology, mental-physical in lieu of imaginary-real, the framework can be also shown as a 2x2 matrix (Figure 5), in which the mental-abstract quadrant can be identified as representing the role which housing plays in the minds of people. The mental-specific quadrant represents then the function of housing. Similarly, one can say that the activities associated with housing are physical but abstract phenomena in contrast to the dwelling itself which is a specific physical facility.

Defining the four quadrants further, the role of housing is to satisfy the idea of a home, a vague notion that varies from culture to culture, from nation to nation, from individual to individual; albeit, as a grand abstraction, the idea of a "decent home" has been a social goal and a political slogan for centuries. On the

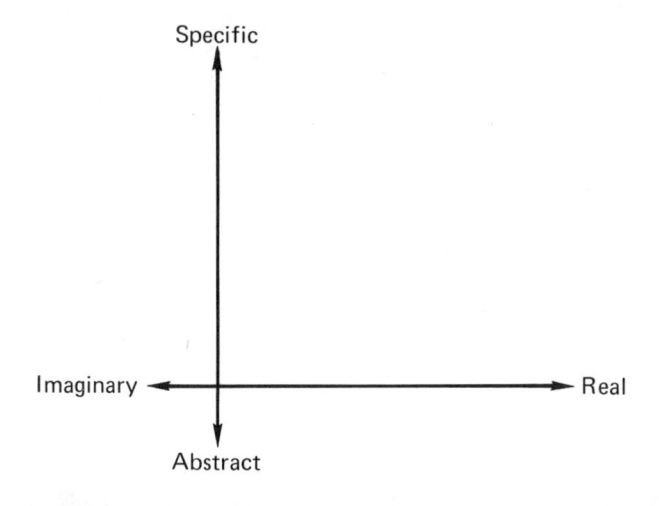

Figure 4. The Conceptual Reference Frame

	Abstract	Specific
Mental	Role	Function
Physical	Activity	Facility

Figure 5. The Housing Concepts Matrix

other hand, the function of housing, simply stated, is to provide for shelter. This too is a concept of the mind. In reality, shelter, as a physical facility, can subsume various physical forms from caves to palaces. Finally, the activities which take place in the physical facility again are varied, ranging from seeking shelter to plain resting; from entertaining friends to elaborate ceremonial functions. Within this framework operational housing policy centers on the question of providing facilities. As mentioned before, at this policy level standards become the control through which the identified and allocated means are distributed and the entire policy range from general objectives, priorities, programs, and locations is implemented. Hence, the development of standards requires that the conceptual housing model be made operational.

In analyzing the concepts underlying the rationale of the four quadrant model, the task of making the model operational requires that the ideas associated with role can be translated into specifications—standards—useful in the design of facilities. It can be submitted that in the past, in traditional societies, this task was simple. Activities in the home were strictly controlled by norms and custom, functions were limited and simple, the role of housing was well defined. Consequently, the "design" and the "supply" of facilities was accomplished through indigenous interpretations of the role of housing. This condition was reinforced by the slow pace of change of the society at large; the field of housing was static or near static.

In juxtaposition, housing in modern societies operates in a dynamic field. The activities in the home have multiplied and are constantly changing. The functions of housing have become more diverse and more complex. Consequently, the role of housing is blurred and subject to numerous interpretations, and the process of translating the multifarious constantly changing role images into standards which would result in a housing stock capable of portraying all the images of "decent housing" seems to be a task beyond our capabilities.

Two distinct, seemingly opposite suggestions have emerged in response to this predicament. On the one hand, the advocates of pluralism propose that at the operational end of the policy continuum standards be replaced by measures of performance developed in the main from observing indigenous interpretations of

Housing Policy and Housing Standards 209

individual and sub-culture concepts of housing. This can be defined as the "behavioral" approach to housing policy formulation. On the other hand, the "technocratic" approach sees a "high-technology" housing industry which relies heavily on standardized mass-production of housing components and construction systems as the answer to the housing problems of modern societies.

Both of the above positions possess their distinct merits. In organized society, however, polarization, though a most helpful analytic tool and a useful catalyst for dialog, must be brought into resolution within a framework which allows for the polar positions to become active members in a total system. One way to accomplish this is to consider them as termini on a continuum or as conceptual variables in a dualistic framework. The housing model presented above may provide this dualistic framework because it can be submitted that in complex societies role cannot be translated into facilities without simultaneous attention to both activities and functions. In other words, the formulation of standards becomes a dual process involving the traversing of the four interfaces in the model.

The two first steps, from role to function on the mental plane, and from role to activity, are abstract. They involve an ideological translation of the concept of home to the concept of shelter in the traversing from role to function; and a cultural translation in moving from the concept of home to the various possible activities within a home. These two moves have one commonality: they require judgments involving values, traditions, and norms. When one moves from function to facility, and from activity to facility, different sets of requirements emerge. In the case of translating the concept of shelter, the function of housing, into a facility for shelter, a wide range of rather precise requirements can be found. Some of these are environmental, e.g., the need for heat or protection from wind and rain; some are related to health, e.g., potable water, drainage, and sanitation; some relate to materials, construction technology, etc. In general, they can be considered technical requirements. They determine, in part, the location, cost, shape, and size of a shelter facility. Finally, the requirements for moving from activity to facility are social in nature, e.g., rest, privacy, recreation, sociality, etc. The commonality between these latter two sets is twofold. First, all these requirements can be measured with relative ease, and general agreement about the nature of these measures seems to exist. Second, as exemplified by the Cologne Recommendations, nearly all attempts to develop standards have focused on technical and social requirements.

In summary, the four sets of requirements fall into two opposites in pairs: one pair can be quantified with relative ease, the other pair with great difficulty. One could also suggest that the former pair of requirements—the technical and the social—determine the quantity of housing that can be provided in a given time/space context. It is the avenue which appeals to the technocrats in their effort to create a high-technology housing industry. The quality of housing is determined by the ideological-cultural set, however. This is the avenue of the behaviorists. The critical task is to converge the two avenues. This task is even more critical in the developing countries not only because of their scarcity in resources, but also because of the unique opportunities for foresighted policy formulation which their incipient states of urbanization, industrialization, and modernization provide.

Before discussing the policy opportunities which are inherent in the dualistic standards formulation process, some additional attention should be given to the concept of standards itself. As mentioned in the introduction, the literature on housing does not provide us with a satisfactory conceptual definition for housing standards. Nor does the literature suggest what measures should be incorporated into the definition of standards or what the nature of such measures might be. Because of the inherent difficulty of arriving at reasonably accurate methods of measurement, broad generalities are applied to the evaluation of existing situations and to the programming of future development. For example, a United Nations expert report on housing makes this statement:

> It is estimated that in Asia and the Far East only 60 percent of the population in urban areas and 50 percent in the rural areas are adequately housed; the remainder are living in unsanitary and overcrowded conditions.[19]

However, the report does not contain a measurable definition for the words "adequate," "unsanitary," and "overcrowded."

A different aspect of generalities in housing standards is represented by the "two-room house." In India this became at one point in time a sacrosanct edict and part of Nehru's legacy because of his continual demand for nothing less than two-roomed units which, in his opinion, were the minimum acceptable standard for India's people. When this view was bolstered by the opinions of international expertise, local planners seem to have accepted it unconditionally. The following excerpt from an editorial in the Journal of the Indian Institute of Town Planners, entitled "Economics Vs. Basic Planning Standards," was indicative of this attitude:

> The basic standards in housing and planning are arrived at not only from considerations of cost but also from considerations of creating the desirable sociological and physical environment necessary for the healthy growth of the individuals and the community. Such standards have been established by various committees and technical missions. The Environmental Hygiene Committee recommended a two-roomed house as the minimum for a family. The U.N. Technical Mission on Housing, the later Seminar and Conference on Housing and Town Planning, and other reports published by national and international agencies concerned with housing and town planning all recommend the two-room house with adequate sanitary and other facilities as the barest minimum if the normal aspirations of healthy living is to be achieved . . .
>
> * * *
>
> These standards cannot be lowered, whatever be the community, whatever be its location and whatever be the economic situation in the country.

Housing Policy and Housing Standards

> Sub-standard housing is but a step towards slums. Deliberate sub-standard housing will defeat the very purpose of housing as it will lead to the creation of future slums; the basic standards must be adhered to at all costs.[20]

Though some changes in attitudes have taken place during the intervening years we still are searching for answers to the proposition made by Latin American planners in a situation where housing conditions were about as deplorable as in India:

> Aside from the scientific criterion of healthfulness that would govern these standards, the public opinion, the culture and the economic structure of the country would have a hand in determining what they should be. Thus, the ideal scientific standards would be modified according to the prevailing social and economic conditions of the time and place. These standards should, therefore, have a basic flexibility enabling them to be adapted to a variety of conditions and the actual situation that prevails.[21]

In contrast to the Indian position this report stresses that cultural, social, and economic conditions in relation to time and place are important factors in the design of a housing program. Also, it recognizes the need for flexibility to allow for regional adjustments.

The above reports and other housing and planning literature seem to agree on one point, namely, that there are four basic areas to consider in any attempt to establish criteria for the measurement of housing deficiency and demand:

(1) The attitudes of political and professional leadership;
(2) The environmental condition of housing;
(3) The occupancy of housing units; and
(4) The cultural characteristics, attitudes, and habits of the population.

These four areas correspond to the four interfaces of our conceptual framework.

The first category relates to the ideological interface between role and function. Nehru's concept of minimum housing and the statement by the Indian Institute of Planners are indicative of the difficulties which must be overcome in order to make the proposed model meaningful in operation.

The second category corresponds to the technical interface. The standards of health and security are predominant. They include environmental engineering factors, such as adequate potable water supply and drainage, and the protection against the elements, against fire, and against structural hazards. Because of the exactness of the factors to be considered, measurable standards can be established in this area easily. However minimal, as in the case of the Calcutta Bustee Improvement Schemes, they can be quantified and agreed upon.[22]

The third area, that of occupancy characteristics of housing units, is less exact. It corresponds to the social interface in the model. The previously discussed overcrowding measures fall into this category, as well as most of the measures on which the "Cologne Recommendations" are based.

The fourth area influencing housing standards and design criteria, that of cultural characteristics, is the one in which quantification is most difficult. Accurate information in this area is scanty and it has been suggested that "much of what has been written on this subject is a product of premature generalization based on limited observations of Western experience."[23]

THE HOUSING CONCEPT IN APPLICATION

Four specific conditions in the developing countries are of major significance in the formulation of housing policy. These are:

(1) The state of urbanization;

(2) The ideologies of welfare;

(3) The cultural rift between the urban, Westernized elites and the masses dominated by recent migrants from rural areas; and

(4) The respective roles of the traditional and modern sectors in the functioning of cities.

Due to the nature of conceptual work these four conditions can be related to the housing model only if they are discussed in similar terms, e.g., as continua, as dichotomous pairs, as systems, etc. Also, the levels of conceptualization should be near identical and, hopefully, the concepts themselves should possess analogous characteristics. The four frameworks selected for providing this larger setting for operationalizing the housing policy model do possess some of these required qualities. However, they create another conceptual difficulty: that of relating Western models to the conditions in Asia. The point one has to make is that these models should not be considered to be applicable as analogs, i.e., directly transferable. But inherent in the models are qualities which can be applied in terms of conceptual transfers.[24]

The four frameworks are:

(1) On urbanization: the author's and Ved Prakash's urbanization policy model;[25]

(2) On welfare: the welfare model applied to the current low income study in Sweden;[26]

(3) On goals conflict: Folke Kristensson's "total model" of regional structure and demand;[27]

(4) On the function of cities: T. G. McGee's socio-economic model of the Asian primate city.[28]

The Urbanization Policy Model

This model is based on the strong correlation which appears to exist among industrial development, technological advances, and urbanization. As Fourastié has pointed out, the two former variables result in the shift of the occupational structure of society from a traditional agriculture-based state of civilization to a tertiary, service-occupation-dominated civilization.[29] Prakash and I, among others, have related the growth rate of urbanization to that of the tertiary sector in Fourastié's schema, though in the initial phases of industrialization, manufacturing employment is the triggering factor of urbanization, in particular accelerating the growth of the larger cities.[30]

The model suggests that in most developing countries, in particular those with an urbanization rate of 20 percent or below, housing policy targets should be immediate, policy content remedial, and the level of policy objectives and implementation standards low, because of scarce resources and high budgetary constraints on implementation. However, the model also suggests that policies should be cumulative, allowing for easy transition from one stage to the next. The incorporation of this cumulative concept into the model is important because it suggests that during certain, or possibly all stages of development, dual or multiple sets of policies may be required.

The Welfare Model

In the recent literature on welfare, the Swedish national study of low income contains a conceptualization of welfare which seems to provide a particularly well-suited definition for the purposes of housing policy formulation. This study, which was initiated by the Swedish Government late in 1965, is examining in detail the nature of income distribution in general, and its impact on welfare goals and social policy in particular. The conceptual design of this study begins with a discussion of the changes which have occurred in Swedish social policy since World War II.[31] Due to the switch from programs which stressed the need for economic growth and productivity as a means for achieving welfare goals to programs which emphasize social and economic equality, the traditional assumption that economic growth leads to increased welfare has been set aside. Instead, the study approaches welfare as a phenomenon to be analyzed from two distinct points of view: (a) from the point of view of income and wealth; and (b) from the point of view of an individual's personal, non-monetary resources. Among these are health, education, access to strategic resources, political participation, the housing environment, leisure, recreation, etc. In diagrammatic form this dualistic concept of welfare can be presented as in Figure 6. The diagram represents two distinctly different views about the ingredients which constitute a measure of an individual's standard of living. In the traditional approach, represented by the left box, a person is seen primarily as a consumer whose standard of living is determined by his opportunities for consumption provided by his income and wealth. This is analogous to measuring a country's standard of living by its Gross National Product.

The other viewpoint is based on the assumption that an individual's resources include, in addition to income and wealth, such components as education,

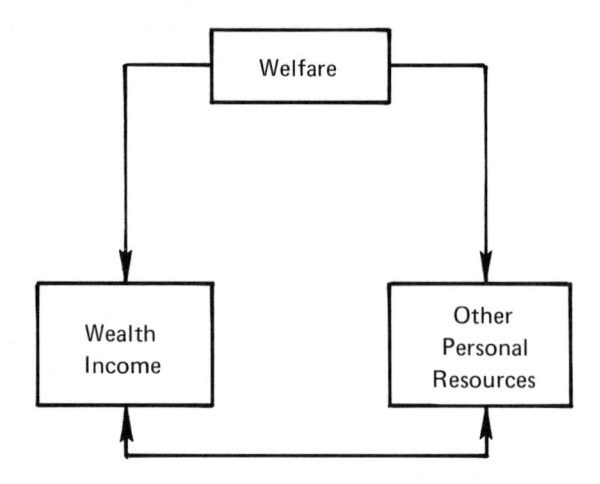

```
         ┌──────────────┐
         │   Welfare    │
         └──────────────┘
         ↓              ↓
┌──────────────┐   ┌──────────────┐
│   Wealth     │   │    Other     │
│   Income     │   │   Personal   │
│              │   │  Resources   │
└──────────────┘   └──────────────┘
         ↑              ↑
         └──────────────┘
```

Figure 6. The Swedish Welfare Model

health, access to socialization, etc. In other words, the term "resources" includes all the means whereby an individual can influence his condition. One could suggest that the latter approach places increased value on the individual as an active person, who is concerned not only about the size and composition of his consumption, but is concerned also with the conditions of his physical and social environment: the conditions of housing, the work milieu, opportunity for relating to other persons, etc.

These two points of view do not conflict. However, if the consideration of all resources becomes the broader viewpoint, including consumption as a part of total welfare, the consequences for policy formulation will differ. If standards of living are equated with opportunities for consumption, the indices which measure standards of living in economic terms—GNP per capita; size of public and private consumption; cars per 1,000 inhabitants; etc.—will suffice. But a dualistic welfare concept would have to be measured differently, and the selection of measures to be used would be difficult because we do not have generally accepted social measures beyond the economic ones.

From the point of view of housing policy the dualistic welfare concept suggests that amenity, in terms of location, environment, cultural tradition, and social relationships, becomes an important variable. In this lies the conceptual analogy between welfare in general and the dualistic approach advocated for the process of establishing housing standards.

The Concept of Goals Conflict

The above dualistic concept of welfare suggests that though its two components in theory support and reinforce one another, in reality they may initially conflict because established welfare practices are based on interpretations of wealth, income, and the individual's role as a consumer.

Swedish literature again provides a useful conceptualization of goals conflicts in society in economist Folke Kristensson's model for regional structure and growth. This model was developed for the Stockholm regional planning program and served as a basis for the formulation of the "1966 Outline Regional Plan." The purpose of Kristensson's "total model" is to create a comprehensive overview of possible and conceivable structural changes in society and to show how these changes affect the demand for regions of various sizes and of varying densities from the point of view of people and establishments. The model differentiates between the goals of people, which have to do with welfare, and the goals of establishments, which are aimed at efficiency. It then seeks to describe the conditions necessary for both elements to achieve their goals. The completed model describes both the demands affecting regional structure and the influence of structure on these demands.[32]

Another way in which the model contributes to the formulation of operational housing policy lies in the recognition of the necessity of taking into account new factors emerging from the changing patterns of society, so that future goals and demands are not interpreted as a mere extension of the present. Kristensson asserts that the crucial task is to predict and foresee the future desires and needs of people and establishments and their possibilities of satisfying these needs within the limitations that technical, economic, and social development will impose. A particularly valuable aspect of the model is the fact that it accounts for the interaction and potential conflicts among goals, as well as the effects of the fulfillment of one goal on the possibility of fulfilling others. In the model an attempt has been made to direct attention to the strongly interdependent relationships. People, establishments, and government, affect with their actions each other's choices, and it seems, from an overall point of view, especially important in the case of decisions with long-range effects, that these inter-relationships are taken into consideration. The most obvious source of conflict arises from the fact that the needs of people and establishments are often opposed; people are concerned with welfare and establishments with efficiency, in addition to which people are a resource, demanding goods and services, while establishments produce goods and services but demand resources. The formation of a conflict situation in posing goals has special merit in that it identifies weak spots at the outset and therefore makes possible the development of more realistic policies. In relation to housing this conflict can be expressed in terms of household needs, preferences, and behavior on the individual's side, and in terms of supply, demand, and resources on the side of establishments. This juxtaposition can be extended to the situation prevailing in many developing countries where the elites represent the establishment, and the masses the people in Kristensson's model.

The Dualistic Economy Concept

T. G. McGee suggests in his discussion of the characteristics of Asian cities that two distinct parts exist in the economy of cities: a modern, capitalist, firm-centered economy, and a traditional bazaar-peasant economy. Based on this dualism he develops a dynamic socio-economic model in which the traditional economy is penetrated by the capitalist production system in varying degrees and at varying speeds in the different countries of the region. After questioning what Hirschman means when he says:

> It is often said that the underdeveloped but developing countries are apt to pass from the mule to airplane in one generation. But a closer look at most countries reveals that they are, and appear to remain for a long time, in a situation where both *airplane and mule* fulfill essential economic functions.

McGee responds by suggesting that

> [I]n fact no such balance between bazaar and capitalist systems of production persists in quite these terms in the Asian cities. The penetration of the capitalist production system is a dynamic fact. This process of capitalist penetration into the peasant bazaar system does not always lead to immediate collapse of this sector; the creation of new-felt needs—shoes, bicycles, etc.—can gradually cause the decline of uncompetitive cottage industries in the city, or it can motivate a young peasant to move to the city to acquire these possessions. This is a dynamic process constantly changing the structure of the city and therefore affecting both its role and its function, and becomes a basic constituent for our model.[33]

A Dualistic Housing Standards Concept

This above dualistic concept of the urban economy corresponds with a proposed dual model of housing. In the context of housing the traditional and modern situation can be presented as in Figure 7. In terms of urbanization, welfare ideologies, and elite-masses conflict, the dichotomy in this model is analogous to the dichotomies in the other models discussed. In regard to the processes and the stages which characterize urbanization, the model is additive, but allows for the simultaneous development of distinct but interlinked sets of housing standards because some parts of the society may have moved from one transitional stage in the urbanization process to the next stage. The Swedish

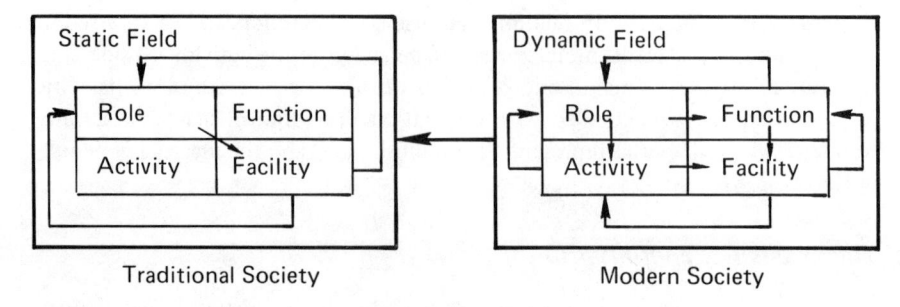

Figure 7. The Dualistic Housing Standards Model

Housing Policy and Housing Standards

welfare framework and the goals conflict models similarly suggest dualistic housing policies. In the welfare model it means the harnessing of the human resources, e.g., through self-help programs and the support of indigenous solutions to housing for that segment of the population where monetary resources are nil. The goals conflict model supports the idea of elitist normative standards for the supporters of the establishment and indigenous performance standards for the large masses. In all cases, however, the additive nature of developmental policy formulation must be kept in mind.

In relation to our earlier conceptualizations, the two streams in the formulation of housing standards are analogous, on the one hand, to the right side box of the welfare model, to the welfare notion of individuals in Kristensson's conflict model, and akin to the grand abstractions on Gross' ladder. In the discussion of concepts for standards they fall into the category which was labeled "socio-cultural characteristics, attitudes, and habits of the population." On the other hand the technical and social requirements are akin to the left side box of the welfare model, and to the efficiency goal of establishments. They will be found at the specificity end of the Gross ladder.

In the following concluding section the conceptual discussion presented in this chapter will be related to a summary of a proposed housing policy for Calcutta. The proposal was originally presented in an unpublished staff note as an alternative to the traditional housing policy proposals embodied in other proposals. Parts of the original note were subsequently presented in a proposal for a low-cost urban settlement program of the Calcutta Metropolitan Planning Organization, and may have influenced some of the housing policies recommended in the Basic Development Plan for the Calcutta area.[34] Though the intervening time has modified some of the premises on which the proposal was based, it is felt that as an illustration of the conceptualizations previously discussed the inclusion of the proposals will clarify some of the difficulties in the interpretation of the models.

An Illustrative Case: Calcutta

One of the premises on which the Calcutta proposal was based was the recognition that in developing countries one finds either a lack of the ability for critical interpretation and evaluation of Western concepts and experience and subsequent development of indigenous solutions, or an unwillingness to accept and admit the fact that social and cultural adaptation to modernization, economic development, and social change is a slow and difficult process which cannot be accelerated by coercion and imposition. No one has stated this problem better than Hilda Selem in her description of some postwar resettlement projects in rural Italy for the social, productive, and moral rehabilitation of communities that were either suffering from the effects of the fighting or from long periods of economic stagnation and neglect:

One must understand that planning of this kind is a new and strange thing in most parts of Italy. In England there exist social habits and relationships that enable the planner and architect to work efficiently without having to consider the inhabitants of their projects as much more than units in a statistical rearrangement. But in the undeveloped parts of Italy such activities may be met with suspicion or even hostility, because planning is either unknown or has been known only as part of an oppressive political regime. The designers of Orto Nuovo (Cutro) and La Martella have had to approach their public with caution, sympathy and imagination, because they are conscious that they are invading patterns of life and social arrangements that are ancient and ingrained, and, however squalid they may appear in some ways, still enshrine warm and valuable human relationships.[35]

The housing situation in the Calcutta metropolitan district was then analyzed in a spirit similar to that of the planners of La Martella; and assessed on the basis of a series of assumptions and time-related goals, present housing deficiencies, and estimated needs of a projected future population. Finally, in qualitative terms, concepts were presented which could be applied in the planning of the residential areas of the metropolitan district, and in the subsequent programing for the provision and construction of housing.

After the demographic, economic, and spatial characteristics of the metropolitan area were mapped and analyzed the following factors seemed to be of major importance in the design of metropolitan housing policies and programs:

(1) The bulk of future growth will take place outside the two central cities, Calcutta and Howrah;

(2) The zonal rates of growth were changing rapidly, therefore planning efforts and programs, including housing development, should concentrate on bringing about organized growth in the outer zones rather than in the central cities which cannot deteriorate much beyond their present state and, therefore, in a scarcity economy, should not be allowed to drain limited resources;

(3) The growth trends indicate that zonal adjustments are taking place in the socio-economic characteristics of the metropolitan population;

(4) It is necessary to develop new and imaginative solutions to housing in the metropolitan district because the magnitude of the problem and the meager resources available will render every conventional solution unworkable;

(5) Housing targets should be minimal and designed to keep the existing situation from further deterioration; subsequently the preservation of existing housing is imperative;

(6) Improvement efforts in housing should be concentrated on the elimination of gross environmental deficiencies only;

(7) Other public improvement schemes should be designed in a manner which would avoid elimination of existing housing stock, however squalid in character;

(8) As a corollary, slum clearance projects and programs are not feasible—the expansion requirements of other urban functions must be solved in a manner that will not encroach on existing housing stock;

(9) The bulk of additional housing needed for the accommodation of projected population increases should be of non-permanent character, for example, in self-help housing on minimal open plots with shared environmental and sanitary facilities and in "urban villages";

(10) Permanent housing should be provided only for that segment of the population which in its socio-cultural characteristics has reached the zero-level of rated indices.

When one relates the above policy formulation factors to the then ongoing practices and programs, they were in conflict with most of them. The only areas in which a degree of consensus was found were in respect to items (2) and (5). The Bustee Improvement Program of the Calcutta Metropolitan Planning Organization presented an illustration of the kind of activities which may be undertaken in accord with factor (2). In regard to factor (5) the Fourth Plan placed more emphasis on open lot development schemes than had previous plans. Open plot development, however, was an area of great controversy. For instance, West Bengal's plan draft for the same period did not include any provisions for this type of housing development. It reflected the tenor of the 1956 conference of the Institute of Town Planners, which passed the following resolution:

> The Open Plot Scheme is merely a housing scheme for the very low income groups, i.e., those that can only pay Rs.2/- or Rs.3/- per month as rent, and does not help to clear slums.
>
> In the considered opinion of the Conference, the adoption of this scheme in bigger towns and cities will lead to the creation of further slums and would also result in an uneconomic use of the land obtained after clearing slums, and hence it should be deleted altogether.
>
> If at all the scheme is applied then it should be confined only to towns having a population of 50,000 or less and the present standards prescribed in the scheme should be revised to conform to the standards recommended by the Conference for villages.[36]

Similar views were expressed by Indian planners attending UN seminars and other international meetings. Also, there seemed to be considerable opposition to any solution which could be labeled "temporary." To avoid a discussion on this subject the words "non-permanent" and "permanent" were used to connote situations where the former expression in actuality means a temporary or a transitional solution and a holding operation. One must, however, point out that many leading analysts of housing in the developing world are accepting the concepts of "non-permanent" and "temporary" as important elements of a housing program. Among those who openly have advocated such solutions, for instance at the 1954 United Nations Regional Seminar on Housing and

Community Improvement in New Delhi were C. A. Doxiadis of Greece, Rafael Pico of Puerto Rico, Ernest Weissmann of the United Nations, and R. B. Gupta of India.[37] However, the concurrent South-East Asia Regional Conference of the International Federation for Housing and Town Planning passed a resolution stating that "it is undesirable to permit temporary housing in urban areas particularly by public authorities."[38]

On the other hand, if the recommendations above merit serious consideration, the questions no doubt will arise: What kind of urban pattern will emerge in the metropolitan district if its housing programs would be based on these factors? And what kind of housing types would be required and in what quantities? And beyond slums is there going to be anything else?

To answer these questions, maybe La Martella can provide another set of clues:

> The budget was too restricted to permit of anything but the simplest of structural methods and local materials. House-types and elements, such as doors, windows, grilles, etc., have been almost completely standardized, and these bring the discipline of repetition into a townscape otherwise characterized by considerable freedom in the disposition of buildings in relation to one another and the roads that serve them.... The result is still, clearly, a town of people living close to the subsistence line and not endowed individually or collectively with any surplus of goods or equipment. Yet for all its dirt roads and simple construction, the town is as rich in character as its inhabitants, and the two characters are complementary.[39]

There are no reasons to suggest that a self-help housing project in India could not be as successful as La Martella in Italy. Nor has one to design public housing in a manner which from quite a distance has to reveal its institutional character as "housing for the poor." There are many spots in the metropolitan Calcutta which despite their "standards" possess a human quality which can be duplicated, without copying, and which can give us clues to the kinds of housing standards and designs which may evolve over time.

In this search for solutions it was suggested that the residential areas of the metropolis should be classified into two basic groups—permanent and non-permanent. Both of these could be broken further into sub-categories as follows:

(1) Permanent development:
   (a) traditional;
   (b) modern;
(2) Non-permanent development:
   (a) improved bustee;
   (b) open plot hutments;
   (c) the "urban village."

In the first group "traditional" connotes the kind of development which Doxiadis has described as follows:

Housing Policy and Housing Standards 221

> For years, Greece has built illegally, according to the by-laws, because the ancient Greek patio style—that is, different rooms round a courtyard— remains popular. You do not need any explanation to realize that this style of building could not be continued under the existing by-laws which were influenced by the building regulations of Western countries. The courtyard has always been the center of our life but it is only recently that we have been able to disentangle ourselves from the burden imposed on us by our foreign education and to give legal sanction to this type of house.[40]

Traditional development should not be limited to the old urban parts of the metropolitan area. It should be allowed in new areas also, as separate entities or in combination with other urban development forms. Design criteria in this category would allow for high land coverage, small and medium size lots, narrow streets with restricted automobile access, and irregular layout in all three dimensions. Open space would be provided in communal facilities. Densities would be high, for instance with 60 percent coverage and 2½ stories average height, net density may be as high as 260 two-room dwelling units per acre. Examples of the visual character of "traditional" housing of this kind can be found in some redevelopment work in the former French North Africa.[41] In terms of the conceptual housing models, standards in this category would be "cultural" and evolve from observation and judgment from role to activity to facility.

"Modern permanent" housing refers to "adapted" Western standards, layouts, and design. "Adaptation" means such modifications in Western concepts as are necessitated by local circumstances, such as climate, materials, financing, etc. It was expected that there would be a growing market for this kind of housing, although it is conceivable that if good traditional design develops, the demand for "modern" could diminish. In relation to the model, the standards for this housing category are technical. They are based on the measurement of the functions a shelter is to provide.

The "urban village" was the most permanent sub-category in the group labeled "non-permanent." It represented a type of housing which would be suited for several components of the metropolitan population. The idea was not new—it had been suggested in Delhi in conjunction with the rehousing of a segment of the slum population—primarily people engaged in home occupations and cottage industries where customer access was not a primary requirement: artistic metalware, handloom weaving, zari and zardausi, tanning, and milk cattle keeping.[42] But in addition to people engaged in the above kind of activities, urban village schemes developed in and around the existing and proposed metropolitan open space reservations would allow the head of the household to pursue an urban occupation, while the members of his household would continue to live a rural way of life, keeping animals and tending to small allotment fields. Housing in these villages could be self-help or could be provided by industry or government. One can say that this is a form of housing that is already taking place all along the metropolitan periphery. This is true. However, the inclusion of it here is consistent with the earlier recommendation which stressed that the emphasis of planning should be on the problems in the periphery and not at the center.

The main difference between controlled and uncontrolled urban village development is that the former will take place according to plan, and that provisions for water supply, drainage, and other environmental engineering features would be made. Also, the location and size of village clusters would be determined according to plan and in regard to other development in the area involved. An urban village would most often be located in the outer zones, its size could be anywhere from a few hundred families to several thousand. The buildings would be of cutcha construction intermingled with an occasional brick building or bamboo hut. The village would be provided with water taps, drainage, and sanitary latrines at the same standards as in the bustee improvement program. The village layout would be irregular and densities would be medium high. In visual character a description similar to that of La Martella should apply. In the proposed model this type of housing corresponds with the traditional in the permanent sector.

The "open plot" development scheme is important because it was estimated that the bulk of all new "housing" for years to come had to be in this category, providing for sites and services only. Although some of the urban villages would be developed along self-help lines, the open plot scheme would basically differ from the village in three ways. First, it would be carried out at a much larger scale and with less environmental control. Second, the layouts for open plot schemes would be more rigid, they would appear to be more camp-like and temporary. Third, it would be less permanent, with a projected life span of 15 to 20 years only. As its standards are highly technical it should be considered a modern schema in the context of the housing model. The virtues of this scheme are: minimal cost, ease of removal, and temporary use of land as a holding operation. It was suggested that this latter factor should be of value in a planning situation like that of Calcutta, where the assignment of land for an immediate, non-permanent use can effectively protect strategic areas from premature development of a more permanent type.

In conclusion, in regard to the overall distribution of the various concepts throughout the metropolitan district, in broad principle, the following policies were suggested:

(1) In the central cities most housing activities should be confined to bustee improvement and the rehabilitation and conservation of rundown non-bustee housing. New development should be primarily in the private sector and designed to fill vacant land and open building lots. A triple standard should be developed for the Calcutta and Howrah zones to meet the simultaneous requirements for traditional and modern new construction, and the requirements for conservation and rehabilitation.

(2) In the intermediate zone, in addition to bustee improvement and the conservation and rehabilitation of existing building stock, most new development should be in the urban village category to provide for housing for a growing industrial labor force and an expanding tertiary sector. Codes and plans should be flexible to allow for simple construction and for minimal space standards.

(3) In the outer zones the bulk of planned public housing should be in open lot developments; such developments should be timed for occupancy for 10 to 20 years depending upon location and estimated land demands for other future uses. Lot sizes and development standards should be kept at a minimum. Permanent new housing sites also should be kept at a minimum and located only after careful comprehensive plan studies in locations possessing potential of becoming strong centers in a changing metropolitan structure.

The Calcutta study preceded the conceptual development of the housing model. In retrospect, it provided the initial impetus for work on the model because it glaringly demonstrated the shortcomings of considering housing a commodity only, and of separating the issue of standards from those of finance, construction, and management. The model presented herein may have little practical value too. As an initial expression of a growing concern for a broader housing policy framework, however, it may provide some guidelines for further work.

NOTES

1. Allan A. Twichell, "Measuring the Quality of Housing," in Coleman Woodbury (ed.), *Urban Redevelopment: Problems and Practices.* Chicago: The University of Chicago Press, 1953, p. 22. One should point out that the fourth room in Twichell's example is the kitchen, which in the U.S. is counted as a room in contrast to most European countries where the kitchen is discounted in the application of occupancy ratios. Most recently, in 1965, the Swedes changed their previous crowding definition of more than two occupants per room excluding the kitchen to more than two persons per room excluding both the kitchen and the livingroom. For a two-bedroom flat this represents a 50 percent higher standard, reducing the number of permitted occupants from six to four.

2. Glenn H. Beyer, *Housing and Society.* New York: Macmillan Co., 1965, pp. 345-346.

3. *Ibid.,* p. 497.

4. "A Decent Home," the Report of the President's Committee on Urban Housing. Washington, D.C.: U.S. Government Printing Office, 1969, and "Building the American City," Report of the National Commission on Urban Problems to the Congress and to the President of the United States, 91st Congress, 1st Session, House Document No. 91-34. Washington, D.C.: U.S. Government Printing Office, 1968.

5. Ministry of Labour and Housing, "Towards a New Swedish Housing Policy: Directives for a Government Commission," Stockholm: September, 1971.

6. *Ibid.,* pp. 4-8.

7. *Revised Cologne Recommendations, 1971,* Standing Committee on Rent and Family Income, International Federation for Housing and Planning. Luxembourg: Private Press of S.N.H.B.M., 1971.

8. *Ibid.,* pp. 15-16.
9. G. M. Desmond and Ved Prakash, *Financing Housing and Urban Development in the UCAFE Region,* unpublished. New York: United Nations Center for Planning, Housing, and Building, 1971.
10. *Ibid.,* p. 14.
11. *Ibid.,* pp. 32-33 (emphasis added).
12. The model discussed here was first formulated in a shoreland development study for a county in Michigan, U.S.A. The principles underlying the model apply, however, to planning situations in general. See: Leo Jakobson, "Conceptual Framework," Technical Report A, Muskegon County Shorelands Study. Madison: The University of Wisconsin, 1971, mimeo.
13. Bertram M. Gross, "Social Systems Accounting," in Raymond A. Bauer (ed.), *Social Indicators.* Cambridge: M.I.T. Press, 1966, p. 263.
14. *Ibid.,* p. 265.
15. *Ibid.,* p. 266.
16. The U.S. Federal Housing Administration's "Minimum Property Requirements" provide, under the headings "Site Planning Requirements" and "Building Planning Requirements," good examples of technical standards for implementation and control, respectively.
17. Arnold Kaufmann, *The Science of Decision-making.* New York: McGraw-Hill, 1968, p. 36.
18. The choice of words denoting the polar positions on the two continua attempts to relate this concept to the work of Bertram Gross, Aselm Strauss, et al.
19. United Nations, *Report of the Ad Hoc Group of Experts on Housing and Urban Development.* New York: United Nations, 1962, p. 9.
20. *Journal of the Institute of Town Planners, India,* No. 3 (July 1955), p. 1.
21. Pan American Union, *Problems of Housing of Social Interest,* Report of Ad Hoc Committee for the Study of the Low Cost Housing Problem, Inter-American Economic and Social Council, Washington, D.C., 1954, pp. 17-18.
22. "A Note on a Massive Bustee Improvement Programme for Calcutta and Howrah," Improvement Programme for Metropolitan Calcutta: 1964-1971, Vol. V. Calcutta: Calcutta Metropolitan Planning Organization, 1964, mimeo.
23. P. M. Hauser (ed.), *Urbanization in Asia and the Far East.* UNESCO Research Center on the Social Implications of Industrialization in Southern Asia, Calcutta, 1957, pp. 92-93.
24. See Kaufmann, *op. cit.,* for a discussion on analogs and concept transfer.
25. Leo Jakobson and Ved Prakash, "Urbanization and Urban Development," in Jakobson and Prakash (eds.), *Urbanization and National Development.* Volume I, South and Southeast Asia Urban Affairs Annuals, Beverly Hills: Sage, 1971, pp. 15-38.
26. Sverige (Income Distribution in Sweden). Stockholm: Bokförlaget Prisma, 1970.
27. Folke Kristensson, *Människor, företag och regioner (People, Establishments and Regions).* Stockholm: Almquist and Wiksell, 1967.
28. T. G. McGee, "Catalysts or Cancers? The Role of Cities in Asian Society" in Jakobson and Prakash, *op. cit.,* pp. 157-181.
29. Jean Fourastié, *Le Grand Espoir du XX Siécle.* Paris: Gallimard, 1963.
30. Jakobson and Prakash, *op. cit.,* pp. 30-31.
31. According to the report, these changes have taken place in response to the several social movements which have gained momentum in the 1960s. Among these are: women's liberation, the political radicalization of the young, the environmental protection movement, the consumer protection movement, the growing debate on the urban living milieu, etc. Leion, *op. cit.,* pp. 7-21.
32. Kristensson, *op. cit.,* pp. 33-45.
33. McGee, *op. cit.,* pp. 166-171.

34. Leo Jakobson, *A Note on Housing in the Calcutta Metropolitan Area,* Calcutta: The Ford Foundation Advisory Planning Group, January, 1965, unpublished, mimeo; Leo Jakobson, "Housing Deficiency and Housing Goals and Standards: Criteria for Measurement and Policy," in *A Proposal for a Low Cost Temporary Urban Settlements Programme,* Calcutta: Calcutta Metropolitan Planning Organization, 1967, unpublished, pp. 47-61; and "Calcutta Metropolitan Planning Organization, Basic Development Plan: Calcutta Metropolitan District 1966-1986." Calcutta: Government of West Bengal, 1966, pp. 80, 85-94, 110, and Schematic Plans 1 and 2.

35. Hilda Selem, "Urbs in Rure," *The Architectural Review,* Vol. 122, No. 727 (August 1957), pp. 91-92.

36. "Brief Report and Recommendations of the 1956 Seminar," in *Journal of the Institute of Town Planners, India,* No. 9 (January 1957), p. 23.

37. "International Action in Asia and the Far East," United Nations: Housing, Building and Planning, No. 9 (September 1955), pp. 44-69.

38. "Report of the South-East Asia Regional Conference on Housing and Town Planning, New Delhi, February 1954," in *Journal of the Institute of Town Planners, India,* No. 2 (April 1955), p. 13.

39. Hilda Selem, *op. cit.,* p. 96.

40. C. A. Doxiadis, "Standards of Housing Accommodation and Density," in *Housing, Building and Planning, op. cit.,* p. 55.

41. For excellent illustrations see *L'Architecture D'Aujourd'Hui,* Vol. 19, No. 20 (October 1948), Vol. 21, No. 35 (May 1951); and Vol. 26, No. 60 (June 1955).

42. "Urban Village—A Plan for Dispersal," Town Planning Organization, Ministry of Health: New Delhi, October 1959, mimeo, p. 45.

CHAPTER 8

Ved Prakash and J. P. Sah
FINANCING HOUSING AND URBAN DEVELOPMENT

Background

As a consequence of rapidly declining mortality and fairly stable fertility rates, a vast majority of the developing countries have been experiencing accelerated rates of population growth since the end of the Second World War. Growth of urban population has generally been much higher than the overall rates of population growth due largely to increasing rural-to-urban migration. The urban population (localities of 20,000 or more inhabitants) in South and Southeast Asia was 104 million in 1960. It is expected to increase to 235 million by 1980 and to 506 million by the end of the present century. In other words, urban population in this region is expected to double itself every two decades during the second half of this century.[1]

A salient feature of urbanization in the South and Southeast Asian countries is the invariable trend towards heavy concentration of urban population in the capital cities and metropolises. To give a few important illustrations: Colombo, the capital city of Sri Lanka (Ceylon), contains about a quarter of the country's urban population. The seven largest Indian cities with over one million population hold one-fifth of the total urban population. The Bangkok-Thonburi urban complex accounts for about 52 percent of Thailand's urban population with these twin cities' individual shares being 40 and 12 percent respectively.

The vastness of the size of Asia's urban population, and more importantly the rapidity with which it has been growing and concentrating in the largest cities and metropolises, have many serious repercussions. One of them is on the problem of urban housing and infrastructure. The imbalance between the need for housing and infrastructure and the supply began with the beginning of World War II when some of the housing stock and infrastructure was destroyed and the rate of new construction reached its lowest ebb. The post-war period began with a legacy of huge backlogs of needs in both housing and urban services. The influx of refugees into cities and towns in several countries, without a commensurate increase in their economic capacity, compounded the situation.

227

No wonder housing shortages in all Asian countries are severe, the quality of housing stock and environment is poor, and basic urban services are either unavailable or are woefully deficient. To cite a few examples: in Sri Lanka years ago, an official committee classed over 40 percent of the urban dwellings as "slums" and nearly half of Colombo's population as living in slum conditions. In Manila, the primate city of the Philippines, about one-third of the city's population comprises slum dwellers and squatters. The urban housing shortage in India as of 1972 was estimated at about 15 million dwelling units. In the seven largest metropolitan cities, over 66 percent of the households live in one-room dwellings. More than one-fourth of the total population of major cities are slum dwellers. About 40 percent of India's urban population does not have a piped water supply and 76 percent have no waterborne sewerage system. The situation in regard to the availability of basic urban services is perhaps even worse in some other countries such as Nepal, Burma, Thailand, and Indonesia.

The phenomenal growth of urban population raises certain crucial public policy issues. The developing countries are undergoing rapid socio-economic changes and most of them are engaged in varying forms of developmental planning in an effort toward achieving socio-economic development. The development strategy in any country is of crucial importance since each "development plan has a spatial dimension in the sense that each newly established installation or activity requires a locational decision."[2] The locational decisions, in turn, largely determine and set the pattern for urbanization and regional development. Furthermore, the locational patterns tend to be self-reinforcing for some time in the future.

Because of the extreme scarcity of resources within the developing countries, the costs of providing infrastructure and other public facilities are of crucial importance in the developmental process. Economic development, industrialization, and urbanization are closely related processes. Many of the urban areas in developing countries either lack or are inadequately supplied with such basic facilities as water supply, sewerage and drainage, transport and transit, power, and housing. These urban areas are, therefore, not able to support industrialization and urbanization. In turn, this lack of industrial activities restricts their tax and revenue base resulting in successive deterioration of municipal services, the replacement and modernization of which is rendered imperative by rapid urban growth.

Shortage of available funds is the major constraint on capital improvements, which once built need proper maintenance. In that capital costs influence and may largely determine maintenance and operating costs, any initial capital investment in infrastructure and other urban facilities has far-reaching implications for future allocation of resources. In the planning and programing of housing and urban facilities, therefore, it is essential to give careful and simultaneous consideration to capital outlays as well as to the long-term impact of these projects on future budgets or maintenance and operating costs.

The interdependence between capital and maintenance and operating costs implies that methods of financing them—capital outlays as well as long-run maintenance and operating expenditures—must be viewed as interrelated and integral parts of the decision making processes for planning housing and urban development programs. The initial capital costs are generally financed through public borrowing (including external and international resources) or on a pay-as-you-go basis or through a combination of the two. The current expenditures (including repayment of principal and interest on loan financing) are financed primarily through public revenues raised by one or more levels of government (central, state, and local) through taxation and receipts from utilities and other revenue-producing public sector activities. To put it in another way, an accelerated program of public investment in urban facilities and services in developing countries may have far-reaching implications concerning the creation of new financial arrangements and institutions (and changes in the existing ones) at all governmental levels, central, state, and local.

Urban growth is a process of demographic, social, economic, and physical change. Solutions to urban problems require that governments cope with complex change, which in turn implies increased governmental activity. It must be recognized that the broadening scope of the public sector in the context of urban development is basically an intergovernmental process and requires both horizontal and vertical coordination among central, state (regional), and local agencies.

Besides the scale and rapidity of the urbanization process in South and Southeast Asia, the problem of financing housing and urban development is further compounded by the extremely low level of incomes, income distribution patterns, and high costs associated with urban infrastructure and housing in most of the countries in the region. As one study points out:

> The acuteness of the shortage of resources in relation to urban growth has probably not yet been fully grasped. On the one hand lie the basic limitations of total resources available for development, on the other the heavy cost of providing urban services, particularly long-life infrastructure to support the rapid increase in urban population. For countries with low income levels and high population growth, the squeeze between these constraints has become intense.[3]

Annual per capita income in five countries of the region—Laos, Burma, Nepal, India, and Indonesia—is less than U.S. $100; in another five—Cambodia, Pakistan, Sri Lanka, Vietnam, and Thailand—the range is U.S. $100-$200; two countries—Malaysia and the Philippines—have per capita incomes between U.S. $200-$400. Singapore is the only country in the region where per capita income is approaching U.S. $1,000. Income distribution pattern is highly skewed so that approximately 80 percent of the households in most of the countries fall in low income groups. A large majority of such households do not have the ability to bear the economic cost of housing even at minimal standards.[4] For example, a study by the People's Homesite and Housing Corporation of the Philippines estimated that only 12 percent of the urban families had the ability to afford the open market costs of housing and the remaining 88 percent could do so only with direct or indirect subsidies.[5] The situation in many other countries, e.g., Burma, Cambodia, India, Indonesia, Laos, Nepal, Pakistan, and Sri Lanka, may be equally serious.

Given the low level of income and pattern of income distribution, the level of net savings in almost all of the South and Southeast Asian countries, is extremely low. Even if urban infrastructure is accorded a top priority in the developmental context, available resources may be woefully deficient. The World Bank in its urban sector paper correctly puts the problem in a proper perspective when it points out that:

> A level of net savings of 10 to 15 percent, fairly typical of the developing countries, implies net savings per head below $25 a year for the majority of them, and below $15 for many. Even if the totality of these savings could be mobilized for the benefit of the additional population, the amount per head of the additional population, assuming a 3 percent annual growth rate, would average from $500 to not much more than $800. By contrast, net national savings per head of population growth in the richer countries of Latin America may exceed $4,000. Obviously, the problems for such countries though serious enough are of a quite different order.

> Such illustrative figures may appear unduly pessimistic in the context of urbanization problems since urban incomes and savings are well above the national average. However, though savings in the major towns are typically two or three times the national average, so also is their rate of population increase. Net savings in the towns per head of urban population increase are accordingly likely to be of the same order of magnitude as the national average. Relative rates of population growth between town and country tend roughly to parallel relative levels of saving.[6]

Comparative cost data for urban infrastructure are extremely scarce. Per capita capital outlays for urban facilities and housing as per the proposed standards in many of the countries in the region may range between $750 and $1,000. A recent publication points out that:

> Available data indicate incremental costs of water supply averaging around $100 per head and sewage about the same. There are considerable variations, but these appear to depend much more on physical conditions than income level. (Conventional "low income" housing costs range from a minimum rarely below $1,000 per family unit for the house construction alone to double this figure or more;) $200 per head is perhaps a typical minimum. Primary school capital costs for projects with which the Bank has been associated range around $450 per student place, or $90 per head assuming one-fifth of the population in this age bracket. Capital costs for employment vary widely from perhaps around $400 per worker in the more traditional urban sectors to over $1,500 in the modern sector and several times this amount in the more capital intensive advanced technology occupations.... Large investments are also needed for trans-

port infrastructure and equipment, health services, electricity, police and fire protection, garbage collection, and other urban services.[7]

Based on 1962-64 cost data for several new towns in India, it was found that per capita capital costs ranged from approximately $500 to $900. Of these, development costs (e.g., land, water supply, sewerage, drainage, street lighting, non-residential buildings, etc.) ranged between $150 and $500 per head and the per capita outlays on housing were between $350 and $500.[8] It is important to note that per capita outlays for urban infrastructure, in general, do not vary too much from one developing country to another. The ratio between the per capita infrastructure and housing costs and per capita gross domestic product may vary widely from one country to another, and this ratio is many times higher for the lowest income countries. In large part, this is due to the unavailability of intermediate technologies relative to the requirements for most elements of urban infrastructure and the economies of the different developing countries.

It may be interesting to note that in most of the Asian countries, in spite of rapid urbanization and concern for the deteriorating urban environment, investment in housing and urban services relative to the gross national product and the total investment has declined during the last two decades. For example in the Indian Third Five Year Plan it is pointed out that:

> Although efforts on an increasing scale have been made in housing during the First and Second Plans, the problem of catching up with the arrears of housing and with the growth of population will continue to present serious difficulty for many years to come. Between 1951 and 1961 there was an increase in population of nearly 40 percent in towns with a population of 20,000 or more. It was reckoned in the Second Plan that the shortage of houses in urban areas might increase by 1961 to about 5 million as compared to 2.5 million houses in 1951.[9]

The Pakistani Third Five Year Plan similarly points out that:

> In the Indo-Pakistani sub-continent urban housing first came to the forefront during the Second World War as a result of rapid urbanization.... By the beginning of [Pakistan's] Second Five Year Plan there was a housing shortage of 600,000 urban dwelling units. Despite the addition of 150,000 new units over the last five years, this shortage has increased to nearly a million on the eve of the Third Plan.[10]

However, the allocation of funds in the plans of the two countries falls far short of the concern expressed for housing and urban development. According to Stanislaw H. Wellisz:

> The feeling of urgency expressed in the plans of the two countries is not reflected in the allocation of funds for housing and for other urban needs. In both India and Pakistan housing is left almost entirely to the private sector, while the burden of providing urban amenities falls predominantly on municipalities and urban Improvement Trusts. Government aid is restricted to grant-in-aid for city planning, help in financing selected major

urban improvements, public building construction, and (on a very limited scale) low-income housing, Thus in the face of rising needs the Indian Second Plan allocated only 765 millions of rupees (1.67 percent of the total public planned outlay) to town planning, slum clearance, and low-income urban housing. In the Third Plan the allocation increased in amount to Rs.1,286 million, but in relative terms it fell to 1.59 percent of the total planned public outlay. The actual expenditure fell so far behind the plan as to approximately equal the Second Plan outlay. The Fourth Plan once again signaled the urgency of India's urban problem and estimated that about 23 percent of the population of India might live in urban areas by 1981 as against 18 percent in 1961 and that the addition to urban population would in all probability increase by 80 million in two decades. Once again the planned contribution of the government is insignificant: Rs.2,550 million, or 1.59 percent of the total planned outlay. The Pakistani figures tell much the same story.[11]

Standards for housing and urban development are of critical importance in the resource allocation context. The Asian countries are caught in the middle in their efforts to defend decent standards of urbanization in the face of growing needs and limited means. If standards adopted are extravagant relative to economic capacity, opportunity costs associated with any level of investment, are bound to be extremely high. There is some evidence to suggest that although in humanitarian terms the standards may not be too high, in terms of economic capacity in general and ability or willingness to pay in particular, the standards are nonetheless excessive.[12]

Capital facilities require proper maintenance and entail recurring costs. Capital outlays largely determine maintenance and operating costs and are of crucial importance in financial as well as physical and programmatic planning, and these in turn are a function of gross capital formation. Similarly, recurring costs are dependent upon and are charges against national/personal income.

There are hardly any systematic studies on maintenance and operating costs for different urban services pertaining to the different countries in the region. On the basis of analysis of rather skimpy data, it is felt that annual maintenance and operating costs may be around 10 percent of initial capital outlays on urban services and housing. The annual cost for land development (excluding utilities) may range between 8-10 percent, utilities between 15-20 percent, and housing between 8-12 percent of the capital costs.[13]

Assuming that annual costs are around 10 percent of capital outlays, and if per capita capital costs for urban facilities and housing are about $400 each, then the recurring (annual) costs may be approximately $80 ($40 for urban services and $40 for housing). Municipal finance theory as well as sound financial principles, demand that urban services should be financed through municipal taxes, service charges, and intergovernmental transfers from higher to lower echelons of governments. The housing costs in turn have to be financed largely through mortgage and other payments in case of owner occupied dwellings and rental charges in case of rented dwellings. It is inconceivable that at the present stage of economic development, the above level of annual costs is within the economic abilities of most of the urban population in the majority of the countries in the region. Nor is it possible to devise a system of financing whereby over 50 percent of personal income of the households can be mobilized for housing and urban development.

If the above situation holds, then the inescapable implication is that the planning standards for many of the urban services may be high relative to economies of many of the countries in the region. The main reason for high standards is that planning has been primarily concerned with the physical aspects of urban development and is based on predetermined standards rather than on any rational investment criteria. It is also true that urban planning, by and large, relies heavily on the concepts and techniques of planning evolved in the 19th and the 20th centuries in North America and Western Europe, notably the United States and Britain. The attempt is to transplant rather than transform Western standards to suit conditions in particular countries. If urban facilities are designed and built to excessive standards, it is very likely that these facilities may be inadequately and poorly maintained.[14]

From the foregoing overview it is evident that problems of financing housing and urban development are extremely complex and that there are important linkages between national income and social account, national, sub-national, and local government revenues and fiscal relations, and capital and annual (maintenance and operating) costs. This in turn implies that costs, resource allocation, and financing questions should be dealt with in the broader contexts of national financial resources and development plans. These questions are discussed in the sections that follow.

CONCEPTUAL FRAMEWORK FOR DEVELOPMENT OF A NATIONAL URBAN BUDGET

At present, development plans in many of the Asian countries lack clearly defined objectives and targets for urbanization and urban development. The treatment of these subjects is fragmented. For example, to identify public policy in India on these problems, one has to refer to isolated discussion in the Five Year Plans on such questions as industrial location, housing, slum clearance, water supply, and so on. To the extent that goals for some of the functional programs are outlined, means to achieve these goals are vague, and resource commitment is meager. These shortcomings, perhaps in large part, are due to inadequate analysis base and information essential for the policy making process.

Attempts towards the development of a national urban budget, ideally should deal with the following issues among others:

(1) Components or elements of urban development program. Should the scope of a national urban budget be limited to urban facilities (e.g., land development, water supply, sewerage and drainage; housing, slum

clearance, improvement and redevelopment; schools, hospitals, and other institutional buildings) or should it also include social and other services?

(2) The size of the total investment both in the private and public sectors, and at all levels of government (central, state, local);

(3) Allocation of local outlays among different regions and urban centers, and among different components of urban programs;

(4) Assignment of responsibilities for financing of initial capital outlays among different regions and urban centers, and among different components of urban programs;

(5) Sources of financing urban services in the long-run (amortization, maintenance and operation), e.g., taxation, utility revenues, intergovernmental fiscal cooperation, and so on;

(6) Integration of urban development policies and programs with the national development plans.

In this section we shall attempt to deal primarily with item (2), i.e., the question of determining the overall aggregative level of urban programs and the size of a budget for urbanization. Although the approach outlined here does not specifically address the other related resource allocation issues, it is hoped that such a framework may provide some important linkages and an integrated policy base for dealing with these questions.

The suggested approach takes into account: goals and objectives of urbanization policies; targets and requirements for different functional programs; alternative programmatic standards; capital costs associated with new programs as well as the depreciated or replacement value of past investments; estimated annual costs associated with amortization (or interest plus depreciation), maintenance, and operation of new and existing programs; and economic capacity which may be expressed as a proportion of projected gross domestic product or income of the urban areas. The process toward the development of a national urban budget is viewed as a continuous one, and the interaction among the above variables is conceived as iterating until the economic capacity and the annual estimated costs are approximately equal (see Figure 1). This procedure attempts to arrive at the total size of the budget in which the capital and operating budgets are viewed as parts of one system.

The formulation of a national policy on urbanization should be based on the explicit recognition and understanding of the indivisible nature of economic, social, political, and spatial aspects of planning needed to tackle the unparalleled growth of urban population—past as well as future. It is imperative that the development design of national plans be evolved on the basis of thorough studies and analyses of the functional importance of, and the interdependence among, different sizes of population centers. In addition, studies on economies of scale and agglomerative motives, as well as costs and benefits associated with alternative patterns of urbanization, can provide an invaluable informational base for formulation of urbanization policy.

Financing Housing and Urban Development

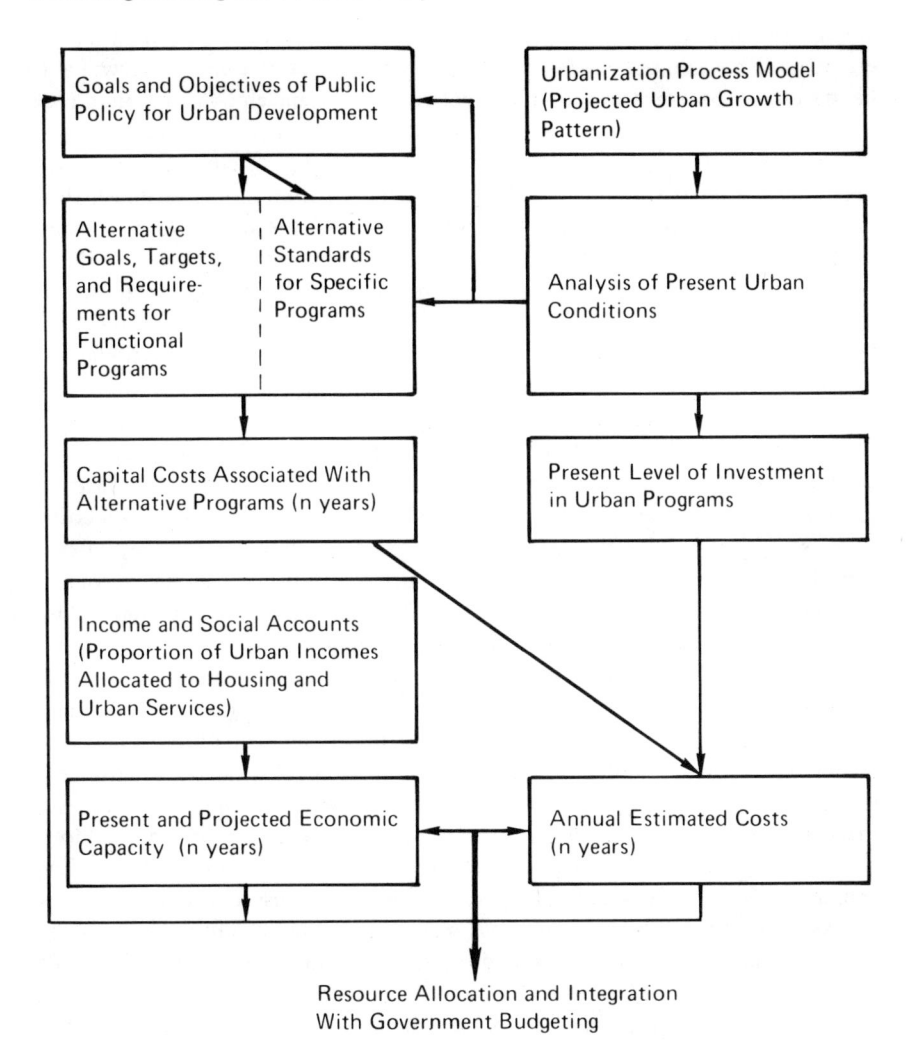

Figure 1. Model Describing the Interaction Between Goals, Targets, Standards, and Economic Capacity Towards Developing an Integrated Policy Base for a National Urbanization Budget

Once the desirable degree of urbanization has been determined and goals and targets for urban development established, it will be necessary to translate the overall policies into workable programs. At this point, based on different assumptions, alternative standards may be determined in order to specify the programmatic requirements for various components of urban development. The next step then is to estimate capital costs associated with each of the proposed alternatives. Although at this stage the main concern is with aggregate capital costs, cost estimates should be made at program level. Engineering personnel can prepare reasonably accurate estimates for inputs of material, equipment, labor, etc. Reasonable assumptions as to prices, wages, production trends, etc., will also be necessary to construct cost estimates. It must be emphasized that cost estimating is a continuous process and may require periodical revision.

There is no firm rule for choosing a planning period to cover the proposed programs and related cost estimates. Ideally, the duration should be longer than the four- five- or six-year national plans. A longer period is preferable since many of the proposed facilities, once constructed, may last more than twenty or thirty years. Thus it may be desirable to select the middle-point of the average life of urban facilities and the relevant period for analysis. Since some countries have "perspective plans" covering periods somewhat longer than the national plans, it may be best to chose a similar span of time for this step.

Having chosen an appropriate planning horizon, it then becomes necessary to estimate the capital costs of the existing facilities and add these costs to the capital costs associated with the proposed alternatives. Ideally, the costs of facilities built in earlier periods should be replacement costs, not historical costs. At present, such information is not readily available. However, in many cases it may be possible to make estimates of such costs using national accounts, economic reports, and economic character classification commonly prepared by the national governments as part of their budgeting processes.

Estimating maintenance and operating costs is an important step in the proposed approach, since these costs are considered crucial for both physical and financial planning. In this analysis, maintenance and operating costs are distinguished from maintenance and operating expenditures as the latter are generally understood. Maintenance and operating costs are required to calculate the annual costs of using the facilities as well as providing municipal services, whereas operating expenditures are relevant for budgetary appropriations. The annual costs for the suggested approach are analogous to accrued costs as utilized in cost-based budgets, whereas maintenance and operating expenditures most commonly refer to cash expenditures. In the short run, both maintenance and operating costs and expenditures may vary widely, but in the long run the variations may be quite small when the cumulative aggregates of maintenance and operating costs and the cash expenditures (especially if these are adjusted to present value) are compared. The annual maintenance and operating costs consist of interest on capital outlays, depreciation, and costs associated with maintenance and operation of municipal facilities and service programs.

For the purposes of this approach an appropriate rate of interest is required to estimate the costs of public funds.[15] The market rate of interest as determined by the forces of demand and supply represents the opportunity cost of funds to the country. At any point in time, there are not one but many rates of interest prevalent. "Traditionally it has been argued that the government should undertake those investments in the public sphere of the economy where the rate of return is greater than the rate of interest on government securities."[16] However, Krutilla and Eckstein argue that the rate of interest on government securities is not an appropriate rate to use in measuring the social cost of funds, since the rate of interest on government securities reflects pure interest exclusive of financial risk. In other words, it reflects only the price level risk and the interest rate risk. Krutilla and Eckstein argue that the social cost of funds is the opportunity cost of these funds to the private sector. They suggest a technique for calculating the social cost which takes into account the changes in the tax structure that may be brought about by governmental borrowing, as well as the prevailing structure of interest rates. "As the opportunity cost of funds depends on the particular tax change and the incidence of this tax change, the social cost of funds to the government is not independent of its own actions."[17] The social cost would be applied to the capital costs of all the projects *irrespective* of whether they are financed out of borrowing or on pay-as-you-go basis or under a combination of these two systems.

The second element of maintenance and operating costs is depreciation, which represents the cost of using a physical facility. The measurement of depreciation may be devised so as to account for salvage value as well as for the major non-recurring expenditures during the lifetime of the asset.

The third component of maintenance and operating costs consists of salaries for the personnel, repairs, insurance, materials, and contingencies, etc. Maintenance may be defined as those costs which are essential to keeping the capital facilities in proper repair, and operating costs are those costs required to operate particular facilities. The former costs are directly associated with the capital facilities and can be estimated fairly easily; engineering personnel can supply certain rules of thumb. The latter costs would vary from one program to another; e.g., operating costs for schools would depend upon the number of children, type of school (whether high school or primary), whereas the operating costs for hospitals would depend upon the number of beds provided in each hospital as well as the type of special facilities offered. Operating costs are thus not directly related to capital costs and would have to be measured on the basis of programmatic requirements derived from program objectives. Relationship between the capital costs and annual maintenance and operating costs may be determined and expressed as ratios between the two. These ratios may be different for alternative patterns of urbanization as well as for different components of the overall urban development program. It will therefore be necessary to develop a weighted average ratio, or ratios, taking into account the above mentioned factors.

The quantity and quality of services that can be made available to the urban population in any country depends upon its economic capacity, which in turn is determined by many factors including the population's total resources—its income, wealth, business activity, etc. If total expenditures on housing and urban services in any given country are related to personal income we find that this relationship changes only marginally over short periods.

The most important goal for economic development is expressed in terms of increasing the real income and standard of living of the people within a particular country. The two crucial variables in the formula for development are: increasing the rate of savings and investment, and improving the productivity of capital. The size of the total investment during a particular plan period is determined on the basis of the relationship between projections of national income and marginal capital-output and marginal saving-income ratios.

In any event, each development plan includes either explicitly or implicitly the projections of national income corresponding to the particular plan period. The next step in our analysis would require further assumptions as to the distribution of income between the rural and the urban sectors. Economic capacity to support urban development programs may be derived from the estimates of urban incomes during particular plan periods. The ratio between the above capacity and urban incomes may be derived by analyzing such relationship in the past. Depending upon the expected rate of economic growth, and anticipated changes in income distribution, a higher percentage of income may be assumed to be available for future urban development. This is justifiable since the demand for public goods and services increases faster than the rise in real incomes and standards of living. In addition, assuming a somewhat higher percentage of income for urban development during subsequent plan periods may be anti-inflationary and may promote capital formation.

Multiplying the amount representing economic capacity by the average ratio between capital and annual costs, we can calculate the total capital investment in urban development programs, which are commensurate with the projected economy during the next plan period. Thus this framework may provide an invaluable informational base for evaluating alternatives, assigning priorities, and phasing different programs. The proposed approach may be relevant in the formulation of local taxation policies, and may also provide suitable guidelines for the formulation of policies for intergovernmental financial relations.

Public Financing of Urban Services

Data on capital investment, current expenditures, and the extent of utilization of different revenue sources for urban development in developing countries in general, and our region in particular, are extremely scarce. Unlike the United States, Canada, and many other advanced countries, published statistics on urban government finance are not available. Whatever scattered information that is available indicates that in many of the countries urban expenditures are a much smaller proportion of their gross national product than is the case in most of the advanced countries. Similarly urban municipal revenues (including intergovernmental transfers) constitute a much smaller proportion of national income in developing countries than in the advanced countries. Some of the cities for which data are available show that per capita urban municipal revenues and expenditures have, in most cases, increased only slightly in recent decades. In all likelihood, per capita urban municipal revenues at constant prices may have remained constant or even declined. If this is the case, then the gap

Financing Housing and Urban Development

between the needed and available municipal services may have in fact widened in recent years.

It may be pointed out that the revenue structure of urban local bodies varies substantially from one country to another. Locally levied taxes generally provide the single largest source of revenue for financing urban services. Non-tax revenues consisting of fees and fines and rents and prices, in terms of their relative importance, generally rank second. Intergovernmental transfers in most cases do not play a significant role in financing urban services. In the last two decades or so, there have been no spectacular changes in the relative importance of the different components of the revenue structure.

TAXATION AND URBAN FINANCE

The taxes levied by urban local bodies for financing urban services may be divided into three main categories:

(1) Taxes assessed in some way on real estate;
(2) Indirect taxes, which in terms of their incidence fall either on consumption or on production;
(3) Taxes on persons, ranging from a flat small poll tax to a progressive income or earnings tax.

It may be appropriate to examine the above tax sources as to their suitability, the potential role they can and should play in the developmental process, and the issues and problems that must receive careful consideration in designing financing policies and programs for urban development.

Taxation of Land and Buildings

Tax on realty in one form or another has been utilized for financing urban services in most parts of the world. It is considered suitable for local purposes since "localization of the tax is automatic, and this is sufficient to keep the tax jurisdictions of different governing bodies from impinging on each other."[18] A carefully designed tax on real estate can be administered quite efficiently and equitably and can provide large recurring revenues to urban local bodies. The realty tax when suitably integrated with other land use regulatory devices can be utilized as a positive tool for urban development.

Local government levies on property generally take, with some exceptions, one of the following three forms:

(1) A tax on the capital value of the property (land and improvements);
(2) A tax assessed on the basis of annual value, which in turn is generally related to the annual rental value of the property (land and improvements);

(3) A tax on the unimproved value of land (land value is taxed but the improvements or buildings are exempt).

The different systems of property taxation, i.e., when the basis is capital or annual value, and when both land and improvements are taxed either at the same or different rates or when improvements are exempt, lead to varying effects and incidences. In an analysis of the effects and incidence of real estate taxation, it must be recognized that land and buildings are two different things. "They are different factors of production—the economic concept of 'land' applying to the one, the concept of 'capital' to the other."[19]

According to Seligman, if a tax is shifted, it cannot be capitalized. On the other hand, if a tax is capitalized, it cannot be shifted. He concluded that the tax on improvements is normally shifted, whereas the tax on land is capitalized.[20] In other words, the tax on land should lead to a reduction in the market price of land. It is on these grounds that substantially higher taxes on land are advocated to reduce speculation in land as well as encourage building activity and promote more efficient and economic uses of land. Since the effect and incidence of taxation on land and improvements is significantly different, and in order to make the system more flexible for achieving rational land uses and other urban development goals, it is necessary to separate the assessments for land and improvements for real estate tax purposes. Different standards of measurement apply for valuation of land and improvements. In fact, "the techniques of appraising land and improvements differ so much that it is necessary for assessors to value each of these major division of real property separately."[21] The appraisal of land is generally made on the basis of sales analysis, whereas the improvements are valued by the replacement-cost method.[22] When the property tax base includes both land and improvements the difference between capital value and annual value is a fundamental one. In theory there is no significant difference between the sale or rental value bases of taxation when land alone is taxed and the improvements are exempt. The salable value of a piece of land is arrived at by capitalizing its future expected rents. However, there is a difference between the taxation of rent actually received and the taxation of rental value. In the former case, if a piece of land is kept out of use, no tax is levied irrespective of the rent such land would yield if used.[23]

Looked at in another way, it can be assumed that any given piece of land at a particular point in time has specific ideal rental value, which is based on its location in relation to other developing land and sites of economic activity, on the existing levels of income and ways of doing business, and on existing transportation facilities and public improvements. In the event that a particular piece of land is developed to less than the highest permissible use, its actual rental value may be less than its ideal rental value. In this sense the ideal rental value is the true determinant of capital or salable value. In countries where annual value is the basis of property taxation, unimproved parcels of land within the urban areas bear an extremely low burden because actual rent in such cases is very low and may even be zero. Under such a system it is very profitable for the

Financing Housing and Urban Development

landowners to keep the land out of use for speculative purposes. The position is substantially the same when a piece of land is developed at levels lower than what is warranted by land values. It is reasonable to believe that when land values are rising, this system encourages speculation and leads to less efficient and uneconomic uses of land. When the tax is based on actual rents, it is less productive of revenues and at the same time it necessitates higher costs for municipal services.

When economic aspects of annual value and capital value as the bases of property taxation are considered, both methods offer certain advantages and limitations over each other. On balance, however, property taxation based on capital value appears to be preferable for the developing countries.[24] The shift from rental to capital value as a basis of assessment would make the real estate taxation more equitable and in all likelihood make the system more productive. Besides, the proposed change would, to an extent, tax the unearned increments in land values and at the same time discourage speculation and promote a more efficient use of land.

Since property values generally rise much faster than the increase in prices of other goods and services, especially in rapidly growing urban centers in the developing countries, an efficient system of property taxation requires that assessments must be kept up to date. It may be desirable that state and/or regional government set up real estate valuation organizations, establish also a number of field offices, and be entrusted with valuation of real estate for local purposes. This would result in more efficient administration and at the same time insulate the local assessments from the political processes.

In the face of rapid urbanization, a long-range land policy is indispensable for urban and regional planning, and property taxation should be an integral element of such a policy. Urban land policies are concerned with land acquisition, development, disposal, taxation, and regulation of land uses. Many of the developing countries have been concerned with these problems and have in the recent years formulated land policies for urban development. These measures are mostly ad hoc and sporadic, however, and do not seem to form part of a well-knit overall policy.[25] On the basis of the information available in the ECAFE region [United Nations Economic Commission for Asia and the Far East] on urban and regional land policies, J. P. Sah concluded that objectives of these policies do not include such basic aspects as controls on speculation and mounting urban land values and that these objectives have not been interpreted in the form of an overall multi-measure policy-frame.

The present system of taxation of real estate whatever its form is not entirely satisfactory for urban development. In addition to separation of assessments for land and improvements, adoption of capital value as the basis of property taxation, and assessment procedures as discussed earlier, some further modifications are necessary. The two such measures are: (1) taxation of land at rates higher than improvements, and (2) a special ad valorem tax at the time of sale and/or transfer of properties. These changes would make the system of real estate taxation more equitable and more productive; they would discourage speculation in land, encourage building activity, and promote more efficient and economic uses of land; they would tax the unearned increment in land values and in all likelihood result in a reduction of the market price of land. These two suggested measures would prove successful only on correct reporting of property values and the assessment administration. It may be desirable that the government or the public authorities concerned should possess and exercise "the right of preemption" or first purchase of property at its voluntarily declared value where it is grossly understated to evade the full tax liability.

Non-property Taxes

Local sales and income taxes as such are more or less nonexistent as sources of revenues for urban local bodies in the region. Several local taxes presently utilized by different developing countries, however, especially in India and Pakistan, do belong to the family of sales and income taxes, e.g., octroi and terminal taxes have certain similarities to sales taxes; taxes on professions, trades, callings, and employment, and various business license taxes resemble ad hoc income taxes. Octroi has certain characteristics common to local sales taxes, and is levied on goods entering the jurisdiction for the purposes of consumption, use, or sale therein. The goods which merely pass through an urban area (whether the exit is immediate or after an interval) are either exempt at the point of entry, or, if a tax is collected, it must subsequently be refunded when such goods leave the area. Exemptions and refunds are thus the distinguishing features of the octroi system. Octroi is an ad valorem tax and is levied by local bodies in several states in India against a selected category of good included in the tax schedules of different local governments. It forms the single largest source of tax revenue of many urban local bodies which levy it.

Octroi has many undesirable features: (1) its incidence is regressive, (2) administration of the tax is cumbersome, and (3) it may have adverse effects on free flow of goods and location of economic activities. In its intent, form, and administration this form of taxation has been subject to serious criticism for over a century.[26] And yet the Council of Local-Self Government Ministers recently recommended that "bad as octroi is as a form of local taxation, it cannot be abolished outright unless alternative sources of taxation which should compensate for the consequential loss of revenue are found."[27]

A superior source of revenue and a suitable alternative to octroi is a local sales tax. It offers a number of advantages for the purposes of financing urban services. It provides a flexible tax base and may be utilized in varying forms—as a general sales tax with or without exemption of items of necessities and/or a selective sales tax on a variety of commodities such as alcoholic beverages, tobacco products, public utility services, motor fuel, etc. It is convenient from the point of view of the taxpayer as well as the tax collector and it has the capacity of reaching economic units otherwise exempt from income and/or

Financing Housing and Urban Development

property taxation. A general sales tax is broadly based and has high fiscal potential and cost of administration and compliance is very low. The tax base is readily measurable, provides a stable source of revenue, and has minimum adverse economic effects. Finally in a majority of the countries the taxpayers are fairly well reconciled to this form of taxation.

Municipal sales taxes have certain shortcomings as well. A general sales tax is regressive and thus is inequitable. If food items are exempt the tax tends to be proportional for middle and upper incomes and may be regressive for the extremely low income ranges. In practice, services are generally exempt and this makes the tax somewhat capricious. Sales taxation places an administrative burden on the retailers who must collect and remit the tax to the governmental unit levying the tax and in the absence of an effective system of audits it may be susceptible to evasion and avoidance. On balance, however, a sales tax is superior to octroi as a source of revenue for urban local bodies. As a potential source of financing urban services in developing countries, sales taxation does merit careful consideration.

Municipal income taxes have not been used as extensively as the municipal sales taxes. Even in the United States these are of recent origin. Philadelphia was the first city to introduce a local income tax in 1939. Presently many large cities impose such a tax and in some of them its yield exceeds any other local tax collection. These local levies are variously referred to as an earnings tax, payroll tax, wage tax, earned-income tax, wage and income tax, occupational license tax, income and net profits tax, and municipal income tax. In general, local income taxes apply only to salaries and wages and net profits of unincorporated businesses and professions. They do not apply to unearned income in the form of interest, dividends, capital gains, and rents. There are generally no personal exemptions and they are typically imposed at low flat rates. Since the tax base is very broad, even at low rates, it is capable of producing large amounts of needed revenues. These levies, being generally on earned income, enable the local bodies to tax persons who live outside the tax jurisdiction but work within the locality and use its services.

As against these advantages, municipal income taxes present some serious conceptual and practical difficulties. These taxes are strongly opposed because they do not relate to personal circumstances or the ability of the taxpayer to pay. In their present form, they are often regressive and discriminate against recipients of small and earned incomes. In the case of persons working in one local government jurisdiction and residing in another, imposition of municipal income taxes by both the local government units will normally result in double taxation.

In most developing countries, power to tax income directly rests with the central governments, and the sub-national, regional, and local governments are constitutionally barred from levying taxes on income. No state or provincial government can grant to its local governments any tax power which it does not itself possess.

It must be recognized that use of sales and income taxes by city and municipal governments does raise some additional problems. First, in all likelihood, the national and/or the state, provincial, or regional governments may already be utilizing these taxes, leaving little scope for local governments to exploit them. Second, the local government jurisdictions, especially in metropolitan areas, may be far too small and form but a part of a much larger economic area which alone may provide a rational territorial base to administer such taxes. Imposition of such taxes by local government units, especially if the tax rates and exemptions are not uniform, would affect the location of economic and other activities, distort the land use patterns, and create unhealthy fiscal competition among them.

And last, but not the least, is the question whether the local government units in most developing countries would have the necessary administrative organization and competence to administer these taxes equitably and efficiently. Their record in this particular regard has generally been very disappointing. Because of all these pros and cons the applicability of local non-property taxes cannot be generally recommended. Nevertheless, there may be situations where their utilization may be possible and even commendable.

Wherever local income and sales taxes are actually levied, their adverse features can and should be mitigated through coordination of central, state/provincial, and local fiscal policies and tax measures. The two fiscal cooperation devices—tax supplements and tax credits—hold great promise in this regard. Under the tax supplement system, a uniform tax base may be used by more than one layer of government. The local rate is added to the state (or central) rate, both the state and local taxes are collected by the state, and the local government's share is credited to its account.[28]

The tax credit is a device similar to tax sharing, under which a taxing jurisdiction (central, state, etc.) invites a subordinate jurisdiction to share with it a prescribed portion of a tax area. The tax credit is to the taxpayer, and not to the subordinate taxing jurisdiction. "Since the taxpayer's liability is the same whether the subordinate jurisdiction uses the tax (which gives rise to a credit) or not, the availability of the credit exerts a strong compulsion on the subordinate jurisdiction to impose the tax up to the limit of the credit."[29] Furthermore, "the tax credit has the tendency to equalize the rates among jurisdictions, thereby curtailing intercommunity tax competition."[30] The advantages offered by intergovernmental fiscal coordination through the tax supplement and tax credit devices in respect of these and other sources of revenue must receive careful consideration, especially in view of the weak position of the local-self governments in the developing countries.

Local governments all over the world have utilized a variety of other non-property taxes. Admission taxes, sometimes also known as entertainment or amusement taxes, and taxes on different types of vehicles and animals are important ones in this category. The admission tax is generally levied on the admission of persons to any place of entertainment either as spectators or audience and/or as participants in the amusements or entertainment. The amusements which are subject to tax may include movies and cinemas, theatrical performances, circus shows, exhibitions, games and sports, and parimutual races. Cinemas are the major source of entertainment in the cities in the developing countries and taxes levied at these places provide a bulk of the admission tax. The tax may be levied at a uniform flat rate, or at a proportional or graduated rate applied to the price charged for admission. In the case of parimutual races, in addition to an admission tax a proportional tax (known as betting tax in India) may be levied on the amounts of all bets. The administration of the tax may be entrusted either to the local bodies themselves, or the state/regional government may administer the tax and share the proceeds with municipal governments on the basis of the geographic origin of such revenues.

This tax has several advantages. The administration is fairly simple. It does not impose a great burden. It is one of the few taxes that directly reaches non-residents and tourists who otherwise do not contribute to city revenues. The tax can provide a fair amount of revenues, especially in large cities. It has no serious disadvantages and is considered a good source of revenues for financing urban services in developing countries.

The municipal tax on animals and vehicles is of minor importance, although some cities in developing countries raise substantial revenue from this source. When a tax is levied on different categories of vehicles, it is not considered an impost on the vehicle but rather a payment for the privilege of using the streets. The animal tax on the other hand is primarily a license fee rather than a tax.

Some of the non-property taxes are good and desirable sources of revenue for the urban governments since they help diversify their revenue system. However, proliferation and indiscriminate use of non-property taxes is not desirable because a good number of them are regressive and bear hardest on those least able to pay. The Asian countries must, therefore, give careful consideration to their equity, revenue productivity, cost of collection and efficient administration, and intergovernmental tax coordination aspects, and move cautiously in this direction.

Non-tax Revenues

Non-tax revenues consist of two major categories: (1) fees and fines, and (2) rents and prices and special service charges. Fees and fines include fee for licenses and permits and fines and forfeitures.[31] The rents and prices include rent of municipally owned property and service charges for utilities and other activities which are owned and operated by local governments.

Fees and fines are not a significant source of municipal revenues because income from this source is incidental to the process of municipal administration, especially regulation of certain activities in the broader interest of public health and welfare. The benefits of governmental activities in this regard are generally widely diffused and the value of the benefits to the community as a whole as well as to individuals and entities is difficult to measure. Thus in designing rate schedules for fees and fines, the benefit principle cannot be strictly applied. However, in spite of these limitations, to the extent it is possible, an attempt should be made to make the fee charges equitable and more productive of revenue. The scope for improvements in this direction is quite considerable. For example, in municipalities where a particular trade is subject to a flat fee it may be rational and appropriate to relate the charge to some form of ability to pay, etc. Once a revised fee schedule is adopted it is necessary to review it periodically.

Rents and prices or user charges accrue to local governments either from their ownership of real estate (lands, markets, houses, etc.) or from their operation of public utility services and semi-commercial undertakings (water supply, sewerage, city transport, etc.). The user charges are theoretically based on the benefit principle and affect only those who really avail of the service or benefit provided. They embody a fair element of *quid pro quo* and are to this extent different from taxation.

Generally speaking, income from rents and prices or commercial revenues does not constitute a significant source of urban development finance in the developing countries. In fact, their revenue potential has not been adequately appreciated nor has any serious effort been made to expand the municipal trade and property sector of the urban economy. It has been so perhaps because user charges have often been viewed only in relation to public utility services such as water supply, sewerage, drainage, etc. It must, however, be emphasized that user charges comprehend a much wider range of charges than merely those for a few public utility services which at any rate cannot be considered or treated purely in terms of revenue.

A specific mention should be made in this context of the role of municipal or public land and real property ownership. In all metropolitan areas and big cities, there is an ever growing demand for urban land and built-up accommodation for commercial offices, supermarkets, shopping arcades, hotels, movie theatres, gasoline stations, houses, etc., etc. The prevailing market rents or prices of such premises are fabulous. There is no reason why the city governments or urban development authorities should not expand their property base and share a sizable part of the tremendous revenue potential of urban real estate business. Land banking by public authorities in particular would not only be a recurring source of substantial revenue surpluses but would also serve as a potent instrument to achieve the objectives of a socially oriented urban land policy.

As regards user charges for public utility services, some economic theorists consider these as inappropriate for financing what are defined as "pure public goods"—services whose dominant characteristics are such that no one is denied their benefits regardless of whether or not he pays for it.[32] It is further argued that in some cases even when a particular public service is not a "pure public good" user charges may be feasible but not desirable. The user charges are also of limited applicability where the service produces substantial public benefits, in addition to those enjoyed by the user as such, e.g., libraries.[33]

Notwithstanding the merits of these arguments, the theory of "pure public good" would need to be viewed as a relative concept. It is doubtful if it would be advisable to apply this approach to developing countries in the initial stages of their development when the accent has to be on resource mobilization and capital formation. Few developing countries can at present afford to provide as pure a public good as potable water free of charge or on a highly subsidized basis. If user charges are not related to the costs of public services, the community will have to finance them through taxation which in most developing countries may well be regressive. While in taxation the citizen has no options, in user charges one has some options in the sense that he may, if possible, not consume the service, or he can at least economize in its consumption. Moreover, most user charges, where desirable, can certainly be made differential in favor of the underprivileged sections of the community.

It is our contention that rents and prices constitute a large and hitherto under-utilized revenue resource and should therefore be exploited adequately by urban development authorities. In the first instance, the authorities concerned should compile and/or update their real estate inventories and establish proper real estate management practices. Effort should then be made to gradually augment the inventories, particularly by procuring or acquiring undeveloped land.

Furthermore, a thorough examination of the existing public utility undertakings in all their aspects—organizational, operational, and financial—should be undertaken and necessary improvements made where necessary. The rate schedule of these services are often outdated and irrational and their rationalization itself may improve their financial picture.

As regards new commercial and semi-commercial activities, the approach should be very very cautious. Priority should be given to projects which yield high return relative to capital investment and have a short gestation period. Feasibility studies, including a thorough assessment of the technical and managerial capacities, should invariably precede any such new activity. Alternatively, a small pilot project may be first experimented with and, if successful, expanded subsequently.

Intergovernmental Fiscal Relations

Planning and financing of urban facilities and service programs is basically an intergovernmental process. The largest proportion of fiscal resources is everywhere controlled by national and provincial governments. The capabilities of urban governments depend therefore not only upon their tax base and non-tax revenues but also upon the intergovernmental transfers from the national and state governments. The intergovernmental relations vary from one country to another depending upon their constitutional and administrative arrangements. The national or central government may transfer funds both for capital and current programs to the local bodies directly or through the state or provincial governments or a combination of the two methods.

Today in most of the developing countries intergovernmental relations are at one of the most important crossroads of their development. The urban local bodies have inadequate revenue base and fiscal powers so that the demand for public services has been outstripping the growth of revenues. In the face of rapid urbanization the gap between needed service expenditures and available resources is so critical that local bodies are already facing a serious fiscal crisis.

Intergovernmental finance is faced with two sets of fiscal problems: (1) a vertical one of how functions and revenues should be shared between different levels of government; and (2) a horizontal one of relations among governments within the same layer—metropolitan cities and their surrounding suburbs. These two problems are extremely complex because local governments have been called upon to perform a number of functions which are touched with extra-local or "spillover" interest. It must be borne in mind that local governments, practically everywhere, are literally the creatures of the state and/or central governments, and legally the latter have the power of life and death over the former. In a sense, local bodies are their agents and undertake the public services which the state governments, etc., would have otherwise to provide. As a consequence of their political dependence, local governments are also dependent in a fiscal sense. The revenue sources of urban local bodies are limited by what is permitted by the state government. The power to tax, and the power to sustain local governments, resides with the state and the national governments. The delegation of authority and responsibility to local governments for carrying out public functions and programs requires an equally heavy duty on the part of higher governments to insure that the local units will have the effective power to implement this grant of authority.

The higher governments' fiscal responsibilities with respect to their local subdivisions may be discharged in two general ways, neither of which is mutually exclusive. First, local government units may be granted power to tax sources which will supply sufficient revenue. Second, the state/central governments may supplement local revenues with those collected by them through their own revenue powers. Since the separation of revenues device tends to favor the higher rather than the lower governments this does not solve the problem of making available adequate revenue to the local unit. In other words, imbalance may be of different degrees from one locality to another. Given the deficiency of the separation device, a mixed approach is most often employed the world over whereby supplemental revenues are transferred to the urban local bodies by the state and the national governments.

There are four major instruments of intergovernmental fiscal transfers and cooperation: (1) tax supplements; (2) tax credits; (3) tax sharing; and (4) grants-in-aid. As pointed out earlier the tax supplement has the advantage of making the higher government's administrative capabilities available to local units and allows them discretion in setting a rate. Like the tax supplement, a tax credit is tied to a state or nationwide tax. The credit, while different in concept from the supplement, usually has the same practical effect. It allows local units

Financing Housing and Urban Development

access to a source of revenue used by higher governments, permits a local tax rate, and provides economy of administration. The shared tax is a third form of fiscal cooperation. The higher government sets aside a fixed proportion of the revenues collected from its tax and distributes shares to the localities on the basis of where the tax was collected. Under a shared tax system the state or the national government specifies the rate and administers the levy; but local units are generally free to use their shares as they wish. Like the supplement and credit devices, the shared tax is primarily a revenue instrument, and does not contribute to the solution of fiscal problems which arise from external effects and inter-local fiscal disparities. Grants-in-aid may be described as payments made by some higher government to a lower one with or without conditions prescribed by the former, to defray either in full or in part the cost of any service or services administered by the latter. Fiscally, a grant is an appropriation of funds from the higher government's budget to local governments. It is not, therefore, a tax or shared revenue: grants have no intentional identification with any particular levy.

Although grants were conceived primarily as a measure of financial assistance, they have acquired a number of important features which add to their usefulness and put them in a distinct class of public revenues. For instance, grants are often used as measures of control and supervision over local governments. They are designed and employed to stimulate local public expenditure to promote certain nationwide goals and objectives or to underwrite the supply of certain public goods provided locally. This is done either because of national interest in a minimum level of service for all citizens or because certain services are touched with external benefits or costs, giving rise to inequities or inefficiencies, or for both of these reasons.

No less important is their role as a device for equalizing costs and opportunities among localities. By allocating more money to local bodies with the least resources or highest costs, some leveling of benefits and burdens is brought about. Grants-in-aid thus represent more than a means of intergovernmental fiscal collaboration; they provide a platform for broad policy coordination and functional cooperation.

There are many types of grants; they differ in many respects and may be classified in several ways, according to the characteristics one wishes to emphasize. For purposes of this discussion, the important distinction is that between grants which are conditional and those which are unconditional. As a class, conditional or functional grants are in for greater use than the unconditional type. Conditional grants may vary somewhat in their provisions, but in general they have two main features. First, they are available only if the recipient government agrees to abide by certain limitations in the use of the funds. In other words, conditional grants provide funds which must be limited in use to a specified program or service. Beyond this constraint there could be other more detailed provisions with certain minimum performance standards.

The second major characteristic of a conditional grant is the requirement that the recipient government make a contribution in support of the aided function or program. This local share is sometimes determined by a formula which includes factors that will take account of the recipient's needs and abilities. Formulas which are sensitive to varying needs and abilities serve another goal, namely, fiscal equalization.

An unconditional grant differs from the conditional grant in that it is not tied to any one given program and may serve general purposes. Second, no matching is required; the general-purpose grant is a lump-sum transfer payment. Since it places no conditions upon recipient governments, the main feature of the grant to consider is the way it distributes funds. The total amount of funds released to local governments under this type of grant would, of course, be fixed by higher levels of governments. The amount of the grant to each local unit may be based on a number of factors. For example, both the total amount set aside and the grant received by each government could be based on population which distributed a fixed per capita payment to local units on the basis of their population. Other factors, such as per capita income, per capita full value of property, population density, etc., might be included as variables. A measure of tax effort could be employed to modify the results.

In conclusion it must be emphasized that intergovernmental fiscal relations are of crucial importance for meeting the challenge that developing countries must face in financing housing and urban development. Intergovernmental fiscal cooperation devices such as tax supplement, tax credit, and tax sharing have necessarily to play a much larger role than they presently do. Although these devices may and can provide adequate revenues to the urban local bodies to supplement locally administered tax and non-tax revenues, they fall short in many important respects, the notable ones being their inability to equalize costs and opportunities among different urban areas within the state and/or the country and to influence the local bodies to plan and provide services according to national or state priorities. A suitable system of grants-in-aid therefore must be developed and continuously reviewed to meet the goals and objectives of urban and regional development.

Financing Capital Outlays

The developing countries already need massive capital investments in housing, infrastructure and several other essential urban services. The coming decades will witness a manifold increase in the demand for capital resources. Because of their life span (durability) capital projects have a long-range effect upon the lives of the urban communities and their local governments. Such projects, therefore, need to be planned with a long-term perspective and within the framework of urbanization and national development goals. In fact, urban development projects have to be integral parts of the overall national and regional development programs, although their detailed planning and implementation may very largely rest with urban local bodies or urban development authorities.

Financing Housing and Urban Development

In the overall context of resource limitations, projects for urban development must compete with other development programs for scarce capital resources. In the prevailing circumstances their share is bound to be grossly inadequate even in relation to their high priority needs. This implies that urban local governments or development authorities must make a herculean effort to mobilize additional resources of their own. Ursula K. Hicks correctly points out that capital investment "lies at the very heart of development from below" and that "local capital formation has intrinsic importance not only from the economic and social points of view, but also on psychological grounds."[34] A bulk of capital projects for urban development are initially financed out of borrowings by public agencies at local, state, and national levels. In some cases, one level of government may borrow or raise the money through taxes, etc., and then transfer it to other level(s) of government as capital grants for specified projects and programs. Initial financing of capital outlays for some other programs (housing, non-residential buildings, etc.) either in part or in their entirety may come from savings, loans, and other sources within the private sector. The long-run costs—repayment of principal and interest on loans and maintenance and operating expenditures—for public sector programs, however, have to be financed through tax and non-tax municipal revenues and intergovernmental transfers.

At present, urban local bodies in developing countries have inadequate revenue powers relative to the responsibilities that are or should properly be placed upon them. This is so notwithstanding the fact that they have quite often not even fully utilized the revenue powers already available to them. The much needed devolution of additional revenue resources on local governments will have, therefore, to be backed with, and even preceded by, their own earnest effort at full utilization of their revenue powers.

An equally serious problem is the insufficient ability and access of the local governments to capital or loan funds. With the exception of a small number of them in very large cities, municipal bodies are unable to secure long-term financing against the issuance of their own bonds for various reasons. Important among these reasons, apart from legal constraints on their borrowing powers, are the weakness of their revenue base and unsatisfactory financial housekeeping.

There are two alternative approaches to facilitate loan financing for urban facilities commonly employed in different countries. First, the municipal governments are granted the statutory authority to borrow in the open market primarily through issuance of different types of bonds. The statutes governing this authority generally place certain limitations on the borrowing powers. Second, the local government units may be granted loans by the state and the national governments for approved projects. The second alternative should by and large be preferable for the developing countries, although large cities with good financial record may also be granted the power to borrow funds directly for certain types of projects. Since the regional and national governments are engaged in large-scale borrowing for development programs, the local bodies, even if granted the borrowing power, would be in a poor competitive position.

If loan funds to urban local bodies in developing countries are largely to be provided by higher levels of government, it may be appropriate to set up different revolving funds both at state and national levels. The revolving fund boards can then loan the funds to local bodies and charge them the interest that the former have to pay plus a nominal charge for management of the funds. It may be expedient to set up a small number of separate funds for different types of projects.

It was argued earlier that intergovernmental fiscal relations must play a much enlarged role in urban development programs. In this context the need for more liberal and extensive grants-in-aid was underlined. Urban infrastructure items, such as water supply, sewerage and drainage, city transport, educational and health facilities, and social housing, requiring large initial capital outlays, especially deserve to be aided by specific purpose capital grants or recurring grants or through a combination of both. It should be conceded that the local governments should be treated more generously in the dispensation of loans and grants. At the same time, we have to appreciate that there are severe limitations to the lending and grant-dispensing capacity of the higher governments. And the limitations of the local governments in regard to loan or grant absorption or utilization and debt-redemption of most of the urban governments in Asia are even greater.

The preceding sections of this chapter have already discussed at some length the nature of reforms and innovations in the sphere of municipal tax and non-tax revenues and intergovernmental fiscal relations which should yield sizable additional revenues. A part of this additional revenue could well be used as capital finance. A hitherto neglected but extremely significant area to conduct the quest for additional capital resources is, however, opened up by the spectacular phenomenon of capital appreciation in urban land values. In several Asian countries urban land values, especially in big cities, have been increasing eight to ten times faster than the rate of increase in the general price level.

A direct, really effective and superior method to capture the unearned capital appreciations in urban land values is for the government or the public authorities concerned to engage in fairly large scale urban land business as a procurer, developer, and dispenser of land for residential, commercial, industrial, institutional, and other purposes. This implies their undertaking land development and land banking functions which would be more justified and better served as one of the elements of a socially oriented comprehensive urban land policy. Besides serving various social objectives, such as promoting planned development and curbing land speculation, this activity would generate sizable revenue surpluses for capital financing. The examples of land business by local governments of Norway, Sweden, and the Netherlands and of the Delhi Development Authority in India's capital city are good illustrations of the point.

This approach has a tremendous potential, and when undertaken in conjunction with a revolving fund concept, can provide a high rate of return investment opportunities for urban development authorities, and requires only small initial capital outlays. This may be illustrated by the example of the "Safdarjung Extension Scheme, 1961-69"—one of the many land development projects of Delhi Development Authority (see Table 1). The scheme involved expropriation and development of 294 acres of land. The income and expenditure statement given in Table 1 will show that on an investment of about Rs.20 million with a provision of Rs.5 million for other expenses, the Authority was able to gain a net surplus of Rs.15 million or a 60 percent return on investment.[35]

For financing certain types of public improvement programs which specifically benefit certain properties and where such benefit can be measured, a special levy or tax widely known as a special assessment or similar cost-sharing scheme may be utilized for financing such capital outlays.[36] The special assessments were used extensively in the United States for financing such improvements as streets, curb and gutters, sewers, sidewalks, etc., during the first third of this century, and are presently used in many communities for new

Table 1. Safdarjung Extension Scheme 1961-1969—Statement of Income and Expenditure (Place: New Delhi; Area Involved: 294 acres)

Expenditure	*Amount Rs.*	*Income*	*Amount Rs.*
Compensation for land acquired (8 Rs/sq. yd.)	11,400,000	Auction sale proceeds of 1,045 residential plots (area = 363,345 sq. yd.)	29,777,441
Cost of land development	8,532,000	Sale proceeds of 47 commercial plots (area = 9,969 sq. yd.)	1,861,100
Expenditure on staff, etc.	1,400,000	Sale proceeds of 223 residential plot (area = 46,943 sq. yd.) allotted on no loss no profit bases	1,821,781
		Sale proceeds of land given for schools, libraries, religious uses, telephone exchange, etc.	1,298,914
		Sale proceeds of land allotted for group housing (area = 52,321 sq. yd.)	2,238,519
Total	21,332,000	Total	36,997,755

Source: P. Prabhakar Rao, "Housing and Urban Development in National Development Planning." Bangkok: ECAFE Document E/CN.11/1 and NR/FINHUD/L.2, (August 1972).

subdivisions. A levy known as valorization tax ("impuesto de valorizaciòn") is being used very effectively in large Colombian cities for financing major portions of capital cash for construction of roads and streets.[37] "Betterment levies" having some attributes similar to special assessments have been tried in some of the Asian countries without much success.

Before concluding this section on capital outlays a few observations on the specific question of housing finance are in order. Public sector housing has so far been concentrated on "social housing" for the urban poor, or for government employees. In both cases the housing programs carry open or concealed subsidies which not only limit their scale but make them financially unattractive. Public housing programs do not as yet cover the upper income group housing except for granting some housing loans to eligible individuals. In all national capitals, metropolises, and rapidly developing industrial towns, the demand for such housing is quite considerable. By catering to a small fraction of this demand for high rental housing, the public authorities could gain appreciable revenue surpluses considering the prevailing high market rents. The revenue surpluses could be ploughed back using the revolving fund technique. The initial seed capital for this activity can be provided to local governments and public or semi-public housing authorities concerned from the plan or non-plan budgetary allocations for housing loans to upper income individuals.

Public housing programs could also be made financially more workable by integrating housing with public land programs and viewing both of them as one financial proposition. Under this proposition public housing schemes will not remain confined to the provision of a few dwelling units at several odd locations as is unfortunately the case at present in most developing countries. These integrated programs will have to be conceived in terms of fairly large, well located, multifunctional neighborhoods in which not only houses of various categories but work places, shopping centers, community facilities, etc., are also appropriately provided. In such developments, public authorities could suitably exploit the revenue potential of commercial sites (for movie theatres, supermarkets, business offices, gasoline stations, hotels, shopping areas, etc.) and high income dwelling units or housing plots.[38]

Some of the suggestions made in this section are somewhat unconventional and may give rise to many issues. We should bear in mind, however, that the present desperate housing and urban development situation in the developing countries has built up over several decades past. It would not have been so had the prevailing conventional theories and measures in this regard been relevant, adequate, and effective. Why not then try the unconventional?

Summary and Conclusions

It has to be conceded that the need to solve the critical problems of housing and urban development is urgent. The financial resources, leaving aside other inputs required for the purpose are, however, so frightfully enormous that most countries in the region are definitely not in a position to make even a sizable part of them available at present. It is doubtful if these weak economies would be able to generate commensurate revenue resources within the next ten years or so. The sad implication then is that viable solutions to the problem should be feasible only in the long run when, hopefully, these countries would have attained much higher levels of economic development. Given these fundamental constraints, can something worthwhile be done in the interim to prevent further deterioration of the desperate situation and, to the extent feasible, improve it? The answer to this question is conditionally affirmative. At least two important pre-conditions to this affirmation are: (1) that the present policies, programs, and priorities governing housing and urban development are thoroughly revamped with a view to making investments in them more productive and purposeful, and (2) that the rate of investment in housing and urban development is stepped up very substantially to enable larger and bolder effort in the matter. Fulfillment of these preconditions involves wide-ranging measures.

In spite of the governments' anxiety in regard to housing so well articulated in government documents and national and international conferences on the subject, no country of this region with the singular exception of Singapore has approached the problem of its totality. The approaches have so far been too narrow or sectoral at best. A strong case can be made that problems of urban development should be viewed and dealt with in the context of national development and resource allocation and financing policies and programs have to be specifically linked with national income and social accounts. To this end, an approach towards national urbanization budgeting has been outlined.

For financing urban services the role of taxation of land and buildings must be viewed in a much broader context than just its traditional role as a revenue producer as has been the case in a majority of the more advanced countries of the world. Real estate taxation should be considered as one of the most critical elements of land policies for urban development. Needless to say a bold and comprehensive urban land policy is an essential pre-condition to any meaningful effort in the matter of housing and urban development. One of the key measures forming an integral part of such a policy is direct government (or public authority) intervention in the land market as a land banker and as a major procurer, developer, and dispenser of serviced sites. This would indeed be one of the most potent instruments for ensuring proper land utilization and to bring land speculation, land prices, and unearned land value increments under social control. The role of real estate taxation thus conceived implies that financing of urban government must also rely on non-property taxation. Local sales and income taxes are the two most important non-property taxes. On balance, local sales taxation may be a more suitable source. However, intergovernmental and interlocal cooperation and coordination through such devices as tax supplements and tax credits may be a necessary and desirable condition for utilization of the non-property taxation.

Suitable pricing policies for public utilities and other urban services are a prerequisite to rational allocation and mobilization of resources for urban development.

With all these revenue reforms, the revenues of urban local governments may increase but not sufficiently enough relative to their heavy functional responsibilities. Many of these responsibilities are of regional and national interest. Urban development is basically an intergovernmental process and requires both horizontal and vertical coordination among central, state (regional), and local agencies. Local governments being the creatures and agents of higher governments with narrowly circumscribed territorial, legislative, and revenue jurisdictions cannot hope to achieve financial adequacy and stability unless higher governments come to their rescue through upward transfer of certain functions and downward transfer of revenue. This consideration requires a radical reorganization of municipal government territories, functions, and finances and a realignment of intergovernmental fiscal relations.

NOTES

1. United Nations Bureau of Social Affairs, Population Division, "World Urbanization Trends 1920-1960 (An Interim Report on Work in Progress)," in Gerald Breese (ed.), *The City in Newly Developing Countries*. Englewood Cliffs, N.J.: Prentice-Hall, 1969, pp. 21-53.
2. John P. Lewis, *Quiet Crisis in India*. New York: Doubleday and Company, 1964, p. 181.
3. World Bank, "Urbanization: Sector Working Paper." Washington, D.C.: June 1972, p. 18.
4. See Jacobo S. de Vera, *Evaluation of National Capacity to Expand Housing Programmes and Investments*. Bangkok, Thailand: ECAFE Document No. E/CNII/18/NR/FINHUD/L.3, August, 1972.
5. *Ibid.*
6. World Bank, *op. cit.*, p. 10.
7. *Ibid.*, p. 19.
8. Ved Prakash, *New Towns in India*. Durham, N.C.: Duke University Program in Comparative Studies on Southern Asia, 1969.
9. India (Republic), Planning Commission, *The Third Five Year Plan*. New Delhi: Government of India Press, 1962, p. 610.
10. Government of Pakistan, Planning Commission, *The Third Five Year Plan, 1965-70*. Karachi: Manager of Publications, 1967, p. 363.
11. Stanislaw H. Wellisz, "Economic Development and Urbanization," in Leo Jakobson and Ved Prakash (eds.), *Urbanization and National Development*, Vol. I, South and Southeast Asia Urban Affairs Annuals. Beverly Hills, California: Sage Publications, 1971, pp. 46-47.
12. See for example Ved Prakash, *New Towns in India, op. cit.*, pp. 42-94.
13. *Ibid.* pp. 54-60.
14. On the problem of maintenance of capital assets, see for example Albert O. Hirschman, *The Strategy of Economic Development*. New Haven, Conn.: Yale University Press, 1964, p. 141; and Ved Prakash, *op. cit.*, pp. 116-117.
15. For a discussion of appropriate rates of interest, see W. H. Brown, Jr. and C. E. Gilbert, *Planning Municipal Investment*. Philadelphia: University of Pennsylvania Press, 1961, pp. 264-272; see also J. V. Krutilla and O. Eckstein, *Multiple Purpose River*

Development: Studies in Applied Economic Analysis. Baltimore, Maryland: Johns Hopkins Press, 1958; O. Eckstein, "A Survey of the Theory of Public Expenditure Criteria," in *Public Finance: Needs, Resources, and Utilization.* Princeton, New Jersey: Princeton University Press, 1961, pp. 439-504; and Robert L. Banks and Arnold Kolz, "The Program Budget and Interest Rate for Public Investment," *Public Administration Review,* (December 1966), pp. 283-292.

16. W. H. Brown, Jr. and C. E. Gilbert, *op. cit.,* pp. 264-265.

17. *Ibid.,* p. 267.

18. U. K. Hicks, *Development from Below.* Oxford: The Claredon Press, 1961, p. 347.

19. Mary Rawson, *Property Taxation and Urban Development.* Washington, D.C.: Urban Land Institute, 1961, p. 8.

20. Edwin Seligman, *The Shifting and Incidence of Taxation,* 4th Ed., New York: Columbia University Press, 1921, p. 277.

21. International City Managers' Association, *Municipal Finance Administration.* Chicago, Illinois: International City Managers' Association, 1962, p. 83.

22. *Ibid.,* p. 83.

23. Harry Gunnison Brown, "Taxing Rental Versus Taxing Saleable Value of Land," *Journal of Political Economy,* Vol. 36 (February 1928), p. 164.

24. See also U. K. Hicks, *op. cit.,* p. 356.

25. For details in the ECAFE Region see "Land Policies for Urban and Regional Development in the Countries of the ECAFE Region," a paper prepared by J. P. Sah for the Seminar on Planning for Urban and Regional Development, Including Metropolitan Areas, New Towns and Land Policies, held at Nagoya, Japan, October 10-20, 1966, (Sponsored by the United Nations and the Government of Japan); and J. P. Sah, *Urban Land Policies and Land Use Control Measures in Asia and the Far East.* New York: United Nations Document No. ESA/HBP/AC. 5/14, September 1971.

26. "Report of the Local Finance Enquiry Committee 1951." New Delhi: Government of India Press, 1952, pp. 145-158; see "Report of the Taxation Enquiry Commission 1953-54, Vol. III. New Delhi: Government of India Press, 1955, pp. 400-406; and "Report on Augmentation of Financial Resources of Urban Local Bodies, *op. cit.,* pp. 48-49. See also Gyan Chand, *Local Finance in India.* Allahabad: Kitabstan, 1947, pp. 46-87.

27. "Report on the Augmentation of Financial Resources of Urban Local Bodies," *op. cit.,* pp. 48-49.

28. For details see Advisory Commission on Intergovernmental Relations, *Local Nonproperty Taxes and the Coordinating Role of the State.* Washington, D.C.: 1961, pp. 46-47.

29. *Ibid.,* p. 48.

30. *Ibid.,* p. 48.

31. See for example J. Maurice Miller, "Service Charges as an Important Revenue Source," *Municipal Finance,* Vol. 26 (August 1953), pp. 49-53; Dick Netzer, *Economics of the Property Tax.* Washington, D.C.: The Brookings Institution, 1966; Dick Netzer, *Economics and Urban Problems.* New York: Basic Books, Inc., 1970; J. A. Stockfish, "Fees and Service as a Source of City Revenue: A Case Study of Los Angeles," *National Tax Journal,* Vol. 13, No. 2 (June 1960), pp. 97-121; and Wilbur R. Thompson, *A Preface to Urban Economics.* Baltimore, Maryland: Johns Hopkins Press, 1965.

32. John A. Vieg, et al., *California Local Finance.* Stanford, California: Stanford University Press, 1960, p. 210.

33. Dick Netzer, *Economics and Urban Problems, op. cit.,* pp. 186-187.

34. U. K. Hicks, *op. cit.,* p. 368.

35. P. Prabhakar Rao, *Housing and Urban Development in National Development Planning.* Bangkok: ECAFE, Document No. E/CN.11/1 and NR/FINHUD/L.2, August 1972.

36. A. G. Buehler, *Public Finance,* 3d Ed., New York: McGraw-Hill Book Co., 1948, p. 528.

37. See William H. Rhoads and Richard M. Bird, "The Valorization Tax in Colombia–an Example for Other Developing Countries," in Arthur P. Becker (ed.), *Land and Building Taxes.* Madison: University of Wisconsin Press, 1969, pp. 201-237.

38. J. P. Sah, *Revolving Fund–A Technique for Financing Public Housing Programmes,* in Selected Papers from Symposium on Housing Finance, National Buildings Organization and U.N. Regional Centre, ECAFE, New Delhi, 1966; and ECAFE, *Finance of Housing and Urban Development in India–Case Study, Document No. I and NR/Sem. FHUD/1, May 13, 1970.*

CHAPTER 9

Leo Jakobson and Ved Prakash

URBAN PLANNING IN THE CONTEXT OF A "NEW URBANIZATION"

THE STATE OF THE ART

The debate on whether or not urbanization is a positive or negative factor in national development, or whether there exists a relationship at all, has its modern origins in the social reform movements of the 1850s and their nationalistic counter movements.[1] In one form or other these questions have been raised in the literature on cities and urban planning ever since. The emergence of the "development cities" of the new nations created in the aftermath of World War II has swelled the literature debating the pros and cons of urbanization to new highs, and a resolution of the questions posed in the debate does not seem to be on the horizon.[2]

The discussion is not confined to the academic scene and the chambers of students of urbanization, development, and planning. The decisions of policy makers and the reports of their professional advisors at the national, the regional, and the metropolitan levels are affected by it, as are the recommendations of various international and bilateral technical assistance programs. Therefore, it is not surprising to find that, by and large, no clearly focused and concisely expressed national urban development goals and objectives have been formulated by any society—large or small, developed or developing.

On the other hand, current literature is full of alarm over the conditions which exist in the few large urban centers of the developing countries and over the prospects which continuous urbanization might bring about. McGee represents this alarmist viewpoint in stating that urbanization in the Third World is "pseudo" urbanization because "the process has not been similar to the one that occurred in the advanced countries at comparable stages of industrialization and economic growth."[3] In the Western countries "the growing cities gradually absorbed an increasing proportion of the total population, until the majority ... was living in cities and an 'urbanized society' had come into being."[4] He goes on to suggest that the Western cities were able to absorb their natural population increase as well as an increased flow of migrants from the countryside because "the industrial revolution ... introduced technical improvements which made possible increased productivity in agriculture and allowed rural population to shift to cities."[5] According to McGee, a great regional "wasteland" will emerge because the cities in the developing countries grow despite low levels of industrialization. At best, he suggests, the Asian city will play an important albeit not a central role in the development process.

In a similar vein, Metcalf and Eddy warn that

> ... certain Asian cities, unhinged from the industrialization that caused Western urbanization, are growing at dangerously fast rates ... growth of this magnitude may cause serious economic and political difficulties for the nations involved. The provision of infrastructure and employment to accommodate the population polarization that this urban centralization will bring may preclude significant overall economic growth for Asian nations.[6]

Ernest Weissmann, the former director of the United Nations Center for Housing, Building, and Planning and currently a senior advisor on regional development to the UN, reinforces the above argument by pointing out that

> The 19th century industrial revolution in Europe and North America ... proceeded at a relatively moderate rate. ... As cities expanded a new social structure emerged gradually. ... Now the rush to the capitals and metropolises of Africa, Asia and Latin America is the most intensive, massive and rapid in countries whose natural resources remain underdeveloped and their man-made counterparts—the economic and technical resources and skills—are insufficient.[7]

At present, those on the opposite side of the debate appear to be in the minority. They question the alarm and assign a positive role to urbanization in the context of national development.[8] Sovani and Dotson challenge the "overurbanization" theme in pointing out that

> For example, when in 1895 the degree of urbanization in Sweden was comparable to that of Asia today (8.2 percent in cities of 100,000 or more), the proportion of the labor force in non-agriculture occupations there was less than 45 percent. Even in 1970, though urbanization had increased slightly to 9.3 percent, this proportion was only 51 percent. Conversely, in Switzerland, though the proportion of labor force in non-agricultural occupations was 60 percent in 1888, there was no city with a population of 100,000 or more in the entire country at that time.[9]

and

> The urbanization/industrialization ratio has not, then, been consistent. A few countries only—notably Britain, France, and the United States— furnish the index. Wide disparities still exist between industrialization/ urbanization ratios in developed countries. Trade disadvantage and

late-starts apparently have not precluded urbanization and rapid national development in Japan, Taiwan, and Australia.[10]

Curie supports the thesis that urbanization is crucial to accelerating national economic development.[11] Similarly, in the first chapter of this volume, Dotson and Teune demonstrate that urbanization yields administrative capacity which in turn yields national development. Finally, Laquian in many of his writings has pointed out that the slum dwellers and squatters in large Asian cities make a positive net contribution to development instead of burdening the urban economy and threatening the existing urban order.[12]

From a policy point of view, Norman Uphoff suggests that the various attitudes on urbanization and its relationship to national development can be summarized as follows:

(1) Urbanization is seen as an evil and its growth should be arrested;
(2) Urbanization is a necessary evil; policy should be directed towards minimizing its negative effects;
(3) Urbanization is a conditional good: policy should facilitate its positive effects; and
(4) Urbanization is an unconditional good and should be accelerated.[13]

However, the national development plans for most of the countries in South and Southeast Asia do not contain clearly defined objectives and targets for urbanization. They concentrate on the problems of economic growth and increasing financial resources, and give inadequate attention to relating economic development to its spatial consequences. Some aspects of urbanization are discussed in the plans in conjunction with industrial location policy; others are mentioned separately, and superficially, as problems associated with housing or slums or the need to prepare "master plans" for all cities over a certain size. Dotson defines this lack of attention to urbanization and urban development in national planning as either unconscious, partial, uncoordinated, or negative.

> It is *unconscious*, in the sense that those involved in formulating it are largely unaware of its overall proportions and features. The great bulk of investments with consequences for urban and urbanizing areas originate in the private, not the public, sector. They represent countless decisions of individuals and associations to concentrate themselves, their houses, factories, offices, services, and talents in confined spaces. They include population movements to and among such areas. Included as well are all of the public expenditures by all levels of government, domestic and foreign, which cause or facilitate these concentrations. The public agencies involved, however, do not have nor do they try to obtain an accurate picture of either the dimensions or the components of this "real" policy. They lack information which might be aggregated into the national urban budget.
>
> Urbanization policy is *partial* in relation to the public sector. Few of the points at which governments might act to affect the course and shape of

urbanization are in fact utilized. The really powerful levers are in the hands of national units, and stem mainly from their economic policies: credit, subsidies, tariffs, taxes, and regional investments. But these are not used to provide direction of urbanization. The intermediate, and especially local, units are left to apply feebler instruments, heavily regulatory, and considerably focused on the physical aspects of the urbanization process. The great majority of private urbanization decisions are untouched by public power.

To the extent that it is conscious, present urbanization policy is *uncoordinated*. National plans are formulated apart from those urban plans that do exist. The national plans are primarily economic and the urban ones, primarily physical—revealing intersectoral as well as intergovernmental and interfunctional detachments. This compound disjunction usually results in competing and conflicting policies. Urban units everywhere attempt to externalize their costs.

The thrust of outstanding urbanization policy is *negative*. Public investments and interventions choose—to the extent that they are conscious and effective—to divert, retard, or stop urban growth. They especially aim to inhibit the expansion of metropolises and primate cities. To that end, a great range of instrumentalities is brought into play: rural community development, cottage industries, alternative growth poles, satellite cities, new towns, and so on. The anti-urban preference extends into political representation, in which rural populations are quite unequally represented. No national policy seeks overall to foster urbanization.[14]

In recent years the lack of coordination between economic and spatial planning on the one hand, and the lack of recognition of their combined importance for urban planning and development on the other hand, have begun to receive some attention. We pointed out some of the emerging concerns, with regard to India, in our article on urbanization and regional planning in 1967.[15] Since then one can note that the Indian Government has begun to recognize the importance of Calcutta to national well-being by making a special allocation in the fourth five year plan to support short-term action programs aimed at arresting a further deterioration of the living environment of the city.[16] The Government of Pakistan considers the current Karachi Metropolitan Planning effort one of three "National Pilot Projects"; this suggests an *au par* ranking of an urban problem—albeit an immense one—with rural agricultural and resource problems like "Agrovilles" and "River Basin Development." Finally one could mention that, at the time of writing this chapter (September 1973), the Indonesian National Development Planning Agency is conducting a two-week seminar on regional development with one of its primary objectives being to discuss Indonesia's problems in regard to the relationship of physical and economic planning within a nationwide regional development framework. Though convening this seminar must be considered a laudable attempt towards a more comprehensive planning effort, three limiting observations should be offered:

(1) The dominance of economists among seminar participants and resource personnel—domestic and foreign;

(2) The conspicuous absence of the members of the Harvard Development Advisory Service from a seminar discussing balanced regional growth and sponsored by the agency they are advising;[17] and

(3) With three exceptions, no reference to urbanization in the twenty or so papers submitted to the seminar, and in subsequent discussion.

Balanced regional development and the elimination of disparities between regions have been major objectives expressed in most national plans. But only in a few instances are concrete suggestions presented in regard to the methods for achieving this objective. The Indian five year plans, for example, include explicit location policies as a means for distributing investment in new industry more equitably among the regions. Similarly, small-scale industry is identified and considered in the context of either rural or small town development. Despite these locational attempts, Indian national planners today admit that the decentralization efforts have failed, that the aggregation of industry of all scales has continued in the large cities and that regional disparities have increased rather than decreased.[18]

Another aspect of this quest for decentralization is evident in the continual interest in the development of new towns, in particular in conjunction with large-scale industrial investment but also in conjunction with administrative reforms requiring new capital cities. The model for planning most of these new towns has been the British "garden city" in its manifold company town varieties; but the two most notable capital cities, Islamabad and Chandigarh, are brick and mortar manifestations of the conceptual schema of their planners, Doxiadis and Le Corbusier respectively, and their firm belief in the universal applicability of their grand designs. The resultant cost of this kind of urbanization is enormous, both in economic and in social terms.[19]

At the metropolitan level urban planning has by and large been modeled along the lines of European and North American examples. As a result most of these "master planning" efforts have produced at best some interesting compilations of information about the nature of urban problems, and at worst colorful map and picture books, some of which have become sought after and hard to find collector's items. The conceptual poverty which has long dominated Western urban planning has been exported to the Asian metropolis despite, or possibly because of, the considerable interest which organizations like the United Nations, the Ford Foundation, and some of the bilateral technical assistance programs have shown in problems associated with the fast growth of the primate centers of developing countries.

There are to date only two metropolitan planning efforts which have begun to develop new conceptualizations and to explore new approaches for metropolitan planning in South and Southeast Asia. The first is the Calcutta metropolitan planning effort, largely financed by considerable grants from the

Ford Foundation over a period of some ten years.[20] The second is the above-mentioned Karachi metropolitan plan project, which is financed, in part, through the technical assistance program of the United Nations Center for Housing, Building, and Planning. The Calcutta experience is described in detail in Chapter 5. It is important, however, to summarize here the main conceptual breakthroughs of that efforts:

(1) A broad approach to "consultative plan formulation" with "emphasis on development action, with detailed development programming, essentially involved the conception of planning and implementation as a single continuous process—with direct and continuous participation of politicians, government departments, municipal bodies and executive agencies in the process of plan and programme formulation."[21]

(2) A shift from the traditional emphasis of urban planning—such as the ordering of land use patterns, transportation networks, and hierarchical activity and service systems—to an emphasis on programming minimal improvements in the existing living environment through the provision of basic utility services, e.g., water, sewer, and drainage at standards far below those considered desirable.

(3) A recognition that slum housing and squatter settlements are part of the existing stock of shelter and therefore should be preserved and improved through the provision of minimal sanitary services.

(4) A recognition that the bulk of new housing would not provide a house at all—only a minimal site with access to communal utilities; and that these "open lot" or "site and services" communities would have to be developed at densities similar to those focused in existing unplanned settlements, e.g., 300-400 persons per gross acre.

(5) A basic understanding that the problems of Calcutta are of national and regional significance requiring national participation in their fiscal resolution and a regional strategy for coping with urbanization in Eastern India to reduce if possible some of the immigration pressure, in order to give breathing time for the metropolitan area to catch up, and to halt the process of gradual economic, social, and environmental degradation.

The Karachi plan builds on the Calcutta experience.[22] It moves even further away from a physical planning emphasis, however, by linking the thrust of its proposals directly with the social and economic objectives of Pakistan's national planning effort. The first phase of the program was devoted to an analysis of two alternatives and their impact on seven identified critical issues facing the metropolis: housing, transportation, utilities, education, health, employment, and income. One of the alternatives emphasized economic growth, efficiency, and production. It was identified as the Concentrated Investment Plan because it focused on improving the condition of that segment of the population which would produce maximum returns per unit of investment, e.g., the small but growing middle class. The lower and lowest income groups would benefit from this plan indirectly through spillover and filtering down effects. The second alternative, the Distributive Investment Plan, reversed the order of priorities by emphasizing the needs of the large masses of low income people and providing them with better access to the bare necessities of survival. This alternative was selected by the Steering Committee of the project as the basis for subsequent planning stages as it best reflected the current national objectives of social justice and equity.[23]

Though the Karachi plan has not yet been published in its final format, the preliminary documentation which we have seen suggests that this plan will become a landmark in the conceptual evolution of urban planning. Nevertheless, a review of both the hitherto produced Karachi working documents and the Calcutta plan reveal inconsistencies in the treatment of their various elements as well as in the overall conceptualization of the urban condition they attempt to improve. We attribute these deficiencies to several conceptual dilemmas in our understanding, and interpretation for planning purposes, of the forces that influence the nature of current urbanization in developing countries, in particular in South and Southeast Asia, and of the role and function, and the structure and performance, of the large city in Asia.

IMPROVING THE ART
EIGHT CONCEPTUAL DILEMMAS

The conceptual difficulties facing urban policy formulation and planning in the developing countries manifest themselves at all three planning levels discussed in the previous section. The problem is made more complex by the fact that at each level the manifestations are quite different. For this reason they are often considered separately and are not perceived as part and parcel of a system of forces facilitating or retarding the process of urban development and change. For the purposes of this discussion we have identified the following specific areas of conceptual difficulty: (1) the lack of balance between the forces that influence urbanization; (2) the role of non-economic factors in the decision affecting the location of investment; (3) the duality in the socio-economic characteristics; and (4) the diffused spatial organization of the large Asian metropolis. Furthermore, (5) the enormous scale of the problems; and (6) the slow rate at which they change or can be changed adds to the difficulties of conceptualization, as does (7) their discrete interdependence. Finally, one must recognize that our capacity to conceptualize is reduced by our (8) anti-urban heritage—particularly regarding the big city.

In the following pages we will briefly examine each of these issues and illustrate their implications for policy formulation and planning.

The Process of Urbanization

As we pointed out in the introductory chapter to Volume I of this series, technological progress has been fastest in the secondary sector affecting not only the various cost variables associated with industrial development but, most importantly from the point of view of urbanization, also affecting the job generation potential and human resource requirements of the industrial sector.[23] While in the early stages of Western urbanization, industrial technology was labor intensive and capable of absorbing rural-to-urban migrants in large numbers, most new industry in the developing countries must follow the latest technological developments in order to be competitive on increasingly competitive world markets. Labor intensive industrial development is, therefore, virtually out of the question and thus the mainstay of the Western urbanization model is broken. But even in industries which still today employ large numbers of workers, the employment situation is different. A striking example of this difference can be seen in Panang, Malaysia, where a new industrial estate has been rapidly developing which provides thousands of new jobs for young, single women. On each plant site there are large signs advertising jobs for unmarried women, ages 16-26, with minimal knowledge of simple English. In observing examples like Penang, one can begin to ask questions about the fit of this women-intensive industrialization with the traditional concepts of relationship between urbanization and industrial development; about its multiplier effects; about its consequences on family incomes, household formation, housing demand, and so on.

A second important difference can be found in the area of health. The take-off and early expansion phase of Western industrialization and urbanization occurred before (or concurrently with) improvements in medicine and health care. In the early phases of the Western experience mortality rates were high not only in the countryside but also in the city, thus keeping rural man/land ratios tolerable and the demand for industrial labor high.[25] In the developing countries today vast improvements in the health sector have preceded industrialization and led to a population explosion in both rural and urban areas.

Thirdly, contemporary national development planning often has assigned highest priority to agricultural development, not only for increasing food production but also in the hope that better incomes, higher standards of living, and more jobs in the rural areas would help to lower the tide of urbanization. The "green revolution" may have backfired in this latter respect, however.[26] Though production has increased and incomes are higher, improved agricultural technology tends to reduce rather than to increase manpower demands. Thus more and more people are freed for migration to the city. This condition also represents a departure from the Western experience, because in the West improvements in agriculture did not begin until the process of industrialization was well under way.

If the urbanization of Western Europe and North America was directly correlated with industrialization and dependent upon it—a "pull" relationship—the present-day urbanization of the developing countries is affected not only by the "pull" of industrial development but also by the "push" generated by improved agricultural technology and improved health, with the latter factors increasing in importance. One of the immediate consequences of this internal shift from "pull" to "push" affects the human resources of the city. For the most part, the "pull" of the city attracts the entrepreneurial and the adventurous—two important human factors in development. Those who are "pushed" to the city are often the destitute and the lethargic. In the city, the latter become an added burden limiting the opportunities of the former.

Finally, one must remember that Western industrialization was exploitive; eventually giving birth to unions, fair labor practices, welfare programs, etc. Most of these, however, became effective during the achievement phase of industrialization when the added cost of "social overhead" could be easily absorbed. The developing countries are industrializing in a social environment which is advanced in comparison with the West at similar stages of development.

What has been suggested here is simply that industry and agriculture will not provide jobs sufficiently fast, and in sufficient quantity, for the exploding populations of the developing countries. Furthermore, their dependency on a worldwide market system does not allow for a retreat to labor intensive methods in the primary and secondary sectors. As population surpluses will continue to grow and will continue to flow into urban centers, national policy must begin to address itself boldly and directly to the problem of overcoming the technological, economic, and social leaps which have taken place since the West began to industrialize and urbanize.

In our estimation there are three basic national policy issues which would address themselves directly to the problems raised. First, in order to overcome the leap in medicine and health services, firm programs must be established to reduce birth rates to manageable levels. To make family planning successful, an effort must be made to develop an economic and social environment conducive to viewing smaller families as an opportunity for improving living conditions. This may have to be combined with parallel programs of economic sanctions against large families as currently contemplated in Singapore. Regardless of approach, family planning must be made co-equal with such national policy issues as increased food production, the utilization of natural resources, and the raising of incomes.

But even if more and successful attention is given to family planning, considerable lead-time is required until the impact of a reduction in birth rates is felt. There is a need, therefore, to introduce interim measures which would keep some of the surpluses in the rural labor force from migrating to cities, particularly to the large ones. As has been advocated by many, and equally challenged by others, massive public works programs appear to be the only way in which new jobs could be created in rural areas in a quantity which would have some influence on migration.[27] These programs would not have to be limited to the improvement of rural infrastructure; they could become part of developmental investment required to overcome existing locational disadvantages between regions. Also, public works programs could be directed towards the management of natural resources, e.g., afforestation, soil conservation and reclamation, etc. Finally, in areas where intensive cropping patterns exist, organized mobile units of farm labor could become part of the labor force in public works programs.

The conceptual difficulty with the two policy areas which are discussed above lies in the fact that to many planners they have no direct association with the problems of cities as traditionally perceived. Nevertheless, they should be given highest priority as critical elements of a national urbanization policy. Both of them are directed towards a common goal: to reduce the impact on urbanization of improvements in health and agriculture.

It can be argued that the proposed policies address the problems associated with urbanization in a negative vein. One can ask the question: are there no "positive," growth-related national policy opportunities with respect to urbanization that would warrant discussion? In answering this question we must keep in mind the earlier suggestion of strong interdependency not only horizontally between sectoral issues at each planning level, but also with respect to vertical interdependency between issues at each level. Thus, the national policy area of job generation in the tertiary sector is directly linked to corollary policies and plans at the metropolitan level. Here we face again a conceptual dilemma: though most of the current job generation in the advanced economies takes place in the service and the service-to-service sectors, in the developing countries the leap from an early industrial to a pre post-industrial state cannot be easily made. The planning for increasing jobs in the tertiary sector must relate to the existing condition in Asia and to the duality of this condition. One could suggest that this presents an opportunity despite the fact that no conceptual models exist for simultaneous job generation in the bazaar and modern components of the tertiary sector. The implementation of policies in this area would require the stimulation of entrepreneurship, the provision of management services, experimentation, and risk capital. All these are alien propositions to modern national planning which heavily attempts to rely on facts and projections rather than conjecture and experimentation. To the best of our knowledge, only Malaysia's second five year plan has discussed job generation in the tertiary sector as a viable proposition for national planning.

At the metropolitan and regional planning levels the job generation opportunities of the tertiary sector are equally ignored. This has been the case in the Calcutta and Karachi plans, which in many other respects have made significant contributions to the advancement of planning in Asia. But in most cases the size of the labor force in the tertiary sector is considered an undesirable, premature phenomenon. For example, the authors of the West Java Development Plan conclude that:

> ... it is a remarkable fact and indeed disturbing that the industrial revolution has so far not taken place in Indonesia; *there is even a danger that it will be skipped altogether,* the working population in the services sector already being two and one-half times as large as in the industrial sector!
>
> It is probable that a 'push' to the tertiary sector has taken place without the necessary economic basis for this being present.[28]

These statements and similar remarks in other planning reports are indicative of a conceptual void in recognizing the distinctions between Western urbanization and the causes and forces of industrialization and urbanization in Asia today.

Paucity in Regional Planning Concepts

Regional planning concepts are mainly derived from economic location theory, which is based on the empirical evidence generated from observations of development in countries like England, France, Germany, and the United States. As these countries are approaching the threshold of total urbanization, new factors have emerged and have begun to influence locational decisions. Most of these factors are non-economic in nature and are related to social concerns, e.g., environment, living conditions, and recreational, educational, and cultural amenity.[29] It can be suggested that an analogous situation exists in most developing countries where national plans emphasize social goals and objectives in discussing regional development, though these objectives often are expressed in economic terms (e.g., the elimination of disparity in personal income between regions). Reference is also made to such considerations as the strengthening of national unity and identity, the preservation of culture and tradition, etc. As the emergence of non-economic location criteria can be attributed to affluence and advanced technologies, the application of such criteria for obtaining social and political goals in the developing countries may not be feasible. However, it may be possible—in the context of a comprehensive national urbanization policy as discussed in the previous section—to direct a rural public works program towards reducing the locational and economic disadvantages of selected regions. This implies the strengthening of regional infrastructure through investment in transportation, power, and utilities according to a desired normative schema rather than on the basis of need.

The difficulties associated with the acceptance, let alone the effectuation, of policies of this kind are obvious because they do go contrary to current practice, as we have pointed out in our essay on regional planning in India.[30] We feel strongly, however, that only normative conceptual regional development policy, rather than the prevailing trend-based and analytic methods, can reduce the economic advantage of aggregation and metropolitan location. Thus regional planning can help to slow down the growth of metropolitan centers and reinforce national urbanization policy. In contrast to "growth pole," "growth zone," "counter-magnet," and other suggestions for the decentralization of economic activity, our regional strategy is based solely on a normative interpretation of national goals. We feel that in a policy context the dichotomy of economic versus non-economic location criteria must be polarized and carried out consistently. Any reference to seeking out the "next best" or "potential" economic location factors (as in the case of growth pole concepts) acknowledges the supremacy of economic considerations in decisions affecting the location of investment. The step from the "next best" location to the "best" becomes a logical one notwithstanding the fact that this logic voids any agreed-upon regional strategy. A concept of "best location" in non-economic terms must dominate policy and the decision process in the implementation of regional development strategy. Only after basic locational decisions have been made should economic criteria be applied toward minimizing the costs and maximizing the returns from the original decision. The conceptual dilemma of this approach is clear: it reverses the current order of considerations in decisions affecting the location of economic activity.

The Duality of Urban Society

Drawing upon Geertz, Boeke, Higgins, and others, McGee has provided us with a most promising description and model of the duality that permeates every aspect of life and activity in the Asian metropolis.[31] An examination of most metropolitan plans reveals, however, that this duality, if acknowledged at all, is considered in a linear temporal context only: the bazaar economy, to use McGee's terms, represents the past and the capitalist economy the future. By definition, planning is concerned with the future. Thus, many plans focus on the modern sector only, in the simplistic hope that the hawkers, the bullock carts, the rickshaws, and all the other manifestations of an unorganized, unhealthy, unclean, and inefficient past will somehow disappear if no provisions are made in the plans for their continual presence. An excellent example of this naivete can be found in the new steel town of Durgapur, where the green buffer space in the plan between the residential area and the industrial area turned virtually overnight into a bustling bustte with a population several times that of the steel town itself—providing all the traditional services for the industrial labor force and their families. The sad part in this transformation of a planned green buffer zone into a human buffer zone is not in the fact that it took place but the fact that it took the Indian planners and project administrators by surprise. Discussions with them revealed that they were totally oblivious to the condition of the society of which they were part and did not understand that the traditional and the modern were not only interdependent as activities but also interlocked in their spatial arrangements.

As we have already pointed out, the Calcutta plan was the first to recognize the duality of the socio-economic system, specifically in its proposals for housing, bustee improvement, and community services, and the Karachi plan has extended this recognition even further through the concept of distributive

Urban Planning in the Context of a "New Urbanization" 271

investment. However, plans fail to recognize this duality beyond the sectors directly related to social development. Thus the discussions and proposals in regard to economy and administration, and in particular with regard to the sectors in which engineering plays an important role (e.g., transportation and utilities), are dominated by concepts, methods, and techniques applicable to the modern sector only. In the Karachi case this has been ably summarized by Sigurd Grava, one of the five panelists invited by the United Nations to review the plan:

> It is unfortunate that very little fundamental thought has been organized in this area by the technical experts in general. Monorails and central secondary sewage treatment plants are, of course, fine, but they have a few serious shortcomings in the developing countries context:
>
> — They require very large (and lumpy) resource investment;
> — They depend on highly sophisticated technology (construction and operation);
> — They are not particularly labor intensive;
> — They require very often the importation of foreign skills, methods, hardware, and habits—they consume foreign exchange;
> — They lend themselves little to incremental flexibility—they are not convertible;
> — They provide service standards that may not always be called for in light of other very pressing needs.
>
> I am fully aware that the technical planners' currently prevailing attitude of favoring high technology solutions is abetted in no small measure by:
>
> — The established procedures of international financing organizations; and
> — Perceptions of national pride as expressed in visible examples of technical progress at the local level.
>
> Yet, much can be done to at least establish realistic approaches and to effectuate more modest solutions that gradually lead to the more sophisticated methods.[32]

Grava's recommendations for incremental solutions and a utilization of less capital intensive traditional utility and transportation methods is supportive of Burton and Lee's concluding admonition in Chapter 6 to be "a little old fashioned."

Incorporating the duality of the socio-economic system into policies and plans for urban development is complicated by the fact that, although the characteristics of the two components can be succinctly described, only the modern sector can be measured with reasonable accuracy. This naturally limits the usefulness of modern analytic methods and techniques. Furthermore, though the interdependency of both systems is obvious, the critical linkages between the two are often discrete and difficult to isolate. The problem is compounded even more by the dual dynamics of the system: the modern sector slowly interpenetrates the bazaar sector and gradually increases its proportionate share, whilst both sectors continue to grow internally, though at different rates. In most metropolitan areas the bazaar sector will remain dominant for a considerable period into the future because of the slowness of change and the sheer size of the sector. We will discuss the conceptual problems associated with rates of change and scale later in this chapter.

The Diffuse Metropolitan Structure

In spatial terms, planning for the Asian metropolis is made difficult by the fact that the two components of the socio-economic system not only coalesce as activity but also tend to utilize the same physical space. In other words, two interpenetrating dynamic systems with entirely different spatial organization and space requirements must be accommodated in the same urban field; not as two separate systems, but as one integrated system. Western planning experience provides no models for this, and to date no Asian plans have attempted to solve this problem. Only in a few isolated instances and for limited purposes can one find examples of indigenous solutions to this problem. For example, the transformation of parking structures serving the modern sector during the day into a lively multi-story market of the bazaar sector at night may be unique to Singapore and Hong Kong at present, but may well serve as a model for experimentation elsewhere. Another example which appears to function reasonably well can be seen in Jakarta, where the main local limited access artery is reserved for modern vehicles and the service roads on both sides carry buses, bicycles, rickshaws, and other slow-moving vehicles. Most new modern construction—hotels, office buildings, manufacturing plants, department stores—is taking place in this linear corridor interspersed with shacks and stalls housing bazaar activities. Though these breaks in modernity will disappear over time, immediately to the rear of the multi-story modern sector buildings there remains a vast hinterland of dense, single story traditional housing and bazaar activity. The physical links remain intimate and intact despite the continual change that takes place.

An examination of the Jakarta Master Plan reveals that though the plan recommends a continuation of commercial and institutional ribbon development along its major thoroughfares, it was not based on conceptualization of the proposed land use pattern as uniquely suitable for accommodating socio-economic duality. To the contrary, one can conclude from the document that the ribbon pattern is a mere expression of expedience rather than logic or an understanding of its inherent merits.[33]

What has been overlooked by the modern planners of Asian cities is that the modern city itself is in a state of flux and that its spatial organization has undergone considerable change in the process of transformation from a pre-industrial to a post-industrial state. In these changes one can see possible cues to the spatial problems created by duality in social and economic activity. For example, the Western metropolis as it progresses toward a post-industrial state of total urbanization becomes more and more diffuse in its spatial structure. As a result, the models of concentric growth and sectoral differentiation which were developed from observations during the stage of rapid industrialization become obsolete. Also, in this process towards a diffuse spatial structure, the functional coalescence and the hierarchical ordering of urban activities is destroyed making the basis for virtually all current land use planning and zoning principles, norms, and standards invalid.

The Swedish architectural historian Göran Lindahl draws a comparison between the diffuse "institutional urban landscape" of the post-industrial city and the spatial structure of the medieval city.[34] Albeit the differences in scale are enormous, the conceptual analogy appears to be accurate. As a conjecture one could then suggest that a diffuse polynucleated urban structure is characteristic of a social order in which growth and change are slow processes. Fourastié, as well as Gross, suggest that one of the basic characteristics of pre-industrial society is stability. They predict that will hold true for post-industrial societies as well.[35] This structural similarity between the existing patterns of the primate metropolis and the emerging patterns of the Western metropolis is quite apparent and may provide a simple model for planning the Asian city: (1) maintain and strengthen its existing diffused spatial organization; (2) constrain centripetal locational tendencies as well as tendencies towards functional differentiation and concentration: in particular the formation (or growth) of a central business district; (3) avoid concentric land use allocation, and single mode radial transportation systems; and (4) allow for the interpolation of the modern with the traditional through ribbon development along major transportation corridors.[36]

We believe that spatial schema based on the four suggestions outlined above would provide for the emergence of land use patterns that would allow for coexistence and development of both components of the socio-economic systems. Locational decisions would not require large-scale analytic studies nor the setting up of an extensive land use control apparatus. Most importantly, they would not impose stifling modern requirements on the bazaar sector.

The Problems of Scale

Ashish Bose has often reminded us that the scale of urbanization in the developing countries is of equal if not greater importance than the level of urbanization and the rate at which it changes.[37] We agree with his concern but would like to add a note to the effect that the conceptual problems associated with scale are more acute at the metropolitan level than at the national level because scale is not only a measure of the absolute but is also a concept associated with the relative. In the context of policy formulation and the setting of priorities, the relative aspect of scale increases further in importance. For example, to the national policy formulator in Indian, 60 million urbanites is a small or modest figure when compared with the 500 million people or more that he must consider. On the other hand, to his metropolitan counterpart the 8 million residents of the Calcutta conurbation become a colossal issue because he judges the scale of his problems not only in comparison to other urban centers but he is influenced also by their concrete and immediate presence, whereas to the man in Delhi the problems of urbanization and urban development are abstract statistical phenomena to be equated with issues like the balance of payments or the gross national product. In each instance the "true" scale becomes then a composite image of the absolute expressed in quantifiable terms, e.g., population size, and the relative impression of that absolute on the observer.

In the case of the city we have developed a size-related descriptive scale ranging from hamlet to megalopolis. We have also developed a clear image of the size of each place related to its urban description. A hamlet would be always defined as very small or minute, and a megalopolis as very large or colossal. In no case, however, are these terms defined in absolute terms, e.g., population size. Urban literature, however, reveals that there are apparent numerical ranges which define the choice of the descriptive terms. If one chooses the five most common descriptive terms for defining urban places, size image, and population range, they correspond approximately as shown in Table 1. The concept of relativity embodied in this table is skewed by one's position in the planning hierarchy. For example, from a local perspective the image of community size will probably be stepped down from the position shown in the table so that anything over one million population is considered very large; the reverse is true when problems are viewed from a national perspective. At the regional level two opposites tend to emerge depending on program emphasis. If the planning effort is directed towards rural-agricultural development, the hamlet and town become important and the bigger cities are stepped down. The reverse takes place when urban-industrial development is stressed. This is shown graphically in Figure 1. Comprehensive urbanization policy should attempt to reduce these distortions in perspective and balance national, regional and local policy.

At the local level scale presents a further problem. As the size of the city increases the issues for decisions affecting development become larger, more complex, and, consequently, more difficult. There exists an internal analogy to the local-national perception gap. To overcome this gap we suggest that at the metropolitan scale simplification is necessary in the materials used for policy

Table 1. Scale of Urban Definitions

Definition	*Image of Size*	*Population Range*
Megalopolis	Colossal (very large)	over 10 million
Metropolis	Large	1-10 million
City	Medium (modest)	100,000-1 million
Town	Small	10,000-100,000
Hamlet	Minute (very small)	under 10,000

Urban Planning in the Context of a "New Urbanization" 275

Figure 1. Urban Scale Perspectives

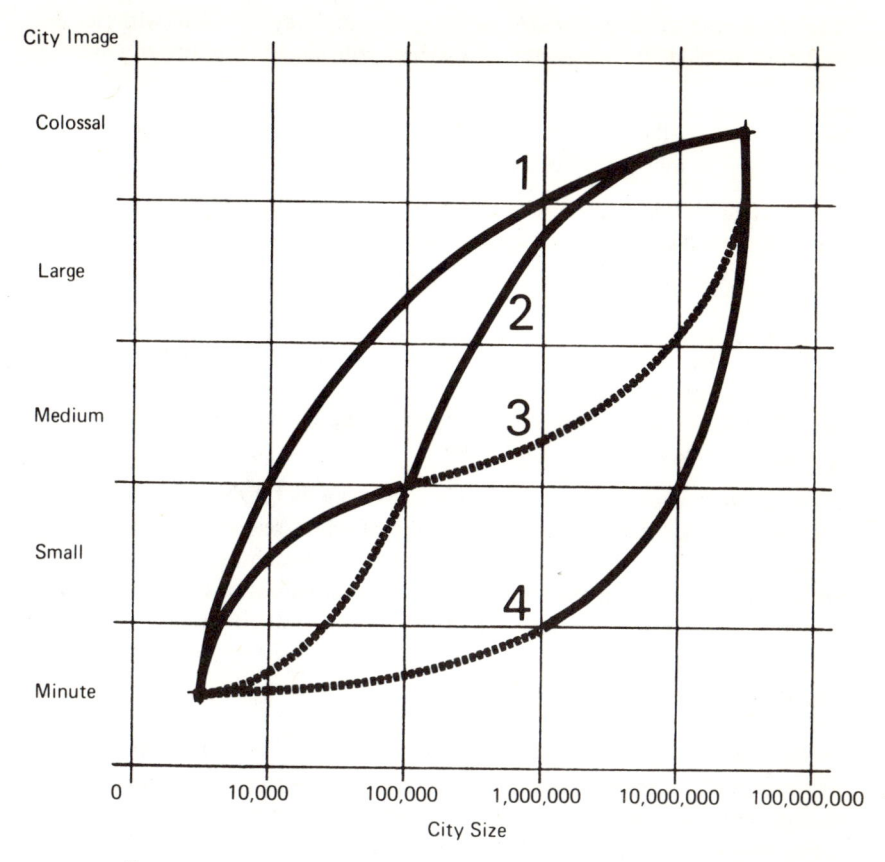

Perspectives:
1. Local
2. Regional Urban
3. Regional Rural
4. National

formation. There are several techniques for doing this, e.g., abstraction, approximation, rounding, comparison, clustering, etc., but in the metropolitan plans which we have examined, we find very little of this. To the contrary, it appears that the larger the problem, the greater the effort to be specific, comprehensive, all-inclusive. And often, after elephantine labor to compile fine-grain statistics disaggregated to the neighborhood level, a mouse is hatched in terms of information useful for metropolitan policy formulation. In fact, the detail and the volume of information tends to obscure critical issues and to confuse the decision maker. Furthermore, as Grava has pointed out in commenting on the statistics of the Karachi plan:

> ... in my opinion, 75 percent of it was of questionable practical, as well as theoretical, usefulness. An aura of scientific precision and careful planning

is attempted, but it should be clear to anybody familiar with local conditions that the apparently logical and convincing structure is a house of cards.

After describing the problems associated with data and information in most developing countries he suggests that:

> ... extensive tables purporting to show the future state of the area to the last decimal place can only be regarded with doubt, if not with scorn,

and concludes with the following recommendation in which we fully concur:

> There is much to be said for order-of-magnitude estimates and prototypical calculations of specific items to show possibilities and consequences, but any study resources beyond that could surely be more profitably devoted to conceptual analysis, original though, and work with official bodies and local organizations.[38]

In this discussion of scale we are simply suggesting that if the urban condition is colossal, it really matters very little if the absolute scale is one of 12 or 15 million. In human terms, both are staggering figures requiring conceptualizations beyond those we are accustomed to. The conceptualizations, however, will be the same for both figures or any other figure in the "colossal" range.

The Snail's Rate of Change

Rates and ratios are often considered in conjunction with scale or as parts of our concepts of scale. They are however entirely different measures. For example, a small town can double in size and so can the metropolis. If they do it in the same time space, their rate of change—in this instance growth—is the same, but their scales are of a totally different magnitude. On the other hand, the metropolis by doubling in size may become a megalopolis—a distinct change in scale but in its internal structure this doubling may have resulted in minimal change. The same may be true of the small town: it could become a city, without significant change except for size. As we are less concerned with size than with effectuating change and improvement, the slowness of change in the internal condition of the metropolis is most frustrating to those who are devoting their energies to the formulation of plans and programs towards these ends. To illustrate this point we will use the income projections of the Karachi "Distributive Investment Plan." As shown in Table 2, the estimates present an income distribution pattern by 1985 which by and large represents doubling of income. In relative terms, measured in percent of population in the various income brackets, the data suggest a significant improvement in the urban condition. But when we translate these percentages into absolute numbers of people as shown in Table 3 the following can be noticed:

(1) If urban growth continues at current levels—resulting in a doubling of the population during the income doubling effort—the number of

Urban Planning in the Context of a "New Urbanization" 277

persons below the nutritional deficiency threshold has remained about constant. This can be considered an improvement because deterioration in nutrition levels has been halted. However, the number of persons below the minimal urban amenity threshold that requires a 100 percent subsidy for all urban services will have doubled. This means, among other things, that if no fully subsidized "sites and services" areas are rapidly developed, squatter settlement will continue to expand and almost double in size. Finally, the population in the partial subsidy range will have quadrupled. This poses a different problem: that of a volatile, vocal, and literate minority of considerable political influence. In this income group, expectations rise fastest and unmet wants easily grow to explosive levels. This is also the group which straddles the border between the traditional and the modern, adding to the problem of planning for their satisfaction.

(2) If growth could be halved (as shown in the last column of Table 3), improvements could be seen more readily. For example, the incidence of malnutrition would be reduced by about one-third and the potential additional squatter population would have grown by only 50 percent. But this target of halving growth means a virtual stoppage of immigration because the natural growth of the existing population would fill the growth quota.

(3) If improvement at the lower end of the income ladder will be hardly discernible—in fact it may appear that the condition will have deteriorated—at the top of the ladder there will be highly visible outward manifestations of growth: the number of private automobiles may triple, so will the demand for housing, offices, shops, etc., at modern space and amenity standards.

For comparison, Table 4 shows that the situation is similar in most large metropolitan centers in Asia. It is therefore safe to surmise that regardless of

Table 2. Projected Income Distribution for 1985—Karachi

Monthly Household Income in Rupees	Percent of Total 1969-70	1984-85	Income Characterization
Below 250	33.6	15.5	Below satisfactory nutrition requirements
250-500	48.6	49.0	Below minimal urban amenity level
500-1,000	12.6	26.1	Below non-subsidized urban amenity level
Over 1,000	5.2	9.4	Above subsidized urban amenity level
Total	100.0	100.0	

Source: Karachi Master Plan, Second Cycle Report, July, 1973 (Income characterization by authors).

Table 3. 1985 Population by Income Assuming Different Growth Rates

Monthly Household Income in Rupees	Number of Persons at Different Growth Rates 1970-1985			
	1970 (Base)	4.8 Percent	3.6 Percent	2.4 Percent
Below 250	336,000	310,000	271,250	232,500
250-500	486,000	980,000	857,500	735,000
500-1,000	126,000	522,000	456,750	391,500
Over 1,000	52,000	188,000	164,500	141,000
Total	1,000,000	2,000,000	1,750,000	1,500,000

growth rate, Asian metropoli, such as Karachi, Calcutta, or Jakarta, will appear to the casual observer 10-15-20 years from now very much the same as today ... only larger in size. To the planner and urban administrator this conclusion is very frustrating indeed. He may well ask, is it all worth the effort? To K. C. Sivaramakrishnan, the able director of the Calcutta Metropolitan Development Authority, the effort is worthwhile:

> If we now can begin to contain the further deterioration of the conditions of life in Calcutta, we will create the opportunity to begin to think about improvements later on in the future.[39]

The Tangle of Interdependencies

Industrialization and its corollary—urbanization—can perhaps be fruitfully studied in the insularity of academic discipline, as can industrial location theory, or the dualistic nature of the Asian city. In the arena of public policy, experts on only fragments of knowledge often limit the perspective of the decision maker. The important thing is to recognize that all these phenomena are part and parcel of development in its economic, social, and spatial dimensions, and that planned

Table 4. Percent Population in Comparative Income Brackets: Karachi, Calcutta, Jakarta—About 1970

Karachi		Calcutta		Jakarta	
Monthly Household Income (Pakistan Rs)	Percent	Monthly Household Income (Indian Rs)	Percent	Monthly Household Income (Indonesian Rs)	Percent
Below 250	33.6	Below 200	46.1	Below 7,500	57.5
250-500	48.6	200-400	27.0	7,500-15,000	27.7
500-1,000	12.6	400-800	16.2	15,000-30,000	11.0
Over 1,000	5.2	Over 800	10.7	Over 30,000	3.8
	100.0		100.0		100.0

Sources: Karachi—Second Cycle Report, Karachi Master Plan, 1973.
Calcutta—A Housing Policy for Metropolitan Calcutta, 1971.
Jakarta—Census and Statistical Office, DCI Jakarta, 1969.

intervention in the form of policy, plan, or program in one component affects the others. The degree of these effects may vary. Nevertheless, their very existence may render the original intervention ineffective or impair the effect of other policies because of the horizontal linkages between the components of a social system like the city and the vertical linkages between, for example, urbanization as a national phenomenon and the growth of a metropolitan area where the abstraction "urbanization" becomes grounded and concrete.

The sorting out of these interdependencies is important for the formulation of policy and for the establishment of priorities. In many instances this becomes a matter of pure judgment because neither available data nor the expert's interpretation of the data allows for a determination of causality or priority. The choice between a chicken or an egg is therefore simply a matter of likes and dislikes. In conceptual terms, the planner builds again a house of cards: not only are his data questionable, but so is the logic of his construct if the chickens and eggs appear in the wrong order in the decision makers' views. The choice of planning method becomes important in this context. Methods which lean on analogies and concept transfers, on dialectic and teratology, and expose conflict through matrices and dichotomous pairing, appear preferable to the traditional planning approaches which mainly rely on methods stressing phenomenological description, linear progression, and causality.

Values and Planning: The Anti-urban Sentiment

The prevailing world-wide attitude among politicians of all persuasions is anti-urban, in particular anti-big-city.[40] As this attitude is commonly shared by planners of all kinds, it is hardly surprising that policies and programs dealing with urbanization and urban development are given low priority in national planning and low attention in implementation at the local level. The actual condition often supports the bias. The statistics on urbanization show that the level is low and the rate slow, hence the logic for a low priority is clear. At the other end of the spectrum an equally convincing logic emerges. The scale is too large, the investment requirements too big; therefore, scarce resources should be allocated to projects which promise quicker returns like building new towns instead of repairing old ones.

In nearly every instance, however, the national decision makers reside and work in a primate capital city, the existence of which they abhor, but the growth of which is contributed to by their very presence! But the creation of new capitals to isolate the decision makers even further from the unpleasant reality of the urban condition is no solution. Nor do we expect anti-urbanism to disappear overnight. What we urge is that the planner, as a professional, not let his personal biases interfere with his judgment. After all, if one dislikes the big city—and this dislike is rather easy for one to acquire—how can one formulate policies, programs, and plans which may render the object of dislike attractive? Urban planning, like all professional work, requires devotion in order to be successful. The bigger the task, the more devotion is required. And when one reaches the colossal scale of the Asian megalopolis even devotion may not suffice. True love may be needed indeed, but how many planners are there who honestly could profess to love Calcutta?

There are a few signs that change is in the offing. For example, the concept of a "new urbanization" emerged during the Pacific Conference on Urban Growth in 1967.[41] It represented a drastic departure from "prior doctrine" in that it viewed urbanization as a positive phenomenon in the process of development which when properly organized should be encouraged. The conceptual dilemmas just described suggest that at the metropolitan level there exists an equal need to discard prior doctrine and current practice. New responses, new conceptualizations, and new methods and techniques are required to cope with problems of scale, time and duality, and analogous means would have to be invented for the administration, financing, and implementation of these new metropolitan plans.

A NORMATIVE APPROACH TO METROPOLITAN PLANNING

According to Erich Jantsch, normative thinking is one of the critical innovative forces in planning. This conception of an integrated planning-forecasting system involves the matching, through successive iteration, of normative criteria, stating needs and desires with available resource opportunities within a framework of purposive goal statements.[42] Though normative thinking in one form or another has been part of planning at all levels of government, its role has seldom been explicitly stated, nor have the requirements on the process of planning of systematic "inventive" planning (in contrast to traditional "projective" planning) been evaluated. In our estimation, a clearly defined normative model like Jantsch's lends itself exceptionally well to overcoming most of the conceptual problems discussed in the previous section. For one thing, the national goals which most often are purposive in nature—like Indonesia's goal of strengthened feelings of national unity—provide the basis for all planning activity. Second, a set of hierarchically organized criteria can be stated which identify the means for obtaining the goal. For example, national unity can be strengthened through the creation of new, expanded, and more diffused sets of economic interdependence. This may require one or more of the following: investment in non-economic locations, establishment of new communication links, change in fiscal policy and incentives, planned population movements, etc. The choice among alternatives is determined through exploratory research examining the specific opportunities and liabilities associated with each of the alternatives, and the general probabilities of goal attainment.

There is then a fundamental distinction in the role and the nature of research between traditional planning practice and a normative planning process model. In the latter the emphasis is shifted from an empirical plane which attempts to describe in great detail all possible phenomena associated with the urban condition to a selective, highly focused plane where the research effort attempts to support, or to refute, normative conceptions about a desired future. In other words, the resource base is scanned for opportunities rather than described in terms of conditions and problems. This exploratory approach to research is conceptually analogous with Grava's earlier quoted remarks about the futility of collecting voluminous statistics of doubtful value when order-of-magnitude estimates and prototypical calculations suffice.

Another, methodological, advantage of normative planning lies in the conceptual and temporal distinctions between forecasts and projections. Most traditional planning utilizing empirical research methods depends on projection as a means of assessing the future. However, if as Ozbekhan has pointed out, "the future should be viewed as a solution to the present, not an extension of it ...," projection becomes useful only for assessing the future magnitude of a condition if existing trends will continue.[43] A forecast, on the other hand, is a probabilistic statement, on a relatively high confidence level, about the future. Exploratory forecasting starts from today's assured basis of knowledge and is oriented towards the future, while normative forecasting first assesses future goals, needs, desires, etc., and works backward to the present.[44] A plan, in this context, represents a statement about the future in which the normative and the exploratory are brought into balance: the felt needs are met by identified opportunities in the area of resources.

The temporal distinction between forecast and projections is important in that forecasts are not bound to a rigidly scaled linear concept of time which forms the basis for all projections. Normally, a forecast would require a sequence of events to take place until the forecast has reached a state of fruition. However, each sequence may have its own time frame, and pauses may occur between them because each sequence may "depend on a configuration of feasibilities, which may have to await maturity in other fields."[45] In relation to the conceptual problems discussed, this freedom from a single, strictly linear time frame allows, for example, for incremental action programs of a relatively small scale to have a slow cumulative impact on the bazaar sector where minimal improvements at equally minimal standards are the only feasible solution, while, at the same time, modern sector development can take place at its own rate, scale, and time frame unhampered by the remedial programs in the traditional sector. The link between the two lies in the spatial organization of the metropolitan area. As we have suggested earlier each system must have its own clearly defined space, however not in widely separated large tracks, as for example in the case of Islamabad-Rawalpindi, nor, on a somewhat less grandiose scale, in Bhubaneswar-Cuttack, but rather in diffuse, intermixed layouts with linear strips of modern development along "high accessibility corridors" lacing the base of dense, traditional urban structure, as is currently most clearly seen in the case of Jakarta.

The distinction between "remedial" improvements in the traditional sector and "developmental" investment in the modern sector leads to the questions associated with the apparent differences between the urbanization processes of the West and the developing countries, in particular the vast difference in the human, economic, and technological conditions at their respective take-off stages. Though we have suggested that there is no way to change the inevitable course of urbanization, and that the stages will be very similar to those experienced by the West requiring policies which recognize the differences in public capacity to deal with the consequences of urbanization at each stage of the process as well as with the cumulative nature of the total process, internally, at the metropolitan level, the duality of the urban condition and the concomitant freedom from rigid linearity in developmental actions, present opportunities for a simultaneous application of policies which in the Western model required temporal succession.[46] For example, the gravitation towards centrality, and its corollary, concentric expansion at lower and lower densities, was a typical structural expression of Western urbanization during its expansion stage. Currently the enormous capital investment in this structure has become an impediment to logical adjustment to new structural patterns attuned to the great advances in technology and social and economic conditions. By maintaining and strengthening the diffused structure of the primate city, the Asian metropolis may be able to "leap" over that stage of Western urban progression which has caused the costliest problems to arise in the history of the Western city. Planning policy must, then, provide for the opportunity to "leap" out of the context of "normal" progression. This supports, again, a normative forecasting-planning approach not only because it is more flexible than the projecting approach but also because it is more capable of accommodating dual dynamic conditions progressing at different rates.

Our final argument for a normative approach to planning is associated with the institutional arrangements and the generation of administrative and fiscal capacity for plan implementation. The duality of the conditions and the multiplicity of incremental possible futures require conceptualizations for urban management which go beyond tradition. Colin Rosser's suggestions for "action planning" in Calcutta are indicative of the nature of these measures. Among other things, he mentions the need to mobilize local voluntary organizations for a concerted effort of local community development within a metropolitan context.[47] The Asian city is not only an agglomeration of people, it is also an agglomeration of associations, and contrary to its Western counterpart the malaise of alienation has yet to penetrate its fabric. An enormous untapped development potential exists therefore which could be unleashed through inventive programs of community organization. The opportunities associated with community organization require planning solutions which are capable of implementation at the self-help level requiring minimal investment, for example "seed money" only. They must, however, possess community appeal and the prospect of instant return. These requirements correlate with the remedial nature of minimal improvements at minimal standards in the bazaar sector where most, if not all, of Rosser's action planning would take place.

The very nature of action planning sets forth another requirement for departure from current planning practice. This is the area of planning controls. We suggest that the traditional sector by the very nature of its intricate socio-economic structure does not lend itself to modern regulation in the form of zoning or other land-use controls. However, the network of associations exercises strong discrete controls over its members and their activities. If mobilized for action planning, this network would also control the nature of such planning—keeping it within an agreed-upon general framework allowing for localized indigenous applications based on community needs, desires, skills, and resources.

What the bazaar sector needs is protection from premature penetration by the modern sector which, in turn, requires internal protection from competing or conflicting land use and abuse, as well as over-utilization and under-utilization of such use. In other words, a dual system of land use regulation is needed: boundary regulation earmarking modern sector ribbons and bazaar sector enclaves requiring monitoring over time to allow for new interpenetrations of modern sector activity into bazaar enclaves when deemed appropriate; and modern building, performance, and occupancy regulation within the corridors for modern sector activity. Lastly, the duality of the metropolitan condition must be recognized in the financial planning component as well. Modern fiscal policy can only be applied successfully to the modern sector. The traditional sector must be dealt with in harmony with its tradition. Conceptually this too presents a dilemma, and to an urban administrator who by virtue of his position will be lodged in the modern government sector it may appear an anomaly if not a nightmare. In reality, it is congruent with the duality of the reality we have described. If no fiscal policy model which recognizes this fact currently exists, one must be invented.

Epilogue

Though the native habitat of the ostrich is not too far away from the countries we are concerned with, to emulate its habit for escaping the difficulties and unpleasantries of the urban problem will not make them disappear. Learning by heart the content of British, Dutch, and American textbooks and applying that knowledge to the production of colorful maps, statistical analysis, and models in clay or symbols, will not help to solve the problems of the metropolis in developing societies. Nor will it be solved by legislation and declaration.[48] In fact it will never be solved, because as history so vividly demonstrates the solution to a problem paves the way for a new problem to emerge. All we can then hope for is that an iterative process of inventing urban futures will provide insights for the formulation of policies and programs aimed at making the transitions from one state of development to the next less painful, and at reducing the levels of human discomfort in a region with less and less elbow room.

NOTES

1. Interesting accounts of early versions of this debate can be found in Adna Ferrin Weber, *The Growth of Cities in the Nineteenth Century*. Ithaca, N.Y.: Cornell University Press, 1964; Werner Hegeman, *Der Städtebau (City Building)*. Vols. I and II. Berlin: Wassmuth, 1913; and R. Baumeister, *Stadt-Erweiterungen in technischer, baupolizeilicher und wirtschaftlicer Beziehung (The Expansion of Cities in a Technical, Legal Control and Economic Context)*. Berlin: Ernst & Korn, 1876.

2. Leo Jakobson and Ved Prakash, "Urbanization and Urban Development: Proposals for an Integrated Policy Base," in Jakobson and Prakash (eds.), *Urbanization and National Development*, Vol. I, South and Southeast Asia Urban Affairs Annuals. Beverly Hills, Calif.: Sage, 1971, pp. 15-38.

3. T. G. McGee, *The Southeast Asian City*. New York: Frederick A. Praeger, 1967, p. 19.

4. *Ibid.*

5. *Ibid.*

6. Metcalf and Eddy, in James E. Bogle, *The Coming of Urban Crisis in Asia*. Saigon: Contract No. AID-VN-86, between the Ministry of Public Works, Republic of Viet Nam and the United States Agency for International Development, 1971, p. 111.

7. Ernest Weissmann, "Introduction" to Aprodicio A. Laquian (ed.), *Rural-Urban Migrants and Metropolitan Development*. Toronto: Intermet, 1971.

8. See for example, Lauchlin Curie, *Accelerating Development*. New York: McGraw-Hill, 1966; Jane Jacobs, *The Economy of Cities*. New York: Random House, 1969; and Aprodicio A. Laquian, *The City in Nation Building*. Manila: Institute of Public Administration, 1966.

9. N. V. Sovani, "The Analysis of 'Over-Urbanization,'" *Economic Development and Cultural Change*, Vol. 12 (January 1964), pp. 113-122.

10. Arch Dotson, "Public Policy and Urbanization," paper presented at Southeast Asia Developmental Advisory Group Urban Development Panel, Ithaca, N.Y.: The Asia Society, 1971.

11. Lauchlin Curie, *op. cit.*

12. See for example Aprodicio A. Laquian, *Slums Are for People*. Manila: Institute of Public Administration, 1969.

13. Southeast Asia Development Advisory Group, SEADAG Reports. Urban Development Panel Seminar, January, 1972. New York: The Asia Society, 1972, p. 10.

14. Arch Dotson, "Urbanization and National Development in South and Southeast Asia," Report of the Southeast Asia Development Advisory Group, Urban Development Panel Seminars. New York: The Asia Society, 1972, pp. 1-2.

15. Leo Jakobson and Ved Prakash, "Urbanization and Regional Planning in India," *Urban Affairs Quarterly*, Vol. 2, No. 1 (1967), pp. 36-65.

16. Colin Rosser, "Urbanization in India," International Urbanization Survey. New York: Ford Foundation, 1972, unpublished, p. 62.

17. The Harvard Development Advisory Service consists of a group of economists attached to BAPPENAS, the national planning board, under a Ford Foundation grant program initiated in 1953 and administered by Harvard University.

18. J. M. Dandekar and Nilakantha Rath, "Poverty in India," *Economic and Political Weekly*, Vol. 6 (1971), pp. 25-48 and 106-146.

19. Ved Prakash, *New Towns in India*. Durham, N.C.: Duke University, Program in Comparative Studies on Southern Asia, 1969.

20. As pointed out by Arthur Row in Chapter 5 of this book, the Ford Foundation's contributions to the Calcutta Metropolitan Planning Organization amount to over $5 million

Urban Planning in the Context of a "New Urbanization" 285

U.S. dollars, the bulk of which has been spent on foreign consultants' salaries and logistic overhead.

21. Colin Rosser, "Action Planning in Calcutta," in Raymond Apthorpe (ed.), *People, Planning and Development Studies: Some Reflections on Social Planning.* London: Frank Cass and Co., Ltd., 1970, p. 127.

22. Alfred van Huyck and John D. Herbert, the principals of PADCO, the United Nations subcontractor for the Karachi project, were among those Ford Foundation consultants who made important contributions to the Calcutta plan.

23. It is of interest to point out that the five-man international panel convened by the United Nations to review the first phase report did not consider the alternatives as a dichotomous pair but rather as two points on a continuum. The panel recommended that in the second planning phase a selective positioning of targets for each sector by made on this continuum. The project's steering committee, consisting of national, provincial and metropolitan officials, preferred the package approach over the selective approach because it provides for easier and clearer internal consistency between the seven sectors and, as a whole, the Distributive Investment package was consistent with national development policy.

24. Jakobson and Prakash, "Urbanization and Urban Development," *op. cit.*

25. See Weber, *op. cit.;* Baumeister, *op. cit.*

26. Wolf Ladejinsky, "Ironies of India's Green Revolution," *Foreign Affairs,* Vol. 48 (1970), pp. 758-768.

27. Among the proponents of this approach are John P. Lewis, who recommended massive rural public works programs in his *Quiet Crisis in India.* New York: Doubleday, 1964; and Dandekar and Rath, *op. cit.* Colin Rosser, a principal staff member of the Ford Foundation's recent International Urbanization Survey (1970-72), in personal discussions, dismisses the idea of rural public works programs as a means to reduce rural to urban migration. For a discussion of the Indonesia experience, see Y. B. deWit, "The Kabupaten Program," *Bulletin of Indonesian Economic Studies,* Vol. 9, No. 1 (March 1973), pp. 65-85.

28. J. L. Giebels and P. L. van Steenveldt, *West Java Development Plan,* The Hague: March 1971, unpublished, pp. 60-61. (emphasis added)

29. A discussion of the increasing importance of amenities and accessibility in location decisions can be found in T. R. Lakshamanan, "An Approach to the Analysis of Intra-Urban Location Applied to the Baltimore Region," *Economic Geography,* Vol. XL, No. 4 (1964), pp. 348-370; and in Justin Gray Associates, *How Industry Selects a Plant Site.* New York: Scientific American, 1970.

30. Jakobson and Prakash, "Urbanization and Regional Planning in India," *op. cit.,* pp. 61-64.

31. McGee, *op. cit.*

32. Sigurd Grava, Memorandum to the Center for Housing, Building and Planning, United Nations, August 1, 1973.

33. Pemerintah Daerah Chusus Ibukota Djakarta, *Rentjana Induk Djakarta 1965-1985 (Master Plan for Jakarta).* Jakarta: 1967.

34. Göran Lindahl, "Staden Och Människan" (The City and Man), in Torsten Frendberg (ed.), *Stadsförnyelse (Urban Renewal).* Stockholm: Svensk Byggtjänst, 1966, pp. 27-40.

35. See Jakobson and Prakash, "Urbanization and Urban Development," *op. cit.,* pp. 23-29.

36. This concept corresponds with the recent suggestions for "high accessibility corridors" in New York and Chicago.

37. Ashish Bose, "The Urbanization Process in South and Southeast Asia," in *Urbanization and National Development,* op. cit., *p. 107.*

38. Grava, *op. cit.*

39. K. C. Sivaramakrishnan, "Calcutta: Problems and Prospects," All University Lecture, University of Wisconsin, Madison, February 2, 1973.

40. Jakobson and Prakash, "Urbanization and Regional Planning, *op. cit.*, pp. 50-53.

41. See Jakobson and Prakash, "Urbanization and Urban Development," *op. cit.*, pp. 21-23.

42. Erich Jantsch, *Technological Forecasting in Perspective*. Paris: Organization for Economic Co-operation and Development, 1967, pp. 29-38.

43. Hasan Ozbekhan, "Technology and Man's Future." Santa Monica, Calif.: System Development Corporation, Report SP-2494, 1966, as quoted in Jantsch, *op. cit.*, p. 93.

44. Jantsch, *op. cit.*, p. 15.

45. *Ibid.*, p. 41.

46. Jakobson and Prakash, "Urbanization and Urban Development," *op. cit.*, pp. 34-36.

47. Rosser, *op. cit.*, pp. 131-132.

48. Jakarta was declared a "closed city" by the Governor of the Capital District on August 5, 1970, which meant that the local chiefs of the city's 229 subdistricts should no longer issue Resident Identification Cards to newcomers not having employment and a place to live. In April of 1973 a detailed consultant's study on residential area improvement reported that only one-eighth of the subdistricts are succeeding in controlling in-migration.

ABOUT THE CONTRIBUTORS

ABOUT THE CONTRIBUTORS

IAN BURTON is Professor of Geography and Associate of the Institute of Environmental Sciences and Engineering at the University of Toronto. During 1964-65 he was a consultant on water resources development with the Ford Foundation Advisory Planning Group in Calcutta. He has also served as a consultant to the World Health Organization and the United Nations. Dr. Burton is currently engaged in an investigation into water supply and sanitation problems in developing countries for the International Development Research Centre (Ottawa). Recently he served as chairman of the Expert Panel on Perception of Environmental Quality of the UNESCO Man and the Biosphere Program. His latest book (with Kenneth Hewitt) is *The Hazardousness of a Place*, 1971.

PETER BUSCH is Assistant Professor of Political Science at Yale University, where he received his Ph.D. in 1972. He did his undergraduate work at Harvard and received his M.A. in political science from the University of Wisconsin in 1966. His major interests include political development in Southeast Asia and regional integration in Europe. He is currently engaged in a research project on European integration and the Common Market. His publications include "Mathematical Models of Arms Races" in Bruce M. Russett, *What Price Vigilance,* and a forthcoming book on Singapore.

ARCH DOTSON is Professor of Government at Cornell University. He received his M.A. and Ph.D. degrees from Harvard University. He was a post-doctoral fellow at the London School of Economics and Political Science. Before joining Cornell University in 1951 he taught at the University of Virginia. During 1967-68 he was Visiting Professor of Public Administration, University of the Philippines. He has served as consultant to various organizations both in the U.S. and abroad, including the Institute of Public Affairs, Washington, D.C., the Ford Foundation on the Delhi and the Calcutta Metropolitan Planning Projects, the U.S. Department of Housing and Urban Development, the governments of Japan and Iran, and the United Nations. He is the author of numerous publications and is currently finishing a book on *National Development Space: Theory, Cases, and Strategies.*

LEO JAKOBSON is Professor of Urban and Regional Planning at the University of Wisconsin. He received his M. Arch. from the Technical University at Helsinki. He also studied at the Royal Academy of Arts in Stockholm and at the

University of Pennsylvania. He has practiced planning in Finland, Sweden, Israel, Puerto Rico and the U.S. In 1964-65 he served as a consultant on regional planning with the Ford Foundation Advisory Planning Group in Calcutta. Since 1972 he has been a member of the United Nations International Review Panel on the Karachi Metropolitan Development Plan. Most recently, he was a Ford Foundation consultant on regional planning education in Indonesia and Thailand. He has taught at the University of Wisconsin since 1958 and has lectured at several universities in the United States, India, and Finland.

T. R. LEE, who received his Ph.D. degree in geography from the University of Toronto in 1968, is currently with the United Nations Economic Commission for Latin America in Santiago, Chile, working on water and agricultural development problems in Latin America. During 1964-65, he worked in India under Ford Foundation sponsorship on problems of water supply and economic development. Before assuming his current assignment, Dr. Lee was at the Canada Centre for Inland Waters, working on pollution problems of the Great Lakes for the International Joint-Commission (Canada-U.S.). His publications include *Water Supply and Economic Development.*

RICHARD L. MEIER is Professor of Environmental Design in the College of Environmental Design, University of California, Berkeley. He studied physical sciences through the doctorate, helped organize the atomic scientist movement, and then joined the staff of the Program of Education and Research in Planning at the University of Chicago in 1950, went on to the University of Michigan in 1957 as a behavioral scientist and resources planner, and in 1967 to Berkeley to teach architects, planners, and landscape architects. He has written mainly on the organization of science and technology and its place in planning, general systems theory, communications theory, and the phenomena of growth in large cities. He is presently writing on the design of resource-conserving cities in developing countries.

VED PRAKASH is Professor of Urban and Regional Planning at the University of Wisconsin. He received his B.A. and M.A. degrees from the University of Lucknow, India, and his Ph.D. from Cornell University. Prior to moving to Wisconsin he was a Lecturer at the University of Lucknow and at the Indian Institute of Management, Calcutta. He has also been with the Town Planning Organization and Tax Research Unit, Government of India. Dr. Prakash has been a consultant to the United Nations and the U.S. AID Mission to Colombia. Most recently he spent a year with the United Nations as an Interregional Adviser in Urban Economics and Housing Finance. His publications include *New Towns in India* and articles on municipal investment planning and urban development.

ARTHUR T. ROW is Chief of the Ford Foundation's Advisory Group in Calcutta. He was educated at Harvard College and the Harvard Graduate School

About the Contributors

of Design. He has served in public planning agencies in Portland, Maine, Detroit, and Philadelphia. For many years he was Visiting Lecturer at the University of Pennsylvania and from 1961 to 1969 he was Professor of City Planning at Yale University. During this latter period he was on leave for two years to work in India. In 1969 he resigned from Yale to return to Calcutta. He has served as consultant to many government agencies and is the author of several articles on urban planning and development.

J. P. SAH is currently a United Nations expert in Metropolitan and Regional Planning and Development in Manila, Philippines. He received his B.A. and M.A. degrees from the University of Lucknow, India, where he also was awarded a law degree and a diploma in public administration. He has been a member of the Indian Economic Service and has served the government of India during the last twenty years in various capacities, including the Taxation Enquiry Commission, the National Planning Commission, and the Town and Country Planning Organization as Chief of its Economic Division, from which position he is currently on leave. He has been a consultant to the United Nations and ECAFE. Recently he was a member of the United Nations Expert Working Group on Urban Land Policies. He is the author of numerous publications including *Urban Land Policies and Land Use Control Measures in Asia and the Far East.*

KHALID SHIBLI is currently Visiting Professor of International Environmental, Regional, and Urban Development at the Graduate School of Public and International Affairs, University of Pittsburgh. He received his Bachelor's and Master's degrees in engineering from the Universities of the Punjab (Pakistan) and the University of California at Berkeley, and obtained the M.S. and Ph.D. in Planning from the University of California at Berkeley and Columbia University respectively. He was also awarded a post-doctoral diploma in Comprehensive Planning by the Institute of Social Studies at the Hague, Netherlands. He was visiting Senior Research Scholar at the West German Akademie Fur Raumforschung Und Landesplanung at Hanover, and at the Department of Regional and Urban Planning of the Royal Academy of Fine Arts in Copenhagen. During 1963-64 he served as a Senior Professor at West Pakistan Technical University at Lahore. Dr. Shibli has been a Sector Chief (Regional and Urban Planning) in the National Planning Commission of Pakistan, from which position he is now on leave. He is currently a member of the UN Secretary General's Advisory Committee on Regional (Sub-national) Development; vice president of the Eastern Regional Organization for Planning and Housing; and chairman of the Commission for Planning in Asia and Oceania. His numerous publications include *Planning in the U.S.S.R., Planning in the Netherlands,* and *Planning in Western Germany.*

HENRY TEUNE is Professor of Political Science at the University of Pennsylvania. He received his M.A. and Ph.D. degrees from the University of

Illinois and Indiana University, respectively. He has been with the University of Pennsylvania since 1961. Among many assignments he has been Associate Director of Research, International Studies of Values in Politics, 1966-70. Most recently he spent a year in Yugoslavia on a Fulbright Research Grant. He has published widely in professional journals and is the co-author of *Values and the Active Community* and *The Logic of Comparative Social Inquiry*.

INDEX

INDEX

Administrative capacity:
  defined, 14
  linked with urbanization, 33, 43
  measures of, 26-28, 32-33
  related to national development, 43
  testing of, 33
Afghanistan, 109
Almond, Gabriel A., 85, 107 (n. 46)
Angkor Wat, 52
Annual costs for urban services and housing, 232-233
Anti-urban sentiment, 279-280
Army, role of, in Thailand, 56-57
Aronson, Elliot, 107 (n. 56)
Asanol/Durgapur urban region, 145
Ashmore, Richard D., 107 (n. 53)
Asian cities, 215, 216, 261, 265, 272, 273, 278, 282
Asian countries, 231, 233
Assam, 145
Attribution theory, applied to Singapore, 98-99, 104
Australia, 64, 68, 261
Aziz, Ungku Abdul, 105 (ns. 18, 20)

Bangkok, 45-47, 51, 53, 56-59, 61-63
Bangkok-Thanburi urban complex, 227
Bangladesh, 109, 138, 140
Banks, Robert L., 257 (n. 15)
Bartholomew, Harland, Associates, 113, 135 (n. 2)
Bauer, Raymond A., 224 (n. 13)
Baumeister, R., 284 (n. 1), 285 (n. 25)
Becker, Arthur P., 258 (n. 37)
Beling, W. A., 136 (n. 25)
Bellows, Thomas J., 106 (ns. 21, 23)
Benda, Harry, 105 (n. 20)
Bengal, 139, 141, 142
Berkowitz, Leonard, 108 (n. 68)
Bernard, P., 136 (n. 11)
Beyer, Glenn, 198, 201, 223 (n. 2)
Bhagwati, Jagdish, 130, 136 (n. 22)
Bihar, 145
Bird, P. A., 196 (n. 11)

Bird, Richard M., 258 (n. 37)
Boeke, J. H., 270
Bogle, James E., 43 (n. 1), 284 (n. 6)
Bombay, 140, 152
Boo, Tan Peng, 105 (n. 6)
Bosch, H. M., 196 (n. 3)
Bose, Ashish, 273, 285 (n. 37)
Bose, Nirmal K., 166 (n. 1)
Bose, Subhas Chandra, 141
Botha, Elize, 108 (n. 76)
Bradley, David J., 196 (n. 10)
"Brain drain," 56, 67
Breese, Gerald, 256 (n. 1)
Brown, Harry Gunnison, 257 (n. 23)
Brown, W. H., Jr., 256 (ns. 15, 16)
Buehler, A. G., 258 (n. 36)
Buddhism, 57, 64-65
Burma, 68, 228-230
Burton, Ian, 271
Busch, Peter A., 104 (n. 1), 108 (ns. 64, 72)
Bustee:
  defined, 149
  environmental improvement of, 149-150
  social and economic development of, 165-166

Calcutta, 137-147, 149-154, 156-160, 162-166, 186, 218, 222, 262, 264, 274, 278
Calcutta Basic Development Plan, 138, 142-143, 146, 147, 149, 150, 153, 154, 161, 165
Calcutta Metropolitan Development Authority, 142, 143-144, 148, 149, 151, 153, 155, 164-166
Calcutta Metropolitan District (Region), 139, 140, 145, 150, 157, 159, 165, 218
Calcutta Metropolitan Planning Organization:
  economic development plan, 146-147
  establishment of, 141
  government reorganization, 152-153
  health facilities and services plan, 148-149
  housing programs, 149-151
  publications, 147, 149, 150

relationship to CMDA, 165
representation on committees, 148
size and budget, 143-144
support to regional planning, 145
California, 54
Cambodia, 66, 68, 229, 230
Campbell, John D., 108 (n. 74)
Canada, 238
Capacity index for family housing occupancy, 200-201
Caruthers, Martha W., 85, 107 (n. 55)
Chand, Gyan, 257 (n. 26)
Chandigarh, 263
Chelliah, D. D., 107 (n. 58)
Chiang, Hai Ding, 53
Chiengmai, 56
China, 46, 55, 132
Chinese nationalism in Singapore, rise of, 80
Chinese secret societies in Singapore, 79-80
Chye, Toh Chin, 81
Cities:
  amenity measures for, 31
  Bangkok, land prices in, 62-63
  Calcutta, characteristics of, 137-138
  degree of urbanization, 34
  factors contributing to development of, 184
  rate of change in, 276-280
  salience measures for, 21-22
  scale of definitions, 274
  Singapore, as city-state, 47, 51, 55, 75-82
  structural differentiation of, 54
City-state, problems of, 75-108
Clavell, James, 74 (n. 3)
Collings, Barry E., 107 (n. 53)
Collins, Mary E., 86, 107 (n. 49)
Colombo, 227
Comber, L. F., 105 (n. 9)
Community water supply:
  benefits of, 179
  deficiencies in financing arrangements, 195
  need for institutional changes in, 195
  new strategy for, 193-196
  planning and design of system, 193-195
  as public utility, 195-196
  related to health, 179-180
  as social science, 193-195
  theoretical guidelines, 180-193
Cook, Stuart W., 86, 107 (n. 50)
Costs, of urban infrastructure, 230-231
Cultural pluralism, and compatability with national identity, 82-87
Cultural values in modernization, role of, 63-67

Curie, Lauchlin, 261, 284 (ns. 8, 11)

Dandekar, J.M., 284 (n. 18), 285 (n. 27)
Davis, Keith E., 108 (ns. 68, 70)
Debul, 110
Decentralization of industry, 116-117
de Goede, J. H., 136 (n. 12)
Dehaven, J. G., 196 (n. 11)
Delhi, 221, 274
Dennis, Jack, 84, 85, 106 (n. 35), 107 (n. 43)
Desmond, Gerald M., 201, 224 (n. 9)
Deutsch, Karl W., 90, 106 (n. 30), 108 (n. 62)
Development:
  by excess capacity or shortage, 184
  role of water resources in, 177
de Vera, Jacobo S., 256 (n. 4)
de Wit, Y. B., 285 (n. 27)
Dieterich, B. H., 190, 192
Ding, Chiang Hai, 104 (n. 5)
Doraisamy, T. R., 105 (ns. 6, 15), 107 (n. 58)
Dotson, Arch, 43 (n. 2), 260, 261, 284 (ns. 10, 14)
Doxiadis, C. A., 220, 225 (n. 40)
Duggar, George, 136 (n. 13)
Durgapur, 140, 141

Earle, Margaret J., 108 (n. 76)
East Bengal, 138, 139, 140
East Pakistan, 109, 116, 139
Eastern India, 144
Easton, David, 84, 85, 106 (n. 35), 107 (n. 43)
Eckstein, O., 236, 237, 256 (n. 15)
Economic growth:
  new planning model needed for, 130-131
  related to poverty and unemployment, 130
  in Singapore, 47-51
Eddy & Metcalf, 260, 284 (n. 6)
Edelman, Murray, 84, 106 (n. 40)
Elder, Elizabeth, 43 (n. 3)
Emerson, Rupert, 106 (n. 28)
Environmental needs, in housing, 199-200
Ethnic attitudes:
  hypotheses of, in Singapore, 97-100
  indicators of, in Singapore, 101-103
  role of, in policy formation, 103-104
Ethnic conflict, between Malay and Chinese, 81-82, 97-103

INDEX

Family life, metropolitan comparisons of, 69-72
Family needs, in housing, 199-200
Family planning and modernization, 68-69, 267
Financing capital outlays, 250-254
France, 120-260, 269
Freedman, Maurice, 105 (ns. 11, 12)
Frendberg, Torsten, 285 (n. 34)
Fourastie, Jean, 212, 213, 224 (n. 29), 273
Furnivall, J. S., 78, 105 (n. 8)

Galbraith, John K., 180
Gamba, Charles, 106 (n. 26)
Gandhi, Indira, 142
Geddes, Patrick, 127, 133, 134
Geertz, Clifford, 90, 106 (n. 30), 108 (n. 63), 270
Geldern, Robert Heine, 107 (n. 41)
Germany, 68, 269
Ghosh, B. B., 142
Giebels, J. L., 285 (n. 28)
Gilbert, C. E., 256 (ns. 15, 16)
Ginsburg, Norton, 105 (ns. 9, 13, 14)
Glazer, Nathan, 83, 106 (n. 31)
Goals conflict, 214-215
Government structure, in Thailand, 57
Grava, Sigurd, 271, 275, 285 (ns. 32, 38)
Greece, 54, 221
Greenfield, Richard, 43 (n. 3)
Greenstein, Fred I., 84
Grima, A. P., 196 (n. 11)
Gross, Bertram, 205, 206, 217, 224 (n. 13), 273
Growth centers, 117
Growth poles, 117
Gupta, R. B., 220

Haldia, 145
Hanrahan, Gene Z., 105 (n. 17)
Harding, John, 107 (n. 56)
Harris, Chauncey, 124
Hauser, P. M., 224 (n. 23)
Hawaii, 52, 53
Healey, J. M., 196 (n. 5)
Hegeman, Werner, 284 (n. 1)
Henderson, J. M., 190, 192
Herbert, John D., 285 (n. 22)
Hess, Robert D., 84, 85, 107 (n. 42)
Hicks, Ursula K., 251, 257 (ns. 18, 24, 34)
Higgins, Benjamin, 270
Hirschleifer, J., 196 (n. 11)
Hirschman, Albert O., 183, 184, 186, 196 (n. 6), 216, 256 (n. 14)

Hofman, John E., 108 (n. 75)
Holland, William L., 105 (n. 18)
Hong Kong, 46, 47, 51, 55, 66, 69, 70-72, 149, 272
Honolulu, 52, 116
Hoover, E. M., 132, 136 (n. 30)
Horowitz, Abraham, 179, 196 (n. 3)
Housing:
  annual costs, 232-233
  application of conceptual model, 212-217
  attempts to reduce cost of, 158
  Calcutta, programs in, 149-151
  conceptualization of, 207-212
  cooperatives, in Pakistan, 121
  ethnic prejudice in, 107 (n. 53)
  function of, 208
  high-technology industry in, 209
  integration in, 86, 89-90
  lack of holistic approach to, 121
  percentage affording various levels of, 61
  performance criteria for, 208-209
  role of, 207-208
  site and services for, 61-62
  steps in formulating standards for, 209-210
Housing policy:
  Calcutta as illustrative case of, 217-223
  conventional objectives of, 138
  formulation of, in developing countries, 212-217
  issues in, 197
  preservation of existing stock, 157
  reformulation of, in Sweden, 198-199
  spatial distribution of housing types, 222-223
  standards in, 197-203
Housing standards:
  capacity index, 200-201
  classification for, 220-222
  Cologne recommendations, 199-202
  concepts of, 210-211, 216-217
  role of, in policy formation, 203-206
  in the U.S., 197-198
Howrah, 159, 218
Hughes, Helen, 104 (n. 6), 105 (n. 7)
Huyck, Alfred van, 285 (n. 22)
Hyderabad, 110

Income distribution, in Bangkok, 62 (table), 229-230
India, 15, 64, 68, 112, 139, 150, 157, 159, 180, 183, 210, 220, 228-231, 242
Indonesia, 78, 82, 97, 228-230, 280

Industrial decentralization, 116-117
Industrialization:
  correlated with urbanization, 41-42
  in the Philippines, 35-36
Innovation, need for, in Singapore, 53-55
Intergovernmental fiscal relations, 247-250, 252
Islamabad, 113, 114, 263
Italy, 54, 218, 220

Jackson, C. I., 196 (n. 11)
Jacob, Philip E., 106 (n. 38)
Jakarta, 272, 278, 281
Jakobson, Leo, 224 (ns. 12, 25, 28, 30, 34), 256 (n. 11), 284 (ns. 2, 15), 285 (ns. 24, 30, 35), 286 (ns. 40), 41, 46)
Jamaica, 85
Jantsch, Erich, 280, 286 (ns. 42, 44)
Japan, 46, 53, 55, 62, 78, 183, 261
Japanese role in Singapore, 52-53
Jaros, Dean, 85, 107 (n. 44)
Jones, Edward E., 108 (ns. 68, 70)
Johnson, J. H., 136 (n. 15)
Jurong, 53

Kahin, George McTurnan, 105 (n. 16)
Kahn, Hans, 106 (n. 30)
Kaohsiung, 72
Karachi, 109-134 *passim*, 274
Karachi Development Authority, 113-115, 121-123, 134, 135
Kaufman, Arnold, 207, 224 (ns. 17, 24)
Kelley, Harold H., 108 (ns. 68, 69, 71)
Kelman, Herbert C., 106 (n. 35)
Khan, M. Ayub, 113-117
Kiesler, Charles A., 108 (n. 68)
Koh, T.T.B., 54, 74 (n. 5)
Kolz, Arnold, 257 (n. 15)
Kristensson, Folke, 212, 215, 217, 224 (ns. 27, 32)
Krutilla, J. V., 236, 237, 256 (n. 15)

Ladejinsky, Wolf, 285 (n. 26)
Lahore, 133, 134
Lakshamanan, T. R., 285 (n. 29)
Land price, in Bangkok, 62-63
Landsberg, H. E., 136 (n. 16)
Langton, Kenneth P., 85, 107 (n. 47)
Laos, 229, 230
Laquian, Aprodicio A., 43 (n. 1), 261, 284 (ns. 7, 8, 12)
Latin America, 186, 230, 260
Lee, T. R., 271, 196 (ns. 8, 10)

Levine, David, 108 (n. 68)
Le Vine, Robert, 85, 107 (n. 45)
Levitan, S. A., 136 (n. 33)
Lewis, John P., 136 (n. 28), 256 (n. 2), 285 (n. 27)
Lewis, W. Arthur, 181
Lian, Pang Cheng, 106 (n. 23)
Lim, William S. W., 54, 74 (n. 5)
Lindahl, Göran, 273, 285 (n. 34)
Lindstrom, 135 (n. 1)
Lindzey, Gardner, 107 (n. 56)
Lipset, Seymour Martin, 83, 84, 106 (ns. 35, 36, 39)
Loan financing, for urban facilities, 251-252
Logan, John, 179, 196 (n. 1)
London, 72
Los Angeles, 72

MacDougall, John, 108 (n. 65)
Magnum, G. L., 136 (n. 33)
Maharashtra, 140
Malaysia, 51, 68, 78, 81, 82, 88, 97, 229
Malaysia, Western, 46, 69
Manila, 228
Mao Tse-tung, 51
Masuda, Minora, 83, 106 (n. 33)
McGee, Terry G., 43 (n. 1), 212, 215, 224 (ns. 28, 33), 260, 270, 284 (n. 3), 285 (n. 31)
McLoughlin, J. B., 136 (n. 31)
Meier, Richard L., 47, 73 (n. 1)
Meow, Seah Chee, 106 (n. 25)
Merelman, Richard, 83, 106 (ns. 34, 37)
Metcalf & Eddy, 260, 284 (n. 6)
Metropolis:
  earnings per worker, 69-70 (table)
  function of broker, 45-47
  intermetropolitan exchange, 71-72
  new approaches to comparative studies of, 69-72
  obsolescence of models, 46-47
  potentials of, 72-73
  primary function of, in Asia, 45-46
  Singapore, images of, 51-53
  stresses of living in, 69
Metropolitan planning:
  Calcutta's experience in, 138, 142-165 *passim*, 263-264
  correlated with urban land policy, 132
  Karachi's experience in, 125-127, 264-265
  lack of effectiveness of, 123
  models for, 263
  new conceptualizations of, 263-264

INDEX

normative approach to, 280-284
standards and costs of, 156-158
Metropolitan structure, 272-273
Migration to cities, in Thailand, 58-59
Miller, J. Maurice, 257 (n. 31)
Milliman, J. W., 196 (n. 11)
Milne, R. S., 106 (n. 24)
Minimum health standards, in water supply, 191
Mirza, Iskander, 113
Mitchell, Robert Edward, 74 (n. 8)
Modernization:
  and family planning, 68-69
  and institution-building, 67-68
  and peasant culture in Bangkok, 56-69
  role of cultural values in, 63-67
Motor vehicles, increased number of, in Bangkok and Singapore, 63
Moynihan, Patrick, 83, 106 (n. 31)
Multinational corporations, role of, in economic development, 45
Myrdal, G., 136 (ns. 27, 34)

Nagpur, 140
Nation-building:
  applicability of Western models in, 104
  problems of multiethnicity in, 75-104
National development, and administrative capacity, 43
National Pilot Project (Karachi Plan), 126
National urban budget, 233-238
Nehru, Jawaharlal, 140, 210, 211
Nepal, 228-230
Net savings and investment in urban infrastructure, 230
Netherlands, 120, 252
Netzer, Dick, 257 (n. 31)
New Delhi, 140
New York, 72, 83, 157
Nisbett, Richard E., 108 (n. 68)
Non-property taxes, 242-245
Non-tax revenues, 245-247
Normative approach to planning, 280-283
Norway, 252
Nowak, Thomas, 43 (n. 3)

Ooi, Jin-bee, 53, 104 (n. 5)
Orissa, 145
Osaka, 52
Oshima, Harry T., 105 (n. 7)
Ozbekhan, Hasan, 281, 286 (n. 43)

Pakistan, 109-121 *passim*, 129, 131, 135, 139, 229-231, 242
Palmer, J. Norman, 105 (n. 16)
Panang, 266
Parenti, Michael, 83, 106 (n. 32)
Paris, 72, 154
Partition of India:
  impact on Calcutta, 139-140
  impact on Karachi, 112, 115
Patna, 140
People's Action Party (Singapore), 81, 89
Per capita income and income distribution, 62 (table), 229-230
Peritz, Rene, 105 (n. 11), 106 (n. 26)
Philadelphia, 243
Philippines, 14, 24, 34, 41, 42, 78, 228, 229
Pico, Rafael, 220
Piped water supplies, access to, 191
Policy formulation process, 203-206
Political allegiance, 89-97
Political socialization, 83-87
Political structure and legitimation, 83-87
Pollution, 124
Poona, 140
Powell, P.W.G., 136 (n. 19)
Prakash, Ved, 201, 213, 224 (ns. 9, 25, 28, 30), 256 (ns. 8, 11, 12, 14), 284 (ns. 2, 15, 19), 285 (ns. 24, 30, 35), 286 (ns. 40, 41, 46)
Property taxation, 239-242
Public ownership of land, and financing urban development, 252-254
Public policy on urbanization, 13
Public water supply:
  "banker's approach" to, 185-186
  investment programs in, 178
  minimal standards for, 185-187
  non-economic criteria for, 185-187
  popular demand for, 186
  scale and timing of investment in, 178
Puerto Rico, 179
Purcell, Victor, 105 (ns. 9, 10, 14, 17, 19)
Pye, Lucian W., 106 (n. 17)

Raffles, Sir Stamford, 77
Rao, P. Prabhakar, 253, 257 (n. 35)
Rath, Nilakantha, 284 (n. 18), 285 (n. 27)
Rawson, Mary, 257 (n. 29)
Regional planning concepts, 269-270
Rhoads, William H., 258 (n. 37)
Richardson, H. W., 132, 136 (n. 29)

Rio de Janeiro, 149
Roberts, Chester F., Jr., 105 (ns. 9, 13, 14)
Rodwin, L., 136 (n. 26)
Roff, William R., 81, 105 (n. 18)
Rosenau, James N., 106 (n. 35)
Rosenfield, Allan G., 74 (n. 7)
Rosser, Colin, 153, 166 (n. 7), 282, 284 (n. 16), 285 (ns. 21, 27), 286 (n. 47)
Row, Arthur, 284 (n. 20)
Roy, B. C., 141
Roy, Ranajit, 140, 166 (n. 3)
Rudduck, G., 135 (n. 7)
Rustow, Dankwart, 106 (n. 30)

Sah, J. P., 241, 257 (n. 25), 258 (n. 38)
Saigon, 51-53
San Francisco, 156
Schools, characteristics of, in Singapore, 87-88, 107 (n. 61)
Segaar, T. J., 136 (n. 12)
Selcock, T. H., 105 (n. 18, 20)
Selem, Hilda, 217, 225 (n. 35, 39)
Seligman, Edwin, 240, 257 (n. 20)
Seng, You Poh, 104 (n. 6), 105 (n. 7, 16)
Seoul, 47, 56, 67, 72
Sherif, Muzafer, 107 (n. 57)
Shibli, Khalid, 136 (ns. 18, 19)
Shute, Nevil, 74 (n. 3)
Sind, 109
Singapore, 45-55 *passim,* 63, 66-98 *passim,* 103, 149, 229, 267, 272
Singkong, 49-51, 69
Sivaramakrishnan, K. C., 142, 278, 285 (n. 39)
Slums:
 Azam Basti study of, 118, 127, 133
 categories of, in Karachi, 119
 clearance programs, in Pakistan, 119
 household definition of, 120
 Karachi Joint Research Project IV, 128-129, 133
 Lahore, Patrick Geddes report on, 127, 133
 role of religious leaders in, 118-119
Social indicators. *See* Social measurement
Social infrastructure, 181
Social measurement:
 approaches to, 15-17
 commercial activity, 29-31
 communications, 22-23, 37, 40
 comparative indicators for, 69-72
 education, 24-26, 36-37
 factor analysis, 19-20
 health, 38
 housing quality, 38-39
 infrastructure, 39-40
 interpretation of, 19-20
 manufacturing activity, 29-31, 35-36
 municipal government effectiveness, 26-28
 operations, 18-19
 principles of, 15-17
 public service institutions, 36
 road development, 23, 38
 service activity, 29-31
 urban amenities, 31
Social overhead capital, investment in, 181-183
South Korea, 51, 62, 64, 69
Southhampton, 52
Sovani, N. V., 43 (n. 1), 260, 284 (n. 9)
Spain, 54
Special assessments, 253-254
Squatters:
 in Bangkok, 59-61
 in Karachi, 113-114
 participation in development by, 120-121
Sri Lanka (Ceylon), 227-230
Steenveldt, P. L. van, 285 (n. 28)
Stockfish, J. A., 257 (n. 31)
Stockholm, 215
Suyama, Taku, 105 (n. 12)
Sweden, 252, 260
Switzerland, 260

Taipei, 47, 51, 55, 56, 69, 72
Taiwan, 46, 66, 69, 261
Taxation and urban finance, 239-245
Tel Aviv, 52
Teune, Henry, 106 (n. 38), 261
Thailand, 52, 58, 59, 62, 64, 67, 68, 228, 299
Tilman, Robert O., 105 (n. 14)
Tokyo, 52, 72
Torney, Judith V., 84, 85, 107 (n. 42)
Torquay, 52
Toscano, James V., 106 (n. 38)
Totten, G. O., 136 (n. 25)
Traggart, R., 136 (n. 33)
Tregonning, K. G., 104 (n. 4), 105 (ns. 12, 16)
Turkey, 54, 183
Twichell, Allan, 197, 223 (n. 1)

Ullman, Edward, 124
United Kingdom, 46, 55, 64, 218, 260, 269

INDEX

United States, 15, 46, 55, 56, 63, 64, 66, 83, 84, 88, 114, 156, 197, 238, 243, 253, 260, 269
Uphoff, Norman, 261
Urban development, related to income levels, 138
Urban growth policy, 117
Urban land policy, and metropolitan planning, 132
Urban planning:
  history of, in Karachi, 110-115
  history of, in Singapore, 54
  organization, methods, and techniques of, 132-133, 134
Urban policy formulation, concepts of, 265-280
Urban scale:
  defined, 274
  related to analytic techniques, 275-276
Urban Society, dual, in Asia, 270-271
Urban Services, annual costs of, 232-233
Urban structure, polynucleated, in Karachi, 123-124
Urban water supply, and disease control, 177
Urbanization:
  attitudes toward, 261, 280
  basic national policy issues in, 267-268
  consequences of, 13
  correlated with development, 42-43
  correlated with industrial activity, 41-42
  debate on, 259-262
  degree of, in Philippine provinces, 34-42
  forces affecting, 266-269
  hypothesis concerning impact of, 14-15
  indicators for, 20-21
  lacunae in planning of, 262-263
  linked with administrative capacity, 33, 43
  measure of, 33
  and metropolitan planning, 263
  and national development plans, 261-262
  and "overurbanization," 260-261
  problem of scale, 273-276
  "pseudo–," 259-260

public policy for, 13
structural differences in, 260, 267, 281-282
tertiary sector, role of, 268-269
U.S.S.R., 180, 183

Valins, Stuart, 108 (n. 68)
Verba, Sidney, 85, 107 (n. 46)
Vieg, John A., 257 (n. 32)
Venezuela, 179
Vietnam, 46, 51, 58, 229

Wah, Yeo Kim, 106 (n. 22)
Walkley, Rosabelle Price, 86, 107 (n. 50)
Water consumption:
  per capita, 189-191
  related to living conditions, 178, 193
Water resources, and development, 177
Water supply, 187-196 *passim*
Weber, Adna Ferrin, 284 (n. 1), 185 (n. 25)
Weissman, Ernest, 43 (n. 1), 220, 260, 284 (n. 7)
Wellisz, Stanislaw H., 231, 256 (n. 11)
West Bengal, 137, 139-142, 147, 157, 166, 219
West Pakistan, 109, 116, 123
Wheaton, W.L.C., 49, 55, 73 (n. 2), 154, 166 (n. 8)
White, Anne U., 196 (n. 10)
White, Gilbert F., 196 (n. 10)
Wilner, Daniel M., 86, 107 (n. 50)
Wilson, David A., 74 (n. 6)
Wolf, Eleanore P., 107 (n. 54)
Wolman, A., 196 (n. 3)
Woodbury, Coleman, 223 (n. 1)
Works, Ernest, 86, 107 (n. 52)

Yarrow, Leon J., 108 (n. 74)
Yarrow, Marian Radke, 99, 108 (ns. 73, 74)
Yew, Lee Kuan, 77, 81
You, Poh Seng, 104 (n. 6), 105 (n. 7)
Yugoslavia, 54

Zak, Itai, 108 (n. 75)